Constructing the Monolith

Constructing the Monolith

THE UNITED STATES, GREAT BRITAIN,
AND INTERNATIONAL COMMUNISM, 1945–1950

MARC J. SELVERSTONE

HARVARD UNIVERSITY PRESS
Cambridge, Massachusetts, and London, England   2009

Library of Congress Cataloging-in-Publication Data

Selverstone, Marc J.
  Constructing the monolith : the United States, Great Britain, and international
communism, 1945–1950 / Marc J. Selverstone.
      p.   cm.
  Includes bibliographical references and index.
  ISBN 978-0-674-03179-1 (alk. paper)
  1. Cold War.   2. Communist countries—Foreign relations—United States.
3. Communist countries—Foreign relations—Great Britain.   4. United States—Foreign
relations—Communist countries.   5. Great Britain—Foreign relations—Communist
countries.   I. Title.
  D840.S346   2008
  909'.097170824—dc22   2008014219

For Bonnie

Contents

Acknowledgments

As I imagine is the case with so many books, this one began as conversation with friends. Along the way, it took shape as a working manuscript—and one that took a lot longer to ferment than the beer that inspired it. It is therefore with great pleasure that I can now thank the legions of friends, colleagues, and mentors who helped to make the aging process so rewarding.

Ray Haberski and Jeff Woods were present at its Ohio University conception, having considered its fitness for one of our *Timestreams* historical projects; they were and remain invaluable friends as well as comrades-in-arms. Steve Remy, Jeff Coker, Jeremi Suri, and Alessandro Brogi helped to push me on several of the work's particulars, both during our time at OU and thereafter, as did a host of outstanding faculty mentors, including Steve Miner, Alonzo Hamby, Jeffrey Herf, Joan Hoff, and Alan Booth. My doctoral committee provided excellent advice, and I would like to thank John Gaddis, Chester Pach, Charles Alexander, David Descutner, and Frank Ninkovich for their insight and support. John and Chester deserve special mention for, respectively, creating and sustaining the dynamic intellectual environment at the Contemporary History Institute, and for providing its students with such exemplary models of teachers and scholars.

I have been extraordinarily fortunate to have moved from one vibrant academic community to another, and I am grateful for the colleagues I have and opportunities available at the University of Virginia's Miller Center of Public Affairs. Tim Naftali, David Coleman, Kent Germany,

Guian McKee, and Ken Hughes—the scholars with whom I have worked most closely as a member of the Presidential Recordings Program—have been sources of constant support, as has our editor, Pat Dunn. Brian Balogh and Mel Leffler have also been very generous with their time; I cannot thank them enough for their help in so many regards. I should also like to extend my appreciation to Philip Zelikow and Governor Gerald Baliles, who, as directors of the Miller Center, have articulated the vision and marshaled the resources that continue to inform such a remarkable work environment.

I have also benefited greatly from the time and energy of several additional scholars and colleagues who have answered the random question throughout the years. Walter LaFeber, Anna Nelson, Anders Stephanson, Richard Fried, Scott Lucas, Beatrice Heuser, Steven Schwartz, Mark Bradley, Robert Beisner, and Seth Center were all very generous in this regard. So, too, were Randall Woods and Robert McMahon, who offered excellent commentary on conference papers I presented; Tony Shaw, David Caute, and Hugh Wilford offered equally insightful remarks at a London gathering that helped to guide my study. In addition, kudos go out to Sarah-Jane Corke and Meredith Hindley, who were gracious enough to sit through truncated versions of this manuscript at more than one professional meeting.

I owe a particular debt of gratitude to the anonymous reviewers of this manuscript whose critiques made it much better than it ever would have been without their sharp eyes. I have also benefited from the help of countless archivists and librarians: Liz Safly and Dennis Bilger at the Truman Library, Dan Linke at Princeton's Seeley Mudd Library, Paul Barron and the late Larry Bland at the George Marshall Library, Jeff Verhey at Frederich Ebert Stiftung in Bonn, Michael Greco at the Miller Center, Lew Purifoy and his staff at the University of Virginia, and the many archivists at NARA's College Park facility and the Public Record Office in Kew.

I would like to extend a particular note of thanks to Richard Adams, whose father, Ware Adams, was the inspiration for much of the book itself. I greatly appreciate Dick's willingness to talk about his father, his generosity in letting me look at Ware's effects, and his encouragement and kind words throughout.

I would also like to thank Kathleen McDermott at Harvard University Press, whose energy and commitment have been invaluable during the publication process. I greatly appreciate her belief in this project and her persistence in steering it toward completion. My thanks also go out to Kathi Drummy, who helped to guide me through the finer points of manuscript acquisition, and to Barbara Goodhouse for her editing acumen.

In the end, it is family that matters most of all, and mine has been a constant source of love, support, and sustenance. My sister Amy has been steadfast in my corner, as have my virtual brothers and lifelong friends Michael Walmark and David Halper. So, too, have my in-laws Marge and Fritz Hagerman, whose forays to Charlottesville helped to make my research trips less guilt-ridden experiences.

None of this would have been possible, however, without the unswerving love and support of my parents, Harriet and Bob Selverstone. They are simply the most wonderful mother and father anyone could hope for, and I feel so very fortunate to have been the recipient of their love and wisdom. I thank them for their own commitments to education and family, for instilling in me the values of compassion and justice, and for giving me the chance to pursue a life of teaching and learning.

It is now within my own family that so much of my good fortune resides. I will always be indebted to Jake and Alison for the joy and meaning they bring to life, and for their patience and understanding when seeing me go off to work again. I am reminded every day of how lucky I am to be their dad.

Luck knows no bounds, though, when it comes to my wife, Bonnie Hagerman, for whom I reserve the greatest of thanks. She has seen this project and its author in all possible states of disarray, and has been my source of strength, inspiration, and comfort throughout. I cannot thank her enough for her love and support, for it is she who has made so much of this, and much of everything else, possible. And I am forever grateful that we may continue to explore those possibilities together.

Constructing the Monolith

Introduction

During the second week of January 1950, with East-West tensions seemingly rising by the day, Ware Adams, a member of the U.S. State Department's Policy Planning Staff, called for a moment of reflection. It was high time, he thought, for his colleagues to reconsider their most fundamental beliefs about the challenges they faced in the postwar world. Given the train of recent events, it was a curious request: nine months after the creation of the North Atlantic Treaty Organization (NATO), five months after the explosion of a Soviet atomic bomb, four months after the establishment of a West German state, three months after the founding of Communist China—at the very instant, in fact, that a victorious Mao Zedong was forging an alliance with Josef Stalin in Moscow—Adams saw fit to question the foundations of U.S. policy in the Cold War. America was forcing countries "to choose sides between us and the U.S.S.R.," he argued, forbidding nations from remaining neutral in the global conflict. While that desire for solidarity might have made sense in years past, Adams reasoned, it now had degenerated into a reflexive impulse, an unthinking, immoderate, knee-jerk response. Policymakers, moreover, were failing to ask and answer the most basic questions about the nature of the Communist challenge. As a result, they were operating on assumptions "which remain ill-defined and often in conflict in the back of the minds of the different action officials."

The notion that every Communist functioned as a Soviet lackey was the assumption that worried Adams most of all. Experience and wisdom, he argued, seemed to demand a more sophisticated approach to the Soviet threat. Hoping to explore the means by which the United States "might more advantageously handle the subject of Communism as distinguished from Russian imperialism," Adams was practically begging his colleagues to revise their view of international communism—an image of universal threat that was, for many, the very engine of the Cold War itself.

After first broaching the issue in March 1949 of how a more subtle brand of rhetoric might weaken the Communist world, Adams watched as his initiative went virtually nowhere within the State Department. Clearly, trends were moving away from the more measured approach to Soviet communism that had characterized U.S. policy over the previous few years—a strategy that had emerged out of planning for the European Recovery Program in the spring of 1947 and accelerated following the expulsion of Yugoslavia from the Cominform in June 1948. Thereafter, the chances for dividing a rapidly hardening bloc of Communist states would shrink as the Truman administration began to regard those nations as members of an increasingly solid movement controlled by the Kremlin. That emergent vision of a highly coordinated, conspiratorial, malevolent force became encoded in the image of a "Communist monolith"—arguably the most dominant representation of international communism during the height of the Cold War.

As a term of political shorthand, the "monolith" helped to shape popular and official conceptions of the Soviet Union and its allies, distilling the often messy realities of international relations into a neat, comprehensible formula. Its lesson was that all Communists, regardless of their native land or political program, were first and foremost tools of the Kremlin. The geopolitical and national security implications of this alignment were immense. On one hand, if local Communist parties (CPs) were nationalist and therefore more concerned with state-centered interests, then Moscow's ability to marshal their resources in the service of Soviet objectives was far from guaranteed. Communist leaders, in fact, had long spoken of national "roads" to socialism, and such rhetoric became even more commonplace during World War II and the early postwar era. The existence, then, of "national communism"—the practice of tailoring Marxist ideology to local conditions—presented the West with opportunities to isolate Moscow more effectively and pursue its own interests with greater ease. On the other hand, if those CPs were internationalist and therefore loyal to the Kremlin, then each of them, in theory, enhanced Soviet capabilities, dramatically altering the global balance of power. Although U.S. and British statesmen were downplaying the likelihood of Soviet military aggression in the near term, the threat posed by Communist political gains and Moscow's ability to capitalize upon them—particularly in the vital regions of Europe and Asia—was enormous. Evaluations of the monolithic nature of international communism thus became central to the strategic calculus of the United States and its Cold War allies.[2]

While the "monolith" grew out of a specific set of historical circumstances, its rhetorical power owed more to its symbolic than its literal properties.[3] The monolith functioned primarily as a metaphor—a simplification of reality—and therefore served as a kind of mental filter or psychological tool, satisfying the very human need to fit voluminous and often conflicting information into manageable categories.[4] But it was more than just a cognitive crutch, for it was grounded in an interpretation of history that made great sense to those living through a harrowing time. In the four years since V-J Day, several developments had suggested that communism was on the march. Moscow's disciples had consolidated power in Eastern Europe, rejected Western economic aid, founded an international, anticapitalist organization, and staged revolutionary warfare along the entire coast of East Asia. Moreover, they had conducted espionage throughout the United States and the British Commonwealth, suggesting that no place was safe from the long arm of the Kremlin.

Those images of coordinated Communist activity are standard fare in scholarly and general treatments of the Cold War. Monographs and texts on the period, written by historians and international relations theorists, frequently note that Americans of the late 1940s viewed communism as a unitary force. Specific reference to the monolithic nature of international communism did, in fact, surface during those early postwar years, shaping the understanding that Americans and others held of the movement and its adherents. The identification of such a perception and the recognition of its importance rightly focus on a key element in the emerging Cold War consciousness, one that was particularly influential in the United States.[5]

Yet, with all that has been written on that era, scholars have failed to examine the image itself and the process by which it came to permeate the language of policymakers and the public. This is a curious omission given the many books that attempt to explain both the origins and the ideological nature of the Cold War. Those works that do cite the grip of a Cold War mentality attribute its strength to various dynamics, such as the demands of domestic politics, the psychology of the foreign policy establishment, and a latent fear of Communist subversion. Although many of these works factor earlier waves of anticommunism into their accounts, they often treat the early postwar years as a kind of *Stunde-null*—a zero-hour—after which the administration of President Harry S. Truman manufactured a Cold War consensus out of a loosely formed public penchant for tolerating, and even promoting, such crusades.[6] At the same time, studies that have delved more deeply into the ideological dimensions of U.S. foreign policy have often focused on the dissemination of those ideas rather than on their formulation. Even the more incisive accounts devote comparatively little time to the origins of the Cold War mind-set.[7] Similarly, inquiries into America's cultural Cold War rarely trace the means by which the monolithic framework emerged within both public and policymaking circles.[8] And none of these works—neither those exploring the diplomatic angle nor those adopting a cultural approach—has adequately addressed the question of whether, or to what degree, that mentality was a uniquely American one.

The absence of this discussion is all the more curious given the evident discord within Communist ranks during the interwar period. By and large, the relevant scholarship has glossed over this intra- and interparty strife when invoking Western belief in a Communist monolith. Not that such conflict was hidden from view; the most famous example—Stalin's assault on the ideas and person of Leon Trotsky, through internal and external exile, and eventually murder—was well known in the West. So, too, were the purges of the mid-1930s, episodes that allegedly pointed not to the "iron discipline" of Bolsheviks but of the need to instill it. Attacks on Communists in the United States and the splintering of the American Communist movement during the 1920s and 1930s are also suggestive of a movement rife with fissures. Why, then, did Americans as well as Britons in the postwar era come to see international communism as a monolithic force when the history of that movement suggested it was no such thing?

This book will seek to provide an answer by examining the emergence of the monolithic image among government officials and opinion makers in both Great Britain and the United States. It will treat that image as the product of several historical trends that were both deeply embedded and close to the surface of the British and American experiences—an amalgam this study will describe as an "Anglo-American historical consciousness" that was very much at work on both sides of the Atlantic during the 1930s and 1940s. Though more pervasive and millennial in its American guise, this understanding also informed conceptions of international communism in Great Britain, the nation most closely allied with the United States during the early Cold War, and cast the Kremlin's challenge as but one more in a long line of threats to freedom and liberty.

This study will also address a topic in the literature that is in many ways a conceptual complement: the process by which policymakers tried to crack the monolith. Serious academic work on this theme began in the late 1980s as historians outlined efforts by the Truman administration to drive a "wedge" between the Soviet Union and its allies. These analyses brought the contours of the "wedge strategy" into high relief and testified to the subtlety and creativity of U.S. policymakers. They also made it increasingly difficult to maintain that American officials, as a rule, viewed all Communists as out-and-out supplicants of Moscow. Two of those works took that discussion one step further. In 1987, John Lewis Gaddis advanced the "provisional" argument that U.S. statesmen, throughout the entirety of the postwar period, "never believed in the existence of an international communist monolith." Three years later, Gordon Chang qualified Gaddis's claim, stating that not since 1949 had a single official in a position of influence ever believed that communism was a monolithic entity.[9]

While Gaddis and Chang demonstrate convincingly that policymakers were highly aware of tensions within the Communist world, they base their claims on a narrow definition of the monolithic mindset. A more expansive understanding of what constituted "monolithic" behavior, drawn from the perspective of those living at the time, suggests that British as well as American policymakers regarded communism as both a monolithic *and* a nonmonolithic force, and that competing notions of the movement's solidarity often existed alongside each other. This study will therefore juxtapose the many conflicting statements policymakers made about the monolith and their ability to crack it, revealing the enormous complexities those individuals had to confront in the process. It also extends the critiques found in these and similar works by offering a comparative perspective—by couching the American and British efforts at driving wedges within their respective evaluations of the bloc they were trying to bust.

Ironically, the monolithic image entered popular speech as a description of Communist solidarity at the very moment when that cohesiveness was becoming shrouded in doubt. Following the Tito-Cominform split in 1948 and the Sino-Soviet split roughly a decade later, reference to the monolith increased as popular and official acceptance of its validity receded. Witness the spate of works published in the 1970s, a time when U.S. policy was actually predicated on the existence of splits in the Communist world.[10] As mentioned earlier, interest in the schismatic nature of international communism continued into the 1980s as historians explored Western efforts to "crack the monolith."[11] The end of the Cold War brought forth still more titles that either invoked the term or set out to gauge its accuracy.[12] Other works, including textbooks and historical monographs, frequently invoked a Soviet or Communist monolith, often in dismissive tones. Indeed, the impact of the monolith on contemporary discourse extends far beyond the realm of geopolitics. In recent years, articles and books have appeared discussing the monolithic aspects of numerous subjects, including television, political correctness, Mexican machismo, the Holy See, Black thought—even death.[13] Clearly, the monolithic image, which arguably gained such currency because of its Cold War application, has cast a long shadow over political and general discourse in the postwar era.

That image emerged in what scholars have referred to as the "public cultures" of the United States and Great Britain. As John Fousek has described it, a nation's "public culture" constitutes "the arena in which social and political conflict is played out and in which consensus is forged, manufactured, and maintained."[14] Beyond the confines of Congress or Parliament, or the White House or Downing Street, it encompasses the many fora in which the presentation and discussion of social and political ideas take place. Its contours are shaped by innumerable agents, including social and business organizations, educational and political institutions, and the mass media. Some, clearly, are more consequential than others and have varying degrees of impact on their intended audiences. For the purposes of this study, the print media, including newspapers, mass-circulation periodicals, and elite journals, feature prominently as sources of information and insight on international communism. So, too, do public events and spectacles, phenomena which themselves contributed to the respective national dialogues on communism in national and international life. It is through these channels that I hope to offer a more nuanced picture of how monolithic communism, in its various representations, came to permeate the American and British Cold War mind-sets.

In order to re-create the manner in which the monolith emerged as a frame of reference, this book will read as a chronological account of the years 1945–1950, with the close of World War II and China's intervention in the Korean War acting as historical bookends. It begins, however, with a broad overview of American and British reactions to socialism and communism up through World War II. Chapter 2 examines efforts to define the threat posed by international communism during the early postwar era; it also charts the emergence of ideology as a key tool in that regard. Chapter 3 explores the rhetorical dimension of Western Cold War policies from the Truman Doctrine through the Marshall Plan. Chapter 4 explores the considerable impact of the Cominform on interpretations of the Communist challenge. Chapter 5 examines the Cominform's June 1948 expulsion of Yugoslavia, a seminal moment in Western thinking about the monolith. Efforts to widen fissures in the Communist world picked up following the Tito affair, though they had also preceded it; Chapter 6, therefore, looks at attempts to drive a wedge between Moscow and other Communist states. Deeper thinking about anti-Stalinist communism became a feature of British and American policymaking circles following the Tito split, and Chapter 7 evaluates the risks as well as the rewards for encouraging its growth. Chapter 8 focuses on the Korean War and its impact on the monolithic image, and a final chapter ties together the book's central themes and arguments. Although this study is not intended as an exploration of Communist solidarity per se, its conclusion will address, albeit briefly, the general accuracy of Western perceptions of the movement's cohesiveness.

A survey of these themes comes at a propitious time in American history. For many observers, the events of September 11, 2001, signaled the dawn of a new era, prompting pundits and policymakers to look upon the early Cold War as a historical analogue.[15] The attendant "War on Terror" also gave rise to a contemporary version of the Communist monolith—the "axis of evil"—stirring a familiar resistance not only to a new brand of totalitarianism but to the dangers of remaining neutral in the face of it.[16] The commonalities between the "monolith" and the "axis" are striking: both terms are abstractions, both emerged at the forefront of what policymakers and the public perceived as a new geopolitical era, and both carried implicit policy assumptions about the threat each sought to describe. Whereas America had once sought to counter the challenges posed by a bloc of allegedly unified Communist states, it now was confronting the "rogue" troika of Iraq, Iran, and North Korea.

In the immediate aftermath of 9/11, the conflation of those more recent threats was, in some sense, understandable. The feelings of shock and revulsion in the wake of the attack, along with the visceral desire for justice and retribution, could well have led policymakers to pursue a comprehensive solution to U.S. national security threats. In that environment, the reflex to strike at Iraq, even when early reports pointed to al Qaeda as the likely culprit of the World Trade Center and Pentagon horrors, might have stemmed from a desire to settle all "family business," as the fictitious Michael Corleone might have put it. If so, then this "Godfather option" of including Iraq in a target list consisting of al Qaeda and Afghanistan's Taliban regime highlights the potential for actions of such horror—of such *terror*—to magnify threats in a way that overrides clarity of thought and coolness of judgment. While 9/11 also might have created a political climate more conducive to military action against Iraq, the pursuit of that option stemmed, by all accounts, from a sincerely held belief in its necessity.

Indeed, popular opinion was generally supportive of President George W. Bush's decision to vilify an "axis of evil" and his preferred response to it. Rallying around the commander in chief in the midst of a national trauma, Americans apparently agreed that the differences among the "axis" states paled beside their similarities. Testifying to the term's persuasive power, Americans continued to regard the nations it comprised as threatening to U.S. interests long after Bush first used the term—with a conviction not nearly as evident prior to its introduction.[17] Lumping those countries together, Bush placed them on one side of a clear moral divide, allowing him to mobilize public opinion—and in one case military might—more effectively against them. Indeed, both prior to the Iraq War and throughout the conflict itself, the Bush administration displayed a marked tendency to conflate its disparate enemies into a single malevolent threat.[18] That need to simplify reality and manage conflicting information also fostered a dualistic approach to the post-9/11 era, one in which the nations of the world, and implicitly individual Americans themselves, were either with the administration or against it.[19]

Those dynamics are all reminiscent of the early Cold War. Like Truman administration officials who ascribed a unity of action among Communists to the movement's ideological affinities, Bush personnel were seemingly wedded to ideas that sometimes developed independent of (and even in spite of) rigorous, evidentiary proof. Notable among those beliefs were its assessments of Saddam Hussein and his programs for weapons of mass destruction. Although Truman and Bush differed in the degree to which they shared a clearly defined commitment to

America's role in the world, their administrations operated within political realities imbued with increasing amounts of stress and uncertainty.
These conditions allowed ideological preconceptions not only to define a
foreign threat but also to shape the response to it.[20] As scholars gain
some measure of distance from 9/11, they will likely comment further
on the emergence of this new perceptual construct, situating it within
the interpretive frameworks embraced by the Bush administration.

The purpose of this study, however, is to re-create the milieu in
which those earlier actors worked and lived so that we can better understand the interpretive framework they embraced. It was this framework that for Americans, Britons, and no doubt legions of others
helped to define an era. By uncovering the manner in which the monolithic image emerged during that period, we might yet generate insights
into the construction of our more recent consensual climate.

[Handwritten margin note: those will prove, and be, proved — much easier to escape]

[Handwritten note at bottom of page: Selective views the "Communist monolith" as an interpretive framework for policymakers and for the larger "public culture" that influenced those policymakers. He traces how the historiography accepted that monolith as a reality without much critical examination until Gaddis and Chay argued that policymakers did not in fact see communism as a monolith after, at least, 1949. Selective takes this latter argument further by saying the monolith was a metaphor whose symbolic power simplifies reality and serves as the context for policies that tended to "drive a wedge" between communist nations, offends few communists—non-monolithic + monolithic terms simultaneously—solved that document to formulate their policy. The rest of the book traces that emergence in the U.S. + G.B. in order to establish the "Anglo-American historical consensus" but to also contextualize U.S. designs.]

CHAPTER ONE

The Inheritance

World War II had been raging for over eighteen months by the time Henry Luce, the publisher of *Life* magazine, delivered what he regarded as a long overdue tonic to the American public. Inserting an essay of his own into a February 1941 issue, Luce called on Americans to realize their destiny as the crowning glory of human achievement. The United States, he pointed out, the "most powerful and most vital nation" on earth, had been neglecting its responsibilities. Shirking the spiritual as well as the practical obligations of leadership, Americans had remained aloof from the global conflict, consigning the world to the chaos of total war. But the fortunes of all nations depended on U.S. management of the international community. Prosperity and harmony could still rain down upon the peoples of the world, Luce wrote, but would do so only if the rest of the twentieth century unfolded as an "American" one.

It was a powerful argument and one that would become familiar to far more than *Life*'s 3 million subscribers. By and large, Americans endorsed its premises: that the world was a battleground between good and evil, that totalitarianism was the modern manifestation of evil, and that the United States—as the culmination of historical progress—had a mission not only to fight that evil but to spread its own ideals far and wide. Rhetorically, Luce had struck all the right chords, tapping into the nation's past in order to prepare Americans for the troubles ahead.[1]

By minimizing the complexities of international life, however, he had reinforced an impulse that would exacerbate the very problems he sought to allay. For Luce had given voice to the "monolithic framework," an interpretive construct that would beget the "Communist monolith," the dominant image of international communism during the formative years of the Cold War. That image was hardly peculiar to those living in the United States. In fact, the manner in which it emerged suggests that Britons, who would soon stand alongside Americans in their resistance to Communist expansion, internalized similar historical lessons and conceived of totalitarianism in comparable ways. Although the monolithic framework took shape in response to contemporary events, it grew out of traditions deeply embedded in an Anglo-American historical consciousness, traditions which held that both peoples had a unique destiny to civilize the downtrodden and redeem the world—and, in a later guise, to halt the spread of communism itself.

For Americans as well as Britons, that sense of national purpose emerged out of worldviews that glorified their respective countries as the engines of historical change. This "whiggish" reflex, an interpretation of history in which the world is seen as following an upward spiral of material and spiritual progress, is integral to the Anglo-American heritage.[2] The origins of whiggism likely stretch back thousands of years, but its contours are clearly evident in English society during the sixteenth and seventeenth centuries. Fears of conspiratorial plots, belief in millennial visions, faith in the redemptive power of Protestant Christianity, confidence in the virtue of republican institutions—all of these impulses were widespread in Reformation England and made their way across the Atlantic to the New World. They would continue to color the British and American experiences thereafter.[3]

The industrial and social upheavals of the late nineteenth and early twentieth centuries exacerbated those dynamics, but it was the Great War of 1914–1918 that gave them an increasingly nativist gloss. In the United States, groups such as the American Protective League, the National Security League, and the American Defense Society sprang up to promote "100 percent Americanism." Federal authorities cracked down on labor agitation as new strictures against immigrants and inflammatory speech radicalized an already tense environment. Americans thus became even more suspicious of movements they deemed conspiratorial and alien-inspired. In Britain, the outbreak of war quashed any enthusiasm for a radical socialist program. Calls for an international general strike fell on deaf ears as the Labour Party supported the British military effort. While the ensuing burst of patriotic nationalism had a unifying effect on Britain's class structure, it also had an ugly side, isolating those groups perceived to be deficient in their

Britishness. The obvious targets at the start of the war were Germans and those with German-sounding names. As the war dragged on, however, anti-German sentiment evolved into a bias against all "foreigners," rendering British xenophobia every bit as virulent as its American counterpart.[4]

Bolshevism

Apart from heightening Anglo-American fears of outsiders and radicals, the Great War had a profound effect on socialism itself. The readiness of many European Socialists to identify with national and bourgeois interests, rather than with international and proletarian concerns, split the movement in two, convincing its extremists that only a more confrontational and revolutionary socialism could establish a workers' paradise. Vladimir Lenin sought to realize that utopia when he and his Bolshevik cohorts overthrew Russia's Provisional Government in October 1917. Not surprisingly, the founding of the world's first Socialist state alarmed a great many observers on both sides of the Atlantic. Communism now had a territorial and ideological home, a development that cast ties between Russian and foreign Socialists—especially those living in the capitalist bastions of Great Britain and the United States—in an entirely new light. In so doing, the Bolshevik experiment gave rise to the more sustained antisocialism, and later anticommunism, that became endemic to American and, to a lesser extent, British political culture.[5]

Adding to Western fears, the Bolsheviks and their European associates had established an international organization to coordinate revolutionary movements all over the world. Founded in March 1919 and embodying all the elements of the idealized foe, the Communist International (Comintern, or Third International) was alien, conspiratorial, socialist, nondemocratic, and every bit as millennial as the Anglo-American project. British and U.S. officials reacted to its creation with horror. Winston Churchill, who regarded Russian—now termed "Soviet"—communism as "a pestilence more destructive of life than the Black Death or the Spotted typhus," saw the Comintern as "a deliberate world-wide, profoundly-conceived conspiracy" that threatened the foundations of Western civilization. British Labour also denounced the Comintern's aim of exporting revolution around the globe; even the party's Left wing rejected affiliation with the organization.[6] From the other side of the Atlantic, President Woodrow Wilson set out immediately to crush the organization. Fearing that delays in concluding the peace treaties at Versailles might embolden Soviet and European Communists, Wilson cut off food supplies to Eastern Europe in an effort to smash the region's Communist parties (CPs). "We are running a race with Bolshevism," he remarked, "and the world is on fire."[7]

Wilson's concern was real, for the Bolshevik revolution had spawned similar upheavals in Hungary and Germany, threatening the president's vision of a new world order as well as the shared values of the Anglo-American liberal tradition. With Russia controlling Comintern affairs and issuing its directives, Moscow sat atop a network of CPs ready to do its bidding. Indeed, the American Communist Party openly admitted its subservience to the Kremlin when, in signing the Twenty-One Points, it affirmed that "the Communist Parties of the various countries are the direct representatives of the Communist International, and thus, indirectly of the aims and policies of Soviet Russia." That declaration of fealty to a foreign power sharpened tensions in the United States, which had already risen to a fever pitch in the wake of labor protests, mail bombings, and the general uncertainties of the postwar world.[8]

The federal government responded by hunting down Communists and radicals in what became known as the "Red Scare." Attorney General A. Mitchell Palmer spearheaded that campaign, with a young J. Edgar Hoover serving as the department's point man for domestic subversion. Hoover, in his 1920 tract *The Revolution in Action,* had portrayed the previous year's disturbances as part of a highly coordinated plan, hatched in Moscow, to foment revolution worldwide. Resorting to the apocalyptic rhetoric that later generations of "Red hunters" would find so compelling, Hoover cited communism as "the most terrible menace of danger" to civilization "since the barbarian hordes overran West Europe and opened the dark ages." With Hoover's words adding more fuel to a highly incendiary domestic environment—Left-leaning figures such as union chief Samuel Gompers and Wisconsin senator Robert LaFollette were equally strident in condemning American Communists as Soviet lackeys—*de jure* recognition of the Soviet Union became a political impossibility. Secretary of State Bainbridge Colby argued that the Kremlin's commitment to revolution abroad, through the medium of the Comintern, disqualified Moscow from joining the family of nations. It was a position the United States would maintain throughout the 1920s and into the 1930s.[9]

While Britain took several steps toward recognition of the Soviet Union, it, too, endured a postwar spate of anti-Communist fervor. By the mid-1920s, the nation's political Right was lashing out at its Left in a spasm of Red-baiting rhetoric that undercut London's acknowledgment of the Soviet state. Publication of the "Zinoviev Letter," a communication purportedly written by Comintern chief Grigori Zinoviev encouraging British Communists to engage in subversive activities, further poisoned bilateral relations and polarized British political culture. A wave of anti-communism swept over Great Britain as politicians and government officials campaigned against the "Red menace." The home secretary arrested the entire leadership of Britain's Communist Party; materials seized during the raids indicated, in the words of the *Times,* a "constant and systematic promotion by institutions in Moscow of a movement directed to the ruin of British trade, the overthrow of the British constitution and the destruction of the British Empire." By the mid-1920s, roughly a decade after the Bolsheviks had seized power, Britons and Americans were largely convinced that Communist parties in England and the United States had become adjuncts of the Soviet regime.[10]

They had ample reason for believing so. From its earliest days, the Comintern had served the interests first and foremost of the Russian Bolsheviks. The body's real power was located in the Executive Committee of the Communist International (ECCI), which was itself controlled by the Kremlin. Moscow was therefore able to dictate the Comintern's various policies, ranging from its 1921 directive to create "united fronts" to its 1928 injunction against collaboration with social democrats to its 1929 condemnation and purging of American Communists for articulating the heretical doctrine of "exceptionalism"—the notion that the American experience invalidated aspects of Marxism-Leninism. From time to time, local CPs did succeed in modifying Comintern directives for their own tactical purposes. During the early 1920s, for instance, parties in Bulgaria, Norway, Italy, Sweden, and Hungary had quarreled with Lenin and carved out some space for tailoring Communist teaching to local conditions. But such detours rarely resulted in meaningful party independence.[11]

Moscow's control over the Comintern became even more pronounced with the emergence of Josef Stalin as the supreme figure in the Soviet Union. Following Lenin's death in January 1924, Stalin used his position as head of the party secretariat to outmaneuver several rivals for the top spot in the Bolshevik hierarchy. His ability to win debates over the direction of Soviet development allowed him to establish the party's ideological line and to marginalize those with whom he differed. By virtue of his increasing grip on the levers of power, Stalin was able to use the Comintern to much the same end, directing its operations in support of the Soviet state. His power to do so only grew as storm clouds, in the guise of Nazi Germany, appeared on the horizon. While the hard work of consolidating the Bolshevik project dictated a focus on events inside the Soviet Union—the call to promote "socialism in one country" had actually emerged out of a 1924 Comintern directive—protecting Moscow's sheer existence from the Fascist threat soon became the imperative of Communists worldwide.[12]

Monolithism

Interest in fostering that solidarity marked Soviet rhetoric from the earliest years of the regime, however. Lenin's "ban on factions," set down in 1921 at the Tenth Party Congress, stipulated the need for Communists to speak with one voice. Enforcement of that new stricture fell to Stalin himself, whom Lenin had endorsed for the newly created post of general secretary of the Communist Party. It was thus Stalin who lorded over the party machinery and ensured the ideological conformity of its members.[13] Yet he was hardly the only member of the Politburo interested in wiping out traces of internal dissent. Gregori Zinoviev, head of the Comintern, also sought to instill "iron discipline" among party members and invoked the image of the monolith to do so. Speaking to a 1923 Party Conference in Leningrad, Zinoviev explained that it was necessary "sometimes to cut off a very considerable section of the Party . . . in order to achieve a single monolithic Communist Party rather than a 'parliament of opinions.' "[14] Similarly, the German Communist Clara Zetkin campaigned for the "monolithism of our discipline and action" at the Fifth Comintern Congress in 1924, the meeting at which Moscow sought to bring the world's Communist parties in line with the policies and practices of the Soviet state.[15] From that point forward, the Kremlin would "bolshevize" the native parties—centralizing their organization and stamping out all factional activity—consolidating its hold on the Comintern and remaking its constituent members into more effective agents of international revolution.[16] And it was Stalin, more so than any of his colleagues, who made the monolithic unity of world communism a top priority.[17]

Stalin's embrace of that position also helped him eliminate his domestic rivals. Not surprisingly, those whom he purged decried the emphasis on total conformity. Leon Trotsky, for instance, maintained that such ideological rigidity was anathema to communism. "When and where," Trotsky asked, "has there yet been in the history of the revolutionary movement such dumb 'monolithism?' "[18] Undeterred, Stalin hammered home the need for uniformity in his *Foundations of Leninism*, published in 1932. The constituent parties of the Communist International, he wrote, simply could not permit the emergence of factions. The Party itself was synonymous with "unity of will" which left no room either for splinter groups or for the division of Party control.[19] According to American Communist Eugene Dennis, that singleness of purpose was precisely what his party needed. Quoting Stalin, Dennis argued that "the Party must systematically improve the social composition of its organizations and rid itself of corrupting opportunist elements, with the aim of making its ranks monolithic to the utmost degree."[20]

The impact of monolithism was not limited to the internal workings of Communist parties or to the relationship between those parties and the Comintern. Pursuit of the monolithic ideal helped to ensure that a particular image of communism—as a highly coordinated, conspiratorial movement, modeled along the lines and in the interest of the Soviet Union—was the only image presented to the outside world. Italian Communist Eugenio Reale maintains that "the term 'monolithic unity' invariably appeared in every Communist declaration" during his days with the Comintern. "By repeating it incessantly for twenty years," Reale notes, "Stalin achieved one undeniable result: many people (above all Westerners) eventually believed in this 'monolithic unity' " as an integral feature of the movement. Indeed, it was an image that Communist leaders sought eagerly to project.[21]

The extent to which Westerners bought into the monolithic image is difficult to gauge, but references to the term began to appear in British and American publications during the 1920s and 1930s. In 1924, the London *Times* cited Lev Kamanev's declaration that " 'our party is more united than ever and . . . will remain compact and monolithic.' " During the purges of the 1930s, it quoted *Pravda*'s announcement that Trotskyist elements were " 'penetrating even our monolithic party.' " In addition, the *Times* described the Red Army as "a monolith—in Moscow's metaphor" and Poland's national assemblies as " 'monolithic,' in accordance with the best totalitarian models."[22]

American publications also began to employ the term. The *Nation*, for instance, in a 1927 article on Trotsky, commented on "the 'monolithism' of the party."[23] The *New York Times*, from the 1930s onward, made frequent reference to the monolithic nature of both the Nazi and Soviet states, and reported on a related theme in contemporary Italian journalism: the tendency to describe the Axis powers as "a flawless monolith."[24] The *Washington Post* was also enamored of the expression, using it in both news and editorial pieces. The *Post's* emphasis, however, was on the Soviet nation and not the Communist movement. As its editors opined in early February 1944, the U.S.S.R. was "the most monolithic state in history."[25] Although the *Post* and other news outlets surely helped to popularize the term, the ideal of socialist solidarity—of Communist parties the world over pursuing and maintaining a posture of "monolithic unity"—originated with Moscow itself and was precisely what many in the West found so threatening. The Kremlin, therefore, bore a large share of the burden for cementing the monolithic image in the minds of Communists and non-Communists alike.[26]

While foreign observers were becoming more familiar with the Soviet political machine, they were also shedding their fear of its revolutionary character. The U.S.S.R., the argument ran, was evolving into a more "normal," less revolutionary state, concerned primarily with is own national interest. Indeed, several events during the 1920s and 1930s seemed to indicate that the Soviet Union was devoting more energy to its internal needs than to its external program. The capitalist initiatives of the New Economic Policy and the power struggle following Lenin's death both pointed toward such a transformation; the emergence of Josef Stalin as the Soviet *vozhd* (boss, or leader) and his ouster of Leon Trotsky further suggested that worldwide revolution was taking a back seat to "socialism in one country."

This evolutionary interpretation of Soviet communism became popular in Britain before it caught on in the United States. Its adherents, inhabiting all sides of the political spectrum, defy categorization; those on the Left viewed it with much regret, while those on the Right greeted it with considerable relief. As London's *Daily Herald* put it, Soviet Russia had morphed into a more imperialist nation. In America, a wide range of voices concluded that the show trials of the 1930s highlighted a struggle in Soviet circles between the forces of retrenchment and those advocating greater revolutionary zeal. Observers now began to portray Moscow's new ideology—Stalinism—as "a Thermidorian reaction," a mellowing of the fires stoking the world's revolutionary movements. Opinion leaders such as the *New York Times* and *Time* magazine each adopted the Thermidorian perspective, as did several other journals. The *Chicago Tribune* even suggested that Stalin's purges marked "the final liquidation of the Red Revolution."[27]

Those views notwithstanding, significant pockets of opinion were wary of such optimistic forecasts. In Britain, the ruling establishment rejected the more strident claims that Stalin had exchanged his socialist garb for Tsarist apparel, though significant pockets in Whitehall were impressed with Stalin's evident pragmatism. To key members in the U.S. State Department, the popularity of the Thermidorian outlook was a troubling development. Officials such as East European specialist Loy Henderson and William C. Bullitt, America's first ambassador to the Soviet Union, believed that Moscow remained undaunted in its pursuit of global revolution. Republicans were similarly convinced that Moscow remained the font of world communism—the only difference being that it now had greater resources at its disposal. Some of those resources, alleged GOP officials, were to be found in the highest levels of the U.S. government. Indeed, Republican hostility to economic planning and social welfare—and to the Left-leaning officials who promoted those ideals—generated suspicions about the ultimate source and beneficiary of President Franklin D. Roosevelt's New Deal measures. Influential figures, including Republican senator Robert A. Taft and former president Herbert Hoover, charged that Roosevelt's policies were "made in Moscow." Critical of the administration and hoping for political advantage, numerous Republicans waved the red flag in an effort to smear the New Deal as un-American.[28]

Though economic depression led Britain to engage in similarly proactive, pseudo-Socialist measures, policymakers in the United Kingdom never had to endure the extreme charges Roosevelt faced. Britons returned the "National Government" to power in 1935 with a diminished but still substantial Conservative majority as one of its own, Stanley Baldwin, replaced Labourite Ramsay MacDonald as prime minister. Thereafter, Neville Chamberlain, Baldwin's successor at Downing Street, would lean toward Nazi Germany in London's quarrel with Bolshevism. Further condemnation of Moscow came from fellow Tory Winston Churchill, who feared that the Soviet Union, by virtue of its role in the Spanish Civil War, would spread "its snaky tentacles through Portugal and France," a view shared by the British media. Yet such anti-Soviet sympathy was out of step in 1930s England. The rapid growth of a Left-leaning press, the heightened presence of a Popular Front, and the support of both by a vocal sect of Labour leaders offered Britons a sympathetic portrait of Soviet policy. Public opinion favored the Spanish Republicans, especially when it became clear that Russia was the only nation willing to resist the Fascists. Thereafter, numerous grassroots committees rallied to the Republican cause.[29]

The Left was far from united in its defense of the Spanish government, however. For both its liberal and conservative wings, support for
Spain meant tacit support of Moscow—a nonstarter for many of its
leaders. Labour stalwarts such as Ernest Bevin and Walter Citrine regarded communism and Communist methods as completely alien to
British democracy, denouncing both in a series of reports published
during the decade. They consistently rejected pleas from British Communists to construct a broad coalition of the Left, recognizing that such
unity would be a sham and merely another way for the Kremlin to undermine its chief ideological competition. Their opposition to communism, a hostility that Spain would engender in broader segments of the
Left, would help shape a broader respect for Western values and political models.[30]

The Anglo-American Historical Revival

It was thus during the 1930s that Britons and Americans gave voice to
much of the imagery that would sustain them through the coming war
and beyond. Both peoples reacted to the challenges of economic depression and totalitarianism by searching their respective histories for
inspiration and guidance. A resultant "Anglo-American historical
consciousness" took root and remained vital throughout the interwar
period, emerging as part of a social process that reached into countless
pockets of American and British life. As such, it both grew out of and
constituted a powerful "public memory," what Michael Kammen has
called the "slowly shifting configuration of traditions [that] shapes a
nation's ethos and sense of identity." A host of personalities, including
journalists, artists, intellectuals, and politicians, were responsible for
creating that identity, and the words, symbols, and images they used
to do so drew their power from the national traditions of both
peoples.[31]

The impulse toward a greater historical consciousness was particularly strong among the American literati. Numerous writers and paint-
ers responded by embarking on an "emotional discovery of America,"
as Stuart Pratt Sherman described it, weaving their narratives around
themes embedded in the nation's history. While the artistic elite expressed that newfound interest in the form of poetry, art, books, and
essays, the American masses found the wellsprings of their heritage in
patriotic organizations and historical roadside markers. Along with a
growing attraction for nostalgic Americana, these developments marked

the emergence of a cultural and historical revival, suggesting that Americans, both high-brow and low, recognized the need to identify and affirm their collective foundations.[32]

Britons, like their cultural kin across the Atlantic, also combed their past for answers to the present. And like their counterparts in the United States, British writers shifted their focus from the more intimate affairs of personal life to larger questions of public importance. This renewed sense of social commitment was not limited to the literary bunch, for it suffused Britain's cultural spirit during the 1930s, manifesting itself in various folk, political, and religious movements. The upper classes, for instance, sought to reclaim the moral certainties of the Victorian Age—virtues that seemed to go hand-in-hand with British imperialism and economic preeminence. Segments of the elite also found that sense of assurance in religion, as the Oxford Group led a spiritual revival. Britons of more modest financial means affirmed their roots through a rediscovery of the land and its history. Still others partook of English traditions through the work of charitable foundations, several of which preserved the integrity and charm of historic buildings, churches, manuscripts, art, and the national landscape. And politicians sought to address the disruptions of the decade by tapping into a widely shared cultural consciousness, invoking images of national greatness that became an ever larger part of civic discourse.[33]

While the search for an historic past sprang from the turmoil of domestic affairs, it was the danger posed by events abroad that locked increasing numbers of Britons and Americans into a reverence for their national traditions. Fascism was on the march: Germany had scrapped the Treaty of Versailles, remilitarizing its society and occupying the Rhineland, and Italy had launched its war of conquest on Ethiopia. The propensity of those states for external aggression, combined with their intolerance of dissent at home, led vast numbers of Britons and Americans to conclude that fascism threatened the liberal values of democratic society. Intellectuals in both countries thus came to embrace the virtues of their native lands. For those in America, that meant supporting the New Deal and the liberal values of free speech, property rights, and democratic governance on which its programs rested. British intellectuals never adopted the celebratory tone of their American counterparts, though several of them eventually struck a more conciliatory attitude toward capitalism or retreated from political involvement altogether.[34]

Both sets of thinkers would also fight "the good fight" in support of socialism and the U.S.S.R. as the solution to the world's problems. When the Comintern called for a "Popular Front" against fascism in 1935, American and British intellectuals—whether Communists themselves or merely fellow travelers—joined hands with others on the Left in defense of the Soviet Union. The Spanish Civil War provided additional reason for their conversion, with several enlisting in the International Brigade to fight the Loyalists of Generalissimo Francisco Franco. American writer John Dos Passos went so far as to liken the battlefields of Spain to those of Lexington and Concord, noting that "a sense of continuity with generations gone before can stretch like a lifeline across the scary present." Thereafter, America's historical resistance to tyranny would become a touchstone for the values that he and his peers sought to uphold.[35]

Yet those who went to Spain soon realized that the fight was not as clear-cut as first imagined. Moscow, the supposed champion of all "progressive" forces, was purging one wing of Spanish Republicanism while simultaneously aiding another. A growing awareness that the Soviets could be just as totalitarian as the Nazis had a profound effect on Western intellectuals, pushing them closer toward the mainstream embrace of liberal, democratic values. By May 1939, American and British writers, fearing that artistic freedom would have no place in a totalitarian world, joined with the illuminati of several other nations to form the Congress for Cultural Freedom. The disillusions of Spain had thus confirmed for many intellectuals what the Stalinist terror had already revealed to others: that there was no meaningful difference between the Nazi and Soviet systems. It was in this context that the Left-leaning Malcolm Cowley, editor of the *New Republic,* urged Americans to reflect on their "great past in order to see the real nature of the traditions that we are trying to save, and in order to gain new strength for the struggles ahead."[36]

Red Fascism

The signing of the Nazi-Soviet Non-Aggression Pact in August 1939 completed that transformation. When Eugene Lyons declared that the agreement "exposed Hitler's Brown Bolshevism and Stalin's Red Fascism as aspects of the same totalitarian idea," he was expressing the sympathies of large numbers of people on both sides of the Atlantic. In fact, the word-symbol of "Red Fascism" merged the features of communism and Nazism into a new, synthetic brand of pure evil, allowing

Britons and Americans—including figures such as President Franklin D. Roosevelt, First Lord of the Admiralty Winston Churchill, and British Labour leader Ernest Bevin—to regard all totalitarians as essentially the same.[37] Although few American writers used the term explicitly in their work, several began to churn out newspaper and magazine articles tying Nazi Germany to the Soviet Union. According to this literature, both states aimed at total control of their populations, relied on terror and forced labor at home, used subversive tactics to spread their influence abroad, pushed for territorial conquest, and governed through charismatic—or at least highly commanding—authoritarian personalities. By early 1939, a growing interest in comparing dictatorial states, among both the academic and lay communities, had generated a widespread consensus that the Nazis and the Soviets were fundamentally alike.[38]

The emergence of the Red Fascist critique was also linked to the rise of totalitarianism as a new political force. As an intellectual problem, totalitarianism did not attract the attention of Americans until roughly a decade after its advent in Italy. Americans invoked the term following Adolf Hitler's ascension to power, and tended to apply it exclusively to Right-wing political movements. Within a few years, however, writers were describing Left-wing dictatorships using similar language. Well before the onset of the Cold War, then, prior to the Nazi-Soviet condominium—at a time, in fact, when Germans and Russians were waging a heated rhetorical war *against* each other—Americans were pointing out the similarities between the two states.

A similar dynamic took hold in the United Kingdom as totalitarianism remained a rather obscure concept for Britons until the middle of the 1930s. Only then, after the Nazis had altered the reference point for the idea, did Britons begin to speak of Germany and the Soviet Union as equally totalitarian powers. While the public made greater use of the term in the wake of Hitler's political triumph, British academics, who were predominantly Leftist in political orientation, reserved it for Germany and Italy; no longer would they group the "progressive" policies of the Soviet Union with those of the reactionary Nazis. Nevertheless, British writers and historians generally recognized that the word "totalitarianism" offered a handy description of a new development in politics: the growing power of the state to reach into the private sphere of the individual.[39]

More important, though, the image of Red Fascism led both populations to treat totalitarianism as equally alien to the liberal values of the

Anglo-American tradition. And it was that tradition—reawakened largely by the rush of contemporary events—that gave the image its explanatory power. American intellectuals, in particular, felt this pull. As Richard Pells writes, they came to regard the United States as "the final repository for their hopes and ambitions," committing themselves to democracy, political pluralism, and the "American Dream." Alfred Kazin voiced much the same idea in his 1942 survey of American literature, On Native Grounds, the last chapter of which is entitled "America!, America!" Although the book appeared following U.S. entry into World War II, its concluding words were equally applicable to a time when the nation had not yet committed itself to the cause: "Never was it so imperative as it is now not to sacrifice any of the values that give our life meaning; never was it so imperative for men to be equal to the evil that faces them and not submissive to its terror."[40]

Put simply, the turmoil of the 1930s—with its political, economic, social, and moral disruptions—prompted that generation of Britons and Americans to express greater reverence for their historic legacy and the values that shaped it. As the world moved closer to war, both peoples saw the coming fight as one between the forces of democracy and those of tyranny. In that context, the symbol of Red Fascism became a useful rhetorical device, not so much to understand the particularities of the Nazi and Soviet systems but to highlight the differences between those regimes and the Anglo-American way.[41]

Wartime Attitudes

The notion that Russia was both a totalitarian and a reactionary state received an added boost from Soviet behavior during World War II. Following the Nazi-Soviet Pact of August 1939 and the subsequent German assault on Poland, Comintern head Georgi Dimitrov ordered the Communist parties of America (CPUSA) and Great Britain (CPGB) to soften their lines toward Nazi Germany, thereby exposing those groups as unvarnished operatives of the Kremlin. Thereafter, the CPGB set out to "work for Britain's military defeat," while the CPA targeted "British and French imperialism," instead of fascism, as the enemy of the moment.[42] While this episode illustrated Moscow's control over comrades around the world, it also strengthened the image of the U.S.S.R. as a status-quo power. Russia's treaty with Germany, in addition to its partition of Poland and its war on Finland, did little to suggest that Stalin was interested in promoting international communism per se.[43] Several members of the Foreign Office hoped that such *realpolitik* might change Soviet policy for the better. And inasmuch as President Roosevelt assumed that the U.S.S.R. and the United States were moving toward a form of government in which elements of the two systems were "converging," he too subscribed to the more chastened view of Soviet behavior. As a result, Britons and Americans—from the diplomat in government service to the person on the street—began to take more seriously the evolutionary view of Soviet foreign policy.[44]

Contributing to this perception was Stalin's decision to fold up the Comintern in May 1943. To congressmen such as Tom Connally (D-TX), chairman of the Senate Foreign Relations Committee, and Martin Dies (D-TX), head of the House Committee on Un-American Activities, the dissolution of the Comintern signaled that Russia would now tend to its own garden—surely a welcome sign for most Americans. Summing up the views of many in and out of government, the *Washington Times-Herald* maintained that it had no problem with the Kremlin's installation of a Communist regime at home; it simply objected to Moscow's efforts to promote Communist revolution abroad. Satisfied that such internationalist behavior was now a thing of the past, the public seemingly dropped its understanding of communism as a Moscow-based monolithic movement. Indeed, Stalin's subsequent call for "many roads to socialism" appeared to indicate that "National Communism" had become an official part of Soviet doctrine.[45]

The break-up of the Third International hardly signaled Moscow's retreat from its position atop the Communist world, however. The Comintern's July 1941 directive urging CPs to form national fronts provided Stalin with the means to manipulate foreign comrades while wrapping his actions in the rhetoric of indigenous control. Construction of those inclusive parties, a Soviet goal not only in Central and Eastern Europe but in Western Europe as well, was accompanied by a shrewd bureaucratic maneuver: the installation of former Comintern chief Georgi Dimitrov as head of the newly created foreign department of the Soviet Communist Party. This new bureau—the Department of International Information—allowed Moscow to direct the Communist movement at a time when it professed to be doing no such thing.[46]

Nevertheless, peoples on both sides of the Atlantic continued to believe that Russia was becoming a more conservative state. Following Hitler's invasion of the U.S.S.R. in June 1941, Britons expressed great admiration for the Red Army's effort to stem the Nazi onslaught.

Opinion polls, moreover, revealed that large numbers of people were expressing the view that Moscow's ideological fervor had waned. Surveys of U.S. opinion from 1943 and 1944 pointed toward a growing conviction that "Russia was aiming not at expanding Communism in Europe, but at achieving national security by the establishment of sympathetic governments in neighboring countries." Only 20 percent of those polled believed that Russia wished to "take over a large part of Europe" to spread communism, while 45 percent thought it would seek to erect friendly governments along her borders. In addition, roughly 70 percent of those familiar with Stalin's mantra of building "socialism in one country" believed that Soviet leaders were firmly committed to that project; only 12 percent thought otherwise. Likewise, by March 1945, less than one-fifth of the American public were worrying about the extension of Russian communism. In fact, far more people disclosed that they had "nothing to fear" from Moscow in the postwar world.[47]

Those expressions of sympathy for the U.S.S.R. owed much to a marketing blitz trumpeting a more benign Soviet state. Hollywood brought the image of a nonthreatening Russia to wide segments of the American public through a series of pro-Soviet movies. Besides *Mission to Moscow,* the celluloid version of the Joseph E. Davies book chronicling his years as ambassador to the U.S.S.R., Hollywood soft-pedaled Soviet communism in films such as *Song of Russia, The North Star, Boy from Stalingrad, Days of Glory,* and *Counter-Attack.* According to the State Department, the media regarded Soviet foreign policy as "actuated primarily by considerations of security" and tended to look at such policy "sympathetically."[48] This sentiment was particularly endemic among the popular press. *Life,* for instance, claimed that Moscow had "embarked on a new nationalist phase in which internationalism was at least temporarily shelved." It also gave Davies a platform to announce that postwar Russia would neither pursue world revolution nor promote dissension in other states. Elite opinion struck a similar chord, with the *New Republic* describing Soviet foreign policy as "defensive, not aggressive," and maintaining that Stalin "had no intention of Bolshevizing Europe" and making it a Russian appendage.[49]

Such rosy forecasts gave way to bleaker ones during the latter phases of the war. The Red Army's sweep across Eastern Europe generated little of the enthusiasm that had greeted its defensive stand against the Wehrmacht. Moscow's apparent indifference to the plight of Warsaw partisans, its cynical approach to the Yalta accords, and its heavy-handed manner in dealing with occupied territories—combined with more bellicose statements coming out of the region's Communist parties—led several officials in the State Department to voice their concerns about Soviet postwar ambitions. Ambassador Averell Harriman, who had once regarded Stalin's disbanding of the Comintern as a sign of growing Soviet nationalism, now viewed it as an utterly disingenuous act, as did East European specialist Elbridge Durbrow; both men began to speculate on how a revived Third International might fit into Moscow's postwar plans. Similarly, State Department counselor and Soviet expert Charles E. Bohlen argued that Moscow would continue to use native Communists to foment revolution around the globe. George F. Kennan, second in command at the U.S. embassy in Moscow, shared Bohlen's concern but was more circumspect in his evaluation of Soviet policy. In fact, Kennan reflected the ambivalence of many officials in their efforts to decipher Soviet behavior. Although he believed that Moscow had abandoned its revolutionary program, Kennan still thought it would seek to spread communism abroad or to impose its rule on neighboring states. Comintern or no Comintern, the Soviets were likely to pursue their interests in an aggressive fashion once the war was over.[50]

In an effort to bring some coherence to high-level thinking on Soviet communism, the department turned to Raymond E. Murphy, its resident authority on fascism and the international Communist movement.[51] Shortly after V-E Day, Murphy produced a lengthy summary of Moscow's postwar intentions, the most comprehensive analysis of international communism prepared for President Harry S. Truman prior to the upcoming Big Three conference at Potsdam. The picture Murphy painted was of a Soviet Union poised to conduct ideological warfare on a grand scale. As he described it, the resurgence of "Marxist-Leninist-Stalinist tactics" among the Communist parties of Europe signaled that the Kremlin would likely resuscitate the Comintern and revert to its revolutionary program of old. For all practical purposes, however, a revived Comintern would have little effect on the workings of international communism since its absence had never seriously hampered Moscow's ability to direct Communist affairs. "In no country after the dissolution of the Communist International," Murphy argued, "was there ever a deviation in loyalty by a communist party towards the Soviet Union." Owing to its military success and enhanced prestige, Moscow was now in a better position to ensure that loyalty and to encourage its growth throughout the world. As such, the Kremlin now posed a new kind of threat: that of a "smoothly-functioning, experienced and disciplined communist machine," poised "to take advantage immediately of any opportunities which may be presented." Murphy had thus articulated, in the department's most comprehensive survey of international communism, the clearest expression of the monolith to date.[52]

British depictions of Soviet communism moved along a similar trajectory. Moscow's sweep to the West eroded U.K. support for the Red Army, just as it had tarnished American images of the Kremlin. Given the changing perception of the U.S.S.R., British officials who had shunned the more benign view of Russia so popular with the masses now began to express even greater concern over Soviet behavior. According to Armine Dew, a member of the Foreign Office's Northern Department, the Soviets had never given up on their internationalist agenda. Contrary to many in the Foreign Office, who saw the disbanding of the Comintern as indicative of Stalin's more nationalistic policy, Dew was highly skeptical of the Soviet leader's motives; he regarded the abolition of the Third International primarily as an exercise in alliance propaganda. Moscow had in no way abandoned its mission to convert the world. In fact, its showing against the Nazi juggernaut would only heighten its ability to pose as a revolutionary city upon a hill.[53]

Other officials in the British Foreign Office were more fearful of the Soviets leading not by example but by force. Assistant Undersecretary of State William Strang noted that the Red Army might simply replace the Nazi Wehrmacht as the totalitarian masters of Europe. According to Roger Makins, who would soon become minister at the British embassy in Washington, the trend of Soviet policy was to extend "exclusive Russian influence" over the eastern half of the continent. Given current territorial realities, the Kremlin could represent its imperial interests as security imperatives in disguise. Furthermore, if Moscow still harbored any ideological ambitions, the Soviet military might be able to secure, or at least create the conditions for, what the native parties could not achieve on own their own: the ultimate victory of Communist power.[54]

What was one to make of communism in the postwar world? Was it still the revolutionary force that aroused the fears of religious and political conservatives? Had it undergone a profound change, as British and American liberals thought? Had it evolved incrementally into a more pragmatic, opportunistic movement, as many policymakers had feared? It was hard to say. No firm consensus had yet to emerge on either the nature of communism or its relevance to Moscow's postwar intentions. As for the Soviet state, it left the war as it had entered it—in Churchill's words, "a riddle wrapped in a mystery inside an enigma."[55]

Still, the vast majority of Americans and Britons had a vague sense of what it entailed. For starters, most understood Soviet Russia to be a resilient force, animated by a repugnant ideology and concerned primarily with ensuring its survival in a world its leaders deemed unremittingly hostile.[56] Newspapers, movies, and other media, sympathetic to the wartime plight of the Russian people, popularized this image of a more benign Soviet state. With Moscow allegedly shorn of its revolutionary zeal, Britons and Americans expected to work with the Kremlin on some kind of collective basis, a belief reflected in opinion polls of the day. Although hope that Russia would be a solid ally of the United States had faded by the winter of 1945–46, both peoples urged their leaders to work out a *modus vivendi* between East and West.[57]

Nevertheless, an influential community of citizens—including those who believed that Soviet communism was "evolving" or entering a "Thermidorian" phase—recognized that the Kremlin would likely aid Communist movements, in some indeterminate fashion, if the costs of doing so were not too high. Key officials in the U.S. State Department and the British Foreign Office believed that ideology still mattered to Soviet leaders, though they also recognized that Moscow would no doubt contravene Communist dogma in the service of *realpolitik*. The Kremlin, they argued, thrived on opportunism and would likely promote its national and ideological interests if the situation presented itself—which was precisely why the emerging geopolitical alignment seemed so problematic: the opportunity was now at hand for Moscow to enlarge its security belt in Eastern Europe and greatly expand the ranks of Communist states. And given the U.S.S.R.'s presumed interest in consolidating its spatial and ideological gains, the Kremlin would no doubt tether its new dominions firmly to the Soviet pole. If Stalin could master not only their Communist parties but the governments they ruled, then the reality of a unified—indeed, monolithic—force was close at hand.[58]

Yet a handful of Americans and Britons, including several working in their respective diplomatic corps, never entirely accepted the idea that all Communists were spies, dupes, or willing servants of the Kremlin. The Foreign Office's Gladwyn Jebb, for example, thought that the Yugoslav Communists, who had liberated their nation without much help from the Red Army, might not align themselves with Soviet foreign policy, especially given the "strong national leanings" of Russian communism.[59] American officials, like their British counterparts, recognized that Communists would face several challenges at war's end that might thwart Moscow's regional ambitions. According to the Office of Strategic Services, local parties would have to grapple with domestic concerns if they were to command the respect of their populations; "national" solutions to national problems were also liable to conflict with the demands of Soviet security. The Red Army's occupation of Eastern Europe, moreover, was not likely to sit well with people who had lived under German rule during the war. Having been liberated from the yoke of foreign tyranny, Europeans would no doubt reject the "quislings and collaborationists," as George Kennan put it, who sought to do the Kremlin's bidding.[60]

But the fear of collaboration would live on as the imagery of "quislingism," which referenced the actions of Norwegian fascist Vidkun Quisling in facilitating Nazi control of Norway, became grafted onto the reemerging vitality of Red Fascism. Not only were the Nazi and Soviet systems recognized as moral and political twins, their use of local citizens as advance agents—"fifth columns," in words originally ascribed to Spanish Fascists—suggested that Moscow was now just as likely as Berlin to benefit from the evils of treason and treachery. Given the broader, global appeal of communism, "fifth column" activity, as instrumental as it had been in securing Nazi rule in Europe, would likely be even more potent and more noxious in the service of Soviet interests. World War II, then, either by giving birth to or further popularizing concepts such as "quislingism" and the "fifth column"—in addition to its role in publicizing terms such as "satellites" and "puppets"—cast the previous actions of "fellow travelers" and Soviet sympathizers in an entirely new light.[61]

Still, the practice of labeling collaborators "quislings" or "puppets" obscured the particular dynamics that might animate Communists in the postwar world. Kennan, for one, failed to entertain the question of whether the Communists native to various lands might buck the Soviets and still maintain their Communist credentials. He was hardly alone in bypassing this matter; most of his colleagues had been focusing their attention on Moscow's growing might without pausing to consider whether its minions would remain faithful to their reputed masters. The same was true of Britain; though individuals such as Gladwyn Jebb might have voiced an occasional objection to the monolithic interpretation, his colleagues in the Foreign Office believed that native Communist parties would invariably serve Soviet interests.[62]

This reluctance to consider the schismatic tendencies in international communism is curious given the movement's brief, turbulent history. Factional disputes seemed to be a regular occurrence during the interwar period, a phenomenon not lost on Western observers.[63] Stalin's removal of the old Bolsheviks, for instance, provided ample evidence of a power struggle within the Soviet Union. The arrests, show trials, and liquidations of countless comrades—high-ranking and low—exposed those tensions on a grand scale. The purges had a similarly divisive effect on Communists around the world as several dissident Marxists, including Jay Lovestone, Sidney Hook, and the staff of the Trotskyist *Partisan Review,* repeatedly criticized the practice of Stalinism. These episodes reinforced the image of international communism as a hotbed of internal intrigue. Indeed, the very public dressing-down that French Communist Jacques Duclos delivered to American Communist chief Earl Browder in Spring 1945 was one of the events that led Raymond Murphy to consider the postwar direction of Soviet communism.[64] Yet that manifest example of division within the socialist camp and the corresponding effort to stamp it out encouraged Murphy, and likely countless others, to focus on the latter dynamic instead of the former, thereby giving more credence to the centripetal tendencies at work in the Communist world. But why?

The answer may be found in the geopolitical fortune Russia had amassed by war's end, which contemporary appraisals of communism had to take into account. While dissident Communists in the West— especially in the United States—could form their own organizations largely beyond Stalin's reach, their comrades in Eastern Europe had no such luxury. The presence of the Red Army in countries that lay virtually prostrate following the war allowed Moscow to organize local Communists more effectively in the service of Soviet interests. Recognition of that fact might well have led American and British observers to conclude that military control of the region would allow Stalin to treat potentially rebellious Communists in neighboring states the same way he handled his former colleagues back home. Thus, the likelihood that East European CPs would resemble the "bolshevized" or "Stalinized" cadres of old probably muted debate over the prospects of a viable, nationalist Communist alternative.

Yet even those who were most critical of communism continued to question Soviet interest in stoking the world's revolutionary fires.

Although the Kremlin might wish to see Communist parties triumph in foreign lands, the argument ran, no longer would it coordinate their activities through some kind of centralized machinery. This is not to say that vast segments of society came to belittle the Kremlin's role in international communism. Hardly anyone in either Britain or the United States questioned whether foreign Communists looked to Russia for inspiration; even without the Comintern, Moscow remained the center of the Communist movement. The U.S.S.R. was still the only functioning socialist state and, as such, commanded an extraordinary amount of respect among the world's Communist parties. That much was clear even to the casual observer. It was far less certain whether Moscow, having secured the allegiance of its far-flung comrades, was interested in leading them into a new round of political and ideological battle.

CHAPTER TWO

Appraising the Enigma

Speaking in July 1945 to an audience at London's Chatham House, home to the Royal Institute of International Affairs, British journalist Paul Winterton announced that "the brief period of idealistic striving for world revolution is long since over." For Moscow, ideology was now "simply an instrument of Russian policy, and a productive one."[1] It was an argument that enjoyed great currency at the time in Britain. Philosopher Bertrand Russell, a fellow at Trinity College, Cambridge, had recently made a similar claim to a much wider audience in *Picture-Post*, Britain's leading mass-circulation pictorial magazine. "Since the fall of Trotsky," Russell noted, "the Soviet Government has ceased to support revolutionary movements" outside the U.S.S.R.[2] Foremost in the minds of the Kremlin leadership, it seemed, were the parochial, national interests of the Soviet state.

American periodicals were offering similar appraisals of postwar Russia. Although *Life* magazine described Moscow as "the No. 1 problem" for the United States, its silence on the matter of international communism suggested that the source of the "problem" itself had little to do with ideology. Indeed, *Life* warned explicitly against the movement of "Russian dynamism" into the power vacuums of Eastern Europe.[3] Ideological interpretations of the Soviet challenge were only slightly more evident among groups closer to the centers of U.S. economic and political power. A newly established working group at the Council on Foreign Relations, for instance, tasked with providing insight into Russian affairs, featured talks from specialists who played up the power-political theme in Soviet behavior. Nevertheless, these conversations also featured speakers whose interpretations were rooted in ideology.[4] Such equivocation came to mark official thinking on the Kremlin as Washington and London struggled to divine the sources and aims of Soviet foreign policy.

For what, precisely, were they? Was the U.S.S.R. a country animated by the same concerns as other countries? Was it the spearhead of an international, millennialist creed backed up by the resources of a nation-state? Some mixture of the two? And beyond that, what was its relationship to Communist parties the world over? To what extent did Moscow control their affairs and, consequently, influence the policies of nations large and small? It had been difficult enough to evaluate the Kremlin's aims in the prewar and wartime worlds; Churchill had indeed begged these questions when he described the Soviet Union as "a riddle wrapped in a mystery inside an enigma." The challenge of deciphering Moscow's postwar conduct, with its power position enhanced, would only add to the task.

The chief stewards of American and British policy—all four of whom were new to their jobs—believed they had some insight into these matters. At the very least, they thought they knew how to deal with the Soviet leadership. While neither President Harry S. Truman nor Secretary of State James F. Byrnes felt any sense of kinship toward the men in the Kremlin, both regarded Josef Stalin as a politician not too dissimilar from themselves; the Soviet *vozhd* responded to incentives, they reasoned, just like an American big-city boss or a U.S. senator. Truman and Byrnes therefore minimized the importance of ideology as a factor in Stalin's and, consequently, Moscow's behavior. This attitude put them well within the range of informed (as well as uninformed) opinion, for it was a perspective shared by countless others throughout the land.[5]

The top officials in His Majesty's Government were only slightly more wary of the role that Marxism played in Soviet policy. According to Prime Minister Clement Attlee, Russia was "a great continental power with an immense heritage in Asia to be developed, but with ambitions in Europe which are essentially imperialist, whether ideological or territorial whether derived from Lenin or Peter the Great." Along with Foreign Secretary Ernest Bevin, Attlee shared a deep-seated hostility to Moscow, stemming primarily from the Kremlin's manipulation of native Communist parties (CPs). Bevin, for his part, had long despised the conspiratorial aspects of international communism, and he was fully prepared to ascribe some measure of Soviet behavior to the dictates of Marxist theory. But he, too, was unsure of the precise relationship between ideology and Soviet foreign policy. Stalin's behavior at the July 1945 Potsdam conference led him to believe that in matters of international affairs, at least, Soviet national interests were paramount.[6]

Yet Bevin needed no grand theoretical schema to grasp the connections between the Kremlin and Communists outside the Soviet Union. As far as he was concerned, Moscow controlled the fortunes of European CPs. He had held this view for some time, owing to his years of fighting British Communists for the political soul of the English working class. Not long after becoming foreign secretary, Bevin warned that Russia would seek to penetrate and influence Western Europe through its coordination of native cadres. In February 1946, he again lashed out at "the incessant utilization of the Communist Parties in every country in the world" as instruments of Soviet policy. His belief in the monolithic nature of international communism was nothing if not deep-rooted.[7]

Still, to get a better sense of how the Kremlin might now relate to their comrades-in-arms, the Foreign Office, in September 1945, sent out the first of several postwar circulars requesting information on the relationship between Moscow and local CPs. Replies to the memo from British missions abroad suggested that native Communists generally served Soviet interests, though the exact arrangement, especially between the Kremlin and the French and Chinese parties, remained unclear. Nevertheless, embassy response revealed that evidence of a truly "national" brand of communism, with party leaders and regulars responsive primarily to local concerns and direction—and resistant to the dictates of Moscow—was virtually absent. That was precisely the argument that Thomas Brimelow, the counselor in the Foreign Office and one of the premier Soviet experts in Whitehall, had made in August 1945. The Kremlin, Brimelow noted, would no doubt use native Communists within its sphere to further Soviet objectives, a practice that local parties would readily support. Although British statesmen detected traces of local initiative among native cadres, they harbored few illusions about the ultimate source of party policy.[8]

American officials were demonstrably less interested in questions of socialist solidarity than their colleagues across the Atlantic. Soviet experts Charles E. Bohlen and Geroid T. Robinson, for example, had relatively little to say about Moscow's utilization of local Communist parties. Their January 1946 report on the Soviet Union, one of the State Department's first postwar studies of Kremlin policy, hardly addressed the subject. While it covered a broad range of issues, including the impact of the atomic bomb, the political economy of Russia, and policy options available to U.S. decision makers, Bohlen and Robinson equivocated on the role of ideology in Soviet affairs. Both Marxism and *realpolitik*, they suggested, "might eventually supply a strong impulse toward a further wide expansion of Soviet power and influence." Compared with the Murphy Report of June 1945, the Bohlen-Robinson paper offered a considerably less alarmist image of Soviet communism. Yet it preserved Murphy's take on the ideological affinities of Communists abroad: underlying its assessment of Soviet strength was the belief that Moscow could rely on foreign Communists to do its bidding. As the authors put it, postwar Russia would enjoy "the discipline and energy, if not the numerical strength, of supporting groups in foreign countries."[9]

With Bohlen and Robinson drawing only tentative conclusions about the role of communism in Soviet policy, the question of Moscow's ideological commitment continued to gnaw at administration personnel. Navy Secretary James Forrestal was virtually consumed by the issue, an obsession that stretched back to the wartime years.[10] At roughly the same moment that the Bohlen-Robinson Report began to circulate within the State Department, Forrestal initiated a separate study devoted almost exclusively to the role of ideology in Soviet affairs.[11] Behind that project lay his fear that the worlds' democracies might repeat the mistakes of the past by ignoring the statements of totalitarian despots. Believing that ideology was a key determinant of totalitarian behavior, Forrestal set out to compare Soviet obeisance to their sacred texts with Nazi adherence to *Mein Kampf*.[12] "I realize it is easy to ridicule the need for such a study," he remarked in a note to *Life* publisher Henry Luce, "but I think in the middle of that laughter we always should remember that we also laughed at Hitler."[13] The resultant paper, written by Edward Willett, a professor of Russian history at Smith College, found that the Soviets had not abandoned any of communism's goals. Just as the West should have taken Nazi aims at face value, Willett wrote, they should now do likewise with the "stated objectives" of the U.S.S.R.[14]

The Ideological Mobilization of America

While Forrestal gave voice to a comparison that was becoming increasingly popular among administration officials, neither the Willett Report nor the Bohlen-Robinson Report had a significant impact on departmental thinking. In fact, by the time that Bohlen put the finishing touches on his paper in early February 1946, various developments in foreign and domestic affairs had created a climate, both in and out of government, less conducive to his call for prudence. Administration displeasure with Byrnes's handling of the December 1945 Moscow Council of Foreign Ministers conference, the continuing presence of Soviet troops in Iran, disappointment with the initial meeting of the United Nations Organization in January 1946, and fears over Communist espionage cells in the State Department had combined to leave U.S. officials less sympathetic to cautious appraisals of Moscow's intentions.

Central to this emerging viewpoint was the growing importance of ideology in Soviet affairs. According to policymakers and journalists alike, Moscow's increasing emphasis on Communist themes suggested that the Kremlin was returning to its doctrinaire if not revolutionary days of old. The speech that Stalin delivered on February 9, as part of the Soviet election campaign, thus became a seminal event for many Americans as they searched for the meaning of Soviet statements and actions. Discarding the rhetoric of the wartime years, with its emphases on allied unity, antifascism, and national self-defense, Stalin peppered his talk with the more antagonistic themes of Marxism-Leninism. Gone were references to the grand coalition, Russian "countrymen," and even the Motherland; in their stead were paeans to Soviet "comrades" and the Soviet system. Perhaps most notably, Stalin stressed the incompatibility of communism and capitalism, and the need for Moscow to undertake a new Five-Year Plan. Although President Truman regarded Stalin's comments as generally unremarkable, his was a minority opinion. Influential segments of both the U.S. diplomatic and journalistic communities found the speech alarming. Thereafter, they would interpret Soviet actions through the lens of ideology, treating Moscow as an expansionist, totalitarian power that lay at the center of a global conspiracy.[15]

It was against this backdrop that the State Department asked George F. Kennan, the U.S. chargé in Moscow, for a more comprehensive review of the election campaign and a wide range of Soviet behavior. Kennan responded by locating both ideology and Russian history at the center of the Soviet mind-set. Communism, he argued, was the glue that held the regime together and ensured its continued existence; without it, Soviet leaders would appear merely as the latest in a long line of Russian despots. Under the "guise of Marxism," the Kremlin had given new life to the "steady advance of uneasy Russian nationalism," challenging the West with a novel and potent force. Although Marxism functioned primarily as a "fig leaf," propping up Moscow's "moral and intellectual respectability," Soviet officials were hardly insincere in their worship of its tenets. Kennan thus warned against underrating "the importance of dogma in Soviet affairs." He maintained that the Kremlin would do all in its power to remain "ideologically monolithic" and advance the socialist cause. And since Soviet policy sprang from the internal workings of the Soviet machine—that is, from both ideological and historical influences—the West could do little to alter its course.[16]

Although Kennan's memo has long been recognized for introducing the principles of "containment" to government circles, equally noteworthy is its depiction of international communism as a monolithic movement. Aside from being one of the first officials in the postwar era to invoke the "monolith" as a reference to the Stalinist project, Kennan was convinced that Moscow was using foreign Communists to further Soviet objectives. The "inner central core" of those native parties, he argued, housed a group of fanatically pro-Soviet Communists who were "in reality working closely together as an underground operating directorate of world communism, a concealed Comintern tightly coordinated and directed by Moscow." Although the Soviets had yet to take the wraps off a revived Third International, there was no mistaking their interest in harnessing its revolutionary potential on a grand scale. This was, indeed, a sobering portrait of Soviet foreign policy: peaceful coexistence as a pipe dream; Soviet behavior as driven by historical and ideological forces; and the international Communist movement—of which Moscow was only its foremost proponent—as a well-oiled global conspiracy.[17]

The "Long Telegram," as the missive came to be known, had an electrifying effect on Washington, becoming standard reading for Truman administration personnel, including the president himself. Secretary of the Navy Forrestal also made sure that countless numbers of military officials became familiar with its theses. As the State Department's Louis Halle recalled, "there was a universal feeling that 'this was it,' this was the appreciation of the situation that had long been needed." Kennan had provided a coherent explanation of Soviet behavior that synthesized generalized fears of totalitarianism and communism while accounting for outward displays of Soviet intransigence. In so doing, he established a veritable "company line" on how to interpret Soviet behavior, confirming the fears of those already prone to ideological explanations and removing the doubts of those more temperamentally circumspect.[18]

Popular opinion toward Moscow was undergoing an equally significant transformation, aided less by the private memoranda of government officials than by the alarmist rhetoric they used in public. Central to this appeal was the language of Red Fascism, a lexicon that dramatized the similar dangers posed by fascism and communism. This vocabulary marked an extended dialogue on U.S.-Soviet diplomacy between Secretary of State James F. Byrnes and Senator Arthur H. Vandenberg (R-MI), a leading Republican voice on foreign policy. Each had been invoking Red Fascist themes since at least the close of the Moscow Council of Foreign Ministers (CFM) in late December 1945, with Byrnes comparing Molotov to Hitler, and Vandenberg criticizing the administration—and, more specifically, Byrnes himself—for "appeasing" the Soviets in the postwar settlement. Vandenberg, in particular, had often compared postwar relations with the Soviets to the prewar situation involving Germany; talk of Truman aides "loitering around Munich" was, for him, a frequent refrain. While the press viewed the Vandenberg-Byrnes dispute of February 1946 as something of a tit-for-tat exchange, observers also recognized that it augured a "toughening" of the administration line.[19]

Indeed, by March 1946, large numbers of Americans thought their government was "too soft" on the Soviets and called for an end to its "appeasement" of Russia.[20] That invocation of the Munich analogy, built into the very wording of a recent Gallup Poll, reflected the popularity of Red Fascist rhetoric. Parallels between prewar Germany and postwar Russia, or comments on the similarities of all totalitarians, appeared frequently in periodicals such as *Time, Life,* and *Newsweek.* Conservative media outlets were particularly fond of the analogy. The *Chicago Tribune,* for instance, noted that Stalin had replaced Hitler "as the scourge of middle Europe.[21] But Left-leaning sheets were equally prone to making those comparisons; journals such as the *Nation* and the *New Republic* did so liberally when commenting on bodies as diverse as the Chinese Nationalists, the governments of Spain and Argentina, and the U.S. Republican Party.[22] With the Munich analogy appearing in myriad public statements and the Gallup organization contributing to its hold on the American consciousness, the totalitarian and ideological interpretations of Soviet behavior gained increasing salience.

The profile of that rhetoric increased in early March 1946 when Winston Churchill came to the United States and articulated a position more belligerent than any yet taken by such a well-respected Western official. Surveying the postwar environment in an address at Missouri's Westminster College, Churchill focused on the ideological and conspiratorial nature of the Soviet challenge. The Kremlin, he argued, was mounting an ideological war on Christian civilization. In words that echoed throughout the world, he declared that an "iron curtain" had descended across the European continent, dividing its central and eastern states from those in the West. All who lived behind it were "subject in one form or another, not only to Soviet influence but to a very high and increasing measure of control from Moscow." The situation was grim: Stalin was constructing a coterie of pliant states, committed to excising Western culture from its ancestral home.[23]

But the picture was even darker, Churchill noted, for Moscow's reach extended beyond Europe and the furthest advance of its armies. Comrades around the world were poised to strike, ready to aid the Soviets in eliminating the last traces of Western civilization. "Communist fifth columns," he maintained, "are established and work in complete unity and absolute obedience to the directives they receive from the communist center." In other words, the Comintern was alive and well. "Nobody knows what Soviet Russia and its communist international organization intends to do in the immediate future," he warned, "or what are the limits to its expansion and proselytizing tendencies." Although the exact sequence of the Kremlin's plan remained unclear, the nature of its challenge was not: international communism, as Churchill described it, was a well-disciplined, global conspiracy, threatening the very existence of Western culture.[24]

The Westminster speech marked a turning point in postwar rhetoric and gave rise to a more hawkish portrayal of the Soviet Union. Central to this development was the media's role in disseminating its message. While commentators rejected Churchill's call for an Anglo-American alliance, they nevertheless repeated his description of Eastern Europe as tucked behind a Soviet-constructed "iron curtain." Journalists began to adopt the bipolar construction implied in that metaphor, a trope no doubt legitimatized by Churchill's political and moral authority as Britain's wartime prime minister. Representations of both Russia and its looming crisis with the West soon became saturated with the imagery of a world rent in two and the malevolence of Soviet leaders. Following the address, media outlets began to interpret the Kremlin's actions with increasing suspicion and in the most negative of lights.[25]

The Ideological Mobilization of Britain

As much as Churchill sought to influence the direction of U.S. foreign policy, he was equally interested in molding opinion back home. British papers were still writing about Russia from the perspective of World War II—to Churchill's chagrin—with its ethos of Allied cooperation and Soviet military valor. Fearing the media and public's tacit acceptance of Moscow's postwar behavior, Churchill thought it necessary to reorient British opinion before England was confronted with another Munich. Officials in Whitehall, however, were already on guard. As Bevin's private secretary Pierson Dixon put it, the Fulton speech "echoes the sentiments of all"—a bit of hyperbole, since the address fell flat among many Conservatives who thought it harmed Bevin's chances of guiding the ruling Labour Party down a more hawkish path. Still, Churchill's emphasis on the ideological and monolithic dimensions of Soviet communism reflected the thinking of Robin Hankey, Christopher Warner, and Orme Sargent, three of the Foreign Office's more influential members.[26]

That outlook also struck a chord with Frank Roberts, the British chargé in Moscow, who soon delivered an extended précis of Soviet behavior to his superiors back in London. In a series of three telegrams dispatched to the Foreign Office in March 1946, Roberts addressed the Soviet challenge to British interests in lines remarkably similar to those offered by George F. Kennan, his opposite number at the U.S. embassy. According to Roberts, Stalin and his cohort were firmly committed to the dogma on which they were raised. While Moscow was seemingly no longer interested in promoting revolutionary socialism abroad, it still aimed to create "a communist or socialist society throughout the world in close communion of spirit with the Soviet Union." The Kremlin, therefore, would undoubtedly use native CPs to further its objectives since each was "directed, if not controlled in detail, from Moscow." Unfortunately, Britain was ill-prepared to meet such a challenge. If it was to do so, Roberts argued, the Foreign Office would have to mobilize the government and press to educate the public about the Soviet threat. To get a clearer picture of what that threat entailed, it would need to produce major studies on all aspects of Soviet policy. Were it even to perform that function, however, the Foreign Office would need to create a new mechanism for coordinating and implementing political strategy.[27]

Roberts and London were clearly of the same mind, for by the time he sent his memos back to Whitehall, his colleagues at the Foreign Office had already adopted a more confrontational posture toward the Kremlin. They also had enhanced their diplomatic capabilities much as Roberts had suggested.[28] In early April, the Foreign Office established the Committee on Policy toward Russia—the Russia Committee (RC), for short—an interdepartmental organization set up to coordinate Britain's Soviet policy. Calling for a more offensive brand of diplomacy, its first appraisal of Russian behavior, a paper entitled "The Soviet Campaign Against This Country and Our Reaction to It," set the hawkish tone of the group. Written by Northern Department chief Christopher Warner, it argued that Britain should now target the Kremlin as well as its animating ideology, a worldview that "we should frankly expose as totalitarianism." More dogmatic than anything Roberts had produced, the paper cast the RC as a center of "hard-line" thinking.[29]

Such talk flowed freely from the Russia Committee, for Warner was pushing the ideological-totalitarian line through the British bureaucracy just as much as James Forrestal was through the American. Echoing Forrestal's belief in the inherent likeness of totalitarian leaders, Warner advised taking the Soviets at their word "just as we should have been wise to take *Mein Kampf* at its face value." This invocation of Munich was endemic to members of the Foreign Office. In March 1946, for instance, the Northern Department's Robin Hankey determined that "appeasement won't pay," for "the more Russia gets the more she will want." Foreign Secretary Bevin was similarly fond of the analogy, telling Attlee that anything less than a firm stance against the Soviets would produce "as much of Stalin's goodwill as we got of Hitler's after Munich." Clearly, the image of Red Fascism—the notion that Nazis and Soviets posed similarly lethal threats—was proving resonant to policymakers on both sides of the Atlantic.[30]

The commonality of that rhetoric was likely to increase as Britain and the United States sought to harmonize their anti-Communist campaigns.[31] Active cooperation between Britain and the United States in countering the postwar Soviet challenge had actually begun in the fall of 1945. Angered by the behavior of Soviet diplomats at the London CFM that September, officials in the State Department began to think more seriously about coordinating policy with their opposite numbers in the Foreign Office. Bevin, for his part, was eager to hitch the British cart to the American horse, and was willing to play the junior partner in some kind of Anglo-American entente. His goal, shared by many in the Foreign Office, was to encourage U.S. leaders to assume greater responsibility in preserving Western security interests. With U.S. officials still reluctant to convey the appearance of "ganging up" on Moscow, however, British and American statesmen began their "defensive/offensive" campaign, as Warner put it, in piecemeal fashion.[32]

The Riddle of National Communism

In the meantime, Britain continued to explore the matter of Moscow's relationship to world communism. The Russia Committee took up the question within just weeks of its creation, maintaining an interest the Foreign Office had been pursuing since the previous summer. In commissioning a study of the Kremlin and its links to CPs the world over, Christopher Warner sought to gauge the extent to which native Communists pursued "national" or "international" policies. This was a matter of enormous importance since the orientation of those parties weighed on the political, economic, and military resources Moscow might one day have at its disposal.

While the exercise appeared to be a straightforward one of research and analysis, the Foreign Office hardly approached it from a position of unbiased neutrality. High-ranking officials had already demonstrated their obeisance to the monolithic framework. Orme Sargent, for instance, the permanent undersecretary for foreign affairs, had previously described communism as "the Soviet gospel" and believed that "Communists everywhere" were the "instruments of Soviet policy."[33] Warner had also spoken of Soviet "puppets" and "satellites," as well as Moscow's ability to mobilize "in every way possible the driving force generated by the Communist 'religion' in foreign countries and in international bodies." Yet comment from British missions abroad suggested that "national" communism was, in fact, a legitimate force in the world. Brian Robertson, for example, Britain's military chief in Germany, maintained that many local Communists were "Germans first and Communists afterwards," a lesson the Russians, as he put it, "may discover . . . one day to their cost." Similar judgments came by way of representatives in Austria and Czechoslovakia.[34]

Sargent and Warner remained unconvinced. To them, "national communism" was a fiction, a belief they shared with their colleagues in the Moscow embassy. According to Maurice Peterson, Britain's ambassador to the Soviet Union, European Communists were undoubtedly doing the Kremlin's bidding, especially in those states overrun by the Red Army. Frank Roberts agreed and tried to convince London that native CPs operated without any autonomy whatsoever. Roberts had grown weary, he remarked, of cables that minimized Soviet control of foreign Communists. Although local parties might all be genuine and led by local reformers, their connection with Moscow "is always found out sooner or later to exist, usually in a pretty close form."[35]

This was indeed the majority opinion of the Russia Committee, for the preponderance of evidence it turned up indicated that Stalin continued to direct the fortunes of comrades worldwide. Although Communist methods, tactics, and direction might vary from country to country, the general pattern was unmistakable. "It had become clear beyond doubt," the committee maintained, "that Communist parties throughout the world followed the general line of policy laid down in Moscow." Individual members of the RC contested that finding when they met to discuss it in November 1946, pointing out that communism varied from country to country—even among those countries under Soviet influence. Such comments only prompted Warner to repeat his charge that apparent manifestations of "national communism" were merely illusions. From time to time, he pointed out, the Russians themselves propagated the myth of "national communism," especially in countries where the local party had yet to gain control over the government; in those situations, Communists would often act as patriots in an effort to satisfy domestic political opinion. But the key to a party's alignment lay in its foreign policy. There, Warner argued, "the Communist line was always directed to serve the Russian interest." His view carried the day.[36]

Warner and others in the Foreign Office had come to believe that Moscow would soon make its ties to native Communists more overt. Several officials concluded that the Soviets would revive the Comintern to provide increasing support to Communist parties abroad. Their claims hardly took the Russia Committee by surprise. Several of its members, including Warner and chair Robin Hankey, not only anticipated the Comintern's reemergence but believed it had already come to pass. The effect of Soviet ministrations on native Communists, therefore, regardless of the present standing of the Comintern—officially defunct since 1943—was to tie them more firmly to the Kremlin line. That was also the view held by the Joint Intelligence Committee (JIC), the body charged with coordinating and consolidating Britain's intelligence operations. While national Communist parties might differ on minor tactical questions, the JIC noted, "on essential issues (and particularly on those in which the Soviet Union has declared its line) the Communist movement acts as a single whole."[37]

American diplomats stationed behind the Iron Curtain, as well as intelligence officers back in the United States, held a similarly jaundiced view of the vitality of national communism. Representatives posted to Bulgaria, Hungary, Romania, and Poland all referred to the respective local governments and their Communist leaders as shills and "quis-lings." Czechoslovakia offered perhaps the lone ray of light. According to Ambassador Laurence Steinhardt, Klement Gottwald, one of the local party's leading figures, was behaving as if he were "a thorough Czechoslovak patriot."[38] Yet departmental intelligence reviews had concluded that all Communists, seemingly by virtue of their being Communists, functioned as instruments of Soviet foreign policy. Al-though native parties might "express a degree of local autonomy" to suit their domestic needs, all came "under one centralized direction." Each followed "without exception" the Kremlin line in foreign affairs. The "discipline" of those parties, moreover, which allowed them to ex-ercise disproportionate influence within their respective governments, reinforced Moscow's ability to project an image of socialist solidarity. As the department noted, "despite the intricate maze of channels through which Soviet foreign policy is administered, it does not lose its monolithic and dynamic character." Supporting the State Department in its findings was the newly formed Central Intelligence Group (CIG), the forerunner to the Central Intelligence Agency (CIA), which also re-garded native Communists as adjuncts of Soviet power.[39]

The Soviets, therefore, constituted both an external and internal threat to Western governments. According to the State Department, Moscow could use its "fifth columns" to influence the domestic politi-cal process in France, Britain, and the United States.[40] Native Commu-nists and fellow-traveling groups could thus promote Soviet objectives through subterfuge, obstruction, or political agitation; in turn, those maneuvers might block the resolution of issues left over from the war and inhibit Europe's economic rehabilitation—and, in the end, sow the seeds of further Communist success. As many in the Truman administra-tion believed, outright sympathy for the Soviet cause, as well as eager-ness to maintain great power cooperation—sentiments more prevalent in Europe than the United States—was allowing Moscow to break its wartime agreements without compunction, presenting Western policy-makers with further evidence of a worsening international climate.

Some of that pro-Soviet support was concentrated in the interna-tional organizations that had sprung up to campaign for a cooperative postwar world. Groups such as the World Federation of Democratic Youth, the National Union of Students, and the World Federation of Trade Unions backed policies in line with Soviet interests and couched their positions in the language of peace. This was precisely the kind of campaign that Western officials feared the Kremlin would wage.

According to Britain's Joint Intelligence Committee, Moscow was seeking to extend its influence abroad without provoking war, using "Communist Parties in other countries and certain international organizations" to do its bidding. British statesmen recognized the dangers such groups posed, particularly those involving international youth organizations, and tried to negate their influence. Policymakers in both London and Washington thought these organizations provided cover for Soviet intransigence in matters relating to the postwar settlement, making it harder to confront the Soviets successfully.[41]

Taking these and other developments into account, Truman aides Clark Clifford and George Elsey set out in July 1946 to catalogue Soviet treaty violations. Although their resulting paper did, in fact, address Soviet infractions, it went beyond that more limited objective to offer a general summary of Russian communism. The "Clifford-Elsey Report," the government's first attempt at a comprehensive, interdepartmental review of Soviet behavior and American foreign policy, maintained the emerging emphasis on ideology that had begun to take hold earlier that year. Its authors were firm believers in the monolithic nature of international communism, maintaining that the doctrinal uniformity of Communists all over the world, including those in the United States, offered Moscow a potent weapon in support of its foreign policy. Not once did the Clifford-Elsey study highlight tensions within the Eastern bloc or within local Communist parties. Although it generally coincided with the president's own thinking on Soviet affairs, Truman promptly locked all copies of the paper in his White House safe. Even with the administration and the American people growing increasingly impatient with Soviet behavior, Truman thought the document was too controversial for official, let alone public, consumption.[42]

Interestingly, the Council on Foreign Relations (CFR), which had recently conducted its own survey of Soviet behavior, also decided to suppress its findings on the subject. Informed by numerous academics, businessmen, journalists, and policymakers, the Council's working group on the Soviet Union began its study in March 1945. By the fall, it had concluded that national considerations overrode those of ideology as factors in Soviet policy. Nevertheless, it also maintained that Moscow dictated the actions of Communists worldwide—the lone exception being the Chinese Communists, who, as discussion leader Owen Lattimore put it, were "too busy solving practical problems of their own to be much influenced from Moscow." In drawing up its final report in the spring of 1946, however, the group hedged its views on the orientation of local

CPs. While noncommittal on whether West European or Asian Communists would be directed by the Kremlin, it recognized that Moscow's "influence on them is tremendous." Moreover, it admitted that "a Communist victory in any of them might well constitute a real danger to our security." That was the position of Geroid T. Robinson, wartime head of the Russian research section of the Office of Strategic Services (OSS), co-author of the Bohlen-Robinson Report, professor at Columbia University, and contributor to the CFR working group. Though an overwhelming majority of the group were willing to sign the document, a handful thought it too "charitable" to the Russians; those holdouts, in turn, either sought to attach qualifying statements to the report or refused to sign it altogether. By late June 1946, with the international situation having grown even more strained, not one member of the committee was willing to endorse its publication.[43]

Asian Communism

The Council's generally skeptical approach to Chinese communism reflected widespread uncertainty about the nature and alignment of Asian communism, at least initially. Throughout the war, State Department specialists in Russian and Asian affairs had regularly minimized the ties between Soviet Russia and the Chinese Communist Party (CCP).[44] Although several observers thought that Moscow and the CCP would draw closer following Russia's entrance into the Pacific War, embassy personnel in China still believed that the United States could wean Yenan, the wartime and early postwar home of the CCP leadership, away from Moscow, encouraging the party to take a more nationalist and independent stand.[45]

At the same time, the American media, far more than government representatives, downgraded the threat that Chinese communism posed to Western interests. During the latter stages of World War II, articles in both mainstream and elite publications repeatedly described the CCP as an assemblage of "agrarian radicals" and "Chinese democrats." Print sources such as the New York Times, the New Republic, Amerasia, and the Far Eastern Survey all portrayed Chinese communism as a reform movement, separate and distinct from the revolutionary program of Soviet Russia.[46] Similar verdicts appeared in numerous books on China, contributing to the popular impression that the Chinese Communists were, as Harrison Forman of the Times concluded, "no more Communistic than we Americans are."[47]

During the early postwar period, however, at virtually the same time that George Kennan was describing Chinese communism as a potentially schismatic force, officials in the State Department were arguing that "minority groups" in Asia were "controlled by the Soviet Government." Other high-ranking personnel were also convinced that Moscow was guiding the fortunes of Asian Communists. Walter Bedell Smith, America's ambassador in Moscow, asserted that Russia's manipulation of "fifth columns" made Soviet foreign policy perhaps more dangerous in Asia than in Europe. The frequency of such reports would increase throughout the year. In July 1946, for example, the Central Intelligence Group characterized the CCP as "an unusually effective instrument of Soviet foreign policy"; six months later it would portray Korean Communists in similar terms. Judgments such as these indicate that a more ideological framework was coming to dominate interpretations of the Soviet challenge.[48]

Such was also the case with regard to assessments of Vietnamese communism and the orientation of its most notable adherent, Ho Chi Minh. Having proclaimed the founding of the Democratic Republic of Vietnam in September 1945, Ho—whom knowledgeable observers recognized as the former Comintern agent Nguyen Ai Quoc—would battle efforts to reimpose French rule over the former colony for the remainder of the year. Part of that project involved a campaign designed to present both himself and the Vietminh, the umbrella organization he had founded, as nationalists. Ho's dissolution of the Indochinese Communist Party in November 1945, his offer of economic and strategic concessions to the United States, and the moderate nature of Vietminh political and economic policies all served the purpose of masking the Communist foundation of party ideology. Ho would hide that reality from public view until the domestic and international environment permitted a more complete statement on its intended direction. Remarks to Western officials downplaying the socialist nature of the Vietminh program thus aided Ho's efforts in portraying himself as more patriot than patsy.[49]

As tensions between Moscow, Washington, and London increased during the course of 1946, U.S. officials repeatedly sought to clarify Ho's international position, an indication that policymakers were not taking Ho's statements at face value. Undersecretary of State Dean Acheson was particularly concerned about Ho's alignment and asked State Department officials to comment on the relationship between the Democratic Republic of Vietnam (DRV) and the Soviet Union. As he put it, Ho's refusal to recant his Moscow affiliation augured poorly for a Vietnam independent of Soviet influence.[50] Still, responses emphasized not only the "uncertain reliability" of reports emphasizing the Ho-Stalin connection but the determination of French efforts to convince Washington of such solidarity.[51] Secretary of State Byrnes could do no more than stress the possibility of such contact with Moscow, as well as with the Chinese Communists.

By 1947, however, newly installed Secretary of State George C. Marshall, on the basis of evidence no harder than that held by his predecessor, interpreted Ho's ideology and organization as "emanating from and controlled by [the] Kremlin." And all of these reports, the optimistic as well as the pessimistic, stressed the internationalist complexion of Ho's ideology. While observers recognized both his nationalism and his communism, none discussed his orientation as that of *national* communism. Nevertheless, disdain for French actions in Indochina and fear of how they might tarnish Western interests in the region led U.S. officials to base their policies more on anticolonialism than on anticommunism, an attitude that kept them aloof from involvement in the region.[52]

In contrast to the Americans, British policymakers were eager to preserve the region's prewar colonial arrangements and were therefore more inclined to support France in its attempt to reimpose metropolitan rule. An interest in beating back America's general challenge to their own crumbling empire certainly contributed to this reflex, but the British decision to aid French efforts also stemmed from the desire to help stabilize Southeast Asia and bolster France as a continental ally. Absent from this mix, however, was the fear that Ho's communism threatened to extend the long arm of the Kremlin into Southeast Asia. London certainly recognized that Ho was a Communist and was hardly supportive of his ideology or of his efforts to promote it. Although the Foreign Office had picked up signs that Ho was in contact with other Communist parties, it regarded Ho as something of a moderate; thereafter, British officials would remain wary of efforts to portray Ho and the Vietminh as handmaidens of Moscow, a campaign the French had been waging since 1945. The Foreign Office argued repeatedly that the increasing popularity of the Communist appeal in Southeast Asia was likely due more to the heavy-handed methods of the French than to the virtues of communism and its most vocal, regional proponent. That appeal would only grow as war broke out between French forces and the Vietminh in December 1946. At that time, however, the matter of Ho's communism was not a galvanizing force in devising British policy for the region.[53]

Nor would Ho's communism be a hot-button issue for Whitehall as it considered Britain's options in China. During World War II, officials in the Foreign Office generally regarded the CCP as a band of pseudo-Communists. U.K. representatives in China, including ambassadors Archibald Clark Kerr and Horace Seymour, even described the Chinese Communists as "agrarian reformers" and "mild radicals."[54] Foreign Secretary Ernest Bevin questioned whether the CCP was working on Moscow's behalf or even if it deserved to be labeled a Marxist organization. In early January 1946, he publicly rejected the notion that Mao Zedong and his ilk were "communists as we understand the term at all."[55] Moreover, as members of his staff pointed out, the ideological affinity between Soviet and Chinese Communists did not automatically create a solid political partnership, since tensions might well develop between the two. Throughout the wartime and early postwar periods, London generally sought to downplay the Communist leanings of the CCP.[56]

British media and pressure groups reinforced that image of Chinese communism among the public at large. Statements coming out of the China Campaign Committee, for instance, portrayed the CCP as moving toward "democratic government" and "agrarian reform." And like the press in America, publications such as the *News Chronicle* and the *Manchester Guardian* were offering favorable portrayals of the Chinese Communists. Similarly, the centrist *Times* claimed that "the Yenan system is not Communism; it resembles an agrarian democracy," a position it maintained into 1946. This was also the stance adopted by the *New Statesman & Nation.* Most British observers were not necessarily inclined to such optimism, but significant pockets of opinion, including that of the business community, believed the CCP would eventually prove more Chinese than Communist.[57]

Nevertheless, key government officials detected greater ideological fervor among Asian Communists and viewed the CCP as either the current or future handmaiden of the Kremlin.[58] Frank Roberts believed that Japanese Communists were at Moscow's beck and call, and that their Chinese comrades were "under the direct control of Moscow." By the end of 1945, the Foreign Office's Far Eastern Committee had surmised that the activities of Communists outside Russia were directed "towards furthering the strategical interests of the Soviet Union."[59] British diplomats, in turn, began to distance themselves from the notion that the CCP was Communist in name only, mirroring the evolving position of their counterparts in Washington. By the close of 1946, Ralph

Stevenson, the U.K. ambassador to China, had emphatically rejected the notion that Chinese Communists were "really agrarian reformers and Chinese rather than Communists in the accepted sense." Its leaders were "Communists first, last and all the time" and could "thus be trusted not only to follow the 'Party Line' in all circumstances, but automatically to serve the best interests of the Soviet Union." Stevenson and his colleagues would argue this position repeatedly in communiqués to Whitehall.[60] Synthesizing many of those reports, Britain's Joint Intelligence Committee recognized a degree of coordination between Chinese and Soviet Communists, though it could not ascertain the precise relationship between them.[61] Even the Left-leaning *New Statesman and Nation* was now describing Mao's clique to its elite readership as a cadre of "Russian-controlled Chinese Communists."[62] By the fall of 1946, therefore, wider segments of British opinion were coming to regard international communism, in both its European and Asian expression, as a monolithic force.

As the year drew to a close, two episodes—one in the United States and one in Britain—illustrated just how salient the ideological and conspiratorial interpretations of the Communist challenge had become. In September, President Truman fired his secretary of commerce, Henry A. Wallace, for stating publicly that America should abandon its "get tough" policy toward Moscow. Wallace had argued that instead of confronting the U.S.S.R., the administration should recognize and accommodate Moscow's security concerns in Eastern Europe.[63] His dismissal brought greater coherence to U.S. foreign policy, but it also removed the administration's sharpest and most public critic of the ascendant ideological approach.

A similar dynamic took root in Britain, where Labour backbenchers were challenging their party's handling of Soviet affairs. Led by MPs Richard Crossman, Michael Foot, and Ian Mikardo, this faction condemned U.S. as well as Soviet foreign policy, and implored Bevin and Attlee to pursue a "democratic and Socialist alternative" to American capitalism and Soviet communism.[64] Their revolt would last from the fall of 1946 through the spring of 1947—longer, therefore, than Wallace's comparable stand. Nevertheless, developments in late 1946 signaled that its duration would be short. Rejecting calls for closer ties between British Labour and the Communist Party of Great Britain, party stalwart Harold Laski noted that such affiliation would turn Labour "into one more instrument . . . of subservient devotion to the dictatorship of the Communist Party in Moscow." Likewise, Victor Gollancz, publisher of the *Left Book Club,* had by mid-1946 embraced an increasingly hawkish view of Soviet behavior. Although he still professed a faith in socialism, Gollancz denounced the "totalitarian" methods of the Soviet state and its direction of Communists the world over. The outcome of the Labour and Wallace episodes, both of which halted internal challenges to government policy, suggests that individuals and institutions that sought to accommodate the Kremlin were facing increasing marginalization in both Great Britain and the United States.[65]

Britons and Americans would thus exit 1946 similarly convinced that Moscow was at the forefront of a monolithic Communist movement. They had not entered it that way. Although officials on both sides of the Atlantic were leaning toward such an interpretation by the close of 1945, neither the events of the day nor the findings of Soviet experts were leading policymakers to adopt such a unified perspective. Developments over the course of that winter, however, helped to spawn the new consensus. Tension over Soviet troops in Iran, a combative first session of the United Nations Organization, and myriad problems with the postwar settlement in Central and Eastern Europe—followed swiftly by the bellicosity of the Soviet election campaign—signaled to officials that the Kremlin would, at the very least, promote Communist power throughout Europe and possibly even renew its commitment to a revolutionary, conspiratorial, international crusade.

But it was nongovernmental actors who sought to popularize that understanding among the general public. At times in conjunction with the Truman administration, organizations such as the Advertising Council and the U.S. Chamber of Commerce were active in promoting the image of communism as un-American and dangerous. Administration officials looked to the Advertising Council (AC), an agency born during World War II and committed to the promotion of free enterprise, to get its message out. So effective was the AC in reaching the public (its warnings about the danger of foreign ideologies appeared in over one thousand magazines and newspapers) that the White House, after hosting an early 1946 meeting with its members, instituted annual conferences with the AC leadership beginning that September. The U.S. Chamber of Commerce was at least as influential as the AC and even more vigorous in its demonization of communism and its adherents. Its call for a broad offensive against un-American activities appeared in "Communist Infiltration in the United States," a booklet the Chamber published in October 1946. By January 1947, drafts of a subsequent handout, entitled "Communists with the Labor Movement," claimed that communism and Communist-controlled organizations served the interests of a foreign power.[66]

Media outlets were also pushing this theme and raising more broadly the specter of communism in America. The journalist Stewart Alsop played a lead role in this effort through an increasing focus on communism in trade unions. His September 1946 remarks on the subject, which appeared in the nationally syndicated column he co-wrote with his brother Joseph, depicted Communists as furthering Kremlin objectives.[67] In a similar vein, the popular radio show "Town Meeting of the Air" built upon the momentum the Alsops had generated, offering an extended discussion of the topic in October.[68] The Alsops were two of several journalists who enjoyed the close company of administration officials, but they took up the issue of Communists in government on their own. Their relationship with administration officials was indicative of the regular contact that existed between media and government: influential journalists were invited to the White House, Cabinet members spoke at industry trade meetings; and journalists received personal notes from the highest officials in the land supporting administration positions. Yet the broader impetus for seeing Communists as foreign agents came from private figures and entities, such as the Alsops and the Advertising Council, and not specifically from the government itself.[69]

Media outlets in both Britain and the United States broadened that discussion to focus on the ideological element at work in global affairs. In numerous articles and columns, journalists echoed the fear that Moscow was returning to the slogans and tactics of world revolution. Press establishments in the two countries diverged, however, over the role ideology now played in Soviet policy. The London *Times* took a decidedly nonideological view of what was transpiring in Eastern Europe, as did the conservative Beaverbrook press.[70] The *New Statesman and Nation* also ran pieces rejecting the ideological interpretation of Soviet conduct, though it did fear that Stalin's February election speech portended a more virulent propaganda campaign and a "clash of ideologies."[71] The American press, by contrast, began to treat the Soviet challenge in increasingly ideological terms. By March 1946, *Life* would note the speed of Moscow's "ideological reconversion" and warned that Russia, which was "not just a nation-state," could be opposed only by a rival ideology.[72] This trend was not limited to the conservative-leaning, mass-circulation journals of the day. Articles in the *New Republic,* for instance, portrayed East-West tensions as a struggle between two political philosophies, and the pull of such thinking became stronger throughout the year.

That drift toward an ideological understanding of global affairs led more and more commentators to stress the dichotomous nature of the postwar era. Talk of "One World," which had been so prevalent in the later phases of the war and remained an aspiration in the months following the end of fighting, now seemed a distant memory. By early 1947, Frederick Lewis Allen, the editor of *Harper's,* would note that journalists were incorporating black-and-white formulations more frequently in their writing. The use of such conventions, arguably, led commentators to maximize the difference between the two camps and to minimize the differences within each of them—a signal characteristic of the monolithic framework.[73]

Emblematic of this reflex toward dualistic forms was the increasing prevalence of Red Fascist rhetoric. Journalists and politicians would frequently point out that Nazi Germany and Soviet Russia were similar, if not identical, evils. With the lessons of World War II fresh in the minds of so many—and with tensions developing between East and West at an alarming rate—it is not surprising that they drew on the recent past to prepare for present and future challenges. That the parallels many drew were inexact was almost beside the point. Although the Nazis and the Soviets represented different kinds of strategic dangers, Moscow posed a potentially more lethal threat than the explicit one that Berlin had mounted earlier. Both systems, moreover, were equally and utterly contemptuous of the democratic values of Western culture. Several voices sought to quash such analogizing—the *New Statesman and Nation* among them—but the comparison caught on nonetheless.[74] Even Frank Roberts, who recognized the many fallacies contained in the Red Fascist image, still regarded Soviet ambitions as similarly and manifestly hostile to British interests.[75]

Having therefore decided on the nature of the Communist challenge, the British and American governments were moving toward a consensus on how best to cope with the Soviet threat. Nevertheless, they still had not formulated a coherent strategy to meet it. Once again, the pressure of external events provided the necessary push.

CHAPTER THREE

Supporting Free Peoples

Pressure for a more explicit Soviet policy surfaced in the context of a renewed cultural crusade to extol the virtues and traditions of the democratic way. That crusade and those pressures would combine to reinforce the image of communism as a monolithic force, a dynamic that was as true in Britain as it was in the United States. Ideological interpretations of the Soviet challenge, which had animated private discussions among government officials in 1946, were now commonplace in public circles and would metastasize into a penchant for seeing the world as split in two. The image of a binary universe was central to the coming British and American publicity offensive, campaigns that served to embed the precepts of the monolithic framework in more dramatic fashion. But it did not take shape simply as a response to contemporary events; those developments, and the meanings they evoked, emerged against the backdrop of recent as well as ancient history. The monolithic framework owed much to a broad ideological and informational offensive that couched the challenge of international communism in the context of a shared historical consciousness.

Leading the charge was *Life* magazine, which, during the first week of March 1947, debuted a series of articles intended to give Americans a much needed "perspective on history." The rationale for the series, according to the magazine's editors, lay in the presumption that "Western man" was currently experiencing a crisis of confidence; if European civilization was to be saved, *Life* argued, Americans needed to know more about the values they had inherited. Readers would learn about that heritage from Whittaker Chambers, a talented if controversial member of the *Time/Life* family. Writing most of the articles in the series, Chambers fashioned his essays into virtual museum pieces, offering exhibits of the rich artistic and literary tapestry of the West. Each of them resonated with the religious and democratic traditions America had come to represent.[1]

Largely unbeknownst to Chambers's audience, the ancient home of that civilization—Greece—was then in danger of losing whatever remained of its democratic legacy. Less than two weeks before *Life* published the first installment of its "Western Culture" series, the British Foreign Office informed the U.S. State Department that it soon would be cutting off economic and military assistance to Greece, as well as to neighboring Turkey. The implications of that policy reversal became immediately apparent: Britain would no longer be able to sustain groups that were resisting Communist domination of the region. Unless aid could be found to support the Turkish government and anti-Communist elements in Greece, both would likely succumb to forces hostile to Western interests and Western culture.

Over the next several weeks, the State Department worked relentlessly on a program of assistance for the Aegean states. At the same time, the president's closest advisers drafted a speech for Truman to make in support of that initiative. Several officials realized the enormity of the moment: they were starting down a path that no U.S. administration had traveled, committing the nation's resources and prestige—during an era of nominal peace—to the security and survival of Europe. Because of the program's novelty and the resistance it would likely meet in Congress, many of them thought it necessary to portray the situation in the most dramatic of terms. The president's address to the nation would therefore employ rhetoric bordering on the apocalyptic and cast the struggle with Moscow in highly Manichean language. The choice facing America, Truman would claim, was between two opposing and irreconcilable ways of life—between the virtues of democracy and the horrors of totalitarianism. It was a tale many had heard before, and one that tapped into a core component of the national saga.

Yet Truman's speech would give that narrative new meaning. Although the East-West conflict had become more ideologically polarized during the previous twelve months, the administration had yet to frame it—at least publicly—in such a binary fashion. Now, however, several officials thought they had little choice but to do so.[2] That was precisely how Undersecretary of State Dean Acheson sold the speech to the congressional leadership. Not since the days of antiquity, he argued, had the world been so divided between two great powers. The choice now facing them was between democracy and dictatorship, between liberty and conformity. Such phraseology held great appeal for Arthur H. Vandenberg (R-MI), the newly installed chairman of the Senate Foreign Relations Committee, for he believed that totalitarianism and democracy were locked in mortal combat. Following Acheson's lurid description of the situation, Vandenberg pledged to support the aid request on the condition that the president employ similarly bold language in his upcoming address to Congress.[3]

On March 12, Truman did just that. "At the present moment in world history," he proclaimed, "nearly every nation must choose between alternative ways of life." Too often that choice was not a free one. It would therefore be the policy of the United States "to support free peoples who are resisting attempted subjugation by armed minorities or by outside pressures." While Truman chose not to cite those minorities or pressure groups by name, he left little doubt as to their identity. Less clear, however, was the nature of the commitment America was about to make. Truman had asked Congress to aid specifically Greece and Turkey, but he also had deemed "the free peoples of the world" equally worthy of American assistance. By implication, therefore, the president's proposal was no mere stopgap to rescue two nations under siege. As many in the press and government realized, it aspired to nothing less than the preservation of Western civilization.[4]

Confronting the Monolith

The Truman Doctrine, as the message came to be called, brought together several themes woven into the national dialogue on the Soviet Union. Although the president had referred to "totalitarian regimes" rather than the U.S.S.R. or communism as the unindicted offender, the image was clear enough; by early 1947, most Americans were willing to identify Russia as the primary threat to national interests. Yet by evoking the menace of totalitarianism, Truman raised the specter of a former foe—Nazi Germany—and linked it to the current regime in Moscow. Parallels between fascism and communism had been floating around for years, but the Truman Doctrine helped to sear that image into the public consciousness, locking in the notion that Soviet Russia and Nazi Germany posed equally mortal dangers.[5]

Administration officials hardly needed a government directive to draw that comparison. The image of Red Fascism came easily to them, regardless of whether they were conscious of its persuasive potential. This was especially true for the president; not long after his speech to Congress, Truman argued that "there isn't any difference" between totalitarian states. "I don't care what you call them," he commented, "Nazi, Communist or Fascist or Franco, or anything else—they are all alike."[6] Talk of "appeasement" evoked similar truths. Individuals such as Acheson and Vandenberg, as well as Assistant Secretary of State for Public Affairs William Benton and Assistant Secretary of State for Inter-American Affairs Spruille Braden, were equally taken with the parallel. Nearly everyone involved with drafting Truman's speech and securing ratification of its attendant legislation saw the world through the prism of Munich.[7]

The press did its fair share to popularize the Red Fascist image. *Life* found the concept particularly revealing and invoked its symbolism on the eve of Truman's address. "To argue that Communism is not so bad as Nazism as some 'liberals' still like to do," it noted, "is a complete waste of time," a charge the magazine repeated three weeks later. By equating the crimes of communism with those of fascism—in effect, by minimizing the differences between any and all totalitarians—*Life* helped to popularize the monolithic framework. At times, the magazine was even more explicit in promoting that understanding, using prominent individuals, including Winston Churchill and philosopher James Burnham, to make its point. Looking back on his Fulton speech, in which he argued that Eastern Europe was largely controlled by the Kremlin, Churchill claimed that such statements "are not seriously challenged in any part of the world today, outside the vast Communist or Communist-controlled regions." *Life*'s editors reiterated that argument the very next week, pointing out that "the nature of Communism was by now pretty well understood."[8]

What the public seemed to grasp particularly well was the relationship between local Communists and Soviet Russia, much of which involved espionage committed by native CPs on behalf of the Kremlin. The mass-circulation press offered readers a steady stream of spy-related stories, thereby encouraging that conspiratorial understanding of Communist behavior. *Life*'s exposé of Comintern agent Gerhard Eisler, then on trial as a Soviet agent, pointed out that Eisler's loyalty, "like that of every Communist must be to the Soviet fatherland." *Collier's* also ran several articles on the presence of "Reds" in government, questioning the patriotism of Left-leaning civil servants. *Look* even helped its readers identify would-be traitors—people whose first loyalty was to the Soviet Union—with a précis titled "How to Spot a Communist." Later that month, the Truman administration would try its own hand at locating Communist operatives. On March 21, less than two weeks after launching a crusade against totalitarianism abroad, Truman began a hunt for subversives at home, establishing a Federal Employee Loyalty Program to ferret out Communists and other rogue elements. At virtually the same moment, the House Committee on un-American Activities (HUAC) was conducting hearings on the menace of internal subversion. The U.S. government's "Red Hunt," an exercise shot through with monolithic imagery, was thus in full swing by March 1947.[9]

Uniting those domestic and foreign programs was the notion that all Communists were tools of the Kremlin. According to pollsters, increasing numbers of Americans, both in and out of government, seemed to be moving toward that conclusion. As of July 1946, 48 percent of the public thought American Communists were loyal to Russia; by April 1947, that figure had risen to 61 percent. Truman himself endorsed the notion that Communists were, virtually by definition, beholden to Moscow. "I am not worried about the Communist Party taking over the government of the United States," he noted, "but I am against a person, whose loyalty is not to the Government of the United States, holding a government job." The reference to the monolithic nature of international communism, with its adherents serving Soviet interests, could not have been much clearer.[10]

Policy specialists also seemed to be commenting more frequently on the subservience of native Communists to Kremlin directives. Several officials, including State Department advisers on the Soviet bloc, believed that all European Communists took their orders from Moscow. Llewellyn Thompson, chief of the department's East European Division, was convinced that this was the case.[11] So, too, was departmental counselor Charles Bohlen; throughout the spring and summer of 1947, Bohlen made numerous statements to that effect, charging that American and West European CPs were all beholden to Russia.[12] The situation behind the Iron Curtain was even more pronounced. Recapping Communist reaction to the Truman Doctrine, the Central Intelligence Group noted that each of the Soviet satellites had dutifully "followed the line laid down by the Moscow press."[13]

The increasing tendency to describe the world as split in two, another impulse magnified by the Truman Doctrine, added further heft to the monolithic framework. As the media focused greater attention on the highly competitive and dualistic nature of the postwar environment, visions of a multilateral, "one-world" system fell by the wayside. Truman himself fed that dynamic, for his March proclamation was full of black-and-white characterizations and either/or formulations. Thereafter, U.S. officials would portray the world as divided "between free and totalitarian or imposed forms of government." Not surprisingly, elements of that dualistic vision seeped ever more into the popular press as the media pounded home the image of a world rent down the middle. This dualism was clearly apparent in *Life,* where Protestant theologian Reinhold Niebuhr declared communism and Christianity to be "the great rival faiths of this desperate time." It reappeared in the magazine courtesy of Whittaker Chambers, as he traced the distinctive and virtuous history of Western culture. And it showed up in a companion piece Chambers wrote for *Time* on the philosophy of British historian Arnold Toynbee. By the time readers had become familiar with Toynbee's ideas on the need to restore spiritual health to Western culture, Truman had already delivered his sermon on how best to reinvigorate the West's material well-being. That speech, reinforced by those articles, helped to launch the United States on its anti-Communist crusade, a campaign that rested in no small measure on a bedrock of monolithic rhetoric.[14]

Policymakers, however, were not altogether pleased with the anti-Communist tone of the national mood. Several officials bemoaned the ideological cant of the Truman Doctrine, believing it too negative and martial in character. Over the next few months, various aides, including George Kennan, Charles Bohlen, and Dean Acheson, helped to inject the more constructive themes of economic reconstruction and rehabilitation into the public dialogue.[15] As Truman speechwriter Joseph Jones put it, "we have a great deal to gain by convincing the world that we have something positive and attractive to offer, and not just anti-Communism." Still, if the United States was going to foot the bill for European recovery, key congressional and administration officials believed they had to overdramatize the region's plight in order to wrench the necessary funds out of Congress. U.S. officials, therefore, found themselves caught in a public relations paradox. On the one hand, they had to let the country know what was happening in Europe; only by "shocking" the nation, they believed, could Americans grasp the issues at stake. On the other hand, the resulting upsurge of anti-Communist sentiment threatened to overwhelm the administration's capacity to manage it.[16]

On May 22, in the midst of such planning and strategizing, Congress passed the Greek and Turkish aid bills, making the Truman Doctrine national policy. Numerous U.S. officials, however, still sought to quash its rhetorical flourishes while preserving its operational element, a sentiment shared by their counterparts in Whitehall. Many within the British Foreign Office had never advocated such an expansive campaign against communism and hence deplored the wording of Moscow's arraignment. Assistant Under-Secretary Gladwyn Jebb, in particular, regretted the president's "flat-footed Red Bogey approach."[17] Media commentary in Britain on the Truman Doctrine reflected that sense of discomfort and ranged from tepid to testy. Although the *Times* and *Manchester Guardian* were generally supportive, the *Guardian* worried about the impact of rising international tension. Several other news journals feared the consequences of an inexperienced and imperialistic America throwing its weight around in global affairs. The *New Statesman & Nation,* moreover, deplored the hysteria generated by the address and the "well-organised propaganda campaign" that followed. If anything, the Truman speech perpetuated existing journalistic opinion on American and Russian behavior.[18]

Still, the British public was comparatively sanguine about its impact. Opinion polls indicated that a sizable majority of Britons did not expect another world war for at least twenty-five years.[19] And while members of the Foreign Office might have blanched at the tone of the Truman Doctrine, few of them had problems with its general thrust. Most senior officials recognized the East-West conflict as ideological at root and fully accepted the premise that Moscow controlled the fortunes of native Communists. Their most recent survey of Soviet foreign policy, released in February 1947, had found Eastern Europe to be "as closed a preserve of the U.S.S.R. as ever."[20]

The Quaroni Question

Against this background of increasingly charged rhetoric, the Foreign Office once again asked its embassies to comment on the alignment of Communist parties worldwide. It was the third such request London had made since V-J Day and the second since the formation of the Russia Committee one year earlier. This time, Christopher Warner wanted to know whether Communist parties divided along "national" or "Moscow" lines, an argument Pietro Quaroni, Italy's outgoing ambassador to the Soviet Union and newly appointed ambassador to France, made to Frank Roberts in early February. The "Quaroni Question," as it came to be called, would dominate Foreign Office speculation on the nature of international communism for the next several months.[21]

Not surprisingly, the British diplomats most familiar with Quaroni's argument were stationed in France. Ashley Clarke, the chargé at the British Embassy in Paris, revealed that it was a subject "on which we constantly reflect." Although he judged the French Communist Party (PCF) to be currently in "the hands of 'Moscow' men," Clarke thought that Soviet control of French Communists—indeed any Communists— might be short-lived. "The stronger Communism becomes in any country," he maintained, "the less subservient will it be to the dictates of Moscow." Britain's ambassador to Paris, Duff Cooper, also found much wisdom in the Quaroni line. He had recently suggested that French Communists "were not necessarily likely to be so bad after all and . . . that they were a good deal more 'National' than 'Russian.' "[22]

The situation behind the Iron Curtain was altogether different, however, and Quaroni's argument had little relevance for that part of the world. The embassy in Budapest detected "no significant deviation from the general line of Soviet policy" among Hungarian Communists. Officials stationed in Germany doubted whether any split "has ever really existed or is likely to occur in the immediate future." Even in Czechoslovakia, where British representatives saw the party as home to both "proved" and "unproved" Communists, the embassy admitted no knowledge "of a single Communist in a position to influence the basic party policy who has not served a long apprenticeship and proved his loyalty to Moscow." In fact, several British officials stationed in Eastern Europe deemed *all* Communists to be Kremlin stooges. Back in London, Soviet specialist Thomas Brimelow found himself in general agreement with those incoming reports. While East European CPs might exhibit signs of local initiative, they nevertheless offered implicit obeisance to Moscow's directives.[23]

Perhaps the most interesting reply to Warner's circular came from Charles Peake, the British minister to Belgrade. Peake contended that the Yugoslav Communist Party (YCP) was even more committed than the Kremlin to a monolithically Communist program, and was promoting an ideological orthodoxy more "internationalist" than the Soviets. Nevertheless, with the YCP committed to socialist solidarity, Peake saw "no chance whatever of useful encouragement to national as opposed to international communism." Nor did other officials who participated in the survey. As Foreign Minister Ernest Bevin later remarked, responses to the circular were "generally negative in character." Communism, at least in its European incarnation, was as monolithic as ever. For many in the Foreign Office, Hungary's installation of a pro-Soviet cabinet in late May 1947 all but confirmed that assessment.[24]

Bevin was not without his critics, however, as members of his own party challenged the increasingly hawkish and confrontational thrust of Britain's Russia policy. Yet even those individuals invoked the rhetoric of the monolithic framework. The Keep Left group, for instance, comprised of Left-leaning Labour MPs and the most visible of Bevin's intraparty antagonists, argued that Britain should play a mediating role "to save the smaller nations from this futile ideological warfare and to heal the breach" between the United States and the Soviet Union. Collective security of the kind envisioned in the Truman Doctrine, they argued, would only sharpen the global conflict. But in criticizing Truman they aped his phrasing, characterizing Soviet methods as "totalitarian" and describing the regimes of Eastern Europe as "puppet" governments. Responding to this internal revolt, Denis Healey, Labour's international secretary, rejected calls for a policy wholly independent of America. In words consistent with those used by opponents of the Bevin line, Healey warned of the hostility Britain faced at the hands of "the international Communist machine."[25]

With the machine's components operating in both East and West, the specter of communism was not just a matter of external policy for British officials. Ever since September 1945, when Igor Gouzenko left his post in Ottawa as a Soviet embassy cipher clerk and defected to Canada, London had known of a spy ring involving citizens of the United Kingdom. After evaluating the damage done and assessing his own political environment, Prime Minister Clement Attlee set up a secret Cabinet Committee on Subversive Activities to begin the process of establishing guidelines for dealing with Soviet espionage in Britain. He was aided in this effort by Britain's Joint Intelligence Committee, whose 1946 study of international communism revealed that CPs the world over allowed themselves to be used as instruments of Soviet policy. Although the U.K.'s "Red hunt" was a mere shadow of the one then under way in the United States, its decision to "negatively vet" British civil servants reflected a similar appreciation of international communism. Central to this understanding was the belief that British Communists, professing loyalties to a government other than their own, were likely no different than their far-flung comrades.[26]

European Recovery and Crackdown

As troubling as the developments in Hungary and Eastern Europe may have been, officials in both the United States and Great Britain could point to positive trends elsewhere on the continent. In early May, the coalition governments of both France and Italy dismissed the Communists in their respective cabinets. The ruling powers in both Greece and Turkey also lurched farther West due to assurances of American aid. Thereafter, hope of continued success rode on an address that Secretary of State George C. Marshall was to make at Harvard University during the first week of June. Speaking at Harvard's commencement exercises, Marshall outlined the situation abroad, warning that the whole European economic system was in danger of complete collapse. The continent simply could not provide for its own basic needs; without additional help, it faced "economic, social, and political deterioration of a very grave character." Marshall proposed that the United States offer Europe a "cure rather than . . . a mere palliative" for its grievous condition, making a program of continuing financial aid the centerpiece of his message. Military assistance and ideological confrontation—the buzzwords of the Truman Doctrine—were nowhere to be found in the Marshall address. As if to put even greater distance between his initiative and the one Truman proposed in March, Marshall asked Americans to greet his proposal with sobriety and restraint. "Political passion and prejudice," he noted, should play no part.[27]

With relations between the West and the Kremlin in steady decline, the aid program was structured so that the United States and its allies could reap the maximum political benefit from Soviet intransigence. If Moscow and its satellites wanted to receive Marshall funds, they would have to join with Western Europe in presenting to the United States a comprehensive aid proposal. Such a plan meant that Moscow would have to open its books to Western eyes and its borders to Western influence, two things the Kremlin was loath to permit. According to George F. Kennan, now head of the State Department's Policy Planning Staff, the Soviets would probably balk at participating, a not unwelcome development as far as he was concerned. By opting out of the Marshall Plan and strong-arming its satellites to do the same, Moscow would no doubt incur the blame for splitting the continent in half—and present the United States with a symbolic victory. But the West also stood to gain from Communist participation, for the economic leverage that came with Marshall aid offered U.S. planners a potentially effective tool in their struggle against Communist encroachment. As Kennan put it, the Marshall Plan could, on the one hand, strengthen the natural forces resisting communism in those countries not yet under the Soviet spell and on the other hand wean those states already within the Soviet orbit away from Moscow's rule. Either way, the Marshall Plan offered the most effective means—rhetorically, symbolically, and practically— of stemming the Communist tide.[28]

None of this was lost on the Foreign Office. British diplomats, like their American counterparts, recognized that Marshall aid offered numerous benefits. Aside from the help it would give to Western Europe, the Foreign Office hoped it might loosen the bonds between the Kremlin and Eastern Europe, and thereby isolate the Soviet Union. If the Russians chose to deny their satellites Marshall aid, they would assume responsibility for splitting the continent in two. Pierson Dixon, Bevin's private secretary, recognized Moscow's dilemma. "The rulers of the Kremlin," he noted, "fear for their own position and the regime if Europe under American water-cans handled by British gardeners blossoms into a happy western garden of Eden."[29] Bevin himself saw the Marshall proposal as "the quickest way to break down the iron curtain" and allow for Western influence beyond it.[30] Speaking to Jefferson Caffery, the U.S. ambassador to Paris, Bevin both anticipated and hoped the preliminary meetings between the French, British, and Soviet foreign ministers would collapse over Moscow's refusal to participate.[31] He got his wish: after signaling initial interest in the European aid program, the Soviets walked out of the planning conference, vowing not to participate in Western schemes aimed at isolating Russia. Days later, the nations of Eastern Europe followed suit, rejecting invitations to a mid-July, pan-European conference on Marshall aid. Moscow's actions in prohibiting its neighbors—particularly Warsaw and Prague—from participating in the Paris Conference, was, for many observers, prima facie evidence of Stalin's growing control over Eastern Europe.[32]

Well before Molotov left the Paris talks, however, it had become clear that Moscow was strengthening its grip on the satellite governments. Communists in Hungary had accused premier Imre Nagy of treason, forcing his resignation. Subsequent arrests in Romania and Bulgaria also indicated a tightening of Soviet authority; according to the Foreign Office, such actions could "only have taken place with the approval, if not on the instructions, of the Soviet authorities." Moreover, the trade agreements that Moscow had been signing with the countries of Eastern Europe indicated Russia's desire to fuse together the various economies of the Communist bloc. Combined with Soviet and East European rejection of Marshall aid, those developments reinforced the belief that Moscow was speeding up the bolshevization of its vassal states. Key Foreign Office members, such as Maurice Peterson, Robin Hankey, Orme Sargent, and Christopher Warner, all believed the Soviets were resurrecting the Comintern and were trying to extend communism "by infiltration into other countries." The events surrounding the Marshall Plan therefore wedded British officials even more tightly to the monolithic interpretation.[33]

War and Communism in Asia

With so much attention being devoted in the spring of 1947 to developments in Europe, observers in the United States wondered about the universality of America's expressed anti-Communist commitment. Several congressmen, in particular, wanted to know whether the rhetoric of the Truman Doctrine was equally applicable to Asia. Their concerns peaked during congressional hearings on Greek and Turkish aid. Speaking to legislators, Undersecretary Acheson sought to differentiate the Chinese and Greek situations in order to dramatize the need for a European focus. The U.S. government, Acheson pointed out, was already providing the Chinese Nationalists with material and financial assistance. Greece, moreover, faced an imminent crisis; China did not. Finally, Acheson argued, if and when the question of aid to anti-Communist Chinese forces reemerged, the administration would deal with that contingency based on its own merits. Suffice it to say that while administration officials sought to fix their gaze on the perils of European communism, voices in both Congress and the media were expressing comparable and distracting fears over its Asian variant.[34] They would do so for the remainder of the year.

To head off further criticism of U.S. policy in the Far East and to bolster its chances of winning congressional support for Greek and Turkish aid, the administration took a more active role in helping the Chinese Nationalists (KMT) in their struggle against the Chinese Communist Party (CCP). By May 1947, the State Department had lifted its bans on selling ammunition and arms to the KMT. Taking advantage of this policy reversal, Generalissimo Chiang Kai-shek, leader of the Chinese Nationalists, announced a general mobilization of his forces. In July 1947, just as the Europeans were meeting to harmonize their proposals for Marshall aid, the Chinese resumed their civil war in earnest.

From the British point of view, renewed fighting between the KMT and the CCP was no cause for alarm. The Foreign Office had previously been critical of U.S. policy in China, viewing America's practice of overt disengagement, combined with covert assistance, as utterly ineffectual. Chiang had to have the means, it argued, to counteract Communist advances. Yet Britain was not eager for him to emerge victorious from that confrontation. What the Foreign Office desired was a stalemate between the KMT and the CCP, for it regarded a Nationalist victory as no more beneficial to British interests than a Communist one; both camps were equally xenophobic. Even after the State Department resumed its military support of the KMT, British officials continued to criticize U.S. policy. According to the Foreign Office, America was taking a middle-of-the-road approach, a policy it saw as guaranteeing failure. Only a full-scale commitment to the Nationalists, it argued, could halt the Communist onslaught.[35]

Still, it was far from clear what a Communist victory, if that should come to pass, would entail. A Soviet-CCP alliance was a distinct possibility, though hardly a foregone conclusion. Asian specialists in the State Department thought the ties between Moscow and Yenan—which were never strong to begin with—might soon show signs of wear. According to John Carter Vincent, who headed the Office of Far Eastern Affairs, the inherent nationalism of the Chinese people—Communists included—would make it difficult for the Kremlin to translate a KMT defeat into a strategic victory for Moscow.[36] Vincent believed that Moscow, like Britain, was more interested in preserving a balance between the KMT and the CCP. Most of all, he argued, the Kremlin wanted China to remain in a state of turmoil. The Joint Chiefs of Staff thought so as well.[37] While U.S. officials presumed that the CCP was ultimately serving Soviet interests, many of them detected potential trouble ahead for the two parties.

Having heard about splits among the Chinese Communists, Marshall hoped to exploit those tensions for America's benefit. In mid-July 1947, he asked U.S. representatives in China to verify the existence of a rift between the "so-called nationalist and 'comintern' CCP members." This was not the first time the United States had thought about weaning the CCP away from Moscow. Raymond Ludden, first secretary of the U.S. embassy in China, recalled that a similar study conducted during World War II had proved less than encouraging: among other things, it concluded that the CCP hierarchy was "firmly Marxist"; that the United States could expect "no ideological deviations" from the Soviet line other than those deemed tactically necessary; and that the likelihood of splits emerging within the CCP between a "Nationalist Group" and a "pro-Russian Group" were slim at best. Still, Ludden and John Melby, the second secretary at the embassy, expected problems to arise between Moscow and the Chinese Communists in the postwar world. In the event that they did materialize, both officials thought that America might be able to "foster the emergence of a regime" amenable to U.S. political interests.[38]

Nevertheless, many administration officials were greatly impressed with the links between Soviet and Chinese Communists and were convinced that the two were in cahoots.[39] A fact-finding mission, undertaken by General Albert C. Wedemeyer at Truman's behest in the summer of 1947, offered several diplomats the chance to repeat that charge. In doing so, however, they based their arguments not on any evidentiary foundation but on a firm belief in the unifying power of Communist kinship. For these officials, evidence that Moscow was supplying the CCP with military assistance—of which there was plenty—was beside the point. According to the U.S. embassy at Nanking, proof of such aid was "in itself not as important as the ideological affinity existing between the Chinese Communists and the Soviet Union." Therefore, as embassy official Raymond Ludden put it, such affinity was "in itself sufficient" to assure that were the CCP to be the majority party in a Chinese government, "its basic orientation would be toward the Soviet Union rather than the United States."[40] The question of direct ties, therefore, was basically an academic one. As an "instrument" of Moscow, the CCP provided, in the words of John Melby, an "effective extension of Soviet foreign policy."[41]

By September, Wedemeyer had completed his tour and submitted his report to Truman. It was severely critical of the Nationalists and argued that further U.S. aid be contingent on Chiang's willingness to reform his government. Wedemeyer's dressing down of the KMT had little bearing on his assessment of the CCP, however, for he described the Chinese Communists as "bound ideologically" to the Kremlin. Invoking the image of Red Fascism, he argued that Soviet doctrine called for a "definite plan of expansion far exceeding that of Nazism in its ambitious scope and dangerous implications." Concluding his report, Wedemeyer maintained that the "Soviet Union, in achieving her aims, is being actively assisted by the Chinese Communist Party, which by its actions and propaganda is proven to be a tool of Soviet foreign policy."[42]

The intelligence and defense communities largely echoed that interpretation of Chinese communism. While the CIA recognized the CCP's latent nationalism as well as tensions between Mao Zedong and other Communist leaders, it also described Chinese communism as "ideologically sympathetic and oriented toward Moscow," rating the CCP as a highly effective instrument of Soviet foreign policy.[43] The Office of Intelligence Research at the State Department found that "a Communist China would be closely aligned, politically, economically, and militarily, with the USSR."[44] The Joint Chiefs of Staff (JCS) offered an even more categorical appraisal of Yenan's foreign policy. As they noted in June 1947, the Chinese Communists were "Moscow inspired" and "should be regarded as tools of Soviet foreign policy." The JCS, therefore, thought the Chinese Communists would likely support the Kremlin in its aim "to expand control and influence wherever possible."[45]

Similar accounts of Vietnamese communism were arriving at the State Department. Like the various interpretations of Chinese communism, these reports often reflected the geographic proximities of the observer, with Washington-based officials generally more wary of local Communists than those stationed in the field. In addition, individuals in significant contact with Paris, such as former U.S. ambassador to France William C. Bullitt and the current officeholder, Jefferson Caffery, frequently painted Ho Chi Minh and his Vietminh cadres in the darkest of hues. Caffery, in particular, gave great credence to French reports that Ho was an agent of international communism. This was precisely the direction in which Paris wanted Caffery to move, for France was seeking to recast its war against the Vietminh from that of an anti-colonial struggle to an anti-Communist one—a project in which they were having increasing success.[46] To some extent, the French effort was aided by the U.S. consul in Saigon, Charles S. Reed, who regularly relayed French reports on the dangers of Soviet opportunism and concurred with Bullitt's claim that a Vietminh-run state would be controlled by Moscow. By and large, however, Reed thought Vietnamese communism more a long-term than a present problem.[47]

Reed's colleague, James L. O'Sullivan, the vice consul at Hanoi, was more skeptical of reports extolling the dangers of Ho's communism and his subservience to Soviet rule. O'Sullivan repeatedly downplayed those concerns, although he did note that Vietnamese Communists would likely be pulled in the direction of Moscow.[48] His assessment was more in tune with British appraisals of Ho and the Vietminh. While London appreciated Ho's background as a Communist, British officials did not dwell on it, nor did they regard Ho as a Soviet stooge. Still, the Foreign Office never shied away from recognizing Ho's ideology when discussing

Vietnam internally or with the Americans. Indeed, it would soon begin to focus on the threat of expansionist communism in a campaign to prod the United States into becoming more assertive in its dealings with Southeast Asia.[49]

While U.S. and British officials largely refrained from demonizing Ho and the Vietminh, the rhetoric Washington and London was directing toward the Kremlin itself was extremely harsh. On both sides of the Atlantic, policymakers and pundits were employing a litany of techniques to depict the Soviet threat, each of which solidified the image of a Communist monolith. Red Fascism remained a staple of allied publicity. Senior officials in the British Foreign Office frequently worked its teachings into their own rhetoric, equating the "Soviet" with the "Hitlerian way" and denouncing the "appeasement of Russia."[50] Similarly, the Joint Intelligence Committee, in a major review of Soviet strategy and tactics, described the writings of Stalin and Lenin as "the 'Mein Kampf' of the Soviet regime."[51] Elements of the British popular press, including the *Daily Mail* and the *News of the World,* also liked the image, even as segments of British political culture condemned its use. The Keep Left group, for instance, adamantly resisted what it regarded as faulty analogizing, which it believed was a key factor in creating an increasingly dualistic world. Its campaign for more sophistication of thought, however, appeared increasingly as a rearguard action.[52]

Similarly, Americans continued to embrace the Nazi-Soviet analogy and worked its assumptions into both official and public correspondence. Truman probably did the most to cement that image in the public consciousness. In vowing to defend free peoples from totalitarian aggression, he reawakened memories of similar threats from the recent past, leaving little doubt as to who the aggressors were in either case. Several officials, including those responsible for U.S. policy toward Russia, returned frequently to the iconography of Red Fascism. Elbridge Durbrow, for instance, chargé at the U.S. embassy in Moscow, saw a connection between the Nazi and Soviet propaganda machines and called on the government to work the analogy more forcefully into its publicity campaigns. Specifically, he urged his colleagues to "publish captured German documents *in toto* to show Soviet aggressive intentions in collaboration with Hitler, which correspond generally with Soviet aims today."[53]

Those projects never got off the ground during the spring and summer of 1947. Although officials in the State Department and the Foreign Office called for a more vigorous response to Soviet behavior and propaganda, members of both staffs, including its most senior personnel, thought such measures should await the outcome of preparatory talks for the Marshall Plan, scheduled for later that June. Even after the Soviet sphere decided not to participate in the recovery program, officials chose to delay the onset of their publicity offensives until at least the November meeting of the London Council of Foreign Ministers. Planning for those efforts continued throughout the year, however. Soviet intransigence at the London CFM, which both Washington and Whitehall fully expected, would no doubt provide a "green light" for the more hostile rhetoric that many sought to implement.

While U.S. and British propagandists focused primarily on those living abroad, many officials, particularly on the American side, saw those living at home as equally important targets. In a sense, the Truman Doctrine addressed both populations. It embraced a more assertive brand of anticommunism, geared specifically toward the international arena; but it also conjured up the specter of domestic subversion, raising the volume and vehemence of such rhetoric in the United States. It is uncertain whether administration officials anticipated either that kind of response or its wide-ranging impact; clearly, they did not like it. Ambassador to Moscow Walter Bedell Smith, for one, was "frightened" by the extent to which opinion in the United States had become "violently anti-Soviet." His colleague at the Moscow embassy, Elbridge Durbrow, was equally worried. Fearing that Americans were acting on their "emotions rather than on objective factual reasons," Durbrow called for a more impartial program of public education. With such schooling, he reasoned, popular reactions to Soviet policies would be "less subject to propaganda influences and emotional extremes."[54]

The "curriculum" for such a program expanded during the summer of 1947, incorporating the expertise that many had deemed so valuable back in 1946. Once again, George F. Kennan sparked this more recent discussion of Soviet communism. His "Sources of Soviet Conduct," published under the pseudonym "X" in the July issue of Foreign Affairs, called for a policy of "patient and firm but vigilant containment of Russian expansive tendencies." Within weeks of its appearance, the State Department had sent numerous copies of the article to its missions abroad. The wider American public would also become familiar with Kennan's arguments as Reader's Digest and Life excerpted large sections of the piece soon thereafter.[55]

Although the "X-article" was silent on the issue of monolithic communism, its most significant and influential critic, Walter Lippmann, was not. Lippmann, who dissected Kennan's arguments in the *New York Herald Tribune,* maintained that "the communist party in any country is the *fifth column,*" the local adjunct of "the Red International."[56] In some ways, Lippmann's remarks capped months of reporting in the popular press highlighting the monolithic structure of international communism. *Newsweek* was commenting more frequently on the links between CPs and the Soviet Union, often describing native Communists as "fifth columns" or "puppets."[57] Even the *Nation* began to criticize the increasingly Soviet orientation of local parties. In March 1947—prior to the promulgation of the Truman Doctrine—British Labourite Harold Laski appeared in its pages, noting the "grave misfortune" that Communist parties the world over were continuing to promote a Soviet agenda even after the dissolution of the Comintern.[58]

The combination of several influences, therefore, was serving to convey the image of communism as a monolithic force, a development that was as much a feature of British as of American political culture. Ideology, which by 1946 had come to shape official discussions of Soviet behavior, would now provide an equally powerful lens for the public at large. Although pockets of opinion had taken up this view prior to the Truman Doctrine, its influence on appreciations of Soviet behavior burst into full flower in the aftermath of the president's address to Congress. Alongside the emergent tendency to stigmatize and dichotomize came a willingness to endow ideology with greater descriptive and predictive power over the actions of Communists themselves. Thomas Brimelow, the Foreign Office's leading specialist on Soviet affairs, spoke for many on both sides of the Atlantic when he pointed out that in reality the Kremlin sanctioned any behavior that smacked of "local initiative" on the part of foreign Communist parties. Moscow's consolidation of its orbit, following its denial of Marshall aid to Eastern Europe, only reinforced that already strongly held conviction. Although government officials undermined the monolithic interpretation from time to time, such as with their commentaries on China, France, or Czechoslovakia, those exceptions, by and large, only proved the rule.[59]

For even those officials who recognized and sought to exploit tensions within the Communist world—Kennan, Bohlen, and Brimelow, to a degree—themselves showed signs of operating from within a monolithic framework. Their visions of what would become known as the "wedge strategy" were based on the assumption that the West needed to wean Communists, including those not under the watchful eyes of the Red Army, away from Moscow. In other words, U.S. and British officials expected that Communists would at first drift naturally toward the Soviet Union; all such parties, they reasoned, whether operating in Europe or Asia, were more or less destined to feel the Kremlin's gravitational pull. Western aid was therefore desirable precisely because it held open the possibility of interrupting, or even reversing, the Soviet magnetic field. But when policymakers detected rifts within local Communist parties and tried to widen those breaches through economic leverage, subsequent developments, at least in Europe, made those splits virtually irrelevant. The Marshall Plan, for example, had led Moscow to clamp down harder on its minions.[60] By the summer of 1947, the Kremlin was urging all Communist parties to practice greater discipline—which they could accomplish by jettisoning or silencing dissident comrades—thus making those parties more effective tools of Soviet policy.

How are we to reconcile the arguments of those who rejected the image of Communist parties as frictionless machines and yet continued to mouth the precepts of the monolithic framework? Perhaps those individuals regarded communism as both a monolithic *and* a non-monolithic movement; at root, they may have believed, it possessed both attractive and repellent forces. As already illustrated, a host of officials in both the State Department and the Foreign Office recognized that nationalism might create rifts within the Communist world, undermining the movement's outwardly placid façade. Yet they also noted the affinity that *all* Communist parties had for Moscow. It is entirely plausible, then, that officials such as Kennan and Bohlen, as well as Roberts and Brimelow, were operating from a framework that saw communism as both monolithic and nonmonolithic. Perhaps a more accurate description of their views would suggest that they saw communism as monolithic in the *functional*, if not in the *literal*, sense. Before long, that perception itself would become solidified within the public cultures of Great Britain and the United States, a development that heightened the apparent dangers of the emerging Cold War.

CHAPTER FOUR

The Cominform

The functional reality of a Communist monolith became increasingly apparent to Britons and Americans during the summer and fall of 1947. Observers attributed its emergence to the imperatives of party discipline and intrabloc cohesion. But ideological interpretations of the Communist threat, more evident in the United States than in Britain, also shaped perceptions of Communist behavior as Soviet and East bloc activities came to be seen as manifestations of Communist teaching. Ideology would also shape the self-perception of those in the West, for the battle against communism took shape alongside the corresponding appeal to a shared historical consciousness. Fueling this development was Secretary of State George C. Marshall's offer of economic aid to Europe in June 1947. To observers on both sides of the Atlantic, the Marshall Plan signaled America's readiness to assume the burdens of Western leadership and salvation. Elevating the rhetoric of U.S. foreign policy, it exchanged the apocalyptic, anti-Communist language of the Truman Doctrine for the more restrained and positive message of economic rehabilitation. American largesse, therefore, would come to the defense of Western civilization and thereby preserve the collective culture and history that *Life* had dramatized earlier that year.

Yet all was not well with the European Recovery Program. The United States might have been ready and even able to lead, but its willingness to do so was still an open question. Neither Congress nor the public was disposed to shell out such large sums of money, nor did they accept the program's importance to America's national interests. Once again, the administration and its friends needed to dramatize the stakes involved. They needed to sell both Congress and the public not only on the virtues of Marshall aid but on the values and traditions it sought to uphold.

The Truman administration launched its campaign in October 1947 with the maiden voyage of the "Freedom Train," the heart of the Advertising Council's campaign to "sell America to the Americans." Dubbed the "caravan of American history" by *Collier's* magazine, the Freedom Train was sponsored by the newly created American Heritage Foundation and backed by several administration officials. It brought the country's most celebrated documents—including the Declaration of Independence and the Constitution—to people all across the nation. Towns and cities marked the train's arrival with "Community Rededication Week," a nonstop celebration that included events such as Veterans Day, Labor and Industry Day, Schools Day, Youth Day, Women's Day, Inter-Faith Day, Freedom of Enterprise Day, and Civil Liberties Day. *Collier's* argued that the traveling exhibit, offered in conjunction with these events, would help the nation understand "what American liberty and democracy really mean, and why we'd be a lot worse off than we've ever yet been if we should trade them in for some kind of totalitarianism." As an outgrowth of the burgeoning public-private network forged in postwar America, the Freedom Train stood as an explicit appeal to the nation's historical consciousness. Presumably, it would lead the way toward more enlightened national and international policies.[1]

Americans were not alone in seeing the world divided by competing political systems. Moscow, too, was acknowledging the conflict between the "democratic" and "imperialist" systems, though the Kremlin had its own version of who merited those labels. That "two-camp" thesis, propounded by Soviet ideologue Andrei Zhdanov, emerged from a September 1947 meeting of European Communists. Held in the Silesian town of Szklarska Poręba, the conference marked the birth of a new communist international organization: the Communist Information Bureau, or Cominform. Although Russia advertised the Cominform as a mechanism for improving communication between Communist states, most observers saw it as a tool for binding those nations more firmly to the Soviet Union—and as the clearest expression of the Communist monolith to date.[2] Its creation ushered in a nine-month period that encompassed some of the most dramatic moments of the early postwar period and helped to transform the Cold War from a clash with the Soviets and their allies into a more general struggle against communism itself.

The Monolith Manifest

American officials generally viewed the new Communist organization as the rebirth of an old one. State Department summaries of the Cominform even appeared under the heading "Comintern," implying that the Cominform would be just as conspiratorial and hostile to capitalism as its earlier version had been.[3] Accordingly, analysts at the Central Intelligence Agency (CIA) thought the Cominform Declaration illustrated the "the clear identification of Communist parties as agents of the Kremlin." The National Security Council (NSC) reached a similar conclusion, arguing that the declaration served notice "on the Communist parties in France and Italy, as well as those in other Western European countries, that they are not their own masters and that they must adhere to the policies and plans of the Kremlin." The establishment of the Cominform therefore reinforced the belief within U.S. government circles that Communist parties were essentially adjuncts of Soviet power.[4]

Most of these arguments also appeared in press accounts of the Cominform announcement. Broad segments of the U.S. media found "nothing new" in this latest Communist parley. According to the *New York Herald Tribune*, the declaration merely gave formal recognition to a policy that "Russia and her friends have been pursuing for the last two years." According to State Department staffers, this was indeed a widespread belief, though the government did not necessarily consider it an unwelcome one. Given its portrayal of a dualistic world, the proclamation served to validate administration descriptions of the Soviet challenge. *Newsweek,* for instance, thought the Cominform dramatized the Communist threat "far more effectively than either Mr. Truman or the State Department had yet been able to do."[5] In fact, Washington's first public remarks on the Cominform were very low-key. Offered by newly installed undersecretary of state Robert A. Lovett, the administration urged Americans to approach this latest development with "coolness and clarity of judgment."[6]

Nevertheless, the wider reaction was an emotional one. A host of commentators regarded the founding as an "ominous" event, tantamount to a declaration of "political and ideological war" on the West.[7] Other voices spoke of the tensions that might erupt within native parties, suggesting implicitly that not all Communists would accept Soviet dictation; those same voices, however, charged that the declaration might strengthen the movement rather than weaken it. Siphoning off national from international Communists, a process that was presumably under way in France and elsewhere, would likely serve Soviet interests. Those Communists remaining faithful to the Kremlin would then represent a "harder core of activists," armed with a philosophy appealing to the downtrodden.[8]

That argument did filter into the public dialogue, but it is hard to know what Americans made of it. Conceivably, they might have rejected it out of hand, since most people—as revealed in opinion polls from the time—regarded virtually *all* Communists as Soviet stooges. Surveys from October 1947 suggest that the public viewed Eastern Europe as a Soviet preserve. Close to 80 percent of the population thought of Poland as a Soviet satellite, and at least 67 percent judged the other "curtain" states, with the exception of Albania, to be similarly colonized. Views of American Communists were no better: 62 percent of the public regarded the Communist Party of the United States of America (CPUSA) as beholden to Moscow, while only 13 percent felt otherwise. In the eyes of the public, foreign support of Kremlin policy could only add to Moscow's strength and fuel its ambitions, and three-quarters of the population listed these aims as global in scope.[9] America's image of Russia was thus an increasingly frightening one: the Soviet Union appeared as a totalitarian power, bent on global conquest, aided by a phalanx of pawns the world over.

Great Britain reacted to the Cominform announcement with somewhat less alarm since key officials believed that the Comintern had never actually ceased operation. Frank Roberts, who had left the Moscow embassy earlier in 1947 to become a personal aide to Foreign Secretary Ernest Bevin, echoed a widespread opinion that saw "nothing new in the declaration which conveniently sums up the whole line of Soviet propaganda since Stalin's election speech of February 1946 and more especially since Truman doctrine."[10] The Kremlin had never given up control of international communism, Roberts argued; the timing of its announcement, therefore, was likely related to the European Recovery Program. To block its implementation, Moscow would probably now take more aggressive steps, such as sparking a heightened campaign of political unrest in France and Italy.[11]

Yet for British officials, the Cominform revealed as much about Eastern Europe as it did about the western half of the continent. Like their American counterparts, most high-ranking members of the Foreign

Office saw the Cominform as a way for the Kremlin to tighten its grip on the satellite states. They recognized, however, that Russia's ability to bind those groups closer to the Kremlin line was becoming highly problematic. As Permanent Undersecretary Orme Sargent pointed out, local parties were "under increasing temptation to support national interests and to play party politics, instead of maintaining the full purity of the Communist faith and subordinating their patriotic instincts to the requirements of Communist internationalism."[12] To some extent, then, and like their peers in the State Department, the Foreign Office welcomed the Cominform Declaration, for it clarified the relationship between the Kremlin and its satellites. No longer could one argue that the native CPs of Eastern Europe were "different" or "national." It was now quite obvious, if it had not previously been so, that those parties took their orders "from Moscow."[13] British media outlets, including the *Times* and the *Manchester Guardian,* shared that assessment. Even the Left-leaning *New Statesman & Nation* referred to native CPs, as well as to communism itself, as instruments of Soviet domination.[14]

Such conclusions left most senior members of the Foreign Office feeling less than sanguine about the Cominform's impact on world affairs. The new body would likely be a "much more effective version of the Comintern," posing "a direct public challenge to America and the West."[15] As several officials argued, its founding presaged the beginning of revolution on a worldwide scale, threatening the remnants of the British empire.[16] The foreign secretary, however, resisted such dire appraisals. By November 1947, Ernest Bevin still had not settled on the ultimate meaning of the Cominform and was reportedly "suspending judgement" on its real significance until he detected any alteration in Soviet tactics. In line with Bevin's attitude, the Russia Committee instructed Foreign Office personnel to "keep their eyes open" for any such changes.[17] None appeared to be forthcoming.

The events of December would put an end to Bevin's hesitation. The collapse of the London Council of Foreign Ministers that month proved the last straw in efforts to reach a workable understanding with Moscow and resolved his thinking about the Cominform. Bevin now found it easier to side with those, like Belgrade staffer George Clutton, who thought its creation "marked the development of the concept of the Popular Front in a certain 'monolithic' direction."[18] Not only was this the case for Yugoslavia, the most loyal of Moscow's satellites; as the Northern Department's Robin Hankey observed, it was also true of the "Soviet orbit as a whole as the result of the developments of this year."[19] Conditions outside the Soviet sphere also pointed to a "mono-lithic" interpretation of international communism. Recent labor strikes in France and Italy, which bore a striking similarity in both tac-tics and in timing, pointed to "direction from Moscow."[20] These inci-dents seemed to influence senior British statesmen as much as they did the foreign secretary; after four separate inquiries into the nature of in-ternational communism, the Russia Committee failed to conduct follow-up study at seemingly a most propitious moment for doing so. Apparently, the Committee had finally settled its long-running debate on the schismatic elements and general alignment of Communists worldwide.

Going on the Publicity Offensive

The failure of the London CFM also led to an informational offensive against Moscow that would alter the volume and tenor of Britain's anti-Soviet rhetoric. Officials in the Foreign Office had been preparing for such a campaign since mid-1946. For the remainder of that year and most of the next, the foreign secretary had taken a more "positive" ap-proach to the propaganda war, emphasizing British achievements rather than Soviet misdeeds. After the December 1947 CFM, however, Bevin moved firmly into the camp of those, including Christopher Warner and his Russia Committee colleagues, who sought to imple-ment a "negative" publicity campaign. On January 8, 1948, Bevin sub-mitted several Committee papers to the cabinet, each of which was highly anti-Soviet in tone, launching Britain on its own anti-Communist crusade.[21]

While those papers charted a new course for British foreign policy, they also provide a window into British thinking on international com-munism. Central to the new publicity offensive was the imagery of Red Fascism. Employed previously on an ad hoc basis, Red Fascist rhetoric now became a more conscious component of British propaganda. Offi-cials would thenceforth play up similarities between the Nazi and So-viet systems, and thereby equate Fascist totalitarian terror with its Communist variant.[22] Members of the Russia Committee believed the parallel would resonate with all who had suffered under the yoke of Hitler. In the ensuing weeks and months, the Russia Committee con-tinued to push the Red Fascist line, making it a staple of Britain's anti-Communist publicity. Whitehall's adoption of this rhetorical strategy meant that Washington and London were now embarked on a shared campaign of public vilification that cast Stalin and Hitler, as well as Moscow and Berlin, as equally malevolent.[23]

While this interest in Red Fascist rhetoric heightened the similarities of Anglo-American propaganda, key members of the Foreign Office wanted to draw a clear distinction between the political economies of Britain and the United States. The desire to distance itself from Washington was hardly a departure for the Labour government; antipathy toward American capitalism as well as Soviet communism had long characterized Labour Party policy and debate. Even during this more frigid phase of the postwar period—and, for some, precisely *because* the Cold War had become a bit chillier—the image of Britain as a "Third Force" continued to tantalize party stalwarts. Prime Minister Clement Attlee himself set out such a vision for Britain in a January 1948 radio address to the nation. As Attlee put it, Britain would seek to advance "a positive rival ideology," offering "Social Democracy and Western European civilisation" as alternatives to both "totalitarian Communism" and "laissez-faire capitalism." Aided by this new informational campaign, Britain proposed to offer its services as a *via media* between the Soviet and American systems.[24]

Yet there was more that united British and American publicity than divided it. For in addition to its employment of Red Fascist rhetoric, Britain would depict communism as a monolithic and alien-inspired conspiracy. Again, this portrayal was hardly new to Foreign Office personnel; in study after study over the previous two years, the Foreign Office—and the Russia Committee in particular—had repeatedly voiced that very belief. And that was precisely how Bevin now presented the new information policy to the cabinet as a whole. Moscow was relying, he argued, "both in the Soviet orbit and beyond, on the unquestioning obedience of the agents whom they have trained in Russia for years past, and whom they place in position of authority wherever practicable." He thus called on Britain to highlight the imperialistic nature of Soviet communism and to portray communism itself as the ideology of "Russia's new colonial empire."[25]

A similar dynamic took hold in the United States as Soviet behavior at the London CFM occasioned a comparable change in U.S. information policy. Secretary of State George C. Marshall actually had gone into those meetings convinced of their futility. Persistent differences on issues such as reparations payments and control of the Ruhr only confirmed for him the need to move ahead with European recovery and the incorporation of Germany into a West European framework. The

United States would now mount its own publicity offensive, exposing the realities of Soviet totalitarianism. Those efforts would go a long way toward supporting American objectives in Europe, particularly in shaping attitudes, both at home and abroad, about the European Recovery Program (ERP).[26]

Selling European Aid

Nevertheless, the prospects for ERP looked dim. Polls from late October 1947 indicated that only 47 percent of the American public were in favor of the program.[27] The failure to mobilize support for ERP was a glaring mistake, since the Truman administration now ran the risk of losing whatever momentum Marshall's original offer had generated.[28] Many of the nation's top journalists, including James Reston of the *New York Times,* had criticized the administration for its reticence in shaping public opinion on such an important matter. State Department officials such as Dean Rusk, who headed the Office of Special Political Affairs, and Policy Planning Staff Director George F. Kennan were aware of the problem and tried to correct it, holding a background briefing for the nation's editorialists in mid-October.[29] European and Soviet specialists John D. Hickerson and Charles E. Bohlen followed up on the matter and recommended that the department establish a mechanism for disseminating information on a regular basis.[30]

Indeed, the machinery at State to implement such a publicity campaign was in disarray. William Benton, the assistant secretary of state for public affairs, had resigned in September 1947 and each of the many individuals tapped to replace him had declined the offer. The most that could be said for the department's efforts was that they had succeeded in spawning a private organization, the Committee to Defend the Marshall Plan, to generate support for ERP. Still, that body was not operative until mid-November. In an effort to stimulate further backing, the administration reached out to the Advertising Council. Following up on its work with the Freedom Train, the AC helped to coordinate an October 1947 White House meeting with scores of business leaders aimed at promoting European aid. Council president Ted Repplier thought that casting the virtues of ERP in more ideological terms would promote public and, in turn, congressional support.[31]

The administration's efforts to shape public opinion still left much to be desired, however. With the vote on ERP scheduled for March 1948—administration personnel hoped to use Marshall aid to influence the Italian elections in April—the department had little time to push through such groundbreaking legislation. From January 1948 onward, senior officials sought to rectify the situation and took their case to Congress and the American people, citing the benefits of the recovery program and the horrors that would attend its defeat.[32]

Central to that campaign was an appeal to the nation's historic and cultural legacy. President Truman had invoked those themes in submitting ERP to Congress in December 1947. Its passage, he noted, was vital to the emerging strategy of containing communism. Quite simply, ERP offered the single, best means of preserving "the civilization in which the American way of life is rooted." Secretary of State Marshall echoed those sentiments in early 1948. Without ERP, Marshall warned, "the historic base of Western civilization, of which we are by belief and inheritance an integral part, will take on a new form in the image of the tyranny we fought to destroy in Germany." Engaged in a struggle between Good and Evil, the United States and its citizens were now contemplating "the greatest decision in our history." Charles E. Bohlen, who managed the department's public relations campaign, also tended toward the apocalyptic in his defense of ERP. Invoking the specter of the monolith, he described the Communist threat as one engineered by "a highly organized group whose loyalties are to a foreign government rather than to their own country."[33]

Adding to the information blitz was the dramatic and repeated use of Red Fascist imagery, highlighted by the publication of captured documents relating to the Nazi-Soviet Pact of 1939. Administration officials, including Undersecretary of State Robert Lovett and Ambassador Walter Bedell Smith, were keen to use those materials as part of a general effort to equate past Nazi behavior with current Soviet practice.[34] The release of those files—many of which portrayed Moscow as an expansionist power—received wide attention in the media, with most accounts treating the move as a propaganda coup.[35] Several commentators drew implicit parallels between the prewar and postwar situations; others argued that Moscow was now pursuing the same goals, such as a controlling influence in Iran and Turkey, that it had sought in the 1939 agreement. More than a few observers noted that publication of those documents would likely strengthen the case for the Marshall Plan, and both Truman officials and congressional leaders used it to that end.[36] Although a number of commentators feared it might further poison U.S.-Soviet relations, the more influential voices had no such qualms. The *New York Times*, for instance, treated the episode as "a warning to the Western World which it can ignore only at its own peril." *Time* magazine recognized the material as "clearly propaganda, but propaganda with the virtue of sober truth."[37]

Only occasionally did U.S. officials express dismay at the use of Red Fascist imagery. George F. Kennan, among others, abhorred comparisons between Soviet Russia and Nazi Germany, maintaining that "parallels between Stalinism and Hitlerism were dangerous."[38] From time to time, however, Kennan himself employed such language to dramatize the perils of Soviet totalitarianism. As he argued in January 1948, a Europe under Stalin's thumb "would be no less hostile to us, and no less dangerous to us in the long run, than would have been the European 'New Order' of Hitler's dreams." Kennan also likened the Soviet use of "fifth columns" to the Nazi method of internal subversion. Apparently, even Kennan found aspects of the image hard to resist.[39]

The propaganda was soon paying off. Opinion polls from early 1948 indicate a rising awareness of the European Recovery Program. Since October 1947, when James Reston had lambasted the administration for its shoddy publicity campaign, awareness of the Marshall Plan had increased, rising from 61 percent during that month to 71 percent in late January 1948. Yet the public still regarded ERP as merely a gesture of goodwill; only 8 percent thought it was designed to "curb communism," while 56 percent believed it was intended "to help Europe." That was not a good sign for the administration, since it was widely believed that Congress could pass the aid legislation only if lawmakers and their constituents believed it vital to the containment of communism. Both the administration and its allies in the private sector were still falling short of generating the necessary public support.[40]

The Vicissitudes of Chinese Communism

Those efforts were also failing because of heightened congressional and media concern over developments in Asia. Ever since the Truman Doctrine had cast postwar tensions in global, Manichean terms, questions had arisen as to why the administration was downplaying its global application and withholding additional aid from the Chinese Nationalists (KMT).[41] Those questions became increasingly pointed as the Chinese Communist Party (CCP) made steady progress in its war on Chiang Kai-shek and the KMT. Reports of greater collaboration between Moscow and Yenan only magnified fears that the Soviets would one day control all of Asia, increasing the political pressure on Truman to offer Chiang some kind of aid package. Numerous statements in the press testifying to the indivisibility of international communism were central to that argument.[42]

Such talk was limited neither to the "China Lobby" in Congress—those legislators particularly supportive of Chiang—nor to the private individuals and groups supplying it with information. The CIA, for instance, regarded the Chinese Communists as "ideologically sympathetic with and oriented toward Moscow," as well as a "most effective instrument of Soviet policy toward China."[43] So, too, did a host of government officials who made their way to China during the previous two years. Now, however, those comments were appearing with greater regularity in the nation's press. Just days after the Cominform manifesto became public, *Life* published an article by former ambassador William Bullitt that held out the prospect of China "falling into Soviet hands." The *New York Times* described the Chinese situation in equally weighty terms, characterizing it as "an immediate battleground in the great struggle" between the Soviets and the West.[44]

Interpretations of Chinese communism were far from uniform, however. Many wartime and postwar reports, for example, characterized Mao and his band as "agrarian reformers," revolutionaries who were likely more Chinese than Communist. To clear the haze swirling around interpretations of Chinese communism, Secretary Marshall asked U.S. officials in June 1947 to comment on the international alignment of the CCP.[45] Responses to that request were still coming in as late as October 1947, which meant they would be read—and some of them written—in the context of the Cominform Declaration. Accordingly, in mid-October, Ambassador to China J. Leighton Stuart informed Marshall that the links between Moscow and Yenan were strong and getting stronger. Repeating a theme that he and his colleagues had voiced on a number of occasions, Stuart argued that actual evidence of Soviet aid was virtually irrelevant to understanding the Soviet-CCP relationship; what really mattered was the "undoubtedly very close and conscious affinity in aims, methods and objectives" that both sides shared. That commonality of purpose, Stuart noted, would likely "become more apparent as the rift widens between the United States and the Soviet Union." By December 1947, Asian specialists in the State Department had concluded that a CCP-led government would "almost certainly seek to ally China with the USSR."[46]

Nevertheless, U.S. officials stationed in both Washington and China thought such a partnership might be short-lived. Economic collaboration notwithstanding, Chinese and Soviet Communists exhibited few traces of mutual friendship. The Kremlin, moreover, had yet to introduce any recognizable figureheads into CCP leadership positions. With Moscow steering clear of direct military involvement in the Chinese civil war, the U.S.S.R. was unlikely to promote a faction of Chinese Communists deferential to Soviet interests. Moreover, the very ties that bound Yenan to Moscow might generate a split among the Chinese Communists between those who followed a more patriotic, Chinese line and those who sought to do Moscow's will. The more likely scenario was one in which a rift would develop between the CCP and the Kremlin. As U.S. intelligence pointed out, the Chinese Communists might rival the KMT in the depth of their nationalism and xenophobia, and prove to be just as hostile to outside influences. Despite its earlier comments on Soviet-CCP affinity, the CIA expected Moscow to have some reservations about Mao and his band achieving complete and utter victory.[47]

Indeed, a Soviet-CCP alliance was hardly a foregone conclusion. Kennan still expected Moscow and Yenan to have difficulties managing their relationship, especially if the Chinese Communists emerged as victors in the civil war. John Paton Davies, a Kennan colleague on the Policy Planning Staff with extensive experience in both Russian and Chinese affairs, agreed. Echoing Kennan's thoughts from early 1946, Davies characterized Asian communism as perhaps "the most subtle and misleading political phenomenon in the world scene today," and different in important respects from European communism. To boost American knowledge of the CCP, he called on the State Department to institute a more intensive program of in-house education covering the whole range of Communist activity in Asia.[48] In the meantime, aid to the Chinese nationalists would go forward. Cognizant of its need to build the broadest possible support for ERP, the administration submitted a China aid package to Congress in mid-February 1948, following through on a promise it had made the previous year.[49]

British views of Chinese communism were similarly contradictory. On the one hand, the Foreign Office drew no specific lesson from the Cominform Declaration about the future of Asian communism. On the other hand, it could hardly have found that statement reassuring. If anything, officials were beginning to regard Mao Zedong and the CCP as dyed-in-the-wool Communists, who were every bit as Marxist as their Soviet comrades.[50] But they were at some pains to get that point across to the British public, which had received a generally sympathetic accounting of Yenan from the British press. According to Sir Edmund Hall-Patch, deputy undersecretary for economic affairs, many Britons regarded the Chinese Communists as "more nationalistic and less subject to control from Moscow than Communist parties in other parts of the world." Patch thought it essential that those arguments "should be wherever possible put in their proper light." Whatever the case might have been in the past, he argued, "there was at present no evidence to show that once the Communists got into power in China they would follow any other policy than one which was agreeable to the Soviet Government."[51]

Although the Russia Committee seemed to have little trouble with Patch's argument, it could not ignore reports of tension between Moscow and Yenan. In early February 1948, Ambassador Ralph Stevenson noted that even with the probable victory of the Chinese Communists, "the process of turning China into an orthodox communist state would . . . be extremely slow."[52] Given the complexity of the Asian scene, therefore, the Foreign Office followed up on its seemingly regular practice of evaluating the solidarity of European communism by commissioning a study of the CCP that would ascertain, among other things, its dependence on Moscow and support for the Cominform. The resultant study found Chinese Communists, Korean Communists, and Japanese Communists to be little more than "stalking horses" for Russia.[53] Yet debate about the CCP's orientation continued to roil the Foreign Office, with its London-based Asian experts rejecting notions that the Chinese Communists would likely chart a course independent of Moscow.[54]

Indeed, the very existence of the Cominform seemed to offer Moscow further means of reining in Asian communism's centripetal forces. Within two months of the Silesian conference, U.S. officials began picking up hints that a Far Eastern Cominform was in the offing. Reports from China throughout the fall and winter of 1947 continued to point toward the establishment of an Asian Cominform, though administration officials began to backtrack on that finding by late December.[55] By early spring 1948, however, the CIA believed that a "Far East Cominform" was, in fact, directing the activities of Communist Parties in Asia in accordance with Soviet objectives.[56] According to the CIA, "the very existence of such a coordinating mechanism," even when allowing for the exercise of greater autonomy by Asian CPs, "implies increased Kremlin direction and control." The NSC concurred; with the CCP acting as "an effective instrument for the extension of Soviet influence," the main beneficiary of a Far Eastern Cominform would be the Kremlin itself.[57] To American as well as British officials, conferences held that February and March in Calcutta were the likely venues for harmonizing Asian Communist policy.[58] British observers were more dubious that a Far Eastern Cominform was responsible for such coordination, though they, too, recognized Mao's interest in uniting the "anti-imperialist forces" at work in Asian lands.[59]

War Scare

Debates over the nature of Chinese communism and aid to the KMT soon took a back seat to more pressing developments as political unrest in Czechoslovakia shifted the focus from Asia back to Europe. On February 20, just days after the administration submitted its China aid program to Congress, the democratic members of the Czech government resigned, protesting the dictatorial methods of their Communist colleagues. In short order, Czech Communists seized the vacated ministerial slots and forced President Eduard Beneš to accept the new, Communist government. The action had all the makings of a *coup d'état*, which came as no surprise to American observers, including George F. Kennan, director of the Policy Planning Staff. Kennan had long assumed that Moscow would clamp down on its satellites; the founding of the Cominform, he reasoned, was itself an indication that the Kremlin would demand greater obedience from the countries in its orbit. Many in the press reached the same conclusion and, like Kennan, did so in the wake of the Cominform Declaration.[60]

Although the crackdown might have been expected, the sheer audacity of the act stoked the fears of Western observers. In sweeping away the last traces of democracy in Eastern Europe—by doing so in *Czechoslovakia,* of all places—the Soviets had rekindled images that had been cemented into the collective conscience almost ten years to the day, giving new and dramatic life to what had since become common rhetorical themes. President Truman enunciated the widely accepted notion that the United States now confronted "exactly the same situation with which Britain and France were faced in 1938–39 with Hitler." As Secretary of State Marshall put it, the coup simply reconfirmed his belief that America was "involved in a world-wide struggle between freedom and tyranny," a situation that made the ratification of ERP that much more essential.[61]

The Czech coup made a deep impact on Congress and eventually ensured passage of the European Recovery Program. Senate Foreign

Relations Chair Arthur Vandenberg used the coup in his defense of ERP, claiming that the Marshall Plan would avert World War III and sustain Western civilization.[62] According to opinion polls, Americans were now ready to hear that kind of argument—a rhetorical line the administration seemed only too willing to put forth. During interviews conducted in the midst of the Czech crisis, more than three-fourths of the population attributed Moscow's actions to aggressive rather than defensive concerns, and almost the same number thought America was being "too soft" on the Russians.[63] With anti-Soviet opinion reaching a crescendo, Congress approved the Marshall Plan, making $5.3 billion available to Europe for the first year of the program. At the same time, it appropriated $460 million in economic aid and "special grants" for China.[64]

The events in Czechoslovakia had an equally profound impact on British foreign policy, inciting Foreign Secretary Bevin to even greater heights of alarm. Within two weeks of the coup, Bevin submitted to the cabinet a paper entitled "The Threat to Western Civilization," an appraisal of Soviet behavior more ominous than the one he rendered in January. It was a document full of fear and loathing, and one that portrayed the Soviet menace in the most dramatic of terms. Total mastery of Eurasia, he noted, "and eventual control of the whole World Island is what the Politburo is aiming at—no less a thing than that." Yet Bevin did not expect the Soviets to achieve their objectives through military means. Rather, Moscow would rely on its "political and strategic advantages"—its legions of lackeys and dupes—to do its bidding. Those like-minded comrades would be the ones to "set the great Communist machine in action, leading either to the establishment of a World Dictatorship or (more probably) to the collapse of organised society over great stretches of the globe." It was a nightmarish vision—a powerful, machine-like organization, bolstered by the unwavering support of comrades the world over, united in a quest to undermine the values of Western culture—in short, the very image of the monolith itself.[65]

British information policy would both reflect and promote that image through the work of the newly created Information Research Department (IRD). As envisioned by it creators, the IRD had two primary functions: to analyze intelligence reports and to provide background material ("briefings," in the departmental vernacular) to foreign officials, trade union leaders, academics, and the media.[66] Much of this data would come from surveying Communist activity abroad, a practice the Foreign Office recommended following the Czech coup. Not surprisingly, one of the IRD's first papers, completed roughly one month after the putsch, declared that national CPs were now "to be controlled by Moscow on a tighter reign" and that "the strategy and tactics of Leninism were to be followed more strictly than previously." More so now than ever before, the Kremlin would seek to harness Eastern Europe as "a single instrument of Soviet policy."[67] British representatives in Moscow found the IRD essay to be of "particular value" for its ability to put Soviet policy in perspective. They passed a copy on to U.S. Ambassador Walter Bedell Smith, who promptly termed it an "excellent report" and sent it along to Washington.[68]

That exchange of information became a more regular feature of the Anglo-American relationship during the early Cold War. Much of it was ad hoc; lacking any formal mechanism for such contact, publicity officers from the State Department and Foreign Office were simply encouraged to cooperate with their opposite numbers.[69] Their interaction revealed a significant disparity in experience, however, for the British publicity apparatus was more mature than that of the Americans. Nevertheless, the rhetoric of the two services often paralleled each other. Those similarities became evident in April 1948, when the United States and Great Britain opposed and ultimately helped defeat the Communist Party of Italy in that country's national elections. Central to their information offensive was the depiction of communism as Red Fascism. Just before voters went to the polls, the Foreign Office supplied its Rome embassy with charts linking communism to fascism, and the Soviets to the Nazis.[70] This tactic was all the more powerful because of the sincerity with which it was employed. British officials routinely saw foreign affairs through the eyes of Munich, invoking its lessons in private as well as public communications.[71] The Information Research Department took the lead in that regard, characterizing Stalin's and Lenin's works as the Soviet equivalent of *Mein Kampf*.[72] British diplomats continued to express interest in such propaganda—this time for use on a much wider scale—when the Foreign Office, in June 1948, asked its representatives abroad to generate a list of prominent Communists with Nazi pasts.[73]

The Impact of Political Culture

Although foreign audiences garnered most of their attention, British and American officials were equally concerned about shaping opinion at home. In the United States, much of the rhetoric used in the service of ratifying the Marshall Plan—often hyperbolic, apocalyptic, and brazenly anti-Communist—became woven into the cultural milieu, largely to the dismay of American policymakers. It was not the first time that Truman administration officials had loosed the Communist bogey on the nation or that they felt obliged to rein it back in. Following the administration's campaign for ERP, however, the tenor of the public debate had shifted considerably. Much of this change was attributable to partisan politics, aided and abetted by groups such as the Advertising Council and the Chamber of Commerce. Numerous Republican legislators—some of whom despised the New Deal, others who disliked its modifications under Truman, and still others who simply realized a politically valuable tool when they saw one—hopped on the anti-Communist bandwagon with few reservations. They would do so even more fervently following the general election that November.[74]

Truman and the Democrats were equally culpable in raising the specter of communism in the United States, having found it a useful tactic in the upcoming general election. While they denigrated Republican efforts to smear the administration with charges of coddling domestic Communists, they were at least as energetic in tarring third-party candidate Henry Wallace with a similar rap. Wallace, whom Truman had ousted from the cabinet following the commerce secretary's 1946 disagreement with Secretary of State James F. Byrnes, had announced his candidacy for president in December 1947. Recognizing that Wallace was a potential magnet for liberal votes, Truman officials and political allies sought "to identify him in the public mind with the Communists," as campaign aide Clark Clifford put it. Influential Democrats, union leaders, and organizations such as Americans for Democratic Action were relentless in hammering home the notion that Wallace was a stooge—an unwitting one but a stooge nonetheless—for the Communists and their Kremlin overlords. Leading newspapers such as the *New York Herald Tribune* and *Washington Post* echoed that theme, with syndicated columnist Stewart Alsop indicting Wallace's movement—the Progressive Citizens of America—as "an instrument of Soviet policy." These efforts to smear Wallace legitimized the use of virulent anticommunism as a political tool, further saturating American public life with images of the Communist-as-mole.[75]

Official manipulation aside, anti-Soviet and anti-Communist sentiment also grew out of sincerely held fears about communism, Communist subversion, and the impact of contemporary events. Following the October 1947 Cominform Declaration, these fears rose in conjunction with a dizzying set of developments that collectively had a profound impact on public life. These episodes included:

The House Un-American Activities Committee hearings and subsequent industry crackdown on Communists in Hollywood, which began that November.

The release of administration and congressional lists of subversive organizations and undesirable State Department employees in December 1947 and February 1948.

The Prague coup of February 1948 and subsequent death of Czech minister Jan Masaryk on March 10.

A bill to outlaw the American Communist Party, introduced in Congress on March 15.

Capping this sequence were the events of March 17, which opened with a declaration by columnists Joseph and Stewart Alsop that the climate in Washington was not postwar but "prewar"; peaked with the signing by French, British, and Benelux representatives of the Brussels mutual defense pact; and closed with President Truman's address to a joint session of Congress on the dangers of the world situation. All of the foregoing took place against the backdrop of congressional hearings on both China aid and ERP—public spectacles in their own right, replete with their own rhetorical flourishes. Taken together, these partisan and not-so-partisan forces generated, for both honorable and dishonorable reasons, an increasingly powerful urge to identify and root out Communists from American life.

Again, this virulent strain of anticommunism did not necessarily work to Truman's advantage. Many of his own employees came under suspicion, and in some cases the president had little choice but to capitulate to the demands of various political lobbies.[76] Now that the administration had secured the release of Marshall aid, however, officials such as Soviet expert Charles E. Bohlen tried to dampen the more egregious displays of anti-Communist rhetoric. Hoping to inject a bit of nuance into public discussions of communism, Bohlen sought to carve out some space on the political Left for those who, though sympathetic to socialist ideas, had no fondness for communism itself. This was not an insignificant goal, given the challenges facing Truman in the 1948 election. Appearing before Congress in late April, Bohlen testified that it would be "suicidal" if the U.S. government began to tar as "Communist" anybody with Left or radical views. Not only was the administration eager to paint American liberals as trustworthy anti-Communists, but two of America's key allies in Western Europe—Britain and France—were themselves home to Left-leaning governments. Differentiating socialism from communism was therefore vital to the creation of a common front.[77]

Bohlen also tried to clarify just who warranted the label—and stigma—of the Communist cadre. The administration, he argued, branded as Communist not just anyone who expressed a "theoretical" sympathy for the doctrine but those who belonged to "a highly disciplined organization who take their guidance and receive their instructions from the same men who rule the Soviet Union." It was a curious argument, for in trying to elevate the public discussion of communism and put it on a more sophisticated plane, Bohlen simplified it in at least one key respect: by tying Communist parties to the Soviet Union and casting them as tools of the Kremlin, he reaffirmed the image, perhaps inadvertently, of communism as a monolithic entity.[78]

That issue of misplaced loyalty—the belief that Communists served the interests of a foreign power—played an increasingly large role in public expressions of anticommunism. Encroaching on a province of the Left, the Veterans of Foreign Wars proclaimed May 1, a veritable holy day in the Communist calendar, as "Loyalty Day." Marchers lined the streets of Brooklyn and Manhattan, paying homage to America and American institutions. Other cities around the country followed suit, encouraging the formation of a National Loyalty Day Parade Committee, chaired by Secretary of Labor Maurice J. Tobin. Less than three weeks later, Congress passed the Mundt-Nixon Bill, requiring the Communist Party and its front organizations to register with the Justice Department. The legislation received wide support; a May survey of public opinion indicated that more than three-quarters of the country favored a law requiring all members of the Communist Party to comply with Mundt-Nixon strictures. An overwhelming belief that American Communists were loyal to Russia (65 percent of those polled in mid-April held that view) no doubt aided the bill's passage.[79]

While Americans were becoming familiar with congressional hearings and loyalty investigations, Britons remained generally immune to the anti-Communist crusade. This disparity stemmed, in part, from the nature of the British parliamentary and American political systems, as well as from the relative openness of the British and American CPs.[80] The lack of the committee probe—Parliament had no body comparable to the House Committee on Un-American Activities, for example—removed one such vehicle for the expression of a more raucous anticommunism.

Also absent from the U.K. scene was the volatility introduced into American politics by the 1948 general election, again providing Britain with a comparatively more tranquil political moment. In addition, the crusading impulse in American society endowed the United States with a moralism not as evident in Britain. The corresponding interest of British Conservatives in swimming with the prevailing Leftist tide also made a comparable anti-Communist campaign less likely in the United Kingdom.[81]

Yet Whitehall would also crack down on Communists and fellow-travelers in the wake of the Czech coup. In March 1948, Prime Minister Clement Attlee formed a Cabinet Committee on Subversive Activities, making made good on an earlier decision to rid the government of employees whose work brought them into contact with secret information. Educational institutions also now came under fire.[82] Britain, moreover, now had its own "professional" anti-Communist to rival those in the United States: Douglas Hyde, news editor of the Communist *Daily Worker,* who left the party in March. Following his renunciation of party ties, Hyde went on a speaking tour, regaling audiences with first-person testimony about the horrors of communism, which he capped off two years later in *I Believed,* his account of life as a Stalinist.[83] The ruling Labour Party was also touched by the post-Prague ethos. Gone was the solidarity of the Keep Left group, which had earlier opposed Bevin's handling of Soviet-American relations; several of its members now embraced the more strident anticommunism of Bevin and the Foreign Office. A number of Labour MPs also felt the sting of the party purge, owing to their support of socialist Pietro Nenni in the Italian election campaign.[84] While Britain was far from awash in the pageantry and spectacle of American anticommunism, these episodes suggest that the anti-Communist impulse also began to shape the contours of British political life.

Accordingly, British officials, especially those in the Foreign Office, portrayed Communists and communism much as Americans did. They continued to push Red Fascist and monolithic imagery, two key themes of Britain's publicity policy as outlined in the cabinet papers of early 1948.[85] Yet the precise wording of anti-Communist rhetoric continued to bedevil policymakers, largely because Bevin himself had failed to settle on a preferred epithet, alternating between "communism" and "totalitarianism" as the most effective terms of opprobrium. "Communism" presented difficulties, since its popular identification as an anti-capitalist and anticolonialist revolutionary force appealed to the downtrodden. "Stalinism," another option floated and rejected, seemed to associate Soviet policy too closely with Stalin himself. In the end, the Russia Committee agreed that British propaganda "could attack Communism, the Soviet Government, totalitarianism, the Politburo, the Kremlin, etc., as occasion demanded." It was a strategy that would require considerable finesse, however, especially if the IRD persisted in portraying Moscow as the fountainhead of international communism while simultaneously denying its capacity for omnipotence.[86]

But publicity officers in both Britain and the United States would soon have further grist for their propaganda mills. The imposition of the Berlin Blockade in June 1948—what America's political adviser in that city likened to a potential "Munich of 1938"—capped nine of the most consequential months of the entire postwar era.[87] Beginning with the creation of the Cominform, that period was filled with monumental events, including the economic division of the continent, the political division of Germany, and the inchoate military division of Europe. For Americans, each of those developments unfolded within an increasingly volatile political climate that conditioned further assessments of communism at home and abroad. Although Britons had comparatively less contact with the professional purge or the anti-Communist zealot, they heard equally sharp language from government leaders; after the Czech coup, they would read similarly harsh rhetoric in the national press.[88] British and American policymakers were more closely aligned, however, as personnel in the Foreign Office and the State Department shared many of the same beliefs regarding the fundamental nature of international communism. Both communities, for instance, greeted the Cominform as proof that the Soviets would exercise greater leverage over the Communist parties within their orbit.[89] Each regarded international communism as a centrally directed movement that took its orders from Moscow.

But neither of these audiences saw international communism as an unmitigated threat. To Western observers, the Cominform was as much an indication of Kremlin weakness as it was of Soviet strength. Although U.S. officials believed that Moscow sought to create a monolithic movement, the founding of the Cominform did not necessarily suggest that it had, in fact, succeeded in doing so. The very need to bind Communist parties closer together—and therefore closer to Moscow— suggested the presence of breakaway tendencies within the fold. This was especially true in the Far East, where the Kremlin had yet to firm up its position. Efforts to capitalize on those difficulties picked up in the months following the Cominform's creation. The Foreign Office and State Department now began to coordinate their respective information policies, as part of the two governments' more general effort to meet the Soviet challenge. The similarities between the two programs, including the timing of their implementation and the form of their rhetoric, were reflected in conversations between U.S. and British officials in March 1948.[90]

Still, the two approaches were not identical. U.S. officials sought to carry their propaganda to peoples behind the Iron Curtain in an effort to incite internal subversion, a policy and region that were off-limits to Britain. The British Foreign Office thought the more appropriate outlets for publicity included those countries, as Christopher Warner put it, "where the struggle with Communism is still in the balance." The nature of their publicity also diverged, given the geographic as well as ideological differences separating the two Western powers. Talk of Britain as a "Third Force" was utterly absent from American propaganda, as were references to the virtues of "social democracy." Although U.S. officials had few problems with Britain championing this line, they were loath to adopt it as their own.[91]

By June 1948, therefore, numerous developments in both Britain and the United States had converged to sustain the image of communism as a monolithic movement. Although many of those processes had long been in the works and stretched back to well before the war, they began to blend most forcefully during the previous two-and-a-half years. The Stalin speech of February 1946, George Kennan's "Long Telegram" from later than month, and Christopher Warner's paper of April 1946 lay at the front end of a historical path that culminated in the founding of the Cominform and the coup in Czechoslovakia. Thereafter, it was increasingly difficult to regard communism as anything but a monolithic movement.

Although the links between government and nongovernment organizations accelerated this trend and helped to frame the issues, the desire for greater public vigilance spawned a host of initiatives aimed at fostering a more organically grassroots brand of anticommunism. New organizations, such as the American Heritage Foundation and the Freedoms Foundation of Valley Forge, worked with older ones to encourage greater vigilance and adherence to free enterprise, civic engagement, and resistance to "foreign" ideologies. Combined with the more combustible political climate swirling around the 1948 election season, public spectacles such as the Freedom Train and the HUAC hearings became part of the national experience and created a hypercharged environment in which dangers abroad, as represented by the events of Prague, Paris, and Rome, were bound up with threats at home. HUAC even published "100 Things You Should Know about Communism," a five-part series that repeatedly portrayed all Communists as Kremlin servants.[92] "A Program for Community Anti-Communist Action," the Chamber of Commerce effort to inoculate Americans against this peril and inspire greater energy in combating it, captured the emerging emphasis on local activity. The Chamber's plan also identified Communists as Soviet lackeys, for it appeared as a booklet with a hammer and sickle adorning its cover. The equating of communism with the Kremlin through the use of the Soviet flag was unmistakable and reinforced the image of an alien-inspired and monolithic cabal of Communists the world over.[93]

This was most clearly the case in Europe, where Communists had often trekked to Moscow to study under the Russian masters. With the end of the war, those pilgrims returned to their lands beholden to the Kremlin. In the course of the next two years, they would bind their countries—always under the watchful eyes of Stalin and the Red Army—to the Soviet line. Yet that process of reorientation was a messy one and differed from state to state. The CIA recognized as much when it noted, in June 1948, that "the Soviet position in the Satellite States is not fully consolidated." Those countries still at arm's length from Moscow, according to the agency, were Hungary, Czechoslovakia, and Finland. But efforts to "perfect" that position, according to U.S. intelligence, were proceeding apace.[94]

One nation, however, stood out from the others as the most Sovietized and most loyal of all: Yugoslavia. Not only did its capital, Belgrade, house the Cominform; its leader, Josip Broz "Tito," was arguably the most doctrinaire and powerful Communist outside the U.S.S.R. Indeed, the British Foreign Office viewed Yugoslavia as "largely a 'monolithic' totalitarian state," firmly within the Soviet camp. So, too, did the U.S. intelligence community. As of June 1948, the CIA regarded the bloc nations of Southeastern Europe, of which Yugoslavia was by far the most influential, as solidly within Moscow's grip.[95] If any fog was still swirling around the nature of European communism, it had long since moved off the Balkan peninsula. Events, however, would soon suggest otherwise.

CHAPTER FIVE

A Break in the Bloc

The expulsion of Yugoslavia from the Cominform in June 1948 constituted a signal development for policymakers in their efforts to evaluate
the relative cohesion of the Communist bloc. Moscow's decision to
exile the Balkan nation from the socialist camp also presented the West
with a propaganda and strategic opportunity of extraordinary propor-
tions. British and American statesmen would now seek to undermine
the Kremlin based on the knowledge that significant opposition to Soviet rule from within the Communist camp had actually arisen—and
might well do so again. Promoting Tito as an example to those within
the socialist fold would prove exceedingly problematic, however. Appeals to Communists had to accord some measure of respect to their
professed creed, lest any potential heretics appear as ideological sell-
outs. But policymakers also had to recognize the security situation of
those situated on or near the Soviet Union. The task, therefore, was
akin to walking a tightrope: preserving Tito's ideological independence
from the West while maintaining his political independence from the
East. These challenges notwithstanding, the split within the Communist
ranks marked the last week of June 1948 as perhaps the most optimistic moment in the emerging Cold War.

It had not started out that way. On June 24, Moscow blockaded the access routes to West Berlin, thereby ushering the Cold War into a new
and more dangerous phase. A "hot war," which seemed unlikely just a
few months earlier, now seemed a distinct possibility, prompting U.S.

officials to consider the prospect of sending Americans boys to fight on foreign soil once again. An equally dramatic battle was raging much closer to home, with international communism reputedly having established a beachhead on America's shores. The HUAC hearings on communism in Hollywood, the attorney general's identification of subversive organizations, and the denunciation of Bureau of Standards chief Edward U. Condon had whipped up fears in the United States of a fifth column poised to do Moscow's bidding. By late June 1948, the National Security Council had outlined a strategy for countering the internal Communist threat. In so doing, it drew explicit links between American Communists and their Russian patrons, depicting both parties as comrades-in-arms. As defined by the NSC, international communism was a worldwide conspiracy directed by "the mother of all Soviets, Soviet Russia."[1]

Although U.S. officials had ample reason to view communism in such terms, they were well aware of tensions that had arisen within the Soviet fold. Much of that unrest had come in the wake of Secretary of State George C. Marshall's proposal to aid the European economy. Poland and Czechoslovakia had expressed an eagerness to participate in the Marshall Plan, only to be stifled by the Kremlin. Moscow's actions generated a backlash of ill will, not only among Czechs and Poles but among peoples throughout the bloc. As a result, Western observers realized that such disquiet was leading Russia to demand even more obedience from its satellites. Within a matter of months, the Soviets had created the Cominform, splitting the world—as Andrei Zhdanov declared at the organization's founding—into two camps. From then on, in an effort to head off further outbursts of resentment, Moscow would patrol its half of the globe with increasingly greater vigilance.[2]

The Monolith Cracked

Yet even as the Kremlin muffled dissenting voices within its sphere, a series of terse exchanges between the Soviets and Yugoslavia—the most Stalinized of East European states—indicated that a more serious row had erupted behind the Iron Curtain. While Yugoslavia's willingness to confront Moscow was both a remarkable and an intriguing development, it had not come as a total surprise. Officials in Washington and London had vivid memories of the Yugoslav partisans' ferocious resistance against the Nazis during World War II. In the postwar world, they reasoned, Yugoslavia might not play the part of a dedicated Kremlin shill. Secretary of State Marshall, for one, was impressed by Belgrade's defiance, characterizing the Yugoslavs in February 1948 as "uncontrollable even by the Soviets."[3]

Aside from their perception of Yugoslavia as a fiercely independent nation, U.S. and British diplomats recognized that more specific tensions had developed between Soviet chieftain Josef Stalin and Yugoslav leader Marshal Josip Broz Tito. By early June, those strains had become readily apparent.[4] American officials in Belgrade, including Ambassador Cavendish Cannon and Chargé R. Borden Reams, detected "genuine disquiet" in Soviet circles at the uncovering of "diversionists" in the Yugoslav Communist Party (YCP). The U.S. ambassador to Hungary, William P. Cochran, saw similar dynamics at work. He thought that Tito would soon be taken to task for considering himself "too important" to be a servant of Stalin and for insisting on his "right to be [an] ally."[5] The British ambassador to Belgrade, Charles Peake, also believed that relations between the two leaders were "decidedly strained." Peake's superiors in London had long suspected that Moscow would soon confront Tito with a sharp rebuke.[6]

They were right. On June 28—the same day, ironically, that NSC officials had characterized communism as a monolithic conspiracy—the Cominform declared that the Yugoslav Communists were creating "a hateful policy" toward the Soviet Union and its Bolshevik Party. Tito, the indictment ran, had spied on Soviet officials, followed a Trotskyist line, advocated a policy of nationalism, delayed the collectivization of Yugoslav farms, and likened Soviet foreign policy to that of the "imperialist powers." In light of Belgrade's anti-Soviet attitude, the Cominform expelled the YCP from its membership ranks, casting adrift one of only eight nations allied with the socialist camp. The monolith had cracked.[7]

Observers on both sides of the Atlantic regarded the Tito-Cominform rift as an occasion of enormous importance and were optimistic about its long-term value for the West. As Borden Reams put it, "no event could be more momentous for the attainment of our foreign policy objectives than the permanent alienation from the Soviet of this key regime." Similarly, the State Department's Russian and East European experts— Charles E. Bohlen, George F. Kennan, and Llewellyn Thompson— identified the split as "a break of the greatest significance—probably the most important single development since the conclusion of hostilities as far as internal Soviet and Communist internal affairs are concerned."[8]

Kennan, in his role as director of the Policy Planning Staff, played a key role in developing America's response to the schism. At the request of Undersecretary of State Robert A. Lovett, Kennan produced a paper on the split that would govern U.S. policy toward Yugoslavia for the remainder of the year. At the outset of this work, designated PPS/35, Kennan described the Tito affair as "an entirely new problem of foreign policy for this Government." For the first time, he wrote, "we may now have within the international community a communist state resting on the basis of Soviet organizational principles and for the most part on Soviet ideology, and yet independent of Moscow." Clearly, the Communist world would never be the same. Tito had broken "the aura of mystical omnipotence and infallibility" that had surrounded the Kremlin's power. "The possibility of defection from Moscow," Kennan argued, "which has heretofore been unthinkable for foreign communist leaders, will from now on be present in one form or another in the mind of every one of them."[9]

Kennan's analysis went out immediately to U.S. missions around the world in the form of a circular telegram from Secretary Marshall. Borrowing liberally from PPS/35, Marshall urged U.S. officials to temper any enthusiasm they might have for exploiting the crack in the bloc. The Tito regime was still "deeply distasteful" to Western sensibilities; as long as it remained in power, Yugoslav-American relations could never assume "quite the cordiality and intimacy which we would wish." Still, as long as Yugoslavia was not subservient to an outside power, its internal regime was "basically its own business." Echoing Kennan, Marshall declared that the international Communist movement would "never be able to make good entirely the damage done" by the Cominform announcement." Tito's example would be "noted by other communists everywhere," and non-Russian Communists would "come to appreciate that they have no future as the servants of Kremlin policies."[10]

The Kennan paper and the Marshall telegram, the first official U.S. statements on the Tito affair, reveal several assumptions American policymakers held about the dynamics of international communism. First, according to administration officials, the Tito split destroyed the image of monolithic unity and utter infallibility that the Kremlin had worked so hard to create. Second, regardless of the particular circumstances facing Communist parties—that is, regardless of whether those groups were in or out of power, or whether they had been installed by the Red Army— each would now begin to question their ties to Moscow, if they had not done so already. Finally, as Marshall had stated in unequivocal terms, American officials would look upon a country's internal regime as less important to U.S. interests than the character of its external relations.

The issue at stake, Marshall seemed to be saying, was not international communism per se but Moscow's direction of it.

While the administration was generally optimistic about the long-term consequences of the rift, several officials worried about its probable short-term effects. Fears that the Tito affair would result in a hardening of the Soviet bloc resounded throughout government circles.[11] As U.S. Ambassador to the Soviet Union Walter Bedell Smith put it, the Cominform statement only confirmed the "completeness of Moscow's intention to rule." CIA chief Roscoe H. Hillenkoetter thought likewise. Although he believed the rift might lead to trouble within Communist parties, Hillenkoetter thought it would have virtually no bearing on the relationship between those organizations and the Kremlin. "The Communist regimes in eastern Europe," he noted, "are firmly under Moscow control and are dominated by old-line Communists trained in Moscow."[12] Nor were the Soviets likely to face many difficulties in stamping out other strains of political independence. The Tito affair thus seemed to dramatize not just the tensions existing within the Soviet orbit but the Kremlin's wish to dominate those peoples inhabiting it.[13]

British officials, like their American counterparts, reacted to the Tito-Cominform dispute with equal parts satisfaction and suspicion. Writing from Belgrade, Chargé Cecil King thought that "Tito and the Yugoslav party have got too big for their boots and have run counter to the aims of Russian nationalism." The rift, as King saw it, was a signal development in the history of communism, a heresy that suggests "the parallel of the opposition of Constantinople to Rome."[14] On the whole, however, the Foreign Office questioned the meaning of the schism and the opportunities it presented. Foreign Secretary Ernest Bevin greeted the split with caution and warned Prime Minister Clement Attlee not to read too much into it; the rift was an intrabloc conflict, Bevin stated, that had little bearing on Communist solidarity in Eastern Europe. He also argued that any differences which might have existed between the Soviets and the Communist leaders in Yugoslavia were "differences of method, not of ultimate aim."[15] Bevin's senior aides shared that assessment. Robin Hankey, along with Gladwyn Jebb and William Hayter, believed the split to be of marginal significance. They, too, treated it essentially as a family quarrel that soon might resolve itself. Indeed, a Russia Committee survey of British missions abroad revealed that native Communists were generally uninterested in pursuing a "Titoist" line. As a result, British officials, like

American officials, were quick to question the meaning and ultimate significance of the Tito affair.[16]

Yugoslavia's behavior later that summer at the Danube Conference, a European-wide meeting held to discuss navigation rights along the waterway, contributed to that shared cognitive confusion. While tensions between the Soviets and Tito remained high throughout the August gathering, Yugoslavia's delegation sided consistently with the Kremlin, granting Moscow virtual command over the river. Russia's ability to control the votes of the Eastern bloc—a "pretty meaningless success," in the words of British assistant undersecretary Gladwyn Jebb—allowed the Soviets to maintain the fiction of a solid front; failure to have done so, Jebb noted, would have meant that "the already observable cracks in the Monolith might become too obvious to be concealed," risking another show of independence.[17] Awareness of that fiction was leading the CIA to move into agreement with the State Department; both now held that the Soviet empire was suffering from fundamental, inescapable tensions which, if allowed to go unchecked, could conceivably lead to the dismantling of the entire structure. Yet the agency persisted in questioning the relevance of the Yugoslav situation to the schisms it saw on the horizon, finding it hard to do otherwise when Yugoslavia, by virtue of its performance at the Danube Conference, was presenting the image "of 'correct' relations and . . . a uniform front to the West." In fact, U.S. intelligence continued to identify Yugoslavia as one of the "Eastern European countries now under Soviet influence," noting "the steady uniformity" with which Yugoslavia supported the Soviet line.[18] Although there might be "strains and stresses in the Soviet system," as the Foreign Office put it, the bloc remained intact. British diplomats, therefore, believed it "wrong to deduce from these symptoms that the Soviet system in Eastern Europe is crumbling." It was a view they shared with their American colleagues.[19]

Asia and the Cominform Split

With the split appearing to have at best an ambiguous impact on Europe, U.S. officials thought it might have a much clearer and more beneficial effect in the Far East. Among the first to discuss those linkages was Ambassador Smith, who regarded the Chinese Communist Party (CCP) as a unified, Popular Front-type party—the same type of outfit the Cominform had condemned in Yugoslavia. Smith thought the CCP's pursuit of a mass-based organization, as well as its slow progress toward collectivization, might well occasion a similar reproach. At the moment, he questioned whether the Chinese Communists were "in imminent danger" of being purged by Moscow. Nevertheless, their leaders had to recognize that a "Yugoslavia-type action toward them [was] possible at any time." According to American sources stationed in China, the Soviets thought that Mao might one day emulate Tito, a fear that led them to harbor a certain distrust of the Chinese Communists. Several factors, including China's distance from Moscow, its tradition of individualism and nationalism, and the CCP's inability to secure total control over the country, meant that China "might indeed cause graver concern than certain other areas."[20]

That line of thinking was even more pronounced back in Washington. George F. Kennan, the U.S. official most responsible for devising America's response to the Tito affair, found the rift equally relevant for the Asian theater, as did his colleague John Paton Davies. The key to Tito's survival, both before and after the break, was Moscow's inability to manipulate either the Yugoslav leader or his associates. By controlling the levers of national power, Kennan reasoned, Tito was able to wall off Yugoslavia from the Kremlin's reach. It was therefore conceivable that other Communists, who found themselves in similar circumstances, could do much the same and thereby destroy "the myth of Stalin's omniscience and omnipotence." Would Asia's Communists serve that purpose? They would have plenty of opportunities to do so: the entire continent appeared to be in turmoil, with civil wars raging along the Pacific Rim and nationalist movements on the rise in South and Southeast Asia. The most important of those battles, however, was taking place in China. With its vast size, home-grown Communist party, and inspirational leader, that nation possessed the requisite conditions for a Titoist movement.[21]

Yet several voices in the U.S. diplomatic community were focusing instead on the points of congruence between Moscow and Yenan. Though eager to spur the growth of Titoism, America's ambassador to China, John Leighton Stuart, continued to place the CCP well within the Soviet camp. Speaking with Nationalist leader Chiang Kai-shek in mid-July 1948, Stuart described the Chinese civil war as "part of a struggle between the fundamental principles of democracy and freedom on the one side and the domination of a minority controlled from Moscow on the other." Ambassador Smith downplayed the potential friction that might develop between Russia and the CCP, noting that the Kremlin's likely objective was to have a Communist China direct the fortunes of the regional CPs. Describing that potential scenario as "a merger of [the] old Japanese co-prosperity sphere with militant Stalinism," Smith revealed the salience of World War II imagery—beyond that of Munich and appeasement—as analogues for the postwar era.[22]

American intelligence also recognized the close affinity between CCP and Soviet goals. Dropping its earlier emphasis on the vitality of Chinese nationalism, the Central Intelligence Agency now depicted Chinese Communists as aligned with the Soviet Union. Analysts believed that a Communist China "would facilitate the extension of Soviet influence throughout the Far East and thus present a direct threat to US security interests throughout the Pacific area." The possibility did exist, however, for tensions to emerge. The CIA wondered whether the Middle Kingdom's size, traditional xenophobia, and penchant for regional identity would ever permit Moscow "to dominate China through the medium of the Chinese Communist Party, as it is able to dominate Eastern European countries" through local CPs. Still, the agency argued, should the CCP ever attain ruling power over China, "it would presumably pursue a foreign policy friendly to and cooperative with the USSR."[23]

U.S. intelligence was slightly more circumspect on the subject of Southeast Asia. While it noted that a regional alignment with the U.S.S.R. would be a major blow to U.S. strategic interests, damaging access to resources, markets, and bases, it recognized that such an eventuality might emerge due to racial antagonism, economic nationalism, and lingering anticolonial sentiment as much as to the machinations of international communism. State Department intelligence also questioned the guiding role of ideology in the area, observing that "if there is a Moscow-directed conspiracy in Southeast Asia, it was an anomaly so far."[24] Yet the department was becoming increasingly concerned about the Vietminh and its direction of the Democratic Republic of Vietnam (DRV). Although it failed to uncover evidence of a direct relationship between Moscow and DRV leader Ho Chi Minh, the department assumed that one existed. According to Marshall, a victorious Ho would "almost certainly" orient his state toward Russia. The current influx of Soviet personnel into Southeast Asia also highlighted the Kremlin's growing interest in the region. While Washington regarded the Franco-Vietminh war as largely a colonial conflict, the thrust of its recent reporting, even in light of the Tito affair, suggested that such a perspective was rapidly waning.[25]

The Rift and the Public

Like the vast majority of government officials, large portions of the national media were characterizing the Tito rift as an event of signal importance. Within days of the breach, the State Department's Office of Public Affairs (OPA) found that most newspapers, including the *New York Herald Tribune* and the *Baltimore Sun*, regarded the Tito affair "as a sign of weakness in what was once considered a solid wall." A consensus had yet to form, however, around what that weakness signified. Several newspapers and magazines, including those that detected "cracks in the monolith," offered competing and discouraging assessments of the split. In fact, in its very first survey of commentary on the rift, the OPA found the national press treating the schism "with a great deal of speculation." Some sources even treated the break as a gigantic sham. On the whole, however, the State Department found the media generally receptive to the notion that the quarrel indicated "a crack in the 'monolithic' eastern bloc."[26]

The *New York Times* echoed these competing assessments. Like other newspapers, the *Times* sounded the familiar refrain that Titoism was spreading. The purges then under way in Eastern Europe suggested as much, indicating that the "monolithic unity among the satellites may be more superficial than real." Yet it also took a pessimistic view of the rift, suggesting that the monolith was alive and well. The Comintern appeared to be fully operative, the *Times* reported, as Communists behind the Iron Curtain were openly avowing their subservience to Stalin. In fact, the purges heralded Moscow's increasing control of the satellites.[27] Russia, therefore, was now likely to fuse those states to the Soviet system—specifically, to enforce "blind loyalty" to Soviet policy and to subordinate the particular interests of bloc nations to those of the Kremlin. Even Belgrade, which the *Times* actually described as one of "Russia's satellites," had affirmed its allegiance to Moscow and would likely continue to base its foreign policy on that of the Soviet Union. Given the ambiguities of the Tito affair, reporting in the *Times,* as in other newspapers, allowed readers to draw multiple and contradictory conclusions about the solidarity of international communism.[28]

The major newsmagazines echoed those competing assessments. While *Newsweek* characterized the split as "the biggest break of the year for the West," it commented repeatedly on Moscow's crackdown behind the Iron Curtain.[29] As *U.S. News & World Report* put it, Yugoslavia remained tied to the Soviet pole. Although Tito had bucked

Moscow's leadership, he and his associates were Communists nonetheless "and go along with the Communist empire on world issues." The split, therefore, could hardly be a portent of things to come. Owing to Tito's "unique" position, there was "little chance that other Eastern European countries [would] break with Moscow in the immediate future."[30] On the whole, these sources generally dismissed the notion that the West stood to gain from Moscow's troubles.

Those views received an added boost from America's elite periodicals. According to the *Nation,* the rift foretold a "prospective crackdown on deviations or signs of independence anywhere." Columnist J. Alvarez Del Vayo attributed total control of the situation to the Kremlin, warning readers not to engage in "wishful thinking" about Moscow's weaknesses or difficulties; the clash was a "family fight" within international communism and thus had little to do "with the future of the Eastern bloc and its effect on world affairs." According to the journal's editors, Tito might even return to the fold.[31] Reporting in the *New Republic* was only slightly more optimistic. To Alexander Kendrick, the affair demonstrated that "the Eastern alliance is not as monolithic as had been supposed," a verdict that stood as an encouraging sign to those who were still holding out for a general European settlement. As with the *Nation,* however, the *New Republic* thought Stalin would now tighten his control over Eastern Europe. The nation's flagship journals of liberal opinion had thus concluded that Tito's defiance was significant primarily for its ability to clarify the true nature of not only the Cominform but of communism itself, a perspective they maintained following the Danube Conference that August. In the words of the *New Republic,* not only was the monolith still rock solid, the Iron Curtain was "to be clamped tight."[32]

The nation's mass publication journals essentially supported the emerging consensus on the split, if only because they had so little to say about it. *Reader's Digest* offered no comment at all on the rift, though its July issue featured a piece from Supreme Court justice William O. Douglas on the "well-disciplined Communists" who "operate from their central headquarters in Moscow, planning domination of the world."[33] *Collier's* was similarly silent, presenting instead its standard fare of factual reporting and fictional dramas. The bulk of its commentary, like that of *Reader's Digest,* continued to celebrate the virtues of Christianity, Western Civilization, and the free market. By contrast, *Life* magazine did give its audience a peek behind the Iron Curtain. In a piece entitled "Good News from Europe," its editors claimed that the lure of ERP aid had contributed to Yugoslavia's desire for greater autonomy. Yet an adjacent article, running under the subtitle "Denounced by the Cominform, It Still Looks Like a Communist State," was hardly encouraging to anyone wanting *very* good news. Given the recent crackdown on Eastern Europe, readers of these and similar publications could well have assumed that international communism was no less monolithic after the split than before it occurred.[34]

At the same time, media comment on how the rift might affect the situation in China was sparse and inconclusive. Elite opinion cast doubt on Tito's relevance for Asia. For instance, on the very day of the Cominform denunciation, the *New Republic* published an article by Walter L. Briggs, a former UPI war correspondent in China and India, that portrayed the Chinese Communists as no different than any other Communists. According to Briggs, Mao was a committed Stalinist who took his cues directly from Moscow. Since Briggs wrote his essay before the Tito rift became public, he had no opportunity to evaluate the Chinese situation against the backdrop of Tito's fall from grace. But the magazine let the entire month of July pass without revisiting Briggs's question, "Is China Different?"[35] Most newspapers, including the *New York Times*, offered little more than the purely technical observation that the CCP had "lined up squarely behind the Soviet Union" in supporting the Cominform's denunciation of Tito.[36] Hardly any publication compared the Yugoslav and Chinese cases in meaningful ways, nor did they show much interest in discussing the CCP's international proclivities. Articles focused exclusively on developments in the Chinese civil war, leaving the general reader to infer some measure of allegiance between the Chinese Communists and their Soviet neighbors.

As summer turned to fall, the nation's leading newspaper became even more explicit in tying the CCP to the Soviet Union. Maintaining that the party derived "both its principles and its potency from a foreign power center—Moscow," the *New York Times* treated Chinese Communist belligerency as part of "a Moscow-directed Communist conspiracy," intent on producing a "Communist world directed from the Kremlin."[37] By Thanksgiving, under the headline "Goal of China Communists Is Same as Russia's," the *Times* had noted that the CCP was increasingly aligning itself with Moscow. Mao's support for Soviet policies indicated that the Chinese leader was "taking extra pains to assure the Soviet Union that he is no Marshal Tito."[38]

Discussion of the Tito affair in the British media echoed familiar themes about the Soviet need for complete subservience to Moscow's dictates. As the London *Times* reported, Stalin had declared "that there must be no 'national' Communism'; it must be 'international,' that is, always at Moscow's command."[39] This was a line shared by print publications across the political spectrum. Both *The Economist* and the *New Statesman & Nation (NS&N)* pushed this reading of the rift, though *NS&N* indicated that it was European Communists, in particular, who aped Soviet policy.[40] As with American outlets, however, equivocation crept into British reporting. Over the course of the next several months, and particularly following the Danube Conference, the *Times* argued that the rift had both consolidated and fractured the bloc, but it declined to speculate on where those developments would ultimately lead.[41]

While the word-symbol of the "monolith" received increasing play in print publications, journals were encouraging policymakers to pursue diplomatic options that implicitly called such appraisals into question. The *Economist,* for instance, called for "re-examining some aspect of the Western Powers' relations with Eastern Europe on their own merits without reference to the supposed advantage or disadvantage of the Soviet Union." It also resisted a reflexively hawkish assessment of communism, urging a more flexible attitude toward Communist nations and rejecting the analogy between Nazi Germany and Soviet Russia. In all, the established and elite organs of the British media were taking a less dogmatic, more speculative approach on the meaning and impact of the Tito split than their American peers.[42]

The orientation of Chinese communism, however, remained as much of an enigma for the British press as it was for the American. While *NS&N* recognized Mao's denunciation of Tito's "deviation," the journal believed it "premature and foolish to take for granted that Communist China is to be a mere adjunct of the Soviet Union."[43] Yet it also maintained that the Communist-inspired violence then raging in Malaya and Burma, the February and March 1948 meetings of Communists in Calcutta, and the general hardening of the Soviet line were all "connected events."[44] The *Times* similarly hedged its bets. Although Mao's ultimate victory might grant the Soviets "wider influence" over Chinese policy, it noted that Chinese Communist leaders were unlikely to submit to foreign control. Likewise, it recognized that while Mao had clear "deviationist" tendencies along Tito's line, the CCP was "one of the first to denounce Tito—when it need not have entered the controversy at all."[45] The *Economist* mirrored that approach. Charging that a victorious CCP "might succumb to 'Titoism' and forget their proper devotion" to the Soviet Union, it also determined that "in their world outlook, and therefore in their foreign policy . . . the Chinese Communists are fully orthodox" and that the West could not safely base its own policy "on such a remote chance."[46] On the whole, and even allowing for the slightly more hawkish perspective of the *New York Times*, American and British outlets were equally ambivalent in their evaluations of Tito's impact on both Asia and Europe.

Titoism Reconsidered

That uncertainty was also present among government officials. British policymakers were clearly at pains to determine the nature and challenge of Asian communism. Of immediate interest were the recent disturbances in Malaya that had led the colonial government, on June 18, to place the entire country under a state of emergency. At a meeting of the Russia Committee several weeks hence, Malcolm MacDonald, Britain's commissioner-general for Southeast Asia, claimed that Malayan Communists were not "Moscow-trained revolutionaries" but "amateurs from the ranks of unskilled bandits." Nevertheless, at the same session, he described the newly established Soviet legation at Bangkok as "the centre of Soviet activity in the whole of South East Asia." Additional statements by colonial and military officials lent further credence to the notion that the Malayan uprising was both Soviet-inspired and directed. Contradictory and inconclusive, such statements offered little guidance to officials in policymaking positions.[47]

Gauging the direction of Chinese communism in the wake of the Tito rift was proving even more problematic. J. H. Watson, of the Foreign Office's Northern Department, reminded his colleagues that Yugoslavia, like China, had not been overrun by the Red Army during World War II. Considering Belgrade's freedom from Soviet military occupation, Watson wondered, "What will happen in France, China etc.?" No answer was forthcoming. But even a CCP victory, as Far East specialist Esler Dening observed, might not redound to Moscow's benefit, at least not in the near term. Given China's size, it would be some time before a Communist system could be imposed on the whole country. Britain's ambassador to China was less optimistic. By staying on the sidelines in the civil war, Ralph Stevenson argued, the Kremlin was still achieving its objective, recognizing that the Chinese Communists "could be relied on to adopt tactics favourable to the broad Soviet strategy."[48]

Foreign Secretary Bevin offered the British cabinet no clearer vision of the Maoist forces. In early December 1948, he admitted to continuing uncertainty about the "ultimate nature" of the CCP and the likely relationship between Moscow and a Communist Chinese government.[49] Still, he thought that the Chinese Communists, if and when they achieved power over all of China, would most likely "adopt the policies of orthodox Communism," a position that illustrates how much Bevin's views on the CCP had changed over the previous two years.[50] Days later, however, Bevin submitted a memorandum for the cabinet, drafted largely by the Far Eastern Section of the Foreign Office, that offered a slightly less dogmatic analysis and harkened back to his earlier statements on the "agrarian" nature of the CCP. Reiterating the impossibility of deriving firm conclusions about Chinese communism or its ties to the Kremlin, he cautioned against adopting any policy which might drive a Communist Chinese government "into the arms" of Moscow.[51] For the moment, the FO took comfort in the notion that a CCP victory, while a defeat for the West, did not necessarily constitute "a positive accretion of strength" for the Kremlin. It was a sentiment shared equally by Soviet specialists in Washington.[52]

British policymakers also questioned whether the war in Southeast Asia would in any way support Soviet objectives. On the one hand, London failed to see the Kremlin's hand at work, viewing the Franco-Vietminh War as a colonial conflict and not a Cold War struggle. At the same time, however, and in the context of the Malayan and Burmese situations, it recognized the danger that expansionist communism posed for the region. Malcolm Macdonald was far from the only British official who expressed such reservations; several members of the Foreign Office engaged in Southeast Asian affairs, stationed both in London and in the field, were similarly alarmed. Whereas opinion had earlier regarded Ho Chi Minh primarily as a nationalist, rising tensions in Asia as well as in Europe, from 1947 onward, had led the FO to focus more readily on Ho's communism and its attendant threat to regional stability. These concerns would also play a larger role in conversations with U.S. officials as Britain played the ideological card in an effort to encourage greater American activity in Southeast Asia.[53] It was a position both sincerely held and tactically useful as part of Britain's strategic posture.

That similarity between British and American opinion on Asia also came to mark their interpretations of Eastern Europe. Although the State Department was initially more enthusiastic than the Foreign Office about opportunities to exploit the Tito rift behind the Iron Curtain, by the end of 1948, members of both communities believed that, over time, Titoism could replicate itself throughout the Communist orbit.[54] Bevin expressed his thoughts on the subject to Secretary of State Marshall in a New Year's message that December. Yugoslavia, he noted, had been home to the first break in the Communist front; it had already "eased the situation in Trieste, embarrassed the Communists all over the world and caused the Soviet Government to initiate in many satellite countries purges and repressive measures which may later recoil upon their heads." But it was in Britain's and America's joint interest, Bevin observed, to see that Yugoslavia remained a Communist state. "As long as the split exists," he argued, "it is bound to hamper and embarrass the Kremlin's policy in the other satellite countries and beyond."[55] Even with all of its ambiguity, the Tito affair offered some measure of hope as the two nations considered their prospects for 1949.

But precisely how much? The paradox of the Tito schism was that the rift simultaneously stripped international communism of its *Soviet* character while confirming, in the minds of many, the movement's *monolithic* nature. Clearly, it revealed tensions within the Communist world and illustrated how animosities, jealousies, ideological differences, and nationalist priorities could split the bloc apart. But it also suggested that further defections, however desirable they might be to Western officials, were unlikely to occur. And if they did occur, they would do so later, rather than sooner, and possibly for reasons other than those at work in the Tito affair. In the end, the rift was no more than an isolated incident, a "surprising freak," as John Paton Davies would call it years later. Those two strains of thought—the notion that the split could replicate itself and the belief that it would do nothing of the sort—were present within government circles from the very moment the break occurred and generated an ambiguity that officials were never able to resolve.[56]

Indeed, the most striking aspect of the whole affair might not have been its ambiguity but its irony. When the *Louisville Courier-Journal* declared the split to be "the first deep crack . . . in the monolithic program of Russo-European communism," it expressed the sentiments of many who regarded the Communist monolith as a thing of the past.[57] The Kentucky paper was not the first to use such terminology, but having done so, it added its voice to others printing similar statements. Thus began a curious trend in which journalists and government officials seized upon the image of the "monolith" at a time when its applicability was becoming increasingly shrouded in doubt. Even more curious was that as the popularity of the term grew—again, ostensibly to denigrate the very concept it embodied—so, too, did the possibility that communism *really was monolithic.* As Stalin replaced so-called nationalist Communists with internationalists more committed to the Kremlin line, and as Mao continued to ape Soviet statements on the impossibility of compromise with capitalist nations, international communism took on the look of a movement very much controlled from a single source. Instead of chipping away at the image of the monolith, then, the Tito affair was having the perverse effect of solidifying its very foundation.

As a result, the episode provided statesmen and journalists with little cause for elation. Most observers did take comfort in the vague notion, made somewhat less fuzzy by Tito's purported validation of containment theory, that the Soviet empire would crumble *over time;* it was the rare individual who believed that Titoism would quickly undermine Soviet authority. To be sure, policymakers continued to cite various disturbances within the bloc—the purge of Polish Communist Władysław Gomułka, tensions with Czech party officials, the scolding of Bulgarian Communist Georgi Dimitrov—as evidence that Tito's heresy was spreading throughout the congregation.[58] Yet each of these developments came with certain caveats: no Communist in Europe had Tito's appeal, none had a comparable degree of control over his nation's military and security forces, and all of them, with the exception of Communists in Germany and Albania, headed states contiguous to Russia. In retrospect, Titoism—the name given to a loosely constructed set of postulates—was no "ism" after all, for it had no universal validity. It referred to a particular set of circumstances that happened to exist in only one country—in Eastern Europe, that is.

Asia was another matter, for Communists in the Far East roamed free of Moscow's coercive reach. As a result, several of its regional parties mirrored the YCP not only in their autonomy but also in aspects of their political programs. The largest of them, the Chinese Communist Party, revealed itself to be a prime candidate for heresy. Several officials in the State Department, including George F. Kennan and John Paton Davies, believed that China might well chart a course independent of Moscow. The CIA, too, reflecting on the impact of the Tito affair, questioned whether the CCP was "an absolutely reliable instrument of Soviet policy." It recognized that "the monolithic control that the USSR is demanding from the Communist parties of the West" had yet to encounter "the regionalism and social incoherence of modern China."[59]

While Kennan, Davies, and the CIA were suggesting that China might veer from Soviet policy, those in the field were moving toward the opposite conclusion. Ambassador John Leighton Stuart, "a perfect weather vane to the gusts of the Chinese revolution," according to one scholar of the era, thought the CCP was becoming increasingly Soviet in its orientation.[60] And as much as colleagues hoped that tensions between the Chinese and Soviet Communists would burst out into the open, they, too, recognized that Mao was uncompromisingly supportive of Soviet objectives. On the other hand, U.S. officials reasoned, perhaps Mao and the CCP would be too disorganized to administer a territory as vast as China, making it largely irrelevant to the projection of Soviet power; maybe the Chinese Communists would have no interest in furthering Soviet aims, or at least in being pawns of the U.S.S.R., and thereby limit Moscow's imperial reach. But each of those hypotheses—the optimistic as well as the pessimistic—seemed to hold grains of truth, for not even the China specialists were convinced that Mao would ultimately take an independent line. With so much uncertainty, with Western statesmen reading the actions and rhetoric of Communist officials as one might read the textures of tea leaves, each new development took on added importance as a clue to the ultimate orientation of Chinese communism.

These developments also prompted government officials and their critics in the press to rethink their approaches to communism in general. If the Tito affair demonstrated that Soviet rule was anathema to both the captive peoples *and* Communist leaders of Eastern Europe, and that Communist leaders (and peoples) might want to remain Communist but independent of the Kremlin, then conceivably those breakaway Communist states might find that they had a friend in the White House. This argument—that communism was a threat only if it became the handmaiden of Soviet foreign policy—was central to the emerging consensus within the State Department. Clearly, it predated the Tito split. George Kennan had repeatedly tried to divorce anticommunism from anti-Sovietism, as had fellow Russian expert Charles Bohlen.[61] Similarly, Walter Bedell Smith had sought to qualify America's hostility to communism, arguing that the United States opposed it not on ideological terms but solely because "we had seen repeated instances of Communist minorities coming into power by illegal means and against the will of the majority of the population in the countries referred to." Kennan had said much the same in PPS/35, the government's initial response to the Tito affair, and Marshall made that position a central tenet of American policy toward Tito, including it in the circular tele-gram he posted in the schism's immediate aftermath.[62]

The same held true for America's Asia hands. Ambassador Stuart, for example, encouraged his colleagues to rid themselves of the "prejudices and fears" that clustered around the word "communism" so that they could fashion a more "constructive and positive approach" to the prob-lems of Asia. John Moors Cabot, the U.S. consul general in Shanghai, repeated Stuart's argument in late December. He recommended that ad-ministration officials inform the CCP that the United States had "nothing against the adoption of Communism as an economic doctrine by the Chinese people if they so choose." However, not one bit of U.S. aid would be forthcoming as long as a "Moscow stooge" was in a posi-tion of authority. Ideology, therefore, was not the main impediment to constructive relations. What U.S. officials really objected to, as Stuart argued, was communism's intolerance, brutality, and treachery, "plus [the] fact that policy is directed from Moscow." Statements such as these reveal the alleged willingness of government officials to work with all regimes, even Communist ones, as long as they were not promoting Soviet policies.[63]

What is intriguing about this debate is the virtual absence of any effort to take it public. Officials frequently commented on the need to educate the American people to the realities of foreign policy and the importance of doing so in a cool, dispassionate manner. Given the tenor of the time, it is hard to imagine a public discussion more in need of cool dispassion than one that sought to defend a policy of supporting certain Communist states while simultaneously vilifying others. Such detachment, however, was in short supply. As John Cabot pointed out in late 1948, his own suggestions on the matter "may be—in fact probably are in certain respects—poison ivy from the domestic political viewpoint."[64]

One episode from early July testified to the dangers of Cabot's posi-tion. Within a week of the Tito split, Stewart and Joseph Alsop, syndi-cated columnists with the *New York Herald Tribune,* floated the idea that America should distinguish between different kinds of Commu-nists. They noted that the Yugoslav crisis would probably lead U.S. of-ficials to adopt the "sensible if somewhat cynical principle . . . that the internal affairs of other nations, however unpleasing to us, are after all their own business." What mattered most, they argued, was a country's external relations—whether it was "with us or against us." Almost im-mediately, however, authoritative voices rejected the idea that America should pursue its interests according to the precepts of *realpolitik.* Both

Harold Stassen, the Republican Pennsylvania senator and aspiring 1948 presidential candidate, and Constantin Fotitch, the former Yugoslav ambassador to the United States, criticized the reflex to support Tito simply because he was opposed to Moscow.[65] Only by embracing democratic ideals and implementing liberal reforms, they argued, could Yugoslavia, or any other dictatorial state, hope to win American friendship and aid.

That domestic context, together with the need to build support for U.S. foreign and military policies, would lead government officials to lump all Communists together, propping up the image of the monolith at a time when several were questioning its very relevance.[66] The demands of American politics, especially in a presidential election season, contributed mightily to this development, narrowing the range of policy options open to administration officials. In such an environment, efforts to inject subtlety and nuance into discussions of complex and emotional matters were unlikely to bear fruit. Policymakers had earlier succumbed to this dynamic in the context of securing ERP funds in the spring of 1948. Recognizing the need to placate fiscal conservatives and the Chinese Nationalists' largely Republican friends in Congress, the Truman administration offered assistance to Chiang Kai-shek, thereby paving the way for far larger sums to be granted to Western Europe.[67] Given the constraints at work in this kind of political culture, initiatives that sought to distinguish between acceptable and unacceptable Communists, or at least between those who were worthy of American support and those who were not, stood little chance of a fair hearing.

In fact, statements from U.S. officials indicate that the administration was anything *but* interested in portraying communism as a heterogeneous movement. Delivering a speech to State Department information officers—the very people charged with explaining the main lines of U.S. foreign policy—the East European Division's Robert Hooker invoked all the key assumptions of the monolithic framework. Before communism had found a "Fatherland," Hooker said, it was both "organized and conspiratorial," two qualities the movement had never relinquished. Commenting upon "the thin veil of fiction that separates the Soviet Government from the Communist Parties," he portrayed the international movement as "wholly dominated by the Soviet Union"; there could be "no question of Soviet control" over its machinery. The Tito split had only pointed out "the grim realities of the Soviet system as nothing else has ever done before," realities that were leading Moscow to pursue "ever more total measures of control." Sprinkling his remarks liberally with references to Nazism, fascism, and their similarities to communism, Hooker likened the Soviet movement to its Germanic forerunner, providing his audience of publicity specialists with further examples of totalitarian and monolithic rhetoric.[68]

American statesmen were no more eager to discuss antimonolithic behavior in public. As PPS member Robert Joyce argued in mid-November 1948, the United States "should assume a wait-and-see attitude" toward the Tito affair. It was true, he noted, that "the block of the Soviet satellite states which had been hitherto considered as a monolith is showing a deep rift." But a policy of general indifference seemed the best way to handle such a development; the less attention the government and the press paid to Yugoslavia, the better. "Everything that could give the impression that the conflict between Moscow and Belgrade is welcome to the USA," and that the United States was trying "to stir the conflict," Joyce wrote, "must be avoided." It was precisely the policy the NSC had established for the government as a whole.[69]

Such a prescription made some sense with respect to the practice of foreign policy, but it might also have stifled a valuable conversation at home about the nature and prospects of international communism. For the United States had not yet "lost" China, the Soviets did not yet have the bomb, and the North Koreans had not yet broached the 38th parallel. Tito was holding on, native Communists were seeking greater autonomy, and even the Berlin situation—so precarious in the weeks following the June blockade—was stabilizing. And through it all, several officials were imploring senior personnel to strike *now*, to engage the public in a discussion of the differences between international communism and Soviet imperialism, while the time was ripe. Recognizing that their window of opportunity was closing, they would soon expand their efforts in ways that highlighted the prospects, pitfalls, and ironies of the Tito split and the forces it unleashed.

CHAPTER SIX

The Wedge Strategy

While the Tito affair sparked considerable debate over its impact on international communism, it provoked an equally vigorous discussion over the propriety of the Western response. Policymakers in Britain and the United States immediately recognized the virtues of exploiting the rift; some of these officials called for utilizing its propaganda value as a way to emphasize the Kremlin's imperialistic rule. Others, however, cautioned against its hasty use as an object lesson, either out of distaste for Tito or fear that his rapid embrace might backfire on the West. Virtually all of them sought to encourage the growth of Titoism itself, what numerous statesmen saw as a ray of light in an otherwise darkening international environment. In an effort to foster and accelerate divisions within the Communist world, they pursued an approach that was every bit as amorphous as the force they were trying to promote: the wedge strategy.

Although policymakers and members of the media regarded it as a reasonable response to the break in Communist ranks, the wedge strategy actually preceded the Tito split. In its earliest formulation, however, it was barely a strategy at all, confined primarily to rhetorical flourishes aimed at labeling the Soviet Union a colonial power. As articulated by British and American officials during the early postwar years, the wedge strategy sought to encourage those nations under the sway of Soviet power to buck their imperial overlords and establish independent foreign policies. Summing up the emerging propaganda line in the spring of 1946, J. S. Steele, Britain's commander-in-chief in Austria, argued that U.K. publicity should demonstrate "that Communist policy everywhere is directed from Moscow in its own interest and bears no relation to the particular interests of the countries concerned." Such publicity, which tried to promote a "more emphatic identification of Communism" with the Kremlin, quite consciously sought to identify all Communists as Soviet lackeys. In so doing, it presaged tactics America would adopt later in the decade. By defining all Communists as satellites of Moscow—that is, by *propping up* the image of a monolithic movement—it hoped to unleash those forces that eventually might tear it down.[1]

The success of that policy was predicated on the notion that communism was not so monolithic as to be immune to Western pressure. Officials on both sides of the Atlantic believed it possible to influence relations within and among Communist states, especially via the lure of Western economic aid. The examples of Poland and Czechoslovakia testified to its potential power. Both nations had shown great interest in securing material assistance and had foresworn participation in the European Recovery Program only after extensive pressure from the Kremlin. In spite of Moscow's position—and perhaps even because of it—British officials thought the "economic weapon" might have a salutary influence on developments within the Soviet camp.[2] So, too, did American representatives, who remained intrigued by the prospect of using economic aid to drive a wedge between Moscow and its satellites. At the very least, they argued, such assistance might nudge individual Communists or even whole parties closer toward the West. Armed with a belief in their capacity to split apart a rapidly hardening Eastern bloc, a substantial number of policymakers in both London and Washington viewed communism as a movement rife with incipient fissures.

And yet even those officials who recognized tensions within the Communist world showed signs of operating from within a monolithic framework. Their visions of a wedge strategy were based on the assumption that the West needed to wean all Communists, including those not under the watchful eyes of the Red Army, away from Moscow. In other words, U.S. and British statesmen expected that Communists would at first drift naturally toward the Soviet Union. All such parties, they reasoned, whether operating in Europe or in Asia, were more or less destined to feel the Kremlin's gravitational pull. Western aid was therefore desirable precisely because it held open the possibility of interrupting, or even reversing, the Soviet magnetic field.

The pressures on Poland and Czechoslovakia, however, at least in Europe, seemed to cast those incipient rifts as virtually irrelevant.[3] Thereafter, throughout the summer of 1947, the Kremlin urged Communist parties to practice greater discipline by jettisoning or silencing dissident comrades, making those parties more effective tools of Soviet diplomacy. British policymakers recognized the implications of this directive and so once again tried to gauge the prospects for exploiting divergences between the national and international factions of native CPs.[4] They concluded that such distinctions (and therefore the possibility of exploiting them) were illusory, at least behind the Iron Curtain.[5] The Prague Coup of February 1948 closed the sole potential breach in the wall of satellite states that Moscow had constructed in Eastern Europe. From then on, as Western observers realized, the Iron Curtain was to be clamped down tight.

Exploiting the Rift

Americans also had that apparent solidity in mind when evaluating the Tito-Cominform split of June 1948.[6] Buoyed by the largely unexpected good news of the Tito affair, Americans both in and out of government sought to speed up a schismatic process they believed already under way. Several media sources, including Joseph and Stewart Alsop, Anne O'Hare McCormick, the *Detroit News,* and *U.S. News & World Report,* called on the United States to widen the rift, recommending "direct action in Yugoslavia."[7] So, too, did several officials in the Truman administration. On the day following the Cominform announcement, U.S. representatives in Belgrade and Washington urged the government to pursue the "boldest possible exploitation of this defection in the keystone of [the] Soviet satellite structure," a recommendation they would repeat throughout the summer.[8] Yet senior personnel thought it wrong to approach the Yugoslav leader at a time when Tito and his associates were still mouthing the precepts of Communist unity and capitalist imperialism. Believing the situation "too fluid" for any overtures toward Tito, Secretary of State George C. Marshall rejected calls for early aid.[9]

Limited support to Yugoslavia did flow, however. Building on discussions dating back to mid-1947, the Truman administration, in July 1948, released Yugoslavia's stockpile of gold that had been frozen during World War II and resolved additional claims between the two governments.[10] The potential to capitalize on these and related measures was not lost on George Kennan. By mid-August, the Policy Planning

Staff director was arguing that policies associated with the Marshall Plan were contributing to the schismatic tendencies inherent in the Communist bloc, opening up greater possibilities for U.S. action. He therefore urged his government to increase the "stresses" in Soviet-satellite relations, allowing for East European governments "gradually to extricate themselves from Russian control" and to work out some form of "collaboration" with the West.[11] It was a strategy that had great appeal to the National Security Council, which embraced it initially in late August 1948 and then more formally that December. From then on, U.S. policymakers would seek to capitalize on the Tito split and encourage schisms within the Communist bloc.[12]

British officials were also interested in shaking loose Communist apples from the Soviet tree. In the immediate aftermath of the Cominform split, they debated the merits of a more "offensive" policy to accelerate any such harvest. Their publicity strategy, as Belgrade chargé Cecil King put it, would highlight the "contradictions of Russian imperialism and international Communism."[13] The nation most susceptible to their ministrations, according to the Russia Committee, was Albania, for the Tito affair had essentially cut its access to the rest of the bloc. In late November 1948, committee members considered the feasibility of detaching the Balkan state from the Soviet sphere by starting a civil war between nationalist Albanians and their Moscow-oriented brethren. Enthusiasm for such an initiative was limited, however. As Frank Roberts pointed out, the assumptions underlying that project—the belief that Titoism was endemic to Eastern Europe—emerged out of very specific, local conditions. If Britain "went for too much" and attempted to force the pace of events, "it would only have the effect of consolidating the orbit." The committee thus shelved the Albanian proposal, suggesting that a subcommittee consider its implications in greater detail.[14]

With Albania out of reach, the Foreign Office recognized that the wedge strategy could only function as a long-term approach to Eastern Europe. Indeed, reports from countries under Communist regimes, which indicated that the "loyalty to Moscow of trained Communists always prevailed," suggested that any effort to siphon off Western-leaning Communists from their East-leaning brethren might yield no returns whatsoever.[15] Still, the Russia Committee thought it worthwhile to sow discord throughout the Communist bloc so that the countries of Eastern Europe would "be a source not of strength but of weakness to Russia and a drain on her resources of manpower and trained personnel."[16] It was a policy that had much in common with the U.S. approach.

Against the backdrop of those events, the West took its first significant steps to wean Yugoslavia away from the Soviet Union. In early December 1948, the State Department instructed U.S. officials "to consider carefully" Yugoslav aid proposals that, as the *New York Times* put it, might help Tito withstand pressure from the Cominform nations.[17] By February 1949, the United States was permitting shipments to Belgrade of aviation gasoline and oil drilling rigs.[18] London had also taken action to preserve Yugoslavia's viability outside the Soviet sphere. Alongside the United States, it had sold crude oil to Yugoslavia in June 1948 and had gone so far as to ink a series of economic agreements with Belgrade in December. Britain would also look to comply with Yugoslav requests for aid, preferably by waiting for such approaches and not seeking them out; as several officials argued, Yugoslavia was no less Communist and therefore no less objectionable to Western observers than prior to the split. British policy therefore remained one of "masterly inactivity," of doing just enough to "keep Tito afloat."[19] And since it hoped to widen the breach in the Communist world through the force of Tito's example, Britain opted for a life vest rather than a complete rescue at sea. It would seek to preserve Tito's viability *as a Communist* in order to boost his standing among wavering comrades throughout Europe.

Yet it was far from clear whether Titoism had any relevance beyond the Yugoslav border. The further Stalinization of Eastern Europe, combined with the increasing belligerence of Mao Zedong, indicated that the Kremlin was imposing greater order on the Communist world. Moscow's decision in January 1949 to form the Council for Mutual Economic Assistance (Comecon), an organization of East European states that functioned as the Soviet equivalent of the Organization for European Economic Cooperation—the body created to help distribute Marshall Plan aid—only deepened that belief. For many Westerners, such overt displays of power merely hinted at the more covert means Moscow was using to bring its domains to heel. Communists in Hungary, for instance, ostensibly carrying out Moscow's desire to eliminate all sources of internal opposition, sentenced Jóseph Cardinal Mindszenty to life imprisonment in February 1949. Outside the Eastern bloc, the Kremlin seemed to be relying on the fealty of key proxies, such as the French and Chinese CPs, to do its bidding in Western Europe and Southeast Asia, respectively.[20]

The apparent bolshevization of world communism, however, offered Western officials a glimmer of hope. To many on the Russia Committee, the purges then under way against Communists in Poland and Bulgaria seemed to indicate that the Kremlin's grip on Eastern Europe "may be less sure than the progress of consolidation would lead the onlooker to conclude." Yet Soviet knowledge of that very fact would probably lead Moscow to crack down even harder on those who might have sympathized with Tito or harbored nationalist goals, thus binding its remaining satellites more firmly to the Soviet Union. Ironically, the very existence of Titoism seemed to be hastening its own destruction.[21]

Asian Titoism

The most intriguing targets for such a bloc-busting strategy, therefore, lay outside of Europe. Chinese Communists, who had long suffered from Stalin's indifference and pessimism, seemed both the most likely and the most valuable of marks. American officials stationed in China agreed. The Cominform denunciation, they argued, might generate rifts within the CCP that the United States should exploit; economic and technical aid could then be offered as inducements not only to widen fissures within the CCP but to "wean a Chinese coalition government away from the Soviets." As Kennan pointed out, Chinese nationalism would inevitably surface and drive a wedge between the two nations, a development the United States should be only too happy to promote. Throughout the remainder of 1948 and into 1949, U.S. policymakers expressed great interest in furthering those trends to heighten tensions between Soviet and Chinese Communists.[22]

So, too did their counterparts in Great Britain, who also believed that Titoism's greatest impact was likely to be felt outside the European theater. As Deputy Undersecretary of State Roger Makins put it, Britain should shift the focus of its wedge strategy to "places the battle was actually joined," such as China and Southeast Asia. The cabinet saw great wisdom in this approach; while the Chinese Communists certainly sounded like Communists, it was impossible to draw any firm conclusions as to "the ultimate nature of Chinese Communism or of the relationship between the Chinese Communist Government and the Soviet Union." Reiterating Bevin's 1946 characterization of Chinese communism as an "agrarian movement," the cabinet concluded that Britain would be "unwise" to adopt policies which might drive such a government into the waiting arms of Moscow.[23]

Indeed, since Titoism appeared to be most contagious when a Communist Party's strength was on the rise, 1949 looked like a propitious moment for the onset of a Chinese variant. By the third week of January, Mao's forces had taken Beijing, leaving the Communists in full control of northern China and poised to capture further regions of the country. But Bevin now painted a darker picture of Chinese communism, declaring it to be "just as orthodox in its ideology and just as highly organised as any of its European counterparts." Siding with his Asian specialists in the Foreign Office, he rejected the notion that communism in China had been modified by "any special 'Chinese' factors," finding it to be "strictly orthodox, confident, mature, and at the highest level very well organized," with "no trace of Titoism." There was simply no indication that they "would pursue policies different from those followed by Communists elsewhere."[24] American policy was similarly pessimistic about the future alignment of Mao and his comrades. As the NSC observed, the United States might have to wait as many as twenty-five years before a Chinese Communist government could establish a policy independent of the Kremlin.[25]

The Adams-Davies Working Paper

These concerns contributed to a broader attempt by policymakers on both sides of the Atlantic to refine their efforts at containing and ultimately cracking the Communist monolith. Their new approach would drop the use of economic leverage, which had apparently worked so well in Western Europe, in favor of a rhetorical strategy geared toward the realities of Eastern Europe and beyond. Part of that strategy would seek to differentiate Communist policies from Soviet imperialism, a practice designed to soft-pedal U.S. antipathy toward theoretical Marxism. By downplaying its hostility to Communist ideology, America could present itself as an enemy of Soviet-directed world communism rather than an obstacle to national Communist domestic reform. Testifying to the high-level interest in this approach, Ambassador to the Soviet Union Walter Bedell Smith—one of a number of officials who had already endorsed that line both publicly and privately—reiterated his claim that the United States "does not fear communism if it is not controlled by Moscow and not committed to aggression." As long as Communists refrained from building a monolithic movement, he intimated, the United States would leave them alone.[26]

Nevertheless, such a message was not the one that had been going out to Communists themselves, at least not on a consistent basis. Nor had it been a theme that policymakers were stressing regularly in their statements to the American people. The public portrayal of communism, even in the wake of the Tito rift, remained that of a unified, conspiratorial movement. As a result, officials who were leery of that image began to question the wisdom of its continued projection. One of their number, Policy Planning Staff member John Paton Davies, had frequently disparaged the notion that the CCP was a mere appendage of Moscow. As recently as January 1949, Davies had smelled "a strong odor of bad fish . . . emanating from Sino-Soviet relations," suggesting that Moscow was less than thrilled at the prospect of a quick victory for the Chinese Communists. Tensions between the two, he argued, were likely to increase. A Communist China might even become the dominant power in Southeast Asia, displacing whatever revolutionary leadership Moscow could offer the region. In fact, if two comparable and even competing power centers were to emerge in the Communist world, U.S. leaders might find themselves in a quandary, for it was far from clear whether American foreign policy was prepared to deal with such a novel situation. Had the administration, Davies wondered, educated the American public sufficiently to grasp the significance of Sino-Soviet tensions?[27]

The answer, it seemed, was "no." The image of a monolithic Communist bloc exerted a powerful hold on the popular imagination—so much so, Davies worried, that it might even be contributing to Soviet success. He therefore co-authored a working paper with Policy Planning Staff member Ware Adams that sought to steer U.S. propaganda in a completely new direction. Forwarding a copy of the memo to PPS director Kennan in March 1949, Adams noted that "certain new refinements on our treatment of 'Communism' . . . might provide an opportunity to 'go to town' on the satellite and other communist areas outside Russia." What Adams and Davies were proposing was nothing less than a fundamental review of U.S. policy toward the Communist challenge, perhaps the most far-reaching reevaluation since the onset of the Cold War.[28]

The Adams-Davies study began by noting that U.S. officials tended to treat communism as "a single, coherent, unitary, self-consistent doctrine or political force aimed at domination of the entire world by the Kremlin, and hence by the Soviet Government at Moscow."[29] The popularity of that image, shared equally by government representatives and media outlets, came from the emphasis that both groups placed on Soviet ideology. Most observers based their analyses of international communism on the movement's sacred texts; it was Communist theory, therefore, that informed "the popular concept of communism as a monolithic threat to our security." But quotations from Communist tracts were only partly representative of Communist behavior and Marxist philosophy. "In fact," the authors noted, "one could even cite selections from that same body of theory to disprove the 'monolith' as a theory." Americans therefore needed to realize that while the Kremlin sought to build such a monolith, the world's Communists did not actually comprise one. Repeated declarations of Communist aims by journalists and government officials, Adams and Davies argued, only obscured the reality of the situation.[30]

Such rhetoric, moreover, tended to play into Moscow's hands. The irony of portraying communism in monolithic terms was that it actually emboldened the Kremlin to construct such a movement. It also abandoned to Moscow those countries stuck behind the Iron Curtain. By directing anti-Communist rhetoric "just as much against the satellite states themselves as against the U.S.S.R.," America gave those nations little reason to throw off the Soviet yoke. Ideological adherents thus had little choice but "to become or remain a part of the monolith, since they would otherwise be helpless outlaws between the two all-inclusive camps of communists and anti-communists." True, Tito had rebelled, but he had done so *in spite of* such rhetoric; the Czechs also continued to resist Kremlin authority without any great shift in American propaganda. In failing to distinguish between Communist governments on the one hand and the Soviet world on the other, U.S. publicity had become "an increasingly great force in aid of the Kremlin's desire to increase and solidify its monolith."

The solution, the authors believed, lay in distinguishing communism from what they termed "Russian imperialism." This approach would "remove [a] major political force binding the satellites to the Soviet Union, and in addition remove from the communists in China and elsewhere throughout the world a strong force tending to compel them to collaborate with the Soviet Union." Such a plan would likely find favor with American representatives abroad. The U.S. embassy in Belgrade, wrote Adams and Davies, had "specifically recommended that we redefine our attitude towards Yugoslavia in terms of Russian imperialism rather than communism." Ambassador Smith had also been arguing that "communism detached from the power center of the Soviet Union" warranted little fear, for America's primary threat emanated from "the combination of that power center with a political monolith extending into other areas of the world." In addition, there was ample basis for popularizing the notion that "communism is not necessarily a part of the Kremlin's monolith." Adams and Davies held out the cases of several schismatic Communists, including Tito and Trotsky, as examples. "There would be many more," they maintained, "if we ourselves did not automatically place all communists in precisely the same category as the Soviet Union in our anti-communist policy and actions deriving from it."

Covering roughly five typewritten pages, the Adams-Davies working paper stood as a ringing indictment of U.S. policy. Almost nine months after the Cominform rift had opened the first crack in the Soviet monolith, the memo charged policymakers with virtually ignoring Tito's value as a propaganda tool. Each member of the Policy Planning Staff received a copy, though apparently that was the extent of its tour around the State Department.[31] Nevertheless, U.S. officials were generally in tune with the thrust of its recommendations. Diplomats stationed in Europe, as well as colleagues back in Washington, endorsed aspects of its argument at a PPS meeting in April 1949. U.S. minister to Romania Rudolf Schoenfeld, for instance, one of numerous American envoys in attendance, was similarly troubled by the ideological nature of the U.S. attack. If departmental propaganda was going to target communism, he argued, it should do so—at least in the orbit countries—by treating it as an alien despotism. Most of those at the meeting also saw the Kremlin–satellite relationship as the logical point of attack; officials would therefore encourage the East Europeans, as well as their political leaders, to resist the "iron control" of the Kremlin. While these arguments largely piggybacked on earlier government statements, including the one Kennan had built into NSC 18, they still fell short of the recommendations Adams and Davies made in their March 8 working paper. The mere mention of a "Kremlin monolith" or "iron control," according to its authors, continued to serve Soviet and not American interests.[32]

The Dilemmas of Rhetoric

At virtually the same time that U.S. officials were considering a shift in American publicity policy, British statesmen were engaged in a similar venture. This was not exactly a novel development, since the Foreign Office had earlier explored the matter of which words and phrases to use in its propaganda abroad. By January 1949, it had generally agreed that Britain should cite "Soviet imperialism" rather than the spread of communism as the more serious problem facing the West.[33]

But the Russia Committee once again took up the question that spring. This time, its ruminations would become the basis of governmental policy, for the document that emerged from those talks went out to virtually all British posts abroad. Its aim, according to Prime Minister Clement Attlee, was "to concentrate and sharpen our publicity by the reiteration of a number of carefully selected graphic words to describe Communism" and the entire Soviet project. These words were to be used "where necessary at home in Ministerial speeches, and in official and semi-official public statements," as well as abroad in "information bulletins, semi-official statements, conversation, &c." Among the favored terms were "Kremlin Imperialism," "Iron Curtain," and "puppets." "Satellite States" also made the cut, since the Foreign Office deemed it to be the most effective label for the "states of Eastern Europe and the Far East under Kremlin control." Terms to be avoided included "Communist," since it held a "vague attraction for many waverers," and "Stalin," since Moscow had built up the Soviet leader as a figure of great benevolence.[34]

Curiously, the memo instructed British officials to avoid drawing parallels between Stalin and Hitler, at least when referring to Soviet internal practices. This rejection of the Hitler-Stalin comparison is intriguing since the Foreign Office still thought it could make use of the Nazi-Soviet analogy. IRD head Ralph Murray thought such comparisons "could be very educative of public opinion" and urged that they be invoked on a wider scale. Murray's term of choice was "Communo-Fascism," a label that conveyed "the fundamental characteristics of a Communist regime more vividly than volumes of argument and analysis." Russia Committee official Christopher Warner thought the image similarly potent, but he favored the more felicitous "Red Fascism" instead. Along with the cabinet's qualified endorsement of Red Fascist terminology, Warner and Murray's more full-bodied embrace of it served to weave such imagery even more tightly into the fabric of Britain's anti-Soviet publicity.[35]

British officials showed little interest, however, in adopting terms that signified the new, schismatic element in world communism. Neither "Titoism" nor "national communism" made the list of recommended labels sent out to British posts abroad. This was perhaps an unsurprising development, given the realization that Titoism itself might be an increasingly failing force. The recent purge of Bulgarian Communist Dimitri Kostov seemed to reveal the limits of Titoism; only in Yugoslavia, where Tito maintained control of the secret police, was such a breakaway movement possible. Foreign Secretary Bevin, who had finally accepted the veracity of the Cominform rift, continued therefore to downplay its overall significance. He was well aware that British officials, in addition to members of the press, often touted its strategic value; observers had suggested repeatedly that Tito's apostasy was creating troubles within the orbit, particularly in Bulgaria and Czechoslovakia, and that the economy of the region was experiencing great difficulties. However, "none of these considerations," Bevin argued, "seems to have any real validity." Moreover, he found "no evidence of any deterioration in conditions" in either Russia or Eastern Europe that the Soviet government could not manage. Asia presented a different set of circumstances, for it was still conceivable that Chinese Communists might chart a course independent of the Kremlin.[36]

But did it make sense to promote Titoism, even in Asia, if in doing so Britain actually *swelled* the ranks of Communist regimes? Officials on the Russia Committee had no good answers to this question. Several members thought it a mistake to support CPs that were independent of Moscow. Not only would Titoist solutions strengthen the appeal of communism to "waverers" on the Left, they argued, but encouraging the growth of such movements would contradict a central tenet of British propaganda: that national Communist parties were inevitably subservient to the Kremlin. A consensus thus formed around the paradoxical effort to "publicise the existence of nationalist splinter parties generally" while condemning all Communists "as in fact tools of Moscow." Clearly, the wedge strategy, at least from a rhetorical perspective, posed very real problems for British policymakers. With the government's chief diplomat holding such a jaded view of the Cominform rift and its lead propagandist touting the necessity of the monolithic line, it is small wonder that Britain's overseas missions received patchy guidance on how best to exploit the Tito affair.[37]

Pursuing Traitors, Promoting Loyalty

Perhaps such direction was not immediately necessary, for Great Britain and the United States were concerned primarily with consolidating their own forces within the Western Hemisphere. By the spring of 1949, the process that had begun one year earlier with the signing of the Brussels Pact, an alliance for the defense of Western Europe, was nearing completion. The United States would now join Britain, France, the Benelux countries, and six other nations in the North Atlantic

Treaty Organization (NATO), a politico-military structure that came into being in April 1949. NATO would offer Western Europe more than physical security; Washington's commitment to Europe also provided a measure of psychological assurance that helped the West withstand continued Communist pressure. Further developments would heighten that sense of well-being. On May 12, Moscow lifted the Berlin Blockade, ending an eleven-month quarantine of the city's western zones. Less than two weeks later, the founding of the Federal Republic of Germany granted the West an added bulwark against Soviet encroachment.[38]

Nevertheless, events within the United States were proving damaging to the administration's stand against the Communist menace. In March 1949, the FBI arrested Judith Coplon, an official in the Department of Justice, for passing government documents to a Soviet agent. Though damning in and of itself, Coplon's subterfuge cast new light on the administration's handling of suspected Communists, particularly its alleged coddling of former State Department employee Alger Hiss. The controversy involving Hiss and Whittaker Chambers, which had burst onto the national scene in August 1948, continued to boil, capturing headlines across the nation. In fact, the press seemed to be filled with stories of Communist treachery during the spring of 1949. That April, the House Committee on un-American Activities pushed ahead with its search for Communist infiltrators; one month later, the government began its prosecution of Harry Bridges, the San Francisco dock organizer, for lying about his Communist ties during an earlier court appearance; and in June, the FBI disclosed that Communist espionage, conducted in 1947, had procured atomic research devices for Moscow. All the while, the trial of leading American Communists under indictment for violating the Smith Act—a 1940 piece of legislation proscribing anyone from advocating the overthrow of the United States government—continued to unfold at the courthouse in New York's Foley Square.[39]

The subtext in each of these cases was the traitorous allegiance that all Communists held toward Moscow. Public concern over such ties would flourish on many levels throughout the year. City and state governments built loyalty oaths into employment contracts and other forms of compensation; the Congress of Industrial Organizations purged itself of Communist-led unions; the nation's leading teachers' organizations deemed Communists unfit to educate America's children; university employees faced loyalty oaths and outright dismissal; and actual hostility broke out in various locales, most notably at a Paul

Robeson concert in Peekskill, New York. In all, individuals suspected of being or sympathizing with Communists were urged to "go back to Moscow."[40]

While those spasms of anticommunism marked key moments in the American national consciousness, equally telling demonstrations were shaping the tenor of everyday life. February 1 became "National Freedom Day"—so proclaimed by President Harry S. Truman—contributing to the rising tide of "Americanism" sweeping the country. That upsurge of patriotic feeling continued throughout the next several months, culminating in a "Loyalty Day" parade in New York City on May 1. Leading the throng of 117,000 down Fifth Avenue was Catholic prelate Francis Cardinal Spellman, a national figure with a long anti-Communist pedigree.[41]

Spellman's presence at the head of the march reflected a broader dynamic at work, for American Catholics, both liberal and conservative, assumed leading positions in the nation's anti-Communist campaign. Figures such as Bishop Fulton J. Sheen and Father Edmund A. Walsh, the founder of Georgetown University's School of Foreign Service, were as vocal as Spellman, preaching the dangers of communism and invoking Red Fascist terminology in the process. Truman recognized the value of their support and, at times, invoked the anti-Communist message specifically for their benefit. His willingness to do so was readily apparent during the 1948 general election. In strategizing for that year's campaign, presidential aide Clark Clifford saw this issue as key for wooing the group; Truman's initial denunciation of Progressive candidate Henry Wallace as a Communist tool came during a St. Patrick's Day address broadcast live to the nation. Although Catholic leaders differed on matters such as nuclear weapons and universal military training, their zeal in stressing the dangers of communism was virtually uniform.[42]

Religion would also animate anticommunism in Great Britain, where the Anglican Church played a central role in the nation's confrontation with the Kremlin. The Russia Committee, almost from its inception, had recognized the virtues of mobilizing religious leaders and institutions as part of its anti-Communist crusade. Since the time of Bevin's informational offensive of January 1948, when the foreign secretary affirmed the need to defend Western civilization, the Church had been integral to the policy of grounding that campaign in the spiritual values of Christendom and the Western experience. Bevin sought to enroll influential Anglicans in that offensive, and key figures voiced support for waging the ideological, dualistic struggle laid out by the Foreign Office. Language emanating from religious leaders aped that of the Foreign Office, invoking Red Fascist themes and dichotomous rhetoric. Some of it, to be sure, was directed across the Atlantic in an effort to ease American doubts about the reliability of a Left-leaning government in combating the Marxist challenge. But the capacity of this "divinely sanctioned" campaign to fire at multiple targets made it no less sincere for the Attlee government and no less resonant for the British public.[43]

Whether they came through religious or other channels, popular expressions of anticommunism continued to define significant aspects of postwar public culture. New York's commemorative celebration, for instance, was hardly an isolated incident as displays like the one in Manhattan took place in many other cities. And just as May Day underwent a transformation from an international socialist holiday to a national capitalist one, other dates on the American calendar became similarly sacralized. The nation renewed its tradition of "Flag Day" and instituted "I Am an American Day" to drive home the patriotic theme. Further appeals to the nation's historical consciousness came from Colonial Williamsburg, the living museum of America's revolutionary past, which called on high school students throughout the land to "Speak for Democracy." The interplay between those commemorations and the headlines of the day made for a heady mix—one that, with its constant focus on high-level espionage, did not please the Truman administration. In June, the president condemned the national "hysteria" over communism, hoping that cooler heads would prevail. It was an ironic development, since he and his administration had done so much to generate that groundswell in the first place.[44]

Although emotions were running high over Communist influence in domestic life, the public seemed to be moving toward a more sober appraisal of its role in foreign affairs. Support for Tito, whose regime in Yugoslavia showed no signs of abandoning its Communist program, appeared to be on the rise. Less than 50 percent of the public actually knew about Tito and his troubles with the Kremlin, but those familiar with the Cominform split thought it wise to pursue trade relations with the Yugoslav leader. So did substantial segments of the national press. The *New York Times* contributed to this campaign by trumpeting the advent of "National Communism" as a new and welcome force on the world scene. The media was hardly unified on this score, but several outlets expressed an interest in cultivating closer ties with Yugoslavia in an effort to put greater distance between Belgrade and Moscow. That impulse left a large segment of the nation in general agreement with officials at the State Department who sought to finalize Tito's defection from the Soviet camp. By mid-1949, when the media entered into its qualified embrace of Yugoslavia, policymakers were describing Tito's defiance as a dagger that struck "at the heart of the Stalinist concept of Russian expansion through the instrumentality of complete Kremlin control of world communism."[45]

British media outlets were also live to the virtues of Tito's nationalist stance. Those on the Left recognized the challenge it posed to Moscow as well as to all socialists, including those who had previously sympathized with the Kremlin. As the centrist *Times* noted, nationalism within the Communist bloc was even more dangerous than the "bourgeois" nationalism found outside of it.[46] These arguments appeared at a time when British political culture was itself exhibiting a more anti-Communist reflex. In May, the Parliamentary Labour Party censored one of its own, Konni Zilliacus, and expelled him from its ranks. Zilliacus had been a longtime critic of Britain's anti-Soviet policy and was the most famous of three Labour MPs exiled that year. But Attlee's problems with potential fifth columns extended beyond the ranks of his own party. A London dockers' strike during the summer of 1949 led Whitehall to fear that that the work stoppage, which carried with it the possibility of serious economic disruptions, would likely benefit Britain's enemies. As the prime minister put it, those who sought to continue the strike were "instruments of an alien dictatorship."[47]

The emergence in Britain of a vigorous program of domestic anticommunism, mirroring a more vibrant strain of that impulse in the United States, highlighted a growing trend within British governing circles of siding more closely with America as partners in the Cold War. This development was particularly evident following the signing of the NATO pact in April 1949. Indeed, the notion that Britain could pursue its security as a "Third Force," independent of both the United States and the Soviet Union, was fading. Britain would now tie its fortunes more closely to those of its cultural kin across the Atlantic and focus its publicity on the defense and promotion of Western values.[48] Foreign Secretary Ernest Bevin said as much in addressing a Washington audience at the National Press Club just days before the NATO ceremonies. British historian E. L. Woodward gave further voice to this idea in both British and American publications when commenting that the fight against communism—a fight for liberty, which he termed the essence of the entire Western tradition—was one that had been fought many times be-fore.[49] Closer proximity to U.S. positions also emerged in Britain's over-seas propaganda, in which the previously celebrated virtues of British Social Democracy and West European civilization were now downplayed in favor of the broader, hemispheric virtues of liberty and democracy. By October 1949, that stance of pursuing "the closest association with the United States," a posture that Bevin regarded as a strategic necessity, be-came the official policy of His Majesty's Government.[50]

East and Southeast Asia

At times, London sought to achieve such coordination by pulling Wash-ington closer to its own position. That strategy was most apparent in Southeast Asia, where the French were engaged in a bitter war with the nationalist and Communist forces of the Vietminh for control of In-dochina. Since the early postwar period, Britain had tried to enlist American support for that project—largely unsuccessfully—in an effort to secure its own interests in the region. Now, with the Chinese Com-munists making a final push to defeat their Nationalist foes, the Foreign Office recognized the dire regional implications of a CCP victory and sought to increase the volume and tenor of its appeal. No longer was the Franco-Vietminh War to be understood as a colonial struggle; it was now a crucial battlefront in the Cold War against "Russian expan-sionism," a rhetorical line the French had also eagerly employed.[51] But it was not one delivered insincerely; British officials had repeatedly ex-pressed their misgivings to each other over increasing Communist ac-tivity in the region, noting that the foreign policy of the CCP and the other regional parties would likely serve the Communists' mutual inter-ests. Internal communications thus began to reflect the ascendance of the anti-Communist rather than anticolonialist reading of events, of-fering an early version of the "domino theory" as part of their analyses.[52]

American statesmen recognized the nature of the publicity campaign London and Paris were waging, but they, too, and of their own accord, had come to see the Indochinese conflict through the lens of anticom-munism. The signing of the Elysée Accords in March, in which France brought former Vietnamese emperor Bao Dai back to rule a united Vietnam, did little to encourage further U.S. support. The State Depart-ment still thought the deal did not go far enough toward granting Viet-namese independence and satisfying the nationalist elements in

Vietnam; department officials warned that the "Bao Dai solution" would ultimately give more succor to the Vietminh.[53] Indeed, Secretary of State Dean Acheson and Ambassador to France Jefferson Caffery were particularly worried about the alignment of Vietminh leader Ho Chi Minh and his Democratic Republic of Vietnam (DRV), as were U.S. officials in Southeast Asia.[54] Their level of concern rose in April and May 1949, following a series of interviews Ho gave to U.S. publications in which he downplayed the depth of his Communist connections. Following the appearance of one such conversation, the editors of *Newsweek* went so far as to characterize Ho as "more of a Vietnamese nationalist right now than a Communist stooge." Acheson deemed Ho's professed nationalism irrelevant, especially given the failure of the Vietminh leader to repudiate his Kremlin connections and Moscow's praise of his movement. The possibility of a DRV developing along "Titoist" lines was remote, Acheson thought, and therefore not particularly worthy of American pursuit.[55]

Such was not the case with China, however, and American officials, like their counterparts in Britain, hoped that the CCP might follow in Yugoslavia's wake. U.S. policymakers thought that Mao himself could already have been "infected with the Tito virus." Public opinion in the United States was equally optimistic about the prospects for a Soviet-CCP rift. According to a February 1949 survey by the State Department, "a sizeable number of influential observers" believed that Mao might become another Tito. By May, several sources, including the *Baltimore Sun, Newsweek,* and the *Christian Science Monitor,* were calling on the United States to maintain relations with a future Communist China—the better to drive a "wedge" between Moscow and the CCP. Opinion polls also revealed that more than twice as many Americans favored a "hands-off" policy toward China rather than an interventionist, pro-Nationalist one. That sentiment carried over into June, as large segments of the media continued to point out that Mao might develop independently of the Kremlin.[56]

Nevertheless, a small but vocal group of Americans abhorred the very premises of the wedge strategy and spoke out against them with increasing savagery and regularity. The "China bloc" in Congress, as well as the "China Lobby" in the press, thought it madness to aid the Communist Chinese in any way. The *China Monthly,* for instance, a staunchly pro-Nationalist journal, repeatedly denigrated the notion that Mao might be an inchoate Titoist. To amplify its point, it cited a recent comment from Representative Donald Jackson (R-CA) that

"Marxists are as alike as peas in a pod." But the overall thrust of political commentary suggested that the wedge strategy had at least the beginnings of a consensus forming behind it.[57]

Successful pursuit of that policy seemed increasingly elusive, however, as hope for a Titoist China took a tumble that spring. The Chinese Communists entered Nanking and surrounded Shanghai in April 1949, with Mao subsequently calling on an army of "one million" to cross the Yangtze and free all of China. Recognizing the increasingly parlous nature of those developments, the Truman administration announced a withdrawal of all U.S. forces from the Chinese port of Tsingtao. Then, in late June, Mao voiced his intention to "lean" toward Moscow's side in its struggle with the West. That declaration made it more difficult to generate a broad consensus for the wedge strategy. As the *New York Times* reported, the Chinese leader had come out wholly in favor of Russia as "China's True Ally." Likewise, *Time* magazine thought that Mao had "settled the dust" swirling about Soviet-CCP relations, proving his deference to the U.S.S.R. beyond a shadow of a doubt.[58]

Mao's statement came at a particularly inopportune moment for wedge strategy enthusiasts. Congressional attacks on the administration's China policy had been mounting since the spring and were being leveled in the context of pending votes on key pieces of legislation, including the North Atlantic Treaty, military assistance funds, and an extension of Marshall Plan aid. Such anti-CCP pressure was not uniform, however, as publications such as the *Nation* and the *New Republic,* as well as the *Washington Post* and the *Minneapolis Star,* lobbied for policies grounded in wedge strategy assumptions. Nevertheless, response from the U.S. government was swift. The Truman administration abandoned its efforts to promote closer ties with the CCP, canceling a proposed meeting between Ambassador J. Leighton Stuart and representatives of the Communist hierarchy.[59]

At the same time, U.S. officials were no more interested in expanding or even continuing their support of the Nationalist government. On August 5, the administration halted all aid to the Chiang regime, explaining its policy shift in a State Department missive released the same day. The "China White Paper" became a *cause célèbre* and received generous media coverage in the weeks and months following its publication. Predictably, members of the congressional "China bloc," including Representative Walter Judd (R-MN), Senator Kenneth Wherry (R-NE), Senator William Knowland (R-CA), and Senator Styles Bridges (R-NH), lined up to denounce it as a long-winded whitewash; so, too, did their journalistic allies at the *China Monthly*. But even moderate administration critics, such as the GOP's John Foster Dulles and Senator Arthur H. Vandenberg (R-MI), found it lacking and unpersuasive.[60]

Such criticism stung the State Department and Secretary Acheson, especially since their indictment of the Chinese Communists, offered most forcefully in the White Paper's letter of transmittal, had seemingly catered to the administration's foes. To be sure, the study was highly critical of the KMT (which was the primary impression that China friends took away from it), but it also described the CCP leadership as little more than Kremlin toadies. The United States would therefore "encourage all developments in China" that would lead its people to "throw off the foreign yoke." While these remarks implied a wedge strategy in the making, they contained no hints of tension between the Chinese leadership and their Soviet comrades. Instead, they conveyed the distinct impression that the Chinese Communists were quite content with aiding "the interest of a foreign imperialism."[61]

With the administration's China policy so clearly in shambles, the State Department began casting about for a new approach and one that would be grounded explicitly in wedge strategy assumptions. Papers generated by the department's Charles C. Yost and former Rockefeller Foundation head Raymond Fosdick, written at Acheson's request, offered divergent means of effecting a Moscow-CCP split. Both agreed that China had fallen into the Soviet orbit, yet they differed on what to do about it. Yost, who took his cues from the Yugoslav experience, thought that isolation from the West, rather than interaction with it, was a primary factor in the Tito split; entreaties to Mao, therefore, would only delay the drifting-away process that was bound to occur. Accordingly, the adoption of an "activist" or "hard" policy toward the Communist Chinese, involving nonstop political and economic warfare, was likely to bind Mao more closely to the Soviet camp. This process would eventually lead the CCP, as it earlier had led the YCP, to regard Moscow as a poor and even malevolent ally, and thus to break away from the Kremlin.

By contrast, Fosdick argued for increasing rather than reducing the initial distance between Moscow and Beijing. The ingredients for greater enmity were already there, he argued; more dramatic portrayals of Russia as an imperialist power would help to widen that natural divide. Fosdick's approach, however, amounted to little more than a recapitulation of recent U.S. measures. In fact, his call for "watchful waiting" brought to mind Acheson's prior interest in waiting for the "dust to settle" in China before the United States took definitive action. Fosdick still hoped the Chinese would come to see Moscow as every bit the ogre Yost had portrayed—just that they would do so through the benign approach of persuasive words rather than through the more hostile use of punitive sanctions. Both policies, however, found favor with Truman administration officials, who would press their cases upon the State Department leadership well into the fall.[62]

Ironically, the "hard" approach was driving as many wedges between the United States and Great Britain as between the Soviets and Chinese. According to Foreign Secretary Bevin, the more hostile U.S. attitude was "diametrically opposite" to the British position. If London were not to throw a Communist China into the arms of Moscow, he argued, it had to maintain contact with Beijing. Doing so would present a real challenge, however, since the Chinese Communists, in their broadcasts and public pronouncements, had reiterated their ideological orthodoxy, their support for Moscow, and their opposition to British and American "imperialism." Nevertheless, Bevin was cognizant of an apparent split within the CCP between pro-Soviet Communists and those who desired a working relationship with the West. Widening the rift—an outcome that still seemed plausible—was therefore contingent on at least a modicum of contact between Whitehall and the Chinese Communists.[63]

Those pushing the wedge strategy in both Britain and the United States can hardly be faulted for thinking that events were moving in a positive direction. Tito's clashes with Soviet communism were becoming increasingly acerbic; his demands that Hungary and Romania halt their vilification of Yugoslavia, and similar calls for Bulgaria and Albania to join in resistance to the Cominform, also signaled a more belligerent and, perhaps, confident leader. Media sources such as the *Philadelphia Inquirer,* the *San Francisco Chronicle,* and CBS correspondent Richard Hottelet welcomed those pronouncements as clear indications of Tito's growing strength. Other outlets, including the *Baltimore Sun,* the *New York Herald Tribune,* and *U.S. News & World Report,* were equally hopeful that "a rebellious Communist-nationalism" might eventually alter "the Soviet monolith." Evidence seemed to suggest, then, not only that the disintegrative forces running through the Communist world were gaining strength, but that wider recognition of the development was in the offing.[64]

In light of this turn, Great Britain and the United States expressed a growing willingness to provide Tito with limited economic aid so that he might consolidate his hold on power. Both nations lifted restrictions on trade with Yugoslavia, with the United States allowing Tito to purchase a steel mill from an American manufacturer in August 1949. Tito, for his part, moved closer to the West, diverting resources away from the Soviet bloc and bombarding its member-states with increasingly hostile rhetoric. In an effort to finalize the split between Belgrade and Moscow, the United States, in early September 1949, agreed to loan Yugoslavia $20 million through the Export-Import Bank. In short order, Russia and the Cominform states abrogated their defensive alliance with Yugoslavia, casting the Balkan nation adrift in the widening gulf between East and West.[65]

Although the U.S. media had been pushing administration officials to provide Tito with economic assistance, the American public remained ambivalent about such an aid program. Of those who had heard about Tito and his troubles with the Kremlin—52 percent of the population, according to a Gallup survey—Americans were evenly divided on the virtues of helping Tito. Many observers, including former ambassador to Poland Arthur Bliss Lane, Senator Styles Bridges, commentators on ABC radio, various Catholic groups, and the Hearst press, railed against this policy, invoking the Munich analogy at will. Other sources, however, thought it might lead some remaining satellites to "deviate" as well. The State Department found that broadcast and print journalists were following the feud with "intense" interest. Most thought it "posed a serious threat to the whole Soviet satellite structure." Many of them interpreted the recent purge of Hungarian Communists as a sign that the Tito "heresy" was spreading.[66] The *Nation* regarded efforts to cement that heresy, through inducements such as the steel mill sale, as reflecting a more sophisticated brand of diplomacy. These policies indicated that America's quarrel was "not with communism as such but with the expansionist drive of the Soviet Union," the very stance senior officials had adopted over the course of the past year. Promotion of that attitude would likely aid Tito in his position atop the Yugoslav hierarchy. Should he fall from power, many believed, Belgrade was likely to drop back into the Soviet fold, a development neither the Foreign Office nor the State Department was eager to contemplate.[67]

Yet the potential for Yugoslavia's re-absorption into the Cominform bloc rested on ideological as well as monetary factors. As Britain's Russia Committee pointed out, communism was by definition a movement that possessed the earmarks of a colonial system; as the purveyors of such a system themselves—albeit a crumbling one—British officials were quick to enumerate the many ways in which Moscow had oriented its legions' economies to that of the mother country. But material interests alone would not fasten the satellites forever to the Soviet pole; according to the Russia Committee, quasi-spiritual pressures were equally compelling, for communism had all the attributes of a religious creed. "There must obviously be a centre of the Communist faith somewhere," noted Deputy Undersecretary of State Gladwyn Jebb, and it was clear that Moscow intended to remain its focal point. Thus, it stood to reason that Moscow would both seek and receive the allegiance of native Communists, including those living in Asian states. The Foreign Office regarded the growing ties between Asian Communists, European Communists, and their Moscow supporters as a "natural development." It therefore expected the Chinese to play an increasingly large role in the global Communist movement. As a result, Jebb found it impossible "to separate the spread of Communism from expansion by Russia," two movements that were mutually reinforcing.[68]

If Britain was to make the most of the Tito affair, therefore, it would have to reduce those forces of attraction intrinsic to the Communist world. Clearly, Yugoslavia presented a test case for such a project. As of July 1949, Belgrade was still basing its policy on Marxist-Leninist doctrines, though it appeared to be modifying its attitude toward relations with the West. "If this process continues," the FO noted, "it may establish a precedent for a *modus vivendi* between the Western world on the one hand and, on the other, States which, without abandoning their Communist beliefs, are not actively working against Western aims and are not part of an exclusive Russian bloc." Accordingly, such a relationship could come about only "as the result of the emergence of a stable, non-Stalinist form of Communism," a development that the Foreign Office admitted was far from guaranteed. Indeed, it was possible that Titoism was a "unique phenomenon, due not only to the situation in Yugoslavia but to the personality of Tito himself." Besides, "wider developments" now demanded "serious consideration" from government officials if Britain was to pursue a policy of driving wedges between Moscow and its minions.[69]

One of those developments involved the dangers inherent in Titoist communism. Revisiting a discussion that had taken place in May, British officials again voiced the fear that Titoism might actually promote the expansion, not the diminution, of Communist regimes and—given the gravitational forces inherent in Communist life—enhance the range of Soviet power. So, too, did U.S. officials, who now offered a more cautious appraisal of national communism. Their goal, according to the National Security Council, should be to "facilitate the development of heretical Communism without at the same time seriously impairing our chances for ultimately replacing this intermediate totalitarianism with tolerant regimes congenial to the Western World." The United States, therefore, could not come out "in unqualified support of Tito or Titoism any more than we can take such a stand in favor of Franco and Fascism." Instead, policymakers should seek to foster "Communist heresy among the satellite states, encouraging the emergence of non-Stalinist regimes as temporary administrations, even though they be Communist in nature." Ultimately, however, those regimes were to be "replaced by non-totalitarian governments desirous of participating with good faith in the free world community." While such arguments were implicit in various policy statements dating back to June 1948, the emphasis on national communism as a "temporary" stage of political development was relatively new.[70]

It would have to be, given the state of U.S. opinion on the wedge strategy. With just a quarter of the nation backing policies designed to widen the Tito rift, Americans remained only mildly enamored of approaches designed to put greater distance between Moscow and Belgrade. Admittedly, such scanty evidence makes it difficult to draw conclusions regarding the interplay between media support for the strategy and public receptivity to its premises. Nevertheless, by making repeated reference to the Tito heresy and its attendant strains, the media appeared to be engaging in a concerted effort to sell the image of a non-monolithic Communist world to the American public. Apparently, few seemed interested in buying it.

The Politics of Neutralism

Part of the problem involved the question of Tito's alignment and his stature as part of neither the Eastern nor Western camps. The fear that some states might declare their neutrality in the Cold War alarmed U.S. officials, who feared that neutralism, whether in Europe or in Asia, would be susceptible to Soviet manipulation. Concerns about neutrality were not new for American policymakers. During World War II, questions about how to handle the independent courses charted by Ireland, Spain, Portugal, Sweden, and Switzerland had occupied statesmen throughout the conflict.[71]

Postwar politics dictated that neutrality would again bedevil American diplomats. Finland represented perhaps the most challenging case, given its geographic proximity to the Soviet Union; in time, policy-makers would acquiesce in Helsinki's bid for independence from both East and West. The Truman administration was not as chary toward Finland's neighbors, however. In September 1948, the National Security Council came down squarely against the neutral aspirations of the Scandinavian states.[72] Thereafter, policymakers continued to take steps to dissuade nations from choosing the neutralist path. In the run-up to the North Atlantic Treaty ceremonies in April, for example, Truman officials predicated the sale of U.S. arms abroad on the willingness of recipient nations to line up with the West, a tactic that leading press outlets, in both Britain and the United States, fully supported.[73] Foremost in their sights were the Scandinavian countries, which had made some noise about entering into a regional, neutral bloc. Officials also expressed unease over the potential of Asian states entering into a similarly exclusive arrangement.[74]

While British press and public opinion might have been critical of the neutralist option, Whitehall took a more nuanced view of such matters. Government officials appreciated the desire of Scandinavian countries, particularly Sweden, to remain neutral in the Cold War but were hardly supportive of it. Like the Americans, British statesmen rejected the idea of a neutral Scandinavian bloc. London, however, recognizing the depth of Sweden's neutralist convictions, worked to effect Stockholm's alignment with the West. A number of factors conditioned that policy, including a belief that increased trade and defense cooperation would help to shape Sweden's orientation. A desire to reduce the distance between U.S. and British positions, as well as perhaps a more pragmatic approach to what was achievable, also led the Attlee government to seek some arrangement short of formal alignment. Clearly, Britain shunned America's strong-arm approach to alliance-building and evidenced little of the contempt shown by the Truman administration. Nevertheless, London shared with Washington a sense that neutralism and neutral blocs were generally to be resisted.[75]

Neutrality seemed no more acceptable for citizens of the West themselves. In March 1949, for example—at the very moment Ware Adams and John Davies were railing against the scourge of dichotomous thinking—the New York City Board of Education forbade teachers from remaining "neutral" in their presentation of American ideals and loyalties. Its decision had come on the heels of the city's school superintendent's avowal that "no institution or free man can be neutral in the world struggle between democracy and totalitarianism," nor did it make any difference if that totalitarianism was of the Fascist or Communist variety. Similar sounds were coming out of Hawaii, where a fact-finding board participating in negotiations over a longshoreman's strike—a strike that growing numbers of Hawaiians believed to be orchestrated by Moscow—came under attack for "remaining neutral in this fight against communism." Sentiments such as these did not augur well for policies supportive of countries inclined toward the neutralist position.[76]

Nowhere was this fear of neutralism more evident than with regard to India, one of numerous states that either had achieved or were moving toward postwar political independence. Having ended its status as a British colony in 1947, India sought to remain above the Cold War fray, favoring neither side in the emerging international structure. Yet policymakers were worried that newly sovereign India and Pakistan, among other nations, might drift into the Soviet orbit. American officials, therefore, had repeatedly urged India's prime minister, Jawaharlal Nehru, to side with the West; their efforts came to nought. By the spring of 1949, fears that India might spearhead the emergence of a nonaligned bloc of nations absorbed U.S. officials, who, along with their British counterparts, saw great danger in Nehru's repeated proclamations of neutralism.[77]

As with their earlier pledges to deny economic and military support to those nations reluctant to join the anti-Communist crusade, U.S. policymakers remained cool to Indian overtures for financial assistance. At the same time, they realized that in the event of hostilities between the two camps, India would side with the West. Rarely, however, did this recognition lead to a broader consideration of how Western interests in the Cold War might benefit from the existence, let alone promotion, of a nonaligned movement. Rather than seeking to preserve some political space between the Eastern and Western blocs, State Department officials were actively seeking to counter the notion that such global partitions even existed. By June 1949, with all that had transpired between the forces of "freedom" and those of "totalitarianism," and with Mao just days away from declaring his allegiance in the global struggle, theirs was a project short on credibility.[78]

At the same time, the Kremlin was actually promoting the virtues of monolithism on which that dualistic world was predicated. Its most recent expression of that ideal appeared in the June 1949 issue of the Cominform journal *For a Lasting Peace, for a People's Democracy*, in which the Soviets directed European CPs to "treasure like the apple of their eye the purity of [*sic*] Marxist-Leninist world outlook" and to refrain from ceding "to the class enemy one single brick from the majestic and monolithic edifice of Marxism-Leninism." To British policymakers, it was a stirring reminder that the Kremlin was willing to sacrifice "numerical strength" among the region's CPs—the consequence of subordinating local interests to those of Moscow—for the likely gain in discipline and control.[79]

The power of the monolithic image was such that members of the Foreign Office began to invoke it with increasing regularity throughout the course of the year. They tarred Communist chieftains as "monolithic," characterized Moscow's orbit as a "monolithic structure," portrayed the Soviet system as a "Stalinist monolith," and described the Kremlin's entire project as "Soviet 'monolithism.' "[80] The frequency with which British diplomats used the term is curious since such language, as London had noted, played into Moscow's hands; the Foreign Office had already proscribed its representatives from using words or phrases alluding to "Russian strength."[81] Nevertheless, it had yet to suggest any term that might have hinted at Soviet weakness. "Titoism" and "national communism" were both absent from the government's directive on anti-Soviet publicity, suggesting that the Foreign Office still had not decided on how it would distinguish Soviet Communists from deviationist Communists, or even whether it was appropriate to do so at all. Britain's chief propagandist, Ralph Murray, had recommended that officials use "Kremlin Columns" as a synonym for Communist movements outside the Soviet Union—hardly an image that smacked of weakness or fragility.[82]

The State Department showed comparable interest in standardizing its rhetorical policy. Searching for greater accuracy in its portrayal of the Soviet threat, at least one of its representatives found "Stalinist communism" or "Kremlin-dominated imperialist communism" as preferable alternatives to "Soviet communism."[83] Yet some officials wondered whether they should lash out at "communism" at all. Paul Hoffman, head of the Economic Cooperation Administration, thought administration personnel were focusing too much on ideology and showing "too much emotion." The real issues, he noted, were power politics and the Kremlin's desire to expand its ring of pliant states. Upon closer inspection, however, it appeared that the ring was actually contracting: according to Hoffman's assessment, the Soviet circle had already expelled Yugoslavia and had yet to envelop China. U.S. diplomacy should therefore focus not on the ideology of states but on the extent of their autonomy. Unfortunately, that strategy assumed "a rather sophisticated point of view," as Hoffman put it—a position that required "considerable explaining."[84]

Indeed, the State Department never settled on the best way to articulate the wedge strategy and the premises behind it. Its failure in this respect stemmed, at least partly, from its inability to gauge popular acceptance of the strategy's basic assumptions. Francis Russell, who directed the department's Office of Public Affairs, admitted as much in remarks to a group of public opinion analysts in March 1949. Discussing the limitations of opinion polling, Russell acknowledged that such surveys were often incapable of providing public affairs officers with the information they needed. For instance, their modes of questioning seemed ill-equipped to deal with the matter of schismatic communism. "Do we inquire," he asked, "how many people are aware of the relationship between the Tito regime in Yugoslavia and the Kremlin, and what the possible effect of a lumping together of all countries behind the Iron Curtain might be?" "No," would probably have been the short answer—his question was merely rhetorical—since polls sought clear-cut responses to specific questions. But if Russell was asking whether the department *should* inquire into such issues, the answer to that question would seem to have been "yes." It was a query that others would soon pose, for just three days after Russell raised the issue, Ware Adams and John Davies completed their PPS working paper on communism and its habitual depiction.[85]

As stated earlier, that paper grew out of a desire to encourage a more nuanced approach to the challenge of international communism. It called on policymakers to refrain from painting the movement in monolithic terms, lest they solidify its adherents at a time when the Eastern bloc appeared to be cracking. Talk of a Communist monolith, the authors argued, amounted to a self-fulfilling prophecy. While the department never adopted the Adams-Davies line to any great extent, aspects of their study seeped into Policy Planning and NSC papers. Still, those arguments were scarcely heard outside the State Department, and for good reason. The consolidation of Soviet power in Eastern Europe, the increasing belligerence and orthodoxy of Chinese communism, and a highly politicized domestic environment limited the appeal of such a sophisticated propaganda campaign, rendering the wedge strategy—or at least widespread acceptance of its fundamental premises—stillborn.

British statesmen were no more likely than American officials to adopt the Adams-Davies recommendations. Although they, too, recognized the dangers of monolithic rhetoric, members of the Foreign Office seemed particularly intent on preserving its assumptions as the bedrock of British publicity policy. Both sets of diplomats were fully aware of the opportunities Titoism presented and were taking actions to foster future schisms, but international trends were not in their favor. Developments in Asia as well as in Eastern Europe were pointing toward the greater integration, not fragmentation, of the Communist world; circumstances in Western Europe and the United States suggested that a similar process was afoot in the non-Communist realm. With each side injecting a more tangible, corporeal reality into the "two-camp" thesis, the international order lost whatever fluidity it might have had during those early postwar years. As it began to harden, so, too, did perceptions about the nature of international communism. And with the hardening of those perceptions came the hardening of the monolithic framework.

CHAPTER SEVEN

Anti-Stalinist Communism

The fall of 1949 opened inauspiciously for the West. On September 23, President Harry S. Truman announced that the Soviets had detonated their first atomic device, ending the American monopoly on the bomb. Yet the "ill wind" of Moscow's achievement, as Secretary of State Dean Acheson termed it, had a beneficial impact in Washington. Within days, Congress approved the Mutual Defense Aid Program, a package of military assistance to U.S. allies it had been debating since late July. The rapidity of that legislative response, however, did not necessarily reflect a general wave of hysteria sweeping the nation. To be sure, leading journals saw the Soviet achievement as a turning point in world affairs, but the public reacted with remarkable calm. Perhaps, collectively, it was gearing itself up for the next phase of the Cold War, one in which both East and West would be in possession of atomic and possibly thermonuclear weapons. Against the backdrop of this increasingly militarized and potentially apocalyptic environment, British and American officials soldiered on, reflecting, in a sense, the dualistic and paradoxical nature of the struggle itself. Over the ensuing weeks and months, they would offer both categorical and nuanced appraisals of the Soviet challenge, with pragmatic approaches to communism coexisting alongside doctrinaire assessments of its malevolence.[1]

Into this mix appeared a political treatise that sought to firm up America's sense of steely resolve. Arthur Schlesinger Jr., who in 1945 had asked Americans to ruminate on "the meaning of democracy" in his Pulitzer Prize–winning *The Age of Jackson,* now called on them four years later to preserve that system's very existence. His new book, *The Vital Center,* would provide the necessary moral and political will for the battle ahead.[2]

Schlesinger was hardly the sole literary oracle preaching against the horrors of totalitarianism. Both Arthur Koestler and George Orwell had offered lurid studies of the subject during 1949. But it was Schlesinger whose more didactic approach appealed to the American public. A founding member of the liberal anti-Communist group Americans for Democratic Action, Schlesinger offered the country a purportedly nonideological approach to world affairs. Criticizing both the Right and Left wings of the political spectrum, he deplored the abuses of the House Committee on Un-American Activities as much as he rejected the naiveté of the Progressive Citizens of America. In their stead he offered the "non-Communist Left," with its commitments to individual liberty and social responsibility, as the most sensible answer to the tyrannies of the age.[3]

Despite his endorsement of moderation and gradualism, and his call to discriminate between liberalism and radicalism, Schlesinger offered a vision of the Cold War that was as bipolar as one might get from the members of HUAC or the leaders of the Cominform. "It is we or they" he wrote, "the United States or the Soviet Union; capitalism or communism," and it was "only in these terms that steps can be taken toward enduring solutions." Invoking phrases reminiscent of an earlier conflict, Schlesinger charged that the difference between the United States and the Soviet Union was "basically the difference between free society and totalitarianism." Like Frank Capra and others who had mobilized public opinion during World War II, Schlesinger depicted the American "free society," what he referred to as "the crowning glory of western history," as locked in mortal combat with tyranny. Here was the dualistic, Manichean vision that American whiggism and American republicanism had long espoused, a vision reinforced through the use of Red Fascist imagery. To be sure, Schlesinger argued, communism and fascism differed in several key respects. Nevertheless, their similarities remained "vastly more overpowering and significant than the differences."[4]

While this rhetoric helped to solidify the monolith's adjoining structures, it also firmed up its very essence. The Communist movement, Schlesinger noted, was conspiratorial by nature and geared toward the Kremlin's grand design. Its constituent parts would soon become indistinguishable from Russia itself. "Today," Schlesinger argued, "the satellite states of eastern Europe are being readied for incorporation into the Soviet Union," while tomorrow, "Soviet power will surely spread everywhere that it meets no firm resistance." It would do so through Moscow's use of the "fifth column" and agents abroad. "Let no one be deceived," he charged, "about the relations of these parties to Moscow." Even a casual reading of the press revealed that Communists "in nation after nation" had vowed to rise "in obedient sequence to pledge their allegiance to the Soviet Union in case of war between the USSR and their homelands."[5] The monolithic framework was thus central to Schlesinger's argument, as it would be for those who came to endorse his perspective. A manifesto of liberal anticommunism, *The Vital Center* provided key segments of literate opinion with a resounding call to arms. In so doing, it echoed several themes running through elements of the non-Communist Left in both Britain and the United States.[6]

Schlesinger's audience included those far afield from the intellectual elite. While excerpts ran in more high-brow publications such as *Partisan Review,* the *Nation,* and the *New York Times Sunday Magazine,* passages also appeared in *Life.* In addition, reviews of the book were published in newspapers around the country. In its hostility to communism, support for liberal values, and faith in the American way, *The Vital Center* incorporated several strands of popular opinion coursing through America circa 1949. To the extent that it both reflected and shaped such thought, it would prove instrumental in sustaining acceptance of a Communist monolith.[7]

The Monolith Fortified

Further reinforcement came early that fall. On 1 October 1949, Mao Zedong proclaimed the establishment of the People's Republic of China (PRC), finalizing a development that Western statesmen had long anticipated. Not surprisingly, Moscow's recognition of Communist China dominated the American press for the next several months. Both print and radio comment took it for granted that all Communist gains, including those of the CCP, translated into victories for the Kremlin. Nevertheless, several papers, including the *San Francisco Chronicle* and the *New York Herald Tribune,* argued that China would not simply bow to Soviet wishes. Media analysts in the State Department found a large section of the press siding with Ernest K. Lindley, the foreign affairs columnist for *Newsweek,* who saw the "wedge strategy" as an idea whose time had come. "Wrong as it may have been in the past," Lindley remarked, "the State Department is now advocating the only feasible China policy for the future, which is to play for a schism between China and Russia."[8]

Although news outlets such as the *Washington Post* speculated on rifts between Communist China and the Soviet Union, most thought the odds in favor of Mao becoming a Chinese Tito were "exceedingly slim." As the *New York Times* maintained, Mao's words and deeds "should make us realize that we are dealing with a convinced and enthusiastic satellite." His visit to Moscow in December only deepened that belief. For the *Herald Tribune,* as well as for many other media sources, the Moscow talks confirmed the existence "of a tightly linked chain of dictatorial power that runs from the Oder to the Pacific."[9]

These assumptions seeped into the American consciousness as the vast majority of those polled regarded Mao as a Soviet lackey. By mid-December, five out of every six Americans believed that the Chinese Communists took their orders from Moscow, a finding not lost on the State Department. According to Francis Russell, who directed its Office of Public Affairs, "no considerable group place[d] any faith in the Titoist tendencies of Mao, particularly after his visit to Moscow."[10] The American media thus furthered public acceptance of the monolithic framework, a perception that government officials did little to undermine. Representatives of the Truman administration were routinely depicting the Communist Chinese as tools of the Kremlin. Secretary of State Dean Acheson, Ambassador Walter Bedell Smith, and Deputy Undersecretary John Puerifoy all intimated that Mao and his followers were acting on the orders of the Kremlin.[11] They and their colleagues were regularly portraying international communism as a stalking-horse for Soviet imperialism.[12]

But this was not the only publicity line coming out of the State Department. Americans did hear government officials speak of tensions within Communist ranks, including those between Moscow and Beijing, and Stalin and Tito. Moscow's experience in Eastern Europe, noted George F. Kennan in *Reader's Digest,* indicated "that in this case Soviet imperialism bit off more than it could comfortably chew." Acheson also invoked the Tito rift in public and mused about its potential effect on the PRC. His Republican consultant on foreign affairs, John Foster Dulles, likewise saw the split as a testament to Moscow's need for total control; the Kremlin's intolerance of diversity, in effect, guaranteed the emergence of tensions behind the Iron Curtain.[13] Nevertheless, the notion that Mao might one day function as an Asian Tito was never a deeply embedded staple of domestic debate.[14]

The dearth of such talk stemmed partly from questions about the value of Titoism itself. To *Foreign Affairs* editor Hamilton Fish Armstrong, its virtue was not as a schismatic force but merely as a retardant to the further growth of the Communist movement.[15] Aside from Yugoslavia, no country under Communist rule had challenged the monolithic framework, nor had any Communist Party adopted a Titoist position. State Department officials, including its information officers, therefore concluded that all such parties "operate as Soviet fifth columns which accept unhesitatingly and without question orders emanating from the Kremlin." In Eastern Europe, those parties and the states they controlled constituted, in the words of the National Security Council, "part of the Soviet monolith."[16] This portrayal of international affairs as a zero-sum contest between democracy and totalitarianism thwarted adoption of a more nuanced policy position, such as the one Ware Adams and John Paton Davies had called for in March 1949. For even support of Tito carried the risk of suggesting that the Yugoslav strongman had "entered the democratic camp," a position, the department recognized, that could be easily lampooned.[17]

To be sure, the Tito schism posed a fundamental challenge to Moscow's control of world communism, and American diplomats were keen to exploit its lessons whenever possible. The promotion of nationalism in both Communist and non-Communist states, especially in the developing countries of the world, seemed the most likely means for creating additional fissures. By embracing that force, noted Acheson, the United States could align itself with that impulse "which more than anything else can oppose communism." Part of the government's strategy, therefore, involved a purportedly more general acceptance of national, communist programs. Testifying before the Senate Foreign Relations Committee in October 1949, Acheson sought to downplay the ideological, anti-Communist cant of U.S. propaganda. If the Chinese want to be Communist, he stated, "that is their business." What the administration objected to most strenuously was the imposition of such an ideology by external forces. Officials would slot this refrain into statements on U.S. policy, declaring in NSC 58, a document outlining the U.S. position on the East European satellites, their penultimate goal of working with communist governments, free of Soviet domination. It was a theoretical position that Truman officials, over the previous three years, had taken publicly as well as privately, though without any manifest enthusiasm for adopting it in practice.[18]

Wedges Open and Closed

Toleration of national communism was nevertheless a basic premise of the wedge strategy, an approach the administration continued to pursue with some degree of confusion. Opinion on how best to create and widen fissures between Communist states and parties, and how to minimize the external control that Acheson talked about, continued to oscillate between "hard" and "soft" variants of that policy. The wedge strategy, at least as it applied to China, still amounted to a program of neither "kindnesses nor slights," as Kennan had phrased it.[19] Yet both kindnesses *and* slights were in the offing for Europe. Albania was the East bloc state regarded as most ripe for detachment, and where U.S. policymakers, along with their British counterparts, now opted for an exceptionally hard version of that approach: the infiltration of antigovernment refugees and the dissemination of antigovernment propaganda.[20]

While officials hoped to dislodge Albania from the Soviet orbit by means of the political stick, Yugoslavia—already dissociated from the Cominform bloc—would have its independence preserved by means of the economic carrot. By the fall of 1949, the further deterioration of Soviet-Yugoslav relations had led U.S. policymakers and the American public to sanction the export of aviation materials to Belgrade. But they saw little to no prospect of Titoism spreading throughout Eastern Europe at that time. The Kremlin's hold over its satellite structure was simply too strong to permit the emergence of a serious threat to Soviet power.[21]

In any event, policymakers were not entirely comfortable with the growth of Titoist movements should they arise. According to the National Security Council, the promotion of national communism actually risked swelling the ranks of Communist states, a conclusion both U.S. and British officials had drawn earlier. The challenge for American statesmen, as they framed it in December 1949, was thus "to facilitate the development of heretical communism without at the same time seriously impairing our chances for ultimately replacing this intermediate totalitarianism with tolerant regimes congenial to the Western World." As if promoting the emergence of national communism were not difficult enough, government officials had to consider whether their efforts in that direction might be compounding the very problem, or at least part of the problem, they sought to address. Beyond that conundrum lay the political and even moral hazards of supporting Communist regimes at a time of increasingly ideological and universalist rhetoric.[22]

By the close of 1949, the ironies of the wedge strategy were becoming readily apparent to U.S. officials. Policy papers from that period reveal a growing awareness that the actions and rhetoric of American statesmen might be playing into Moscow's hands; in other words, by mouthing Soviet platitudes about the rigidity and discipline of Communists, policymakers were actually hardening a bloc they were trying to crack. The tendency of Western officials, therefore, to reinforce the myth of Soviet strength left Communists with "no future" for themselves "outside the Stalinist camp." By the time Truman officials had sanctioned that argument, eight months had elapsed since its introduction by Ware Adams and John Paton Davies. Meanwhile, Russia had exploded an atomic device, China had become a Communist state, Moscow had stepped up its purges in Eastern Europe, and revelations of Soviet espionage had become fixtures in the American press. If there was ever a chance of educating the public along the lines Adams and Davies had envisioned, the time for doing so had long since passed.[23]

Davies, however, continued to search for ways to elevate the discussion of communism and inject further subtlety into considerations of the topic. In late 1949, he offered the scientific model of "complementarity" as a metaphor for various manifestations of the Communist movement. Just as physicists recognized that light could be both a particle and a wave, U.S. officials might have to reconfigure their understanding of communism—especially given its Russian, Yugoslav, and Chinese incarnations—as both an international *and* a national phenomenon. Davies, in other words, was suggesting that the Stalinist model of monolithism, with all parties bound to a central authority, provided at times a less valuable guide to Communist behavior than a Maoist or Titoist model, which posited a rival center. While the metaphor offered an innovative appraisal of international communism, it apparently held little sway within the State Department. Davies himself regarded the Chinese as "confirmed Marxist-Leninists" who had "unequivocally declared themselves as in the Soviet camp."[24]

Being in Moscow's camp was not the same as being Moscow's stooge, however, and the belief that Chinese Communists would never subject themselves to external control was as much a consistent feature of British thinking, if not more so, as it was of American. Media comment in England espoused that general argument, as journals and newspapers such as the *Times,* the *New Statesman & Nation,* and the *Manchester Guardian Weekly* made clear.[25] In many ways, this was the line adopted by the Foreign Office, which was generally circumspect in its evaluation of Sino-Soviet relations. Deputy Undersecretary of State Gladwyn Jebb thought it "not yet proven that recent developments in China were a Russian triumph." On the one hand, Jebb recognized the Chinese Communists' "exclusive devotion" to Russia and questioned whether Mao's need for Western aid would outweigh his desire for closer relations with the Kremlin. Still, there was reason for hope. According to Ambassador Ralph Stevenson, "most Chinese communists were Marxists but not all were primarily pro-Russian." In addition, Moscow was likely to have trouble infiltrating the CCP and controlling its security organs as it had done in Eastern Europe. That argument had great appeal to members of the Russia Committee, including Jebb, who found Stevenson's words "reassuring as far as the danger of an extension of Moscow-controlled communism was concerned."[26]

Such reassurance was short-lived. In mid-December, Mao began a visit to the Soviet Union with an eye toward signing a treaty of friendship. As the Russia Committee noted, the Moscow talks marked the first time that Mao had dealt with the Kremlin as the ruler of roughly 450 million people—an event that might "in retrospect be seen as a turning point in history." Guesswork of this sort continued to mark London's approach to China, for British officials persisted in questioning the nature of the Sino-Soviet relationship. Even though the Kremlin had apparently adopted a "forward policy" in the region, it was still "too soon to tell" whether it was engaged in a "co-ordinated political offensive or merely the customary Soviet policy of using opportunities for pressure wherever they occur."[27] Officials stationed closer to Moscow took a more pessimistic approach. David Kelly, Britain's ambassador to the Soviet Union, evinced little hope for an outcome favorable to British interests. The Chinese had adopted a "correct attitude" toward the Kremlin, denounced Tito, and acknowledged their debts to Moscow and Stalin. "I do not suggest that this honeymoon must last for ever," Kelly noted, "but I think it would be folly for the West to base any present calculation on expectation of a 'nationalist deviation' in China." With the signing of the Sino-Soviet treaty in February 1950, and the accompanying propaganda blitz trumpeting socialist solidarity, the Communist monolith, in Britain's eyes, appeared to be alive and well.[28]

American statesmen were less impressed with the Moscow summit. George F. Kennan believed that it actually revealed the fissures inherent in Sino-Soviet relations. The length of Mao's stay in Moscow— roughly six weeks—indicated that the Kremlin "would have difficulty establishing the same sort of relationship with a successful Chinese communist movement that they have established with some of their eastern European satellites." The Policy Planning Staff, now under the direction of Paul Nitze, shared Kennan's assessment. It, too, attributed the duration of the talks to Stalin's attempts to undermine Mao's hold on power—efforts which, the PPS argued, would ultimately fail. Acheson himself held out for a split between Stalin and Mao, though he recognized it would likely come several years, not months, in the future.[29]

That collective sense of strain within the Sino-Soviet relationship led the National Security Council in December 1949 to throw its full support behind the wedge strategy, calling explicitly for the promotion and exploitation of rifts between Moscow and Beijing. In order to encourage such division, Acheson used his press contacts to emphasize Soviet aspirations in China, with the objective of having those rumors then broadcast into China through the Voice of America. The secretary's comments on the Sino-Soviet relationship, made during a January 12, 1950 speech at the National Press Club, were lauded by *New York Times* journalists C. L. Sulzberger and James Reston, and especially by columnist Walter Lippmann, who had been calling for the administration to adopt such a farsighted policy. These actions suggest that Acheson was reluctant to slam the door completely on the possibility of opening wedges between Moscow and Beijing.[30]

A National Communist Alternative

In the midst of Mao's pilgrimage to Moscow, Britain and the United States undertook their most comprehensive reviews to date of "Titoism" and its offshoots. These efforts reflected the bureaucratic momentum for such a project as well as the increasing dualism of the postwar world. The resulting British study, a document entitled "Anti-Stalinist Communism," was, in a sense, years in the making. Its origins lay in the immediate postwar period, when the Foreign Office questioned scores of representatives on the alignment of Communists worldwide. But it also built on later work, including Christopher Warner's queries of 1946, Russia Committee interest in the "Quaroni Question" during 1947, and the many papers and analyses produced in the wake of the Tito affair itself. Written and rewritten throughout the winter of 1950 by the Information Research Department (IRD), "Anti-Stalinist Communism" stood as Britain's most focused comment on the implications of the split within Communist ranks.[31]

The paper began by detailing the two main currents, as well as the minor tributaries, of this ideological offshoot. The first branch took its cues from old Bolsheviks such as Trotsky, Zinoviev, and Bukharin—men whom Stalin had long since eliminated. The second strain derived from "Titoism" itself, a dynamic that had emerged as "a national schism outside the Soviet Union" and revealed the tensions at work within the Communist world. These tensions were sure to persist due to the very nature of Stalinist rule. By the time the IRD had finalized the document in mid-February 1950, it had recast "Titoism" as "National Communism," a linguistic turn that would allow Britain to define the movement as a generic force, independent of time and space.

According to this new formulation, China could now inherit the mantle once worn solely by Yugoslavia. Drawing together the overall implications of the Tito split, the IRD argued that international communism, "organised and controlled by the Kremlin as an instrument of Soviet foreign policy, is such a threat to peace that we should make use of any force capable of disrupting it. National Communism, which involves a split in the Communist ranks, is clearly a force of this nature. Indeed it represents a peculiarly dangerous threat to international Communism, depriving it of that 'monolithic' character which is one of its chief attractions both to the political strategist and to the intellectual." The value of national communism, however, would need to be evaluated on a case-by-case basis "against the risk of its encouraging aspirations, whether nationalist or Communist, which are in themselves dangerous, though less so than Stalinism." With China exerting a potentially powerful influence on its neighbors, national communism "might well present an even more serious threat to our interests in the Far East than would a Chinese régime openly subservient to Moscow." Europe, by comparison, was relatively immune to the dangers of this force. A propaganda offensive west of the Iron Curtain would likely "weaken existing Communist Parties without themselves constituting a serious Communist menace." East of that divide, it would probably have no impact whatsoever.

Regardless of where it took root, the emergence of national communism would remain Britain's penultimate goal. "We should regard the estrangement of national Communist Parties from Moscow," declared the IRD, "not as an end in itself, but as a step towards the disruption of Communism in all its forms." In metaphorical terms, Britain would seek to light several brush fires in order to snuff out a rampaging firestorm. This was precisely what the National Security Council had said in its NSC 58 series, prepared during the fall of 1949.[32]

By March 27, when Foreign Secretary Ernest Bevin posted the memo to U.K. missions abroad, "Anti-Stalinist Communism" had become Britain's definitive statement on the subject.[33] But representatives of His Majesty's Government were not the only ones to receive the document, for the Russia Committee had recommended that the State Department also be given a copy. Officials at the British embassy in Washington had actually discussed the project with their American counterparts back in January 1950, at which time they became aware of U.S. interest in conducting a similar study. According to the State Department's G. Frederick Reinhardt, deputy director of the Office of Eastern European Affairs, Washington was going to "wait upon developments for a little longer," perhaps a month or two, before soliciting such information from its missions abroad. In the meantime, he wondered if he could see whatever material Britain had produced on the subject—a request the embassy was eager to grant.[34]

The Americans, nevertheless, regarded national communism with great skepticism. Possessing neither "the missionary sense of world communism" nor "the advantage of a link with Russian imperialism," the movement—according to U.S. officials—was likely to be a weak force over the next several years, especially in Eastern Europe. Much more influential would be Tito's example, whose effect "on other Communist countries outside Russia would be dangerous." According to Oliver Franks, Britain's ambassador in Washington, the State Department seemed to attach more significance to the manifest power of a charismatic leader than to the strength of an ill-defined, theoretical doctrine. This apparent split between British and American appraisals of Titoism and national communism is intriguing given Britain's alleged penchant for eschewing theory in favor of empiricism, for favoring the concrete over the abstract. Regardless, both sets of statesmen were skating on thin methodological ice, positing the existence of a new form of international behavior on the basis of a single example.[35]

Although Franks had given his colleagues an overview of American attitudes, he said nothing about State Department efforts to produce its own version of "Anti-Stalinist Communism." In fact, the department was hard at work on such a document. By January 1950, the Policy Planning Staff had begun to consider precisely how and where national communism "might be a force inimical to Stalinism." That project was not a new one; since June 1948, policy planners had extolled the virtues of Titoism and had worked its implications into their papers. Yet American officials had never analyzed the nature of that force in any great depth, nor had they conducted a far-reaching study of its meaning for U.S. national security policy. To foster a broader and more incisive discussion of the subject, the PPS charged staff member Robert Joyce with outlining its elements in further detail.[36]

By the third week of January, Joyce had completed his initial study of anti-Stalinist communism, using the terms "Titoism" and "national communism" interchangeably as labels for the movement. Curiously, given the fact that he was evaluating a schismatic force, Joyce began his paper by invoking the very image of the monolith itself. By definition, he wrote, international communism served as "the instrumentality of Russian imperialism," and it was Moscow's control of the movement that constituted a "primary danger" to U.S. security. The time was ripe, however, to examine the broader implications of Tito's brand of "national communism," to assess its impact on the "world communist movement," and to gauge the "effectiveness of Stalinist communism." At the very least, it was in the nation's interest to keep Tito "afloat" to preserve the viability of a heretical branch of the faith.[37]

But the value of an independent Tito seemed to be diminishing steadily, a conclusion policymakers had recognized as early as the fall of 1948. According to parallel but separate departmental studies conducted during the winter and spring of 1950, the forces of world communism were actually moving toward greater centralized control. Various internal developments were damaging the movement's cohesiveness, but they were doing so "not nearly as much as was believed after the first news of the Tito defection." Policymakers thus had little reason to anticipate the emergence of "any general class of potential Titoistes." Tito himself was unlikely to form an "anti-Stalinist International of Communist Parties," nor were there indications of further schisms on the horizon. The unfortunate truth was that no other Communist chieftain had successfully applied Tito's lessons to his own nation. "This does not, of course, mean, that it could not be done," for some such leader would most likely emulate Tito's stand in the future. But how far into the future, and under what conditions, remained a mystery. The department thus did little more than equivocate on the subject of national communism, holding out only the faintest of hopes for its emergence.[38]

It also conveyed a sense of desperation, for the State Department was beginning to think that the time for driving wedges between Moscow and the Communist world lay in the near and not the distant future. According to a mid-1950 study from the Bureau of Intelligence and

Research (INR), the situation could "well get out of hand" in the short term as Moscow sought to rein in troublesome comrades. In the long run, however, "the leaders of the Communist Parties will be reconciled to their roles as complete puppets of Moscow and then the international organization will be an efficient one." This was a remarkable statement, for in making it INR reversed the prevailing assumption that the wedge strategy required a patient, long-term commitment. Apparently, government officials were beginning to talk about Titoism and the U.S. atomic stockpile in similar ways: both seemed to be rapidly "wasting assets."[39]

Capturing the Psychological Initiative

While the Joyce study was designed primarily to help the Truman administration gain the psychological advantage abroad, sustaining its message at home had also become a major concern. Senator Joseph McCarthy (R-WI) had recently launched a series of attacks on the executive branch, scoring administration officials for covering up Communist influence in Washington. On February 9, 1950, he charged the State Department with employing over two-hundred Communists in positions of power; in March, he went after John Stuart Service, one of the "China Hands" who had endorsed a rapprochement between Chiang Kai-shek and Mao Zedong; one month later, he identified Owen Lattimore, a former government official and present head of the Page School of International Affairs at The Johns Hopkins University, as "the top Russian espionage agent" in America.[40] At first, Americans generally dismissed those accusations as political grandstanding. *Life* saw them as part of a "lynching bee" and treated McCarthy as an "irresponsible" opportunist—a partisan politician who was exploiting the ancillary issue of internal security while avoiding the primary one of foreign policy. But support for McCarthy's crusade picked up following his hounding of Lattimore. By May, the national media, and the Luce press in particular, had begun to divorce the recklessness of the man from the alleged righteousness of his cause. While McCarthy's tactics might have been reprehensible, many observers believed his instincts remained praiseworthy nonetheless. Communism was simply "wrong," *Life* argued, and "hostile to all that is good, solid and enduring in the American spirit."[41]

Once articles and opinion polls appeared suggesting that McCarthy was doing more good than harm, the national consciousness underwent a subtle shift that boded ill for any sophisticated approach to international communism. In that highly charged environment, in which anyone critical of McCarthy risked being branded a Communist, the promotion of national communism—even as a weapon against Soviet communism—was bound to fail. The issues of the day had become too black-and-white for those nuances to permeate the public dialogue. As a result, the emerging conservative and Republican consensus, which had crowded out the "grays" of American political culture, added further heft to the rapidly hardening monolithic outlook.[42]

Public life had long been saturated with such talk, however. From at least March 1947 onward, dichotomous rhetoric—often employed consciously to win over legislators skeptical of America's newfound international commitments—had marked administration statements on Soviet affairs. Purveyors of that language included everyone from Truman, Marshall, and Acheson to officials lower on the pecking order. They also included individuals living behind the Iron Curtain; indeed, the war of words between the "two camps" of East and West—a geographic division that was itself part of a binary universe—reinforced the prevalence of the dualistic outlook. By early 1950, that binary reflex was firmly entrenched as part of the Cold War consensus.

Its hold on the public consciousness became even more secure in the wake of Moscow's decision to boost the volume of its "peace" campaign that March. Sponsored by the World Congress of the Partisans of Peace, the resulting "Stockholm Peace Petition," which called for the prohibition of atomic weapons and the criminalization of their use, allowed its sponsors to identify all nonsignatories as members of the warmongering camp. Whitehall recognized the "peace offensive" as a Soviet-inspired effort to disarm the West and continued to regard that campaign as part of an international Communist movement directed by the Kremlin. So, too, did the Truman administration, which construed the initiative as conceived and directed by Moscow. The "Peace Appeal," which the *New York Times* likened to one of Hitler's tactics in the 1930s, soon became part of a global effort to secure further "Signatures for Peace," a pledge designed to disarm the West rhetorically and generate greater sympathy for the Eastern bloc.[43]

Truman's response to the Soviet peace offensive marked a significant shift in U.S. information policy. Addressing the American Society of Newspaper Editors in April 1950, the president called for a corresponding U.S. plan to "promote the cause of freedom against the propaganda of slavery." What was needed, Truman argued, was a "great campaign of truth."[44] U.S. resources would now be mobilized more vigorously to combat Soviet disinformation. Accordingly, the federal government ratcheted up its publicity program, systemizing what earlier had been an ad hoc series of measures.[45] American journalists joined in the crusade, with Truman largely receiving commitments from the nation's editors to exhibit greater energy in counteracting Soviet propaganda.[46] And the language of that crusade reflected the evolution of the Cold War's war of words. With "peace" set off against "war," "truth" against "falsehood," and "freedom" against "slavery," the spate of binary oppositions that flowed from the mouths and pens of persons of influence became even more ingrained as part of the rhetorical landscape.[47]

To heighten the new offensive against Communist propaganda, U.S. officials sought to coordinate their methods more tightly with those of their European allies, a project that had been in the works since 1948.[48] Discussions about harmonizing U.S. and British information policy toward the Soviet bloc became more serious in early 1950, culminating in a meeting of their respective publicity chiefs at the May 1950 London Conference of Foreign Ministers. As part of those talks, Assistant Secretary for Public Affairs Edward Barrett, who had traveled to London with Secretary of State Acheson, met with the Russia Committee's Christopher Warner and proclaimed that both Britain and the United States would seek to widen the fissures in the Communist world. They would do so by "shoot[ing] at the same target from different angles," which was a stance the Foreign Office had adopted back in 1948. Britain would focus its fire on those areas where the battle was still joined, that is, Western Europe and Southeast Asia, while the United States would set its sights on peoples behind the Iron Curtain. To provide for better communication and cooperation, both governments agreed to station information officers in their respective embassies abroad.[49]

While Acheson and Barrett were seeking to refine administration policies in London, Americans were experimenting with more grass-roots initiatives at home. One of the more celebrated took place on May Day 1950, when the residents of Mosinee, Wisconsin, put themselves "behind an iron curtain" to demonstrate the horrors of Communist rule. Mosinee's simulation of a Communist *putsch* captured national attention; over 1,200 newspapers and radio shows advertised the stunt. As the "coup" unfolded, the trappings of Soviet society—and the identification of communism with Sovietism—came to the fore: school-children carried signs proclaiming Stalin as their leader; movie theaters featured his image in their run of Soviet propaganda films; and newspapers such as the *Red Star,* the journal of the "revolution," warned of a Secret Political Police beholden to the Kremlin. Combined with the mock arrests, purges, and confiscations that hit the town, those references to Soviet power left little doubt as to who was really in charge. The fealty of Communists, especially those living in the United States, belonged solely to Moscow.[50]

If the Mosinee experiment was one of America's more notable public comments on international communism, surely its most prominent secret analogue was NSC 68, the National Security Council's landmark reevaluation of U.S. national security objectives. NSC 68 has rightly been characterized as sweeping in its recommendations for a strategic overhaul, as well as in its depiction of communism as a universal threat. But its treatment of communism was not without qualification. As described in NSC 68, bolshevism was not an all-powerful, unstoppable movement; rather, Soviet power, having solidified the monolith not "by any force of natural cohesion" but through the use of armed might, contained the seeds of its own decay. Moscow therefore lay vulnerable to the power of nationalism, the intensity of which the "free world" could potentially heighten. Accordingly, the United States would seek to promote "mass defections" from the Soviet camp, thereby eradicating the "myth" of Soviet might.

That myth, however, was the primary image of communism that came through in the document. Allusions to Soviet weakness appeared infrequently throughout NSC 68; more common were references to "the Soviet-directed world communist party" and the Kremlin's use of native Communists, themes that marked the paper's discussion of Communist China. NSC 68 thus likened the PRC to a Soviet "springboard," a tool for "further incursion" into Southeast Asia. Although it recognized the potential for schisms in the Communist movement, NSC 68 was no primer for the wedge strategy. This most recent, comprehensive statement on U.S. security policy was largely silent on the Tito split itself. Given the absence of such a discussion, its readers could well have deduced that Russia, more so than ever before, controlled the fortunes of a worldwide Communist monolith.[51]

Indeed, the "monolith" itself, or some derivative thereof, was becoming the term of choice within the U.S. and U.K. diplomatic communities to denote Soviet control of international communism. A sampling of British documents reveals the increasing popularity of the expression within the Foreign Office. The Russia Committee, for instance, had charged Moscow with creating "the 'monolithic' parties" of Eastern Europe. Not even the purges, it argued, had altered the view that Stalin controlled "a monolithic power bloc," responsive to his every command. Although it would be exceedingly difficult to gauge the frequency with which British officials used the term, the vast majority of its senior diplomats and policymakers saw its processes at work in ever greater parts of the globe.[52]

Americans were becoming equally prone to incantations of the term. Dean Acheson, who saw the Yugoslav affair as an opportunity to undermine the "Soviet monolith," employed it on occasion.[53] This was a curious move for the secretary, who had long appreciated the restiveness within the Kremlin universe. While Acheson was receptive to the politics of tarring Communists with such broad strokes, he may have operated from a position of doubt regarding the prospects for a truly national Communist movement; comrades were to be regarded as guilty of Kremlin fealty until proven innocent. His references, therefore, to Moscow's international Communist "apparatus" and the toadyish behavior of local cadres suggests that Acheson was not merely engaging in such talk to placate congressional and media critics. Along with Soviet specialists George Kennan and Charles Bohlen, two of the department's more bullish advocates of the wedge strategy, Acheson likely believed in the primal attraction of all Communists to Moscow's pole. Paul Nitze, arguably, was even more beholden to this assumption, having worked its particulars into NSC 68.[54] With Mao seemingly proving his Stalinist bona fides by the day, the monolithic image framed the State Department's thinking on the subject.

More frequently, Acheson and fellow policymakers invoked the image without actually using it in speech. Testifying before the Senate Foreign Relations Committee in January 1950, Acheson maintained that native Communist Parties were in "every sense of the word the instrumentalities and agents of Russian foreign policy."[55] Similarly, the U.S. embassy in Moscow charged the Kremlin with "waging total war . . . under strict unity of command, using the USSR as base and world communism as fifth column." Officials in the State Department had also accused Soviet propagandists of directing "the skilled and disciplined fifth column operating within non-Communist states."[56] Each of those references—the "unity of command," the existence of foreign "agents," and the image of "fifth columns"—implied complete subservience to Soviet rule, the central tenet of the Communist monolith.

Allusions to Red Fascism embedded the monolith even further into popular discourse. By calling attention to "fifth columns," for example, U.S. policymakers continued to parallel the Nazi and Soviet systems. As a result, they reduced the differences between totalitarians of different and, by inference, similar stripes. So argued Assistant Secretary of State Dean Rusk, who claimed that Moscow's "true purpose" was "just as clear and understandable as the designs of Hitler came to be." Even Kennan, who earlier had denigrated such analogizing, likened the effect of a Soviet breakout beyond the Iron Curtain to a "major catastrophe, comparable to that which would have occurred had the Nazis won their war in Europe and forced England's surrender." Critics of the administration were also invoking historical precedent in their attacks on Truman's China policy. An "Oriental Munich" was how Representative Joseph Martin (R-MA), the House minority leader, described the abandonment of Chiang.[57] The illustrative power of Red Fascism exerted a similar hold on key elements of the British government. In May 1950, the Russia Committee declared flat-out that "a characteristic of the Communist State, as of the Nazi State, was the feeling that it was not secure unless it was expanding all the time." Committee members believed that both systems shared a "fully conscious" tendency toward aggression.[58]

Aside from the discursive impact of Red Fascism, references to the apocalyptic and dualistic nature of global affairs furthered the prevalence of monolithic imagery. Such rhetoric was commonplace following the twin shocks of Russia's atomic test and the establishment of Communist China. With the political momentum swinging toward the Communist camp and the fate of the world appearing to hang in the balance, U.S. officials injected a string of hyperbolic statements into their public remarks. America would thenceforth engage in "total diplomacy," as Acheson proclaimed in February 1950.[59] Two months later, the U.S. embassy in Moscow would accuse the Kremlin of "waging total war against the Free World," claiming that Russia's position as a revolutionary power meant it must either "succeed or perish."[60] The National Security Council would marshal that rhetoric as part of an equally sweeping call to arms. According to NSC 68, the Cold War had become a "worldwide" struggle pitting the forces of "freedom" against the agents of "slavery," a zero-sum game in which "a defeat for free institutions anywhere" amounted to "a defeat for free institutions everywhere." Given the "totalizing" nature of its language and its explicit rejection of ambiguity, NSC 68 stood as a model of monolithic thought.[61]

Total Diplomacy

The notion that all threats were equally perilous reflected emerging notions about the indivisibility and seamlessness of modern life, a dynamic that also buttressed the monolithic framework. As Acheson put it in April 1950, "there is no longer any difference between foreign questions and domestic questions . . . . All the problems of the United States are related to the problem of preserving its existence as the kind of a country which we know and love."[62] The *New York Times* had alluded to this dynamic the previous fall. Commenting on Acheson's redesign of the State Department's publicity machinery, it reported that primary and peripheral issues were melding into a conception of national interest that called for a more universal—in a word, "total"—approach to U.S. strategic and information policies. The financier Bernard Baruch even called for a "total peace" drive as a means of winning the Cold War. As Truman put it, America would thenceforth meet the false propaganda of Communist totalitarianism "with truth all around the globe."[63]

This language of commitment made it increasingly difficult for the United States to support countries that were trying to remain on the proverbial fence. Accordingly, the realization that some governments might choose the neutralist option continued to alarm U.S. officials. This fear burst out most openly with Indian prime minister Jawaharlal Nehru's visit to the United States in October 1949. Concern over Delhi's alignment was not as apparent in the immediate postwar period. In January 1947, prior to the promulgation of the Truman Doctrine, Secretary Marshall seemed nonplussed by India's decision to chart an "independent but cooperative" course in foreign policy. By the end of the year, however, and with superpower relations in deep decline, U.S. ambassador to India Henry Grady was disparaging that very policy in talks with Nehru. Thereafter, Washington's concern about neutrality rose in tandem with the level of East-West tension. Nevertheless, the State Department's Office of Intelligence Research viewed India's adoption of a neutral stance as more a theoretical than a practical matter. As Nehru himself had proclaimed to a joint session of Congress, India would forego neutrality "where freedom is menaced, or justice threatened." Yet Delhi's oft-repeated private pledge to side with the West in any armed struggle between the two camps was insufficiently comforting as voices in Congress, including those of Representative Walter Judd (R-MN) and others critical of the administration, condemned Indian neutrality in public.[64]

While appeals to partisanship and engagement dominated the administration's public line, in private Truman officials admitted greater tolerance for claims of neutrality, India included. Acheson received kudos in the press for his reluctance to shove nations, particularly Yugoslavia and Spain—which the United States had begun to court despite its fascist government—into one or the other camp. U.S. officials were unhappy with Nehru's neutralism, but they recognized its virtues, limited as they were. Accordingly, in late 1949, the NSC described India as a "bulwark against communist expansion." Contributing to that description, perhaps, was Nehru's newfound recognition of Ho Chi Minh's Moscow connections. U.S. officials had long been trying to educate the Indian leader on Ho's Communist orientation; by the fall of 1949, they had succeeded.[65] India's status as a nonaligned power, moreover, dovetailed neatly with American objectives, for the Truman administration had repeatedly made national sovereignty a key political goal. That stance of fierce neutrality was precisely the position the State Department was taking with regard to Yugoslavia, with officials basing their policy toward Tito largely on pragmatic, nonideological grounds. Insofar as they considered Marshal Tito's communism at all, their primary concern was that he remain a believer.[66]

But by the spring of 1950, U.S. officials and media outlets were pushing a more categorical line. Public affairs chief Edward Barrett, for instance, bemoaned the lack of unity he saw among the nations of the free world. As a whole, the non-Communist states failed to appreciate that "they are part of the battleground on which the struggle for the allegiance of man is going forward." Congress also took a more dogmatic position, as a bloc of senators declared that "no nation can be neutral" in light of the Soviet threat, "nor could any nation hope to remain neutral if a conflict were to break out." As the *New York Times* editorialized, that argument was "a plain statement of fact."[67]

One of the more public appeals for neutralism came by way of influential columnist Walter Lippmann, who took his campaign to the pages of the *Atlantic Monthly* magazine in January 1950. Lippmann based his argument on the notion that Soviet possession of the atomic bomb invalidated aspects of the NATO alliance. Previously, the prospect of mutual security had provided NATO members with a sense of protection from the nuclear umbrella; no country in Europe allied with the United States—nor any tied to the Kremlin, for that matter—wanted to be caught "between two lines of fire" without absolute assurance that their patrons would come to their defense. According to Lippmann, those security guarantees had now lost their certainty. As a result, the United States should get behind "the general tendency towards national independence, towards military neutrality, and towards diplomatic disengagement," and thereby encourage the break-up of the "two-camp" world that the Soviets were wont to affirm.[68]

Lippmann's arguments fell flat among the policymakers and the public. Perhaps this was inevitable, given the prevalence of dualistic rhetoric and a resistance to nuanced argument. The power of these dynamics was evident in the growing reluctance to distinguish between international communism and Soviet imperialism. Rarely did administration officials differentiate between the spread of communism, as an effort to further the class struggle the world over, and the extension of Moscow's power. Policymakers and journalists were also targeting the ideology of communism with increasing regularity and using it as a synonym for Soviet aggression.[69] Acheson attempted one such refinement in his January 1950 remarks to the National Press Club. While that speech is usually remembered for the secretary's exclusion of South Korea from the U.S. defensive perimeter, Acheson hoped to use it partly to quash the notion that the United States was interested merely in halting the expansion of communism around the globe. Yet in doing so he rationalized America's anti-Soviet policy in terms that described communism as "the spearhead of Russian imperialism"—a distinction without much difference. He would adopt the same stance two months later with regard to developments in Asia, asserting that the United States did not intend to tell the Chinese "what ideologies or form of government they should have," and then turning around and charging that communism was the tool "by which Soviet Russia is attempting to extend its absolute domination over the widest possible areas of the world."[70] Even though such a clarification would have served the cause of a wedge strategy, the frequency with which U.S. officials equated the two forces reflected the broader challenge not only of staying on message but of having tangible reasons for doing so.[71]

A prime example of that potent amalgam was on display in Southeast Asia. With communism and Soviet imperialism linked inextricably to each other, American officials were exceedingly wary of the newly proclaimed Democratic Republic of Vietnam (DRV) and its leader, Ho Chi Minh. Acheson had long been troubled by Ho's connection with Russia; he regarded Ho as an "outright Commie" who would inevitably throw his country into Moscow's arms—or at least Beijing's—once Vietnamese independence had been achieved. Recognition of Ho's government, Acheson argued, would inevitably strengthen Kremlin imperialism, the implication being that true Communists served the internationalist cause. As Far Eastern Affairs head Walton Butterworth put it, Ho was "working toward extending Soviet domination in Asia."[72] Several other departmental officers focused on Ho's relationship to the Kremlin.[73] Perhaps the best example of this position came from the department's William Lacy, who directed its Office of Philippine and Southeast Asian Affairs. As Lacy maintained, "our policy identifies Ho Chi Minh as a communist, therefore as an enemy and I think he should be accorded all the rights and privileges of that identification." Since such statements were not part of any "hard wedge" policy toward Ho, they reflected less a tactic designed to cause his ultimate rupture with Stalin (and/or Mao) and more an assumption of the workings of the Communist world. It was an argument that U.S. officials would make frequently in public.[74]

While Asianists in the State Department backed U.S. support for Asian nationalism, Europeanists thought such a policy would injure French efforts in Indochina, paving the way for a fully Communist DRV. Moreover, as Ambassador to France David Bruce put it, "no responsible American official" could afford to bet that Asiatic communism would be any more friendly to Washington than to Moscow.[75] Regardless, French ratification of the Elysée Accords in January 1950 led America and Great Britain to abandon any such effort as both recognized the Bao Dai government sitting atop the Associated State of Vietnam (ASV). Backed by a surging wave of anticommunism in the United States, President Truman earmarked $15 million in military assistance for Indochina. A subsequent NSC paper explicitly, and for the first time, pledged the United States to the defeat of communism in Southeast Asia.[76]

This was good news for Britain, which had been angling for such an American commitment. Whitehall desperately needed U.S. economic and perhaps military help if it was to protect Malaya (part of present-day Malaysia) from Communist expansion; its need for dollar earnings and success in convincing Washington to import Malayan rubber and tin thus marked a major step in the right direction.[77] Yet the defense of Malaya also depended on support for the French struggle against the Vietminh, support that British political and economic realities made highly problematic. London, as well as Paris, therefore recognized the value of internationalizing the Indochinese war so as to elicit American aid. Obtaining American help, as they saw it, was the key to securing

French and British interests in Southeast Asia.[78] France's restoration of former emperor Bao Dai as the new Vietnamese head of state—an attempt to undercut popular support for the Vietminh—was also instrumental. This nod in the direction of Indochinese independence paved the way for greater American involvement, helping to allay U.S. contempt for French colonial practices and Britain's remaining imperial pretensions.

More consequential, however, was the impending victory of the Communist Chinese over Chiang Kai-shek, which threatened to augment the capabilities of their ideological brethren in Vietnam. Against this background, conversations between French, British, and U.S. officials about the war in Indochina became increasingly laced with the rhetoric of anticommunism, casting the struggle as one between communism and democracy and not, as had been the case in those early postwar years, as one between nationalism and imperialism. The change in British and French rhetoric, coming in the context of a more volatile and highly charged Cold War climate in the United States, allowed for the emergence of a more hawkish American approach to Southeast Asia.[79]

Britain's interest in targeting communism itself marked a linguistic evolution designed for both local and global consumption. Although the Foreign Office had long recognized the need to invoke the specifically Communist threat on a case-by-case basis, Cold War developments now called for the tarring of its adversaries with a more ideological brush. The Malayan insurgency, which Britain had been fighting since 1948, was the proximate cause for this change in rhetoric. During the previous two years, information officers had been treating Malayan Communists as "bandits"; by the spring of 1950, they found it necessary to recast the insurgents as Communists, spurred on by and beholden to Moscow. It was both a sincere appraisal of the threat and one designed for Washington's consumption. As was true of the war in Indochina, U.S. support for British actions was much more likely if the Malayan challenge was depicted as one rooted in the exigencies of the Cold War rather than arising out of merely local grievances.[80]

This rhetorical shift was equal parts pragmatic and cynical, since British officials recognized that communism and Communist subversion presented dangers much closer to home. Although Britain never experienced an anti-Communist crusade of the magnitude waged by U.S. senator Joseph McCarthy and fellow Republicans, the Attlee government did embark on its own energetic and invasive program of surveillance and investigation. Known as "positive vetting," this enhanced effort to minimize security risks in Britain was established by a cabinet committee in the spring of 1950. The January arrest of atom spy Klaus Fuchs (and his subsequent conviction and sentencing in March) was the proximate cause for the initiative, though the momentum for "positive vetting" had increased since the creation of cabinet committees on subversive activities and communism in 1947 and 1949, respectively. Although its formation was designed to address the very real question of Soviet espionage, as demonstrated by the Fuchs case, the system was also intended to reassure the Americans, who feared British laxity on the question of domestic anticommunism. For Whitehall, the prospect of greater Anglo-American cooperation on a host of subjects, from atomic matters to military postures to informational policy, made such procedures all the more vital.[81]

That focus on communism, both domestic and foreign, became an all-consuming project and led to a more strident brand of rhetoric, especially in the United States. Even Ware Adams, who had tried so hard to inject greater subtlety into U.S. policy, found the image of Soviet Communist imperialism hard to resist. While Russian imperialism and Soviet communism were "in some ways incompatible and in conflict with each other," Adams noted, "they strongly reinforce each other in that they share in common an imperialistic drive to bring as much of the world as possible into one political system under one central control."[82] That was precisely the message going out to the American public. According to the State Department, the national press had begun to downplay the specifics of U.S.-Soviet relations in lieu of placing more emphasis on "the broad conflict between western democracy and Soviet communism."[83] By the summer of 1950, then, U.S. officials had backtracked on their earlier professed toleration of communism as an alternative, albeit misguided, program for domestic reform. Now, both they and the media would present it as indistinguishable from the Soviet worldwide offensive.

This discussion of the monolithic aspects of U.S. and British rhetoric should not obscure the many instances in which members of both governments pointed to tensions in the Communist world. The Tito heresy, as Acheson argued in private, remained "the single greatest problem to the people in the Kremlin." Commenting on the purges ravaging the French and Italian Communist parties, Acheson saw the apostolic process as already well-entrenched. Preservation of the Tito split would only increase the likelihood of similar schisms emerging elsewhere.[84] Similarly, a rift between Moscow and Beijing continued to tantalize U.S. and British diplomats, as both based their policy on one of two hopes: that Mao would break from the Kremlin along Titoist lines or that traditional Chinese dynamics would diminish the CCP's ability to govern China. With an eye toward fostering those developments, U.S. officials would try "to convince the Chinese that Communism was another name for Russian imperialism." Britain would also operate on the assumption that "Russian Imperialism and the aspirations of Chinese Nationalism" were incompatible. Provided that China was not driven further into the arms of Moscow, the Russia Committee thought "it might be possible ultimately to secure a divorce between the two."[85]

British and American officials fully recognized the disintegrative process at work and invested considerable time in cataloging its impact. Of the two diplomatic services, the Foreign Office devoted greater energy to the matter; its work on "Anti-Stalinist Communism" occupied its most senior statesmen over a period of several months and resulted in a circular memo that Bevin posted to all missions abroad. Nevertheless, the State Department had also shown great interest in the topic. Policy planners had begun to refine their position on Titoism early in 1950; intelligence analysts followed up with a similar paper in May; and both of these studies built upon earlier works dating back to June 1948. But departmental officials produced no study comparable to "Anti-Stalinist Communism," nor did their findings circulate with anything like the breadth and reach of their British counterparts. By and large, the American critique of national communism remained a compartmentalized affair, limited to relatively few officials in terms of both input and output.[86]

That disparity between the British and American approaches reflected a more general appraisal of Tito's overall significance. According to U.S. statesmen, Titoism was actually fostering as much as undermining the cohesion of the Soviet bloc. This irony was not lost on Paul Nitze, who, along with his staff, built its implications into NSC 68. It was "despite (and in part because of) the Titoist defection," they argued, that "the Soviet Union has accelerated its efforts to integrate satellite [sic] economy with its own and to increase the degree of autarchy within the areas under its control." Moreover, it was far from clear whether potential Titoists would follow in Belgrade's wake. To be sure, numerous statesmen had touched upon China's trouble with Soviet policy. Acheson had spoken of it, as had John Davies, who thought the CCP would likely split into "national" and "Kremlin" factions by the summer of 1950.[87]

Publicly, however, the United States and Great Britain continued to lump those two together. A joint statement on the subject, which emerged from the London conference of May 1950, recognized China as one of Moscow's "satellites."[88] This position remained a feature of both U.S. information policy and American trade policy throughout the spring and into the summer of 1950.[89] And it was one that officials held to in private. As Dean Rusk explained, China's leaders were "junior partners of Soviet Communism." Likewise, the U.S. consul-general in Shanghai, Walter P. McConaughy, had ventured that "no break be-tween Peiping and Moscow [was] in the offing." Although McConaughy was aware of friction between various elements of the CCP, he thought "the monolithic power structure of the party" was likely to continue.[90]

British officials remained similarly dubious of Mao's latent Titoism, as they were of Tito's impact on all of East Asia.[91] From their perspec-tive, Russia was no doubt pleased with developments in the Far East. Signs that the revolutionary process, especially in Southeast Asia, was "maturing fast" in Moscow's favor were borne out by reports of Ho Chi Minh "drawing steadily closer to the Soviet-Chinese bloc." Indeed, international communism appeared to be growing more belligerent with each passing day. When the Cominform lashed out at "deviation-ists" in the Japanese Communist Party, it marked the first time, ac-cording to British officials, that the Bucharest-based organization had endeavored to control the activities of nonmember parties.[92]

The following month, June 1950, would provide Americans and Britons, as well as their allies, with further reason to believe in the exis-tence of a Communist monolith. Once again, indications of Communist solidarity would come from Asia, the seeming focus of Soviet attention for the previous year and a half.

CHAPTER EIGHT

Korea

The call to arms that Arthur Schlesinger, Arthur Koestler, and George Orwell sounded in 1949 rang once again during the summer of 1950 as American and European intellectuals debated the future of artistic freedom in the Cold War. Gathering in Berlin for the inaugural meeting of the Congress for Cultural Freedom (CCF), a stellar cast of writers, philosophers, politicians, artists, and religious leaders gave broader, international sanction to Schlesinger's "Cold War liberalism." Identifying the "totalitarian state" as "the greatest challenge which man has been called on to meet in the course of civilised history," conference attendees condemned a wide range of Soviet practices and propaganda. As American philosopher Sidney Hook explained, much of the talk had galvanized participants into rejecting neutrality as a defensible position in the struggle for freedom. "In the face of a totalitarian threat," he wrote, "either you decide to oppose or appease." Hook's position highlighted the extent to which intellectual opinion was embracing dualistic forms. His appeal for concerted action adorned a "manifesto" the congress ratified on June 30, the fourth and last day of the event.[1]

Although many of its themes had long been central tenets of the non-Communist Left, the manifesto emerged out of specific historical circumstances, rendering it far more than just a recapitulation of liberal dogma. On June 25, 1950, just days before the conference began, the armed forces of North Korea crossed the 38th parallel into South Korea. Although North and South had skirmished repeatedly over the previous two years, this engagement was categorically different from the others, with units of the Korean People's Army (KPA) driving south across a broad front. Western leaders regarded the invasion as a new and violent manifestation of the Communist threat, signaling the emergence of a more dangerous international environment: the Kremlin's "peace" campaign had apparently given way to one of war. From the perspective of those convening in Berlin, the monolith seemed to be on the attack.

Hot war in Asia would magnify the difference between U.S. and U.K. policy toward the Sino-Soviet alliance, a relationship that had become a litmus test for American and British perceptions of international communism. Although Britain joined the American-led coalition resisting the KPA invasion—a coalition authorized by the U.N. Security Council to defend South Korea—London would now voice more stridently its commitment to wooing Beijing away from Moscow, a position that flowed logically from Britain's January 1950 decision to recognize the PRC. Washington, meanwhile, remained intransigent, rebuffing calls for a more conciliatory stance. For U.S. policymakers, the Korean War served to legitimize the hard version of the wedge strategy they had been pursuing since the previous autumn. This approach became all the more acceptable given its convergence with American political currents. Although the administration could now pursue the wedge strategy without appearing to be doing so, its policy of slights over kindnesses took on a more punitive cast. With Communist Chinese killing American and British troops above and below the 38th parallel, there was simply no constituency for pursuing a wedge strategy of any sort, much less the one favored by the Foreign Office. In the end, both British and U.S. policymakers realized that if such a break were to occur, it would likely take place much later than they had originally hoped.

The Monolith Confirmed

In the immediate aftermath of the North Korean invasion, Washington viewed the attack much as the CCF attendees had seen it from Berlin. Accordingly, U.S. officials stepped up their rhetorical assault on communism. President Truman led the barrage, ascribing the KPA assault to the predatory and opportunistic nature of the ideology itself. "The attack upon Korea," Truman argued, "makes it plain beyond all doubt that communism has passed beyond the use of subversion to conquer independent nations and will now use armed invasion and war." Secretary of State Dean Acheson and departmental consultant John Foster

Dulles were more specific in their remarks. Both attributed the invasion to a Soviet-coordinated offensive.[2]

The precise nature of the attack also buttressed the image of the monolith at work. North Korea's push along a line extending the width of the Korean peninsula seemed eerily reminiscent of a Nazi-style blitz. This action reawakened fears, barely a decade old, of naked aggression and the dangers of it letting it go unchecked. As a result, the Red Fascist analogy became encoded with new and deadly meaning.[3] Truman would thus point to an explicit link between "Fascism, nazism, [and] Soviet communism." Acheson invoked a related theme, as did Dulles, who maintained that Stalin's *Problems of Leninism*—the "present-day Communist bible except in Yugoslavia"—offered the same "preview" of world affairs that Hitler had provided with *Mein Kampf*. The frequency with which the president and other government officials appealed to both the Munich analogy and totalitarian imagery suggests that Red Fascism, during the weeks and months following the North Korean attack, was becoming an even more potent weapon in the rhetorical arsenal of American statesmen.[4]

Media comment from around the nation offered similar images of Communist behavior. Speculating on whether Korea was the "Austria of the next war," *Newsweek* wondered what "the Kremlin's precise motives may have been in stimulating this aggression." Included in its reporting were descriptions of how the "Kremlin-controlled armies of North Korea" drove south of the 38th parallel. *Time* echoed those assumptions, relaying what it termed a widespread belief that Russia "launched the Korea attack" as a "test of American determination." Political cartoons, depicting the Kremlin as the driving force behind the assault, offered further support for that view. Both *Time* and *Newsweek*, as well as publications from around the nation, welcomed Truman's decision to resist Communist expansion in Asia, with most sources attributing that expansion to a coordinated Soviet offensive. As far as the State Department's opinion analysts were concerned, the invasion was "almost unanimously considered as directed from Kremlin, as part of world-wide scheme." Commentary and observations such as these indicate that the monolithic framework had become deeply embedded in America's cultural consciousness.[5]

The fighting unleashed by North Korean leader Kim Il Sung had a similar though uneven effect in Great Britain. Reporting in the British press likened the attack to Nazi aggression, with its rapid and massive thrust along a wide front. Moreover, according to the *Times*, the invasion had come "no doubt after consultation with Moscow," a finding that placed Russia at the center of the operation. Even the Leftist *New Statesman and Nation* saw the Kremlin's hand at work, with Moscow sanctioning the invasion "to present the Americans with a fait accompli."[6] Comment in official circles was much less uniform. Although Foreign Secretary Ernest Bevin viewed the assault in the context of similar provocations in Southeast Asia, the British cabinet was unwilling to treat those incidents as part of a single piece. Its decision to downplay the conspiratorial elements of the invasion and to limit official censure to North Korea grew out of tactical considerations rather than a belief in Moscow's innocence. Pinning the blame on Russia, it believed, would only heighten international tension and open the door to a wider conflict. As a result, the Attlee government opposed the original UN statement condemning the attack. Sponsored by the United States, that resolution ascribed the invasion to "centrally directed Communist imperialism." Britain nevertheless supported the American-led coalition in its opposition to armed aggression, a position endorsed widely throughout the nation.[7]

While London was soft-pedaling the monolithic interpretation in public, British officials were taking a different line in private. Their more secretive comments testified to a belief in Soviet culpability for the attack. Officials taking that line were just as certain as their American counterparts that Moscow was calling the shots, with the Foreign Office suggesting that the Kremlin had "connived at, if they have not instigated, the aggression." It therefore embraced the U.S. military initiative with all deliberate speed. Still, the motives behind Britain's support for the UN coalition had as much to do with the past as with the present; having failed to confront Hitler during the interwar years, London would no longer acquiesce in the face of totalitarian pressure. Standing with the United States in the maintenance of collective security also suited Britain's geopolitical need to be seen as Washington's primary partner within the Western alliance.[8]

Efforts to cement that relationship picked up in the weeks following the outbreak of full-scale fighting. As part of its information campaign, the Foreign Office now pushed a more conspiratorial interpretation of the Korean War—a switch in policy that reflected growing unease over developments in Britain itself. A series of domestic disturbances, combined with mounting criticism from the British Left, had prompted the government to speak out against "fifth columns" at home and their corrosive influence on the body politic; Attlee himself warned of "the enemy within." As a result, the Information Research Department

(IRD) became more active in providing several sources, including the British Broadcasting Corporation (BBC), the Labour Party, and union leaders, with material denouncing the Korean War as a Soviet-inspired plot. It hardly needed to do so, however, to marshal support for the war. Prior to the IRD's August 1950 shift in tactics, British opinion had registered a 70 percent approval rating of the UN action. Even as public qualms became evident following the coalition's October push north of the 38th parallel, surveys continued to show widespread endorsement of the allied mission.[9]

The Wider Context

Britain had few interests in Korea proper, but its fear over the security of U.K. holdings further south elicited a more general concern over Communist encroachment in Asia. Worries that Moscow might exploit a series of national liberation movements gripped the Russia Committee within weeks of the North Korean attack. The instigator for that subversion was likely to be the People's Republic of China (PRC), which was showing no signs of divergence from the Kremlin. "Indeed," the committee noted, "the war in Korea, over which the Peking government has faithfully followed the Soviet line, has thrown China further into the Soviet camp." Various statements emanating from the PRC had confirmed for British statesmen the close coordination existing between Moscow and Beijing. And the notion that Russia remained at the center of Communist activity in Asia became a staple of British public rhetoric. Representing the United Kingdom on the UN Security Council, Sir Gladwyn Jebb cited Moscow as the motive force behind the Korean War, describing the KPA attack as Soviet-inspired aggression.[10]

American officials were equally troubled by the broader meaning of the Korean conflict. Acheson, who believed that Moscow sponsored the invasion, wondered whether Communist forces, again on the likely instigation of the Kremlin, might attack elsewhere on the continent. Southeast Asia was a prime concern for U.S. policymakers, especially for the secretary of state, who repeatedly condemned Vietnamese Communist Ho Chi Minh as a Stalinist lackey. In a similar vein, departmental counselor George F. Kennan, as well as officials responsible for Southeast Asian affairs, saw Beijing working hand-in-glove with Vietnamese Communists to undermine stability in the region. Such evidence continued to indicate that a highly coordinated, if not finely tuned, working arrangement existed within the Communist world.[11] As a result, the United States extended its defensive perimeter to Indochina, the Philippines, and Taiwan, and provided an additional $16 million in military aid for the French effort in Vietnam.[12] Policymakers deemed the aid essential as the Vietminh stepped up its effort. In September, it attacked French posts near the Chinese border, inflicting severe damage to French troops and morale. With the situation deteriorating, U.S. officials representing the State Department and the CIA found that a French defeat would turn Vietnam into a Communist satellite.[13]

Hope for a schism between Moscow and Beijing, which had been in a free-fall since late June 1950, persisted nonetheless. Since the mid-February signing of the Sino-Soviet Treaty of Friendship, U.S. efforts to drive a wedge between Stalin and Mao edged toward the "hard" version of that strategy by encouraging the Chinese to move even closer to Moscow. Washington's approach had come to resemble the process of thermonuclear fusion: the State Department would pressure China to bond with the U.S.S.R. with the aim of creating a highly combustible mix. Policies to foster such a split would now take an even more combative form, reflecting Kim Il Sung's attack on South Korea and Sino-Soviet support for the invasion. No longer would the department follow the more passive course of "watchful waiting." Truman's decision to neutralize Taiwan during the first days of the Korean War, which was sure to draw the wrath of Communist China, signaled the president's willingness to drop any pretense of cordiality toward the PRC.[14]

Whitehall, however, maintained its interest in a "softer" approach to the Chinese Communists. The differences between the U.S. and British strategies, evident since late 1949 in discussions over PRC recognition, had resurfaced in April 1950 during talks between Charles E. Bohlen, one of the State Department's Soviet experts, and Esler Dening, an Asian specialist at the Foreign Office. According to Dening, Britain would maintain an open channel to Beijing, hoping to increase its chances of driving a wedge between the two Communist states. "Unless Mao were assured of some possibility of contact," Dening warned, "he might reach the conclusion that there was no other course than to turn himself exclusively to the Soviet Union." Bohlen thought the United States could not afford to base its policy "on the expectation of Communist China splitting away from the Soviet world." Although he failed to raise it in his exchange with Dening, that was precisely the outcome the "hard wedge" strategy sought to effect.[15]

U.S. officials, therefore, were closing the very doors that Britain wanted to leave open. Nowhere was this more clear than in the depiction of communism and Soviet imperialism as identical evils. Interest in disentangling those two forces, which had begun to ebb prior to the Korean War, had all but disappeared after June 1950. America's more aggressive rhetorical campaign thus featured international communism as one of at least four terms that U.S. statesmen were using as shorthand for a Soviet-led Communist conspiracy. The others—Communist imperialism, Soviet imperialism, and Soviet communism—all seemed to work interchangeably. Truman himself was fond of citing "Communist imperialism" as a force capable of weakening and overthrowing free nations; Ambassador Warren Austin used the same phrase liberally at the United Nations, as did John C. Ross, Austin's deputy on the Security Council. Ross actually melded the various epithets together, referring to the "imperialism of Soviet communism" and derivatives thereof to make his point.[16] None of those constructions emerged simply by happenstance. The public affairs staff at the State Department was hard at work crafting guidance papers, offering these and other stock phrases to information officers at home and abroad.[17]

Recapturing the Psychological Initiative

The administration's rhetorical campaign received added institutional support in early July 1950 when Senator William Benton (D-CT) sponsored a resolution calling for a greatly expanded program of information and education to counteract Soviet propaganda. Benton, who ran the State Department's Office of Public Affairs from 1945 to September 1947, had previously expressed the need for such an initiative in March 1950, and his earlier remarks had helped clear a path for the administration's "Campaign of Truth." The North Korean attack now made that crusade all the more important. Depicting the Cold War as a "contest for the minds and loyalties of men," Benton and his colleagues likened their project to a Marshall Plan in the field of ideas. It was a theme that U.S. publicity officials, including Director of Public Affairs Francis Russell, would often repeat.[18]

Further aid for that program came in August when the State Department announced the establishment of a national psychological strategy board. As the Benton group noted, the board and the attendant Campaign of Truth would require the "total mobilization and total engagement" of the nation's psychological and spiritual forces. While the Psychological Strategy Board (PSB) did not begin operations until April 1951, planning for its creation accompanied a series of measures,

including the organization of East European émigrés and radio broadcasts into their homelands, designed to accelerate the forces of disintegration that Tito had loosed behind the Iron Curtain. It was a policy
that built on previous interest in using the Voice of America and on
joint Anglo-American planning.[19]

But Tito himself was not proving to be the disruptive force that officials had envisioned. His interest in charting a course independent of
both East and West, moreover, worried American statesmen. On the
whole, they appreciated the merits of a truly neutral Communist
state—in contrast to the demerits of a neutral democratic state—and
recognized, however grudgingly, the value of Yugoslavia's "no" vote on
the Security Council's Korean resolution. Yet Belgrade's position at the
United Nations presented U.S. officials with the problem of how to sell
"Titoism" to the American people. This was an especially difficult task
during the summer of 1950. Given Yugoslavia's resistance to the Korean resolution and its reluctance to contribute to the coalition force,
the benefits of supporting a nonaligned Tito, particularly when American boys were dying in East Asia, seemed minimal. The State Department's Roy Melbourne, a member of the Office of Eastern European
Affairs, realized how such a scenario might have looked to the public.
Americans, he argued, "may increasingly feel that fundamental issues
should be clear-cut between democracy and Communism." If Yugoslavia continued to pursue its own self-interest, maintaining its distance
between the eastern and western blocs, U.S. citizens might come to regard Titoism as a force of questionable value. In the event they did so,
the public's ability "to distinguish between Titoism and Kremlinism,"
as Melbourne put it, would probably shrink to nil.[20]

If the administration was eager for the public to make such fine distinctions, its portrayals of communism as the great evil—and its tendency
to equate communism with Soviet imperialism—hardly encouraged
such subtle thought. The paradox was not lost on Charlton Ogburn, a
member of the Bureau of Far Eastern Affairs, who, like Ware Adams
and John Davies before him, wanted policymakers to revise their
image of the Communist movement. Boiler-plate attacks on ideology
and pledges to save the Far East from communism, Ogburn maintained, only strengthened the appeal of what must appear to native
populations as forbidden fruit. Moreover, such rhetoric seemed to run
afoul of U.S. pledges to refrain from meddling in the affairs of independent states. Ogburn therefore saw little choice but to present communism as "basically a well-meaning political philosophy which has

never worked and never will, but that if it is what a particular people wants to try, we cannot object." In fact, he argued, U.S. officials should stop referring to the Soviets as Communists at all. "In our new lexicon," Communists were to be treated as "misled zealots," naïve idealists with unworkable political and economic doctrines who either sold out their country to the Russians or were eliminated by their Soviet handlers. The "thugs" in Moscow, however, were to be labeled as "Red Fascists."[21]

As Ogburn's memo indicates, the image of Red Fascism continued to appear in official statements, assuming a prominent place in American rhetoric on the Korean conflict. Truman invoked it again in a September radio address to the nation. Only a few years ago, the president observed, "Hitler and the Japanese generals" had wrongly assumed that the West would roll over in the face of totalitarian aggression. "Let would be aggressors make no such mistake today," he warned. The Munich scenario—a riff on the Red Fascist theme—was currently the most potent strain of such imagery and appealed to a wide range of officials and publicists. But that image dovetailed with those of Soviet and Communist imperialism. During his September radio speech, Truman pinned full responsibility for the fighting in Korea on Moscow, indicting "Communist imperialism" for the threat it posed to the "free world." Ambassador to Russia Alan G. Kirk thought it a "great forward stride" in the effort "to convict [the] Soviet Union as [an] active and ubiquitous inciter [of] present world tension." According to Kirk, "neither China, North Korea nor any other satellite would move without impulse from Moscow and that is what we should make clear to world public opinion." He therefore recommended that future statements continue to employ "Soviet imperialism" as the administration's term of choice since "communism," as Ogburn had earlier pointed out, carried positive connotations with many peoples.[22]

Kirk's peers at the British embassy in Moscow conveyed similar thoughts to their superiors back in London. The word "Communist," they argued, was ill-suited for use abroad, especially "in propaganda directed to any 'Communist' country or fellow-travelling audience."[23] Nevertheless, it had "the right sort of connotation for an average Western audience," precisely because it had come to stand as a term of abuse. So, too, had Red Fascism, for just as U.S. officials recognized the value of pairing the Soviets with the Nazis, leading members of the Foreign Office, such as Ralph Murray and Christopher Warner, were calling for an even more vigorous application of such imagery.[24]

Although British officials had long demonstrated a preference for this phraseology, the language of Red Fascism seemed contrary to their preference for a more benign approach to communism in Asia. Analogies that presented totalitarian movements as mirror images of each other seemed more tailored to the ends of the "harder" policy the Americans were pursuing. By locking all Communists into a single category, London appeared to be pushing each and every Marxist toward Moscow. While the Americans showed little conscious interest in suffusing their "hard wedge" propaganda with Red Fascist imagery, the two brands of rhetoric complemented each other, indicating a degree of strategic consistency. The British, however, while trying to tease the Chinese away from Russia through a more "benign" policy, continued to employ the more hard-line rhetoric of Red Fascism, a development attributable to hawkish cant of the IRD.

Titoism Reconsidered—Again

While British and American officials were trying to finesse the rhetoric of bloc-busting, the UN military coalition was hoping to create some wedges of its own. By late summer, its troops had achieved a remarkable turnaround in its war against the North Koreans. Those victories had come only after dramatic losses during the opening rounds of the conflict. Throughout the last week of June and all of July, the KPA had driven the combined forces of South Korea and the United Nations far to the south of the 38th parallel. Allied commander General Douglas A. MacArthur had managed to stave off defeat by holding onto Pusan, the southeastern tip of the Korean peninsula. After retooling his armies over the next several weeks, MacArthur launched a dramatic offensive from the western port of Inchon, cutting the KPA in half. His mid-September gambit was a stunning success; coalition forces recaptured Seoul within the week, pinned down the North Koreans, reclaimed previously lost territory, and began to go on the offensive. By the first week of October, MacArthur was advancing beyond the 38th parallel into North Korea.[25]

With the coalition having successfully split the various units of the KPA, Western policymakers continued to ruminate on strategic approaches to fracturing the Communist world. American plans for psychological warfare proceeded apace, rooted in the general assumption that Titoism, or national communism, remained a thorn in Russia's side. According to the CIA, the cleavage between Belgrade and the

Kremlin had widened appreciably over the last two years, paving the way for additional splits. From its vantage point in September 1950, the agency believed that "the Titoist alternative to Kremlin-dominated Communism" still constituted "a dangerous ideological threat to the Soviet monolithic structure." Yet the viability of Titoism was largely bound up with the ongoing existence of Tito himself, and the prospects for his survival appeared shaky. Yugoslavia's economy was in shambles, due mostly to a tremendous shortfall in food production. Belgrade's attempt to collectivize its agricultural sector had been a disaster; the onset of drought conditions only worsened the situation. Indeed, the CIA and the State Department argued that the continued economic deterioration of Yugoslavia would undoubtedly weaken Tito and limit the overall appeal of national communism. Continued sniping from the Kremlin and its satellites added to the fears of a people under siege. Hoping to get out from under those clouds, Tito appealed to the West for economic aid and military support.[26]

The Truman administration rallied to his cause. U.S. officials convinced the Export-Import Bank in August 1950 to approve another credit, this time for $15 million, toward the purchase of vital American goods.[27] Over the next several months, they also succeeded in securing funds for Tito through the Economic Cooperation Administration and the Mutual Defense Assistance Program, actions that found "widespread agreement" in the national media.[28] The wedge strategy, therefore, assumed multiple guises, including one for Communists who had already left the Kremlin fold and another for those who still remained part of the Stalinist program.

The administration raised cautionary flags, however, indicating that such policies were not likely to yield quick returns. Warning the public of the challenges inherent in cracking the Soviet monolith, Secretary of State Acheson delivered a sobering message during a mid-September television appearance. Answering questions on the talk show *Diplomatic Pouch*, he thought it "very difficult to expect the sort of break between the Communists in the Eastern European satellite states and the Russians such as you have in Yugoslavia." Poles, Czechs, Hungarians, Romanians, and Bulgarians had all "pretty well lost the power to revolt at the present time." While those peoples might one day reacquire that strength, they were not likely "to declare their independence as the Yugoslavs have." Helping them to realize their freedom would require patience. "This isn't going to be a short effort and it isn't going to be an easy one," Acheson told his interviewer. "This is a tough job."[29]

And so government officials continued to pursue the wedge strategy, by tangible as well as rhetorical means, in the face of numerous obstacles to its success. John Paton Davies, one of its more forceful proponents, argued that the United States should exploit the "organic lines of fission in the Soviet monolith" that ran between the Kremlin and the Soviet public, between the Great Russians and the peoples of the Soviet republics, and between the U.S.S.R. and the satellite states. Policies to subvert Communist rule, such as those being undertaken clandestinely, were to be accompanied by pointed verbal attacks. Davies therefore suggested the use of various phrases to promote further discord among East European cadres. "Liberation from Kremlin tyranny," he noted, "should be the central idea," a policy designed to chip away at the Soviet bloc. With the emergence of Chinese "Titoism" only a "remote" possibility, Davies supported the administration's "harder" approach toward Chinese communism, advocating a more hostile and interventionist stance against the PRC. It was a posture fully in accord with the U.S. trade embargo on China, imposed prior to the war, as well as with Truman's decision to insert the Seventh Fleet in the Taiwan Straits, an action he took during the first week of fighting.[30]

China Intervenes

That more antagonistic approach to Beijing would become even more hostile as a result of wartime developments. Having pushed the North Koreans back across the 38th parallel in September 1950, UN forces regrouped and planned their next move. MacArthur and Truman met at Wake Island during October to establish military strategy for the ensuing campaign. Continued operations in the north, the general promised, would bring the war to a close by Christmas. With Truman's blessing, MacArthur returned to Korea and pursued the enemy toward the Yalu River and the Manchurian border. But his forces soon found themselves confronting not only North Korean but Chinese fighting units. By the first week of November, elements of the People's Liberation Army (PLA) were streaming across the Yalu, lending credence to Mao's earlier promise of protecting Chinese interests. London and Washington considered a joint response; in the interim, MacArthur took his fight to the PLA, making it difficult for him to disengage even if ordered to do so. By the end of the month, he was confronting a force of more than 200,000 Chinese Communists, rendering hollow his earlier promise of a December victory.[31]

Although it was the PRC that had intervened in the conflict, U.S. observers still saw Soviet hands at work. Both the State Department and CIA regarded Beijing as a willing accomplice of Moscow. U.S. media outlets were equally convinced that China was acting as a Soviet pawn and regarded its military intervention as an ominous development. The *New York Herald Tribune,* for instance, sought to hold Moscow and "its Chinese Communist satellite" to a full and public accounting of their actions. The *New York Post* took a similar though tangential line, describing China's entrance into the war as "a blow to those who have confidently depicted Mao as a budding Titoist." Columnist Anne O'Hare McCormick, writing in the *New York Times,* anticipated a coming "Mao-Stalin partnership" for the conquest of the West.[32]

The administration was only slightly less explicit in its public comment. Truman defined the Chinese intervention as "part of a worldwide pattern of danger to all the free nations of the world," leaving little doubt as to where he stood on the question of its conspiratorial origins. Not all government officials adopted this line, however. Dean Rusk, Truman's assistant secretary of state for Far Eastern Affairs, stopped short of calling the invasion a Chinese-Soviet plot. He ticked off several reasons why China might have acted as it did, only one of which included an outright charge of collaboration between Moscow and Beijing. Acheson also sought to check public talk of Soviet-Chinese collusion, suggesting that reference to Soviet perfidy would only complicate efforts to end the war. Nevertheless, both he and Rusk continued to see Stalin as the prime mover. Acheson urged Chinese leaders not to be "dupes," while Rusk was quick to point out that Kim Il Sung and the KPA were receiving assistance from Soviet and Chinese sources, a development that was highly suggestive in and of itself. Although the consistent application of "hard wedge" rhetoric called for blanket condemnation of Communist treachery, such language, when used in a hot-war scenario, created problems that the secretary apparently preferred not to face. A frank discussion of actual Soviet involvement in the Korean War—which was substantial—would only have made a terribly difficult situation that much more challenging.[33]

In contrast to the United States, Great Britain tended to see the intervention as a product of national rather than international concerns. Security imperatives and not ideology, argued the British media, were the primary forces behind China's push south of the Yalu.[34] The Foreign Office shared that assessment and questioned whether Moscow desired a widening of the war. If discussions about the proposed offensive had taken place between Moscow and Beijing, argued British policymakers, there was good reason to think the Kremlin would have counseled *against* it. China's war against the Western powers increased the risk of a general conflagration; yet such a conflict, according to the Russia Committee, "is believed to be contrary to current Soviet policy." Still, officials noted Moscow's interest in "leaving China, in appearance, to make the running in the East." Presumably, Russia was getting what it wanted out of the PRC. British statesmen even described China's invasion of Tibet in October as "a carefully calculated part of the Russia plan," the objective of which was to increase "Communist infiltration into India." Bevin himself thought it "reasonable to assume coordination of policy between Moscow and Peking, particularly as this is provided for in the Sino-Soviet Treaty."[35] While Chinese actions might well have originated out of nationalist or security concerns, British observers still believed that Mao was operating according to an internationalist agenda.

Divergent Appraisals

With the tables now turned on the UN coalition, Truman intimated that he might spin them right back on the Communists in a most dramatic fashion. At the end of November, he raised the possibility of using nuclear weapons to alter the course of the conflict. This was a startling proposal to be sure, but not so much as it might have seemed; the bomb, Truman told a reporter, was always under "active consideration." But America's partners would have nothing to do with atomic warfare. Truman's comments gave rise to a full-fledged peace movement in Britain, capturing the sympathies of voters across the political spectrum. Conservative members of Parliament joined with their Labourite colleagues in voicing objection to Truman's bluster, wondering where their relationship with America was leading. Hours after learning of Truman's remarks, Prime Minister Clement Attlee requested an urgent meeting with the president. Before the end of the week he would be in Washington, where he would represent the interests of several nations determined to rein in a government that was quickly losing credibility with its own allies.[36]

The difference between British and American thinking became readily apparent as the Washington talks got under way. Most evident was the allies' divergent interpretations of Chinese belligerence and their implications for policy toward the PRC. Attlee called for a complete reversal of U.S. strategy in East Asia: the United States should abandon its protection of Taiwan, pave the way for China to gain admission to the United Nations, and accede to the North and South Korean armies resuming their positions on opposite sides of the 38th parallel. Secretary of State Acheson rejected the approach out of hand, believing it was grounded in a fundamental misreading of the Sino-Soviet working relationship. Whereas Attlee believed it "a mistake to think that the Chinese would necessarily be subservient in all things to Moscow," Acheson, as well as newly installed defense secretary George C. Marshall, regarded China as "little more than a Russian satellite."

President Truman was even more categorical, vowing that Beijing would continue to function as a Soviet appendage; the only way the West could deal with communism, he argued, was to "eliminate" it altogether. Regarding the "nationalist aspirations" of formerly colonial peoples, Acheson doubted whether Britain or the United States could give more weight to these concerns, as Attlee had recommended, "in the immediate future." The Truman administration had to remain committed to the Korean War and its hostility toward China if only to maintain a consistent forward posture in both Asia and Europe. To do otherwise, he believed, would "fatally undermine the whole moral basis of American policy" and confuse public opinion. Any conciliatory approach toward Beijing was now out of the question. Having been "bloodied" by his belief in the possibility of a Sino-Soviet split, as well as by Republican attacks on his handling of China and State Department "subversives," Acheson now saw no way to achieve that goal in light of the toxic political environment.[37]

Political realities, therefore, were working against a more subtle approach to foreign affairs. American policy would therefore continue to vilify China; it was almost beside the point that such hostility coincided with the administration's "hard" approach to the wedge strategy. In due course, the United States tightened its embargo on exports to Beijing, prohibiting all shipments to the mainland, and froze all Chinese assets in the United States. According to Acheson, those measures were necessary as long as the PRC continued to aid the objectives of international communism.[38]

Yet the American public was hearing that China might not always furnish such aid. Rekindling aspects of the wedge strategy's more benign strain, Truman began to suggest that Chinese and Soviet interests really *were* different. One month after China had entered the Korean War, the president still held out hope that its people would resist being "forced or deceived into serving the ends of Russian colonial policy in Asia." Edward Barrett, the administration's point man on public affairs, also summoned the ghost of policy past. "We do feel," he argued, that "we can make at least an appreciable impression on some of the Communist leaders and subleaders with information designed to convince them that, if they persist in their present course, it will eventually mean their own ruin."[39] Apparently, the wedge strategy, or at least its rhetorical component, was still in a state of flux. While neither the "hard" nor the "soft" approach had emerged as the clear choice of administration personnel, both versions were grounded in the assumption that the strategy, if it was to be effective at all, would reap its rewards at some later date.

Aid to Yugoslavia

Support for the wedge strategy was dependent, in part, on the continued survival of Tito's national Communist state, which served as the very symbol of what the strategy sought to achieve. By December 1950, public backing for Yugoslavia appeared to be on the rise. According to opinion analysts at the State Department, press comment was focusing on Tito's economic and humanitarian troubles, as well as on pressure he was receiving from the Soviet bloc. Such reporting tended to emphasize the strategic rather than the ideological objectives of U.S. policy. As portrayed in the media, American action was "not directed at the overthrow of Communism per se, but at checking Soviet aggression." Nevertheless, several observers held that communism was not only a bane wherever it existed, but that Truman officials were actively supporting Communist regimes. The McCormick press, for example, headlined by the *Chicago Tribune,* demanded that aid to Yugoslavia be contingent on Tito's abandonment of his "whole Communist program." By and large, however, the media seemed to have bought into the assumptions of the wedge strategy. Its recognition that Tito was worth supporting, if only for his "nuisance" value, suggests that national communism, as a legitimate force independent of Kremlin control, had achieved general acceptance among the public at large, even if it had lost particular relevance for the Communist Chinese.[40]

While the State Department had long been aiming at such a response, it was now even more skeptical of Titoism as a bloc-busting force. By early November, its Office of Intelligence Research (OIR) had evaluated the prospects for dissension in the Communist world and found them to be sorely lacking. The Stalinist system had "met the test," for Tito's actions had not resulted in "broad or deep factional dissension within the world Communist movement." Additional defections in vital areas were unlikely, since "the basic requirements for defection appear only in China, Vietnam, and Albania, and in these countries there is little immediate prospect of it." Although Yugoslavia's continued existence outside the Soviet sphere sent a powerful message to potential heretics, its status as an independent carried little real weight. The Soviets would therefore "continue to command the instrument of world Communism." A CIA study completed two weeks later arrived at a similar conclusion. Analysts had detected considerable patriotic sentiment in Eastern Europe, but they found "no present evidence to indicate that it would give rise to further successful nationalist deviations on Titoist lines."[41]

Against the backdrop of these studies, Truman submitted to Congress a $38 million emergency aid package for Yugoslavia. It was a curious proposal, for having just discounted the impact of Titoism on the Communist world, the administration was now seeking to promote it nonetheless. In so doing, policymakers displayed the various tensions that marked their policies toward schismatic communism. And once again, the quixotic belief in its theoretical value trumped the many indications of its practical irrelevance.[42]

Congressional hearings on Yugoslav assistance brought these discussions of Tito and national communism out into the open. Although both had been subjects of debate during the administration's wrangles with Congress over aid to the Chinese Nationalists, this was the first time that the legislature was explicitly considering the prospect of supporting a Communist state. President Truman, anticipating the arguments against the aid bill, declared that support for Tito did not indicate support for Tito's policies; the United States was "unalterably opposed to international communism wherever it exists." Nevertheless, the administration sought to extend such aid because "Tito espouses nationalist communism rather than imperialist communism, which seeks to bind all Communists to the Kremlin." Although he was crediting Titoism with more energy and agency than it had thus far displayed, Truman made the case, in the most basic terms, for fighting fire with fire. In November 1950, administration officials and friendly legislators joined him in that effort in testimony before the Senate Foreign Relations Committee and the House Committee on Foreign Affairs. George W. Perkins, assistant secretary of state for European Affairs, described Yugoslavia as one of America's best assets in its struggle with the Kremlin. Further support for the aid bill came from Democratic senators Brien McMahon (CT), J. William Fulbright (AR), and Foreign Relations Committee chair Tom Connally (TX). According to Connally, the United States simply had to preserve Tito's independence in the face of "Soviet imperialism."[43]

Backers of Yugoslav aid appeared to hold commanding majorities in both houses of Congress, but opponents of the bill, most of whom were Republican, attacked its assumptions with gusto. According to Representative Lawrence H. Smith (R-WI), working with Tito would be like doing "business with the Devil." It would rank as an "unadulterated compromise" if the administration was to embrace the Yugoslav leader in order to counter Stalin, Mao, and like-minded dictators. "Do we favor just a little bit of Communism?" Smith asked. If so, such cynicism was "diabolical" and would eventually "lead to the same failure as our appeasement policy has with Stalin." Senator John L. McClellan (R-AR) took an even more dogmatic view of the situation. "A Communist is a Communist," he maintained, an assumption that cast the Tito-Stalin feud as entirely superficial. Representative Owen D. Brewster (R-ME) made much the same point and criticized the administration for believing otherwise. He repudiated the notion that Mao and his ilk were proto-Titoists, observing that Chinese Communists were presently "butchering Americans in cold blood" on the Korean peninsula. "If that is what Titoism means in China," Brewster asked, "why should we expect something different in Yugoslavia?" Given what the State Department and CIA had already concluded about the prospects for Titoism in both the near and distant future, it was a question for which the administration had no easy answer. Nevertheless, Congress passed the bill with large majorities in both houses, and Truman signed the legislation—the Yugoslav Emergency Relief Assistance Act of 1950—just days before the start of the new year.[44]

The Framework Finalized

The political environment of late 1949 onward had not been very conducive to the public conversation that figures such as Ware Adams, John Davies, and Charlton Ogburn deemed essential. But the climate of post-June 1950 proved entirely inhospitable to any such discussion. The year ended with President Truman delivering a series of alarming addresses on what he called the "national emergency." Raising the pitch of contemporary rhetoric, Truman declared that "our homes, our Nation, all the things we believe in" had been endangered by "the rulers of the Soviet Union," the masters of "Communist imperialism." The nature of that threat was plain for all to see. Amplifying themes that had become part of his Cold War rhetoric, the president defined the Cold War as an apocalyptic struggle between the forces of freedom and those of communism.[45]

In personalizing that struggle for Americans, Truman depicted the Cold War as an allegory for the national saga. According to the president, the "revolutionary idea" that had guided the American experiment—the "idea of human freedom and political equality"—was entirely antithetical to the one propounded by "the forces of Communist imperialism." Repeated reference to the Liberty Bell, to the concept of freedom as enshrined in the Constitution, and to the nation's early stand against tyranny grounded administration rhetoric in America's historic legacy. Secretary of State Acheson even treated the Korean War as an opportunity to reaffirm the virtues of American political life.[46] But officials also placed the Cold War within a much larger and more enduring framework extending back to antiquity. As Truman told the nation in early September, the soldiers fighting in Korea were "engaged once more in the age-old struggle for human liberty."[47]

Although British leaders clearly differed in their assessment of China's role in the conflict, the Korean War sparked similar though more muted rhetorical flourishes from the Labour cabinet. As Foreign Secretary Bevin had proclaimed in Parliament earlier that March, "Western civilization is worth saving." Indeed, it had to be saved, and the only way to do so was in concert with the other nations of the West. "If that combination grows," he stated, "I visualize a long peace." Likewise, Prime Minister Clement Attlee maintained that "the preservation of the free and democratic life of the peoples of the world" depended on Anglo-American cooperation. Such talk was part and parcel of efforts to depict the Cold War as a timeless struggle for the safeguarding of their historic legacy. In Britain, it was a rhetoric shorn of the providential content that was so conspicuous in the United States, but its focus on freedom and liberty resonated in Britain nonetheless. In its American guise, it was a microcosm of the timeless battle between good and evil—the Manichean struggle that, for generations of Americans as well as Englishmen, was the very engine of history.[48]

That struggle took form according to the events of the day. Contemporary rhetoric, therefore, evoked the image of totalitarianism as the source of modern servitude, with the onset of the Korean War injecting new life into the language of Red Fascism. Britons continued to invoke its lessons in their publicity efforts. Patrick Gordon Walker, for example, the secretary of state for commonwealth relations, saw the writings of Lenin and Stalin as the keys that would unlock the mysteries of the Kremlin. As he observed, "from these fundament teachings the whole of Communist and Soviet behaviour draws its inspiration." Accordingly, those works stood "in the same relations [*sic*] to Soviet foreign policy as Hitler's *Mein Kampf* did to Nazi policy." As illustrated previously, IRD and Russia Committee members frequently resorted to Red Fascist imagery and considered several of its variations before settling on the most potent one of the lot.[49]

Americans were at least as fond of the analogy as the British and perhaps were even more prone to view totalitarians as part of a single breed. Not surprisingly, the Korean War launched a new and more substantial wave of such rhetoric upon the United States. From *Newsweek's* provisional depiction of Korea as the "Austria" of the next war to Truman's proscription of "appeasement," the lessons of the past seemed supremely relevant to the troubles of the present. Munich, Truman argued, had taught the world that security came with costs. But the perils of yesterday seemed only a faint shadow of the more current threat. According to William Sanders, a State Department official for UN affairs, the "Axis totalitarians" were mere novices compared to "the Kremlin experts." Delineating the nature of the two evils, Sanders remarked that "the geopolitical doctrines and the *lebensraum* of the Nazis" had been "replaced in our time by the ideological claustrophobia of the Soviets as a threat to world peace."[50]

Some of the government officials who criticized the rhetoric of Red Fascism warned that the condemnation of all totalitarians—be they red, black, or brown—risked sabotaging aspects of administration policy, especially those elements that depended on the strategic use of former Nazis and Communists. Washington had long recognized the utility of individuals such as Louis Budenz, Elizabeth Bentley, and Whittaker Chambers—one-time Communists turned professional anti-Communists—as witnesses for the prosecution of Soviet imperialism. The services provided by former Nazi Wernher von Braun to the U.S. missile program would prove arguably even more valuable. As Charles Bohlen stated in April 1950, those formerly tied to totalitarian movements were in "the best position to expose the realities of how Russian-controlled international communism really operates."[51]

The Internal Security Act of 1950, however, proposed by Senator Pat McCarran (D-NV), would have prevented the administration from employing onetime fascists for scientific, propagandistic, or other vital purposes. According to the State Department's Policy Committee on Immigration and Naturalization (PCIN), this "indiscriminate classification" of reformed totalitarians "with our real enemies, the Communists, threatens the whole fabric of our policies and objectives, including the primary objective of assuring the security of the United States." While Congress chose not to incorporate these objections into its security legislation, the PCIN nevertheless illustrated the drawbacks of promoting the imagery and substance of the Red Fascist idea.[52] More than that, however, it highlighted the shortcomings of the monolithic framework itself—a flaw that was becoming more difficult to correct now that the Korean War had embedded its assumptions and premises more deeply into the American political consciousness.

Efforts to disentangle the workings of ideology from those of state behavior virtually disappeared as American officials equated international communism and Soviet imperialism with greater regularity. As portrayed by the State Department's Office of Intelligence Research, the indivisibility of those two forces had become an article of faith among administration personnel. According to the OIR, the machinations of both the Soviets and the leaders of the East European CPs had tied international communism "indissolubly . . . to the thread of Russian imperialism." Even in the best of times, isolating one dynamic from the other would have been no mean feat. In the context of Communist aggression—by the North Koreans, by the Communist Chinese, and with the seeming acquiescence and encouragement of Soviet Russia—it had become a practical impossibility.[53]

And so government officials littered their public statements with those ideological formulations. Truman continued to attack "Communist imperialism," describing it as "a reactionary movement that despises liberty and is the mortal foe of personal freedom." Congressional supporters such as Tom Connally also spoke out against Communist imperialism, characterizing it as an "organism of evil" that was "attacking the international body at many vital points." State Department officials were even more explicit in their depiction of communism as the handmaiden of Soviet rule. Attributing China's intervention in Korea to "the decision of international Communist masters," publicity chief Edward Barrett treated that development as a problem "of almost unprecedented gravity." Dean Acheson and Dean Rusk were equally condemnatory in their remarks, with Acheson characterizing the North Korean aggression as "part of the world-wide operations of the international Communist movement." The Korean conflict therefore gave an added boost to the identification of international communism with Soviet imperialism, compounding the problems of those who sought to isolate "national" Communists from "international" ones.[54]

The Foreign Office was similarly fond of the parallels between international communism and Soviet imperialism, and became increasingly so throughout the course of the war. In the immediate aftermath of the North Korean attack, the British cabinet had specifically rejected this phraseology, but with the war's twists and turns such rhetoric soon became more acceptable. The conflation of Russian and Communist impulses was particularly evident in Britain's overseas propaganda. Officials in the strategic outpost of Malaya deemed it "no longer necessary to avoid making clear publicly the connection between the Malayan Terrorist Movement and Communism as an internationally organized and centrally controlled force."[55] Although they recognized the limitations of invoking "communism" as an epithet in their foreign broadcasts, British officials retained its use for publicity at home. Apparently, no one in the Foreign Office was prepared to remove the word from Britain's domestic information program.[56] In England, as in America, the image of a monolithic communist movement prevailed. Given the range of opinion on how best to prosecute a wedge-busting strategy, however, it was an image more suited to U.S. than British tactical objectives.

As for the term itself, U.S. public relations officers continued to make specific reference to the "monolith," though in a limited way. Perhaps its most promiscuous use came at the hands of Francis Russell, director of the State Department's Office of Public Affairs, who during the course of a single August speech spoke of a "monolithic organization," a "monolithic structure," and a "monolithic state." By invoking the term, Russell seemed to be endowing it with multiple meanings. For as much as he used it in a literal sense to describe contemporary "Soviet" and "Communist" realities, he appeared to be questioning its usefulness in future situations. Over the long haul, Russell noted, "the effort of the Kremlin to make all decisions affecting the daily lives of hundreds of millions of people over vast stretches of territory will result in stresses and strains and progressive disintegration." Edward Barrett, Russell's immediate superior in the department, harbored a similar ambivalence about "monolithic" rhetoric. Like Russell, Barrett portrayed the Communist system as a "monolithic dictatorship." But his depiction of Soviet power revealed soft spots through which Western propagandists might target Moscow's dishonesty and duplicity. Publicity officers, therefore, sought to undermine the monolithic image by challenging the notion of Soviet omnipotence. Seeking to highlight Soviet "blunders," Barrett, in October 1950, noted the "psychological opportunity" that Tito provided the West. Moscow no doubt would continue to commit blunders, but given the global prospects for Titoism, capitalizing on those missteps would not be easy.[57]

For neither British nor Americans observers were optimistic about the possibility of driving wedges between Communist states and parties. Mass support for the wedge strategy seemed to hinge on the public's willingness to court potential as well as actual heretics. But the American public, as British officials realized, was unlikely to accept such a scheme. According to the Southern Department's Sir Hugh Stephenson, Americans were "less likely to distinguish between brands of Communism and more likely to agree to help being given to a Communist State if that State has already come out into the open and aligned itself with the United Nations against Soviet Communist aggression." Yugoslavia had certainly denounced such aggression, but it had also spoken out against *all* imperialist aggression, whether it was Eastern or Western in origin. From Stephenson's perspective in July 1950, neutralism thus posed a problem for Americans, which he ascribed to their "having heard of the evils of Communism in and out of season."[58] That was precisely the argument that State Department official Roy Melbourne had made the same month. Yet the virtues of anti-neutralism appealed to high-brow and low-brow alike. Delegates to the founding of the Congress for Cultural Freedom, a purportedly more sophisticated lot, were equally contemptuous of the well-meaning bystander. "Indifference or neutrality in the face of such a challenge," they maintained, "amounts to a betrayal of mankind and to the abdication of the free mind."[59]

But if the goal was now to take a more active, interventionist position toward Communist states—in effect, to *welcome* their hostility—did it not actually pay to whip up indiscriminate anticommunism in the service of a highly discriminating policy? As the State Department noted in late September, "there has been almost universal acceptance of the assumption that the Soviet Union bears responsibility for the North Korean attack." The press rendered a similar judgment after the Chinese

intervention in November. Put another way, did administration officials embrace, if not outright promote, a simplistic view of the Communist world in order to help them manage its complexity?[60]

The documentary record is still silent on this point. Moreover, it is
far from clear whether policymakers approved the emerging "hard" approach toward Communist entities. The generally positive reaction to
Charlton Ogburn's memo of September 1950, in which Ogburn called
for a moratorium on anti-Communist rhetoric, suggests that they had
their doubts about the "hard" wedge solution. Cover notes to the brief
indicate that the Policy Planning Staff had "carefully considered" its
contents, endorsed its recommendations, and sent it up to several assistant secretaries of state. Suffice it to say that U.S. officials were not entirely settled on the "fusion" tactics of the "hard" approach.[61]

British statesmen, who had also moved toward a harder brand of
propaganda, apparently did so without grounding their rhetoric in the
counterintuitive strategy endorsed by some of their American colleagues. The IRD, for example, had stepped up its campaign to publi-
cize the expansionist, aggressive nature of Soviet communism just as
the Russia Committee was affirming the conspiratorial roots of the
Chinese intervention.[62] Yet those initiatives and judgments emerged at
virtually the same moment that Prime Minister Attlee was in Washington
pushing a policy of carrots over sticks. Attlee's desire for a Sino-Soviet
schism was no weaker than Truman's or Acheson's, but his conception
of the best way to promote that development clearly differed from that
of the Americans.

Both sets of statesmen, however, agreed on one thing at least: the key
player in the schismatic movement, Tito, had to be handled delicately.
Any indication that he was tilting toward the West might reduce his influence on potential heretics.[63] In the end, however, Tito's example did
not matter to any great extent, for as the IRD noted in late August
1950, weaning national Communists away from the Soviet Union was
"more a noble aspiration than a feasible aim."[64] The Chinese intervention later that year only made the task more difficult. This gloomy reality defined the general consensus on international communism during
one of the darkest phases of the Cold War—an era that, for Britons and
Americans, was arguably the high point of the Communist monolith.

Conclusion

Scholars and statesmen began to speculate more freely about the basic assumptions of Communist solidarity during the concluding phases of the Korean War. Some of their earliest musings took place at a conference (held, coincidentally, in the immediate aftermath of Stalin's death in March 1953) on the practice of totalitarianism in the modern world. Papers and commentary by George F. Kennan and political scientist Karl Deutsch, among others, focusing on the emergent cracks in the Soviet camp, raised the question of whether communism was ever as monolithic as many had first thought.[1] Their findings reflected a growing interest in exploring the image of the monolith and its relation to actual events during the 1950s.[2]

After tensions between the Soviets and the Chinese became more pronounced during the early 1960s, several scholars set out to invalidate altogether the notion of a Communist monolith.[3] Among this group was Arthur Schlesinger Jr., whose 1949 *The Vital Center* was in part responsible for promoting that image in the first place. By 1962, Schlesinger had concluded that the Communist world was not the tightly coordinated, frictionless machine that he and others had once feared. "Communism," Schlesinger now proclaimed, "is not a monolith; it is a spectrum." Recent visits to Poland and Yugoslavia had led him to admit the possibility of what he "had always supposed to be impossible—'liberal communism.'" Looking back, he discovered the source of his mistake in the dualistic rhetoric that was so common at that time. The problem was one of representation. Americans had "accepted the mystique of either/or," he argued, "and, in endowing essence with greater actuality than existence, we have committed what A. N. Whitehead used to call the 'fallacy of misplaced concreteness.'" This attitude marked a significant change from Schlesinger's writings of a previous decade; just six weeks prior to the U.S. presidential election of 1948, he had criticized Henry Wallace for believing that there were "as many kinds of Communists as there are kinds of Republicans and Democrats." For the Schlesinger of the 1940s, there was only one kind of Communist—Moscow's kind—the only kind possible in a totalitarian structure.[4]

Although Schlesinger offered his later findings as something of a revelation, policymakers and pundits had been warning of the dangers inherent in ideological abstractions even at the height of Cold War tensions. Schlesinger himself had been alert to these dangers when, in *The Vital Center,* he referred specifically to Whitehead's fallacy. While the Harvard historian and paragon of the non-Communist Left failed to heed his own advice, various members of the State Department were apparently more committed to reexamining the assumptions of the monolithic framework and their impact on national policy. Ware Adams, for example, the Policy Planning staffer who raised the issue with John Paton Davies in March 1949, did so again in early 1950. "Too often," Adams noted, "underlying realities become obscured by word-symbols which tend, in so far as they are imprecise, to generate the heat of passion, and, more important, to lead to mistaken or self-defeating conclusions regarding the best means of combatting the very threat for which they stand." Adams recognized that "simple 'anti-communism' backfires in Yugoslavia, tends to press the European satellites tighter into the Soviet monolith as desired by Stalin, and tends to prevent in advance the development of Titoism in China." He thus called on policymakers to avoid "any loose impression that we are endeavoring to organize a part of the world into our own political system in order to combat other political systems *per se* apart from their imperialistic effort to gain control over other peoples." For Adams, the simple fact remained that communism no longer functioned as a "monolith," if it ever did at all.[5]

Adams's 1950 memo raises as many questions as does his earlier joint effort, several of which stand out. For instance, why was the image of a Communist monolith so attractive to government officials? Why did it exert such a powerful hold on the collective imagination? How did it form in the first place? Did American policymakers, and the American public in general, embrace it more readily than the masses and corresponding elites in Britain? And how accurate was it as a representation of the Communist world?

The Monolith in History

The monolithic image of international communism drew on a number of long- and short-term historical dynamics, some of which stretched back generations while others were much more contemporary in origin. The more deeply rooted among them comprised something approximating an "Anglo-American historical consciousness." For the United States, that sentiment became operative even before New World settlers had made their way across the Atlantic. It would persist throughout the colonial and revolutionary eras, often endowing the public culture with a palpable spirit of crusading zeal, and would last straight through the 1800s as leading figures in national life conceived and described their land as a "New Israel," destined to remake the world. The manner in which Americans fulfilled their mission would change according to circumstances, but that whiggish sense of destiny remained largely unbowed. By the last years of the nineteenth century, it combined with a growing capacity for technological innovation and a rapidly expanding financial base to produce a spirit that was more activist, more interventionist, and more internationalist than any that had previously animated the American scene.[6] Britons, too, heeded the call of providence, constructing an empire on which the sun never set. Assuming the burdens of civilizational uplift, they also crusaded on behalf of national glory, expanding the reach of British customs, political institutions, and imperial clout. While the American expression of that spirit carried more evangelical overtones, the Whig tradition exerted an equally powerful hold on Britons. With its vision of unending progress and its faith in the redemptive power of the state, whiggism encouraged both populations to regard their destinies as biblically ordained.

As beacons of light, Great Britain and the United States were destined, even commanded, to cast their lamps out onto the world. Yet that projection of national purpose assumed the existence of an opposite force that blocked the path toward global enlightenment. The Whig tradition thereby reinforced the habit—one that is perhaps hard-wired into the human condition—of dividing reality into two distinct spheres. In its most exaggerated formulation, that dualistic vision is predicated on the coming of an apocalyptic struggle against devious and treacherous foes. These agents of darkness, moreover, are not simply static entities, amenable to education and conversion; they are actively working to subdue the "elect," conspiring to weaken the forces of re- demption. Operating from a historical narrative that encouraged such thinking, Americans and Britons of the postwar generation described communism as the latest and most dangerous enemy of liberty. With its avowedly secretive, conspiratorial, internationalist, millennialist, and anticapitalist tenets, communism possessed all the earmarks of the ide- alized adversary, threatening national security as well as Western values and traditions. It is no wonder, then, that the rhetoric of the early Cold War was so dichotomous in form—a feature of the discourse that po- larized the atmosphere still further, enhancing the Manichean nature of the struggle itself.[7]

As influential as those whiggish sentiments had become, the mis- sionary traditions in both Britain and the United States did not *cause* their populations to treat communism as a monolithic movement. It would be folly to argue that those impulses were always conscious in the minds of both peoples, or that they were singularly—or even primarily—determinative of individual and collective actions. But it would be equally shortsighted to conclude that they had only a mar- ginal impact on the public consciousness. Those dynamics constituted a powerful framework for understanding, providing the backdrop against which Britons and Americans interpreted the Communist threat. Their emergence in the early postwar years should come as no surprise. In times of great upheaval, when crises lay bare the most salient features of national lore, the public dialogue may become satu- rated with increasingly greater reference to historic traditions—so much so, that those mythic lessons and traits may shape the very tenor of an age.

The late 1940s was such a time in both England and the United States. An entire epoch was on the way out as Britons saw their impe- rial past disappear before their very eyes; a new one was dawning on the other side of the Atlantic as Americans assumed responsibilities rarely contemplated just years earlier. Such change was no doubt dis- orienting for both peoples and contributed to a general uneasiness about what lay ahead. Literary figures from both cultures admitted as much. British poet W. H. Auden gave voice to a generation's lament in *The Age of Anxiety*, his Pulitzer Prize-winning work of 1947; the fol- lowing year, historian Richard Hofstadter drew a direct link between those feelings of insecurity and the revival of a historical conscious- ness; and in 1949, Arthur Schlesinger opened *The Vital Center* with the declaration that "western man" was "tense, uncertain, adrift," making the era "a time of troubles, an age of anxiety." As Schlesinger noted, anxiety had become "the official emotion" of the time.[8]

Of the many problems Americans faced in the postwar world, among the most vexing were the ambiguities that such anxiety provoked. Absolute truth, so confidently expressed through the ideological sloganeering of the 1930s, now appeared to be a foolish—even dangerous—notion when linked to the Holocaust and other atrocities of the age. Americans thus began to enshrine the processes and institutions of democratic society as much as the values underlying it. Pragmatism became the philosophy of the day as intellectuals and commoners applied a "realistic" approach to life's problems, shelving doctrinal truths for more experiential methods. Accordingly, fixed certainties fell away as Americans contemplated the morally ambiguous and highly charged terrain of loyalty oaths, human sexuality (Alfred Kinsey's study of male sexuality appeared in 1948), and atomic bombs. As Eric Goldman observed, "a nation accustomed to the categorical yes or no found itself in the nagging realm of maybe." It was not an enviable place to be.[9]

Nor was it for Great Britain, whose citizens were no less susceptible than those of the United States to the troubles of the day. England, too, had to grapple with an altered moral landscape, yet the dangers it faced and the wartime destruction it endured meant that Britain would consider those questions on different terms. Its citizens were consumed with bread-and-butter issues—at times, quite literally—and were engaged in rebuilding a country torn by the strains of war. Looming over those challenges lay perhaps an even more daunting test: the British Empire, that enduring symbol of national pride, was collapsing, and the accompanying need to recalibrate British identity would demand a fundamental shift in the nation's sense of self.

To deal with the complexities of the postwar era, Americans and Britons had to adopt new ways of thinking. According to former State Department official Louis Halle, Americans, at least, had to drop their habits of moralizing, of dividing nations into "peace-loving" and "aggressor" states, and accustom themselves to the game of power politics. "Such a conceptual change as this," Halle notes, "while it might take place more rapidly in the subconscious mind, could hardly be explicitly formulated and adopted as such until after an interval of intellectual confusion and inner conflict." The passage of time, absent the presence of any great mortal threat, would thus be required for the necessary psychic—even emotional—reorientation.[10]

History afforded no such luxury. It is highly questionable, however, whether the collective education Halle longed for could possibly have taken place during those first years of the Cold War. For the dangers Moscow posed resided not only in the more obvious displays of Russian brutality but in the deeper meanings those actions evoked. The Soviet Union seemed both a country and a creed, a nation-state capable of marshaling a range of human and material resources as well as the font of an ideology with potentially global appeal. The possibility that Moscow would pursue both a national *and* an ideological mission, and harness domestic and foreign resources to do so, was central to the emerging chill enveloping Washington and London. And so the intersection of dramatic current events with the deep historical dynamics of republicanism—both of which, especially in America, were themselves filtered through the lens of domestic politics—constrained the ability of opinion makers to evaluate the Communist challenge from the standpoint of sober, reasoned, analytical detachment. As a result, the "nagging realm of maybe" that Goldman had discerned simply vanished. While it lived on in public discussions of various social issues, it lost whatever hold it might have had on attitudes toward the Kremlin.

The conditions necessary for seeing communism as an international, conspiratorial, monolithic movement had thus fallen into place. The impact of long-term dynamics such as British imperialism, American republicanism, and the Whig tradition had created a context in which Soviet behavior appeared in the most malignant and dangerous of lights. Those dynamics did not function as inert elements; they were alive, active in the collective consciousness of both nations, and came to shape the manner in which both peoples understood the Soviet challenge. In the process, they helped to construct a framework that offered a compelling account of how the Soviets might act in the postwar world.

That framework would also draw on recent experiences with a similarly totalitarian state. To unravel the mysteries of the Soviet enigma, Americans and Britons would interpret Russian behavior through the lens of Red Fascism, a context that grew out of several historical pressures, the most powerful of which clustered around World War II and the word-symbols of "Munich" and "appeasement." As a "cognitive script," the Munich experience led Britons and Americans to generalize from a particular experience to a more universal one, suggesting that aggression unchecked gave rise to further aggression unleashed. Yet it was the source of that aggression that endowed the Munich analogy with its interpretive power; the Communists of the postwar period bore a striking resemblance to the Nazis of the prewar years. Although their systems differed in many respects, their mutual disdain for liberal values and Western culture, their reliance on terror as an instrument of rule, their professed desire for global dominance, and their use of foreign agents suggested that both regimes were equally totalitarian and equally dangerous. With their inclusive, internationalist, and quasi-humanitarian creed, the Communists actually seemed the more threatening of the two. The images of totalitarianism and Red Fascism, so powerful in their ability to evoke fears of universal threat, thus became mainstays of anti-Communist rhetoric.[11]

So, too, did the similarly potent construct of the "fifth column" subverting the nation from within. Numerous examples from World War II pointed to the treachery of citizens serving foreign masters, a threat even more plausible in the Cold War fight against international communism. Although the term originated with the Spanish Civil War, the actions of Vidkun Quisling in facilitating Nazi control of Norway not only gave the expression new life but provided a synonym for such traitorous behavior. Those references to appeasement and subversion, which connoted the manner by which Nazism expanded its reach and power, lived on in the postwar era and lay at the heart of epithets targeting Communists around the world. The description of Bulgaria, Hungary, Romania, and like collaborative nations as "satellites" further highlight the centrality of World War II to the rhetoric that was to follow. In conflating the image of various kinds of totalitarians, including those within the Communist camp, such talk contributed to the emergence of the monolithic framework.[12]

That construction received further support from the network of media and private organizations that sought to popularize these messages, especially in the United States. The interplay between opinion leaders, the public, and the policymaking community is complex, and it is difficult to prove the precise direction and intensity of influence among the actors involved. Nevertheless, with Americans in the postwar years generally rallying around their presidents in times of crisis, the Truman administration set the standard for such a dynamic. Seeking to mold popular attitudes throughout the emerging Cold War, the administration recognized the need for executive action in the field of publicity, and a growing belief in the malleability of public opinion spawned further efforts at manipulating it. Yet, by the time Truman set out to shape such opinion in March 1947, public perceptions of communism had already begun to coalesce, largely through the influence of grassroots and nongovernmental organizations, as well as through private groups affiliated with administration personnel and projects. Thereafter, official and nonofficial actors reinforced the messages that each were sending, for both parochial and nonparochial reasons. Later in the decade, when the administration and its partisan opponents began to target communism itself as the enemy, the ground had already been laid for seeing communism as a monolithic conspiracy. The Truman administration had thus moved from being out in front of public opinion, at least on the Soviet Union, to walking in step with it.[13]

At the same time, neither the Red Fascist image nor the Anglo-American legacy, nor even the Truman administration and the events of the day, were wholly responsible for creating the word-symbol of "the monolith." Communists themselves, having introduced the term during the interwar period, bore some responsibility for its continued projection. Figures such as Leon Trotsky, Grigori Zinoviev, and Klara Zetkin all invoked it, as did Georgi Dimitrov and Eugene Dennis during the era of the Nazi-Soviet Pact. British and American writers also employed the word, although it appeared infrequently in Western publications. Not until the onset of the Cold War, however, did the monolith emerge as a widely used reference for international communism. Although policymakers in Britain and the United States resorted to using the term occasionally during the first three years of the postwar era, the monolith seems to have entered the public dialogue most forcefully during the second half of 1948. And when it did emerge, it functioned in an ironic rather than a literal sense. Describing the Communist world after the heresy of Tito's Yugoslavia, several publications invoked the term as an image of communism that had suddenly become obsolete. The greater irony, however, was soon to follow: while the monolith was now supposed to refer to an archaic notion, subsequent developments in the Cold War reversed its message once again, endowing the term with its more conventional and more ominous meaning.

The Monolith in Comparative Perspective

Although they became part of the public cultures of Great Britain and the United States, references to the Communist monolith were limited neither to the American nor even the Anglo-American experience. Germans, for instance, accepted its precepts in the immediate aftermath of World War I and beyond.[14] The emergence of the Nazi Party during the interwar period radicalized the language of anti-bolshevism in German political life, but German Social Democrats (SPD) were prone to equally inflammatory rhetoric in castigating the German Communist Party (KPD) as an outpost of Moscow.[15] Following World War II, a revitalized SPD repeatedly invoked Red Fascist themes in its propaganda, comparing German Communist Wilhelm Pieck to Adolf Hitler and labeling German Communists as "Kremlin creatures."[16] By the time the Cold War had reached its more frigid stages, West Germans were already accustomed to viewing communism as a social, moral, and political evil. The monolithic image, which Germans of several stripes had embraced quite easily on their own, seems to have resonated powerfully outside the Anglo-American sphere.[17]

Still, it is hard to ascertain whether the image was more popular in Germany than elsewhere on the continent, or whether it was any more endemic to U.S. or British political culture. Both American and British statesmen used it, as did commentators in their respective national media. A generally more volatile American political scene, with the ideological and rhetorical "pendulums" swinging more dramatically in the United States than in Britain, might well have occasioned its more frequent invocation on the western side of the Atlantic.[18] Pointing out its ubiquity in American discourse, Ware Adams maintained that "discussion of communism has tended toward the belief that it *is* a solid monolith, as the Kremlin would wish it to be."[19] More frequently, however, policymakers and pundits in both countries referred to the monolith not by name but by its attributes.

In Britain, those anti-Communist impulses, though pronounced, never turned into the crusade that swept the United States. As a result, grassroots efforts to depict communism as monolithic were correspondingly lacking in British political culture. Although elements of this trend did appear from time to time, they had far less salience in Britain than in the United States. This absence of a comparable British lobby highlights the two political cultures' differing views on anticommunism. The distinction is likely attributable to a more populist and participatory ethos in the United States, as well as to the structural elements of the respective political systems. In the end, McCarthyism simply could not take root in British soil. Yet given the popular perceptions of communism and the threat it posed, the United States and Great Britain were more united than divided in their support of the monolithic framework. The anticommunism of Americans and Britons, at least during this stage of the Cold War, differed in degree more than in kind.[20]

Another area of Anglo-American divergence involved their respective interest in evaluating the monolithic nature of international communism. During the years 1945–1950, the Foreign Office devoted more time and energy to the issue than did the State Department. British attention to this matter stretched back at least to the close of World War II, when London queried its missions abroad on the ideological leanings of native Communists. By mid-1946, the Russia Committee had conducted a similar study on the disposition of Communists worldwide. Several officials detected factional splits in Communist parties outside the U.S.S.R., dividing them into "Muscovite" Communists who blindly followed the Soviet line and "national" Communists who favored local concerns. The Russia Committee would revisit the matter the following year, conducting two such surveys on the "Quaroni Question," neither of which turned up significant traces of independence among native parties. Nevertheless, the Foreign Office would commission additional studies, repeatedly evaluating the monolithic, Soviet nature of international communism. The fruits of these investigations emerged in early 1950 in a widely disseminated paper on the practice of anti-Stalinist communism.

The State Department would also probe the nature of international communism during the period in question. Raymond Murphy concluded his report on Communist objectives within three weeks of V-E Day, offering a preliminary appraisal of likely Soviet and Communist activity in the postwar era. American officials would further analyze Communist behavior over the course of the next year; the Bohlen-Robinson Report, the Long Telegram, and the Clifford-Elsey Report all commented of the nature of international communism, and all found it to be a monolithic movement coordinated by the Kremlin. Studies emanating from the Policy Planning Staff were equally suggestive, at least up through June 1948, as were periodic inquiries into the leanings of various Asian Communists. Yet there is no record of U.S. officials conducting comprehensive surveys such as those commissioned by the Russia Committee either prior to the Tito split or within eighteen months of its occurrence. Apparently, the department never addressed the issue in any systematic way.

This absence of an American equivalent to the British effort likely stems from several dynamics, including structural differences within the respective diplomatic establishments. The Policy Planning Staff was first created in 1947, a full year after the establishment of the Russia Committee, and even when it did emerge, the PPS had to concern itself with subjects running well beyond the purview of the British working group. The cultures of the two diplomatic corps might also have shaped their responses. British statesmen, having worked to prop up a troubled but no less functioning empire, might have been more sensitive than their American counterparts (Kennan and perhaps a handful of others, excluded) to the presence of nationalism within imperial structures. Perhaps also at work was the mythical British penchant for empiricism, an impulse that might have led the Foreign Office to cast about repeatedly for signs of national Communist behavior. American policymakers, however, regularly displayed the empirical touch of their British counterparts, lapsing only occasionally into their own alleged habit of reasoning deductively. Still, it was not until mid-1948 that U.S. policy planners began to focus on communism's international solidarity with anything like the energy of their British counterparts.

Even so, their different approaches did not lead to significant departures in policy, nor did they reveal the American position as the more doctrinaire of the two. From early 1949 through the close of 1950, it was the Foreign Office that took the more monolithic view of Eastern Europe. British officials frequently described the region as a "closed preserve" of the Soviet Union, rejecting the possibility that it might become home to further schisms. The situation in Asia was not much different, as Bevin saw few traces of Titoism among Chinese Communists and their neighboring comrades. U.S. officials took roughly similar positions, but they seem to have been marginally more enthusiastic about promoting presumed heretical tendencies behind the Iron Curtain. In addition, their thoughts on encouraging Chinese Titoism did not sour until late 1949 and early 1950. Eventually, Britain would become more optimistic about China's schismatic potential, owing partly to Bevin's declining health and Attlee's growing influence on foreign policy.[21] But the Foreign Office rank-and-file seemed comparatively less enamored of Mao's breakaway propensities. In the end, American and British policymakers shared generally similar ideas on the prospects for Titoism. Both saw additional schisms as features of some distant future.

Of greater note, perhaps, is the air of confusion attending their respective analyses. Take, for example, a British memo from August 1950 citing the Soviet Politburo's control of an "international Kremlin-controlled Communist movement." According to the paper, Moscow drew no distinctions "between the interests of international communism and the interests of the Soviet Union." Several pages later, however, the Foreign Office warned that "in studying communism in South-East

Asia, it would seem especially important not to over-estimate the strength of armed communism in the field, or the extent to which it is controlled and co-ordinated by the Kremlin." Soviet rule was "often tenuous or remote; the advice often inappropriate; and the picture complicated by local rivalries." In other words, international communism was at all times controlled by the Kremlin, except for when it wasn't. State Department analyses were no less rife with such equivocation.[22]

How are we to reconcile these statements, elements of which are at odds not only with previous analyses but at war with themselves? Part of the answer lies in the scale of resistance presumed to be coursing through the Communist world. Granting the possibility that a schismatic, though latent, brand of communism might well have existed behind the Iron Curtain, Eastern Europe, the most visible site of Soviet power, was devoid of any meaningful resistance to Soviet rule. Cracks existed, and officials speculated that events such as Stalin's death might release the energies of independent Communist or non-Communist movements. Yet as long as Stalin was alive, no high-ranking official in the Foreign Office or the State Department thought of Eastern Europe as particularly fertile soil for the growth of national communism.

Solidarity and Discord in the Communist World

Were these statesmen correct in their presumption of iron-clad solidarity within the socialist sphere?

On the face of it, no, for the experiences of the interwar period demonstrate that communism was replete with internal tensions and schisms. A host of developments, both before and after World War II, provided ample evidence of a movement rife with fissures. Even if one were not versed in the factional disputes between Trotskyites or Stalinists, for instance, or even between Lovestonites or Browderites, the Moscow trials of the late 1930s suggested that communism, both within the Soviet Union and without, was not monolithic in the literal sense. Observers need not have believed in the legitimacy of those trials, for instance, to have recognized the existence of intraparty fissures. The protests these proceedings engendered, especially in the West, were testament enough that all was not well within the Communist world.

World War II, however, was the starting point for evaluating the solidarity of postwar communism. The dissolution of the Comintern in 1943 encouraged observers to view that act as the latest in a long line of developments signaling that the Soviet Union was evolving into a more "normal," less revolutionary state, concerned primarily with its own national interest rather than with the fate of international proletarianism. Moscow's wartime declaration that there existed "different roads to socialism," moreover, indicated not only that factional differences were now the norm, but that national communism was the reigning mantra of the movement.

Notwithstanding the quarrel between French Communist Jacques Duclos and his American comrade Earl Browder over the direction of communism in the United States, the rhetoric of "national communism" persisted into the postwar era. In February 1946, former Comintern chief Georgi Dimitrov declared that each nation would indeed "take its own road to the socialist utopia," a pronouncement that was accompanied by demonstrations of independence from the Soviet line.[23] Many of these displays concerned territorial and colonial issues left unresolved at war's end. French Communists, for instance, repeatedly sought to separate the Rhineland from Germany, a policy Stalin opposed after July 1946. PCF leader Maurice Thorez would regularly invoke the mantra of a "French road to socialism" in the early postwar period, all the while taking ambiguous positions on the propriety of Vietnamese Communists opposing France in a quest for Indochinese independence.[24] Italian Communists likewise adopted positions that were at odds with those of their socialist brethren; wrangling between PCI leader Palmiro Togliatti and Yugoslavia's Tito over control of Trieste remained a long-running source of interparty tension. Further squabbling emerged between Polish and East German Communists over the Oder-Neisse lands, between Poland and Czechoslovakia over Silesia, between the Czech and Hungarian governments over Hungarian nationals in Slovakia, and between Hungarian and Romanian Communists over the fate of Transylvania. Taken together, these scenarios suggest that national interests were at the very least colliding with, if not trumping altogether, those of socialist solidarity.[25]

Additional trouble was apparent within the Communist parties themselves. Given the varied fates of their membership during the wartime years (some cadres remained in-country, some emigrated to the West, some sat out the war in Moscow, while some were interned by the Nazis), postwar visions of political change and opportunity reflected, in part, those often wrenching experiences.[26] Inside the Soviet occupation zone in Germany, for example, serious differences were evident among local Communists both prior to and following the 1946 forced merger of the Socialist and Communist parties, at both the leadership and base levels. Some of the faithful even rejected the Soviet model of development.[27] In Western Europe, the Italian Communist Party was almost torn asunder as a result of Togliatti's positions on Trieste.[28] In the weeks and months following the end of the European war, neither the intra- nor interparty relations of European CPs were suggestive of entirely monolithic behavior.

By 1947 and 1948, Soviet interests would emerge as paramount and guide the direction of local party policy, an outcome facilitated by the Kremlin's actions during the war itself. Following the dissolution of the Comintern in 1943, Moscow created a foreign department of the Soviet Communist Party to continue its work through covert means; the arrangement persisted after the war had ended.[29] And by and large, comrades in Western Europe subsequently and repeatedly expressed their fealty to Moscow in both words and deeds, even at their own expense. The French Communist Party, for instance, came to regard the Soviet international position as virtually sacrosanct; Maurice Thorez's September 1948 declaration that the PCF would never take up arms against Moscow was the most public expression of this sentiment.[30] The leadership of the Italian Communist Party was so committed to promoting Soviet positions that it was almost wrecked by its wartime position on Trieste; to the consternation of his comrades as well as Italians outside the PCI, Togliatti maintained this line for nearly a year-and-a-half following V-E Day.[31] British Communist leader Harry Pollitt also offered virtually uncritical deference to Soviet positions, making his party utterly loyal to the Kremlin.[32]

Soviet influence was even more pronounced in Eastern Europe, largely because the Red Army occupied so much of it. Although the anti-Fascist credentials of local CPs added to their political clout, it was Soviet military power that ensured their ultimate political victory. While that show of force enabled Stalin to grant native Communists the initiative for establishing Communist governments, he was likely more interested in dominating than communizing neighboring states. Moscow therefore assented to a healthy degree of local initiative partly because, as in the case of Eastern Germany, it expected to be welcomed as a liberator.[33] Yet Stalin's decision to give party chieftains such latitude seems to have been a purely tactical maneuver—a recognition of the power of nationalist sensibilities in lands that had recently come under foreign rule.[34] The Soviet leader also realized that a heavy-handed approach to Eastern Europe would look highly distasteful to Americans and Britons, and Stalin very much wanted to maintain cooperation among the "Big Three" in the postwar era. Various geopolitical objectives related to the military settlement, as well as a financial windfall from German reparations, argued for the preservation of the wartime working relationship.[35] Stalin, moreover, wanted to avoid giving the Western powers any reason to unite against him before the "contradictions" of capitalism rent those nations asunder. By encouraging East European CPs to adopt a "national front" strategy for gaining political power, the Kremlin was able to promote its agenda with little difficulty.[36]

Moscow pulled the reins tighter following the Marshall Plan proposal of June 1947. The period from Marshall's address through the establishment of the Cominform was critical to the Stalinization of continental CPs and to Eastern Europe itself. The decision to prohibit the East Europeans from participating in the ERP rested with Stalin alone. His demand that Poland and Czechoslovakia reject U.S. aid was a particularly brutal reminder of who controlled the levers of power behind the Iron Curtain. Western officials, therefore, were on target in attributing the rejection of Marshall aid to a Kremlin-based directive.[37] They were also correct in evaluating the political fallout from the Marshall proposal. While the origins of the Cominform were not wholly attributable to the recovery plan itself (sources from the former East bloc reveal that Stalin had expressed a desire to reestablish an international Communist organization as early April 1946), the timing of its appearance was an altogether different matter.[38] Coming less than four months after Marshall's speech at Harvard and two months after Moscow had forbidden its neighbors from participating in the European Recovery Program, its emergence during the fall of 1947 was a direct outgrowth of the U.S. initiative, as many in Britain and the United States had suspected. Stalin saw the new body as a mechanism to support West European Communists in their efforts to sabotage Marshall aid and thereby wreak havoc on Western plans for European reconstruction.[39]

During its early days, the infrequency of Cominform meetings and the irregular publication of its journal suggest that Moscow was not committed to using the new organization as a method of control. In time, however, the Cominform would morph into a Russian tool for stamping out heretical tendencies in the Communist world, both real and imagined. Its establishment thus marked another step on the road toward the Stalinization of the Soviet bloc, bringing greater cohesion to Eastern

Europe in its stand against the West. In due course, the East European CPs crushed the few remaining pockets of political opposition, ending the practice of governing by coalition. Similar developments ensued in Western Europe; the late-1947 strikes in both France and Italy stemmed from Cominform directives urging the PCF and PCI to wage unbridled warfare against bourgeois governments. Moscow's ability to make its wishes known—and to have them granted without issuing explicit tactical instructions for their realization—indicates that the Kremlin exercised an extraordinary degree of control throughout the region.[40]

The U.S.S.R. would receive added support for its global objectives from the Chinese Communists, who now chose to align themselves more closely with the Soviet Union. The relationship had not always been so harmonious. Although the CCP had looked to Moscow for inspirational and doctrinal guidance ever since its founding, it differed sharply with the Kremlin over questions of revolutionary policy. Those distinctions became apparent following the CCP's defeat at the hands of Chinese Nationalists in the late 1920s. Leading Chinese Communists criticized Stalin for insisting that the party merge its interests with those of the Nationalist Chinese. This policy had enabled the Nationalists to rout their Communist rivals, leaving remnants of the CCP to head to the hills for protection. Thereafter, Moscow would have slight influence on the CCP, as the Kremlin's manifest display of bad advice led many in the party to pursue policies tailored more closely to Chinese realities. The primary beneficiary of the chill in CCP-Soviet relations was Mao Zedong, who would emerge as the party's leading figure.[41]

Although the Chinese Communists failed to march in lockstep with Moscow, neither did they break ranks in any fundamental way. Proletarian internationalism remained the mission of Chinese communism, and it was a goal its leaders articulated frequently. Mao, for instance, had declared in 1935 that he and his colleagues were "not an independent communist party" but a "branch of the Comintern, while our Chinese revolution is a part of the world revolution."[42] Later, during World War II, he would align CCP practice with Comintern slogans. Although Mao saw the disbanding of the Comintern as a sign that Stalin would sanction more local initiative, he still sought to harmonize his own statements and policies with those of the Kremlin.[43]

The Chinese Communists maintained their ties with Moscow after the end of World War II. As the CCP resumed its struggle with the Nationalists, Mao regularly consulted with the Kremlin on matters of political and military strategy. His forces also received captured Japanese war matériél, courtesy of Soviet units stationed in Manchuria. Such aid was not necessarily meant to further the chances of a Chinese Communist victory. Stalin's main objective with regard to China was to keep the country in a state of disarray; by prolonging its internal disruption, he thought he could ensure China's continued political irrelevance. In this way, Stalin believed, the West could be kept out of Asia, leaving Moscow as the power broker in the region. Western statesmen were aware of those dynamics and, therefore, rightly pointed to inchoate fissures in the Soviet-CCP relationship. But that relationship continued to deepen from 1946 onward as Chinese cadres traveled to Moscow for study and military training, and as Mao "Sovietized" the ways and means of Chinese communism.[44]

Soviet-CCP ties grew stronger as the Cold War became a more institutionalized feature of the international system. Mao's anti-imperial and anti-Western struggle accorded neatly with the more hostile environment of the "two-camp" world that emerged rhetorically in the fall of 1947. The Cominform's expulsion of Yugoslavia in June 1948 coincided with an even greater degree of cooperation between Mao and the Kremlin. Thereafter, discussions of military tactics and strategy, as well as more general talks about foreign policy, became more frequent. Moscow increased its military assistance to China (aid that the Soviet wished to conceal), allowing the CCP to prosecute its war against the Chinese Nationalists with greater vigor. Publicly, the Chinese issued a statement condemning Tito's regime, launched a campaign against "bourgeois nationalism," and proclaimed the impossibility of neutralism in the world conflict. The Kremlin, for its part, became intimately involved in the workings of Chinese Communist policy, hoping to situate the emergent PRC squarely on the eastern side of the ideological fence. In addition to military aid, Moscow provided the CCP with medical, technical, political, and even psychological assistance, helping Mao consolidate his victory over the Nationalists. While Mao had no interest at that point in a rapprochement with the United States and Great Britain, Stalin's support for that policy of coolness toward the Western powers contributed to their mutual alienation.[45]

Nevertheless, the Sino-Soviet relationship was hardly devoid of suspicion. The Communist Chinese were wary of the Kremlin and questioned the depth of Stalin's interest in aiding their revolution. On several occasions, the Soviet leader criticized the CCP for moving too quickly, for resuming its civil war against the Chinese Nationalists, and even for adopting Soviet economic and political models. Once Soviet support began to flow more freely, Mao's displeasure took root in Stalin's failure to grant the CCP leader an audience during the early postwar years. The January 1949 visit of Soviet diplomat Anastas Mikoyan helped to placate Mao, but a face-to-face meeting between the two party chieftains would have to wait until the Chinese Communists had consolidated their victory. Even then, at the outset of Mao's journey to Moscow in December 1949, Stalin rebuffed calls for a new Sino-Soviet treaty to replace the now obsolete pact between the Soviets and the Chinese Nationalist government. When Stalin finally did express interest in such a deal, the ensuing negotiations were marked by a range of divisive power-political issues as much as by the presumed harmony of ideological kin.[46]

Strains such as these surely indicate the presence of tension between the two powers, but evidence of a coming rift now seems less representative of their partnership—at that stage in its history—than does proof of a more cooperative alliance. The Chinese Communists sought to hide their connections to the Soviets and spread disinformation among the Western powers to convey the image of a split between Moscow and Beijing. Furthermore, Mao repeatedly acted as supplicant to Stalin, frequently expressing his gratitude to the Soviets and his interest in supporting Moscow's leadership of the world revolution. Cast in this light, his various entreaties to the United States, involving contact between U.S. and CCP officials, appear to be aspects of a larger propaganda campaign rather than indications of a desire for closer ties with Washington.[47]

Against the backdrop of these realities, the wedge strategy seems to have been doomed from the start. By the latter 1940s, Mao sought to limit his contact with the United States and Britain; further interaction with those countries, he believed, would have compromised China's ability to realize its revolutionary potential. Western officials, therefore, had virtually no chance of weaning China away from the Soviet Union during the years in question. Although British and American observers continued to hope for the development of some future schism, the PRC and the Soviet Union had formed a tacit alliance that appeared to be every bit as monolithic as many had feared.[48]

The signing of the Sino-Soviet Treaty of Friendship in February 1950 all but locked in that belief. Had Western statesmen been privy to Chinese and Soviet conversations during the run-up to its signing, they might have taken an even harder line against China at an earlier stage and done so in tandem. For Chinese officials went to great lengths to assure Moscow of their fealty. Deputy CCP chair Liu Shaoqui, for example, paid full obeisance to the Kremlin during his June 1949 trip to Moscow, maintaining that the CCP would, even in the face of interparty differences, "submit" to Moscow and "resolutely *carry out the decisions of the Soviet Communist Party*."[49] By all measures, the PRC seemed to stand foursquare with the Soviets. One of the allegedly obvious signs of tension between the two powers—the delays in signing the Sino-Soviet pact—apparently resulted from mundane, logistical problems as much as from any unpleasant diplomatic wrangling: it took Zhou Enlai nearly three weeks to make the trek from Beijing to Moscow, slowing down the finalization of treaty arrangements.[50]

When Mao and Stalin finally did formalize their relationship in February 1950, their ideological affinity was only partly responsible for the summit's successful conclusion. A shared belief in Marxism clearly paved the way for the Sino-Soviet alliance—perhaps even mandating the PRC's pro-Soviet position—but both Moscow and Beijing recognized the strategic value of such a partnership. Mao's anti-imperialist streak was just as strong as his veneration of communism and left him fully committed to eliminating the Western presence in Asia. It also engendered a fear of Western intervention, prompting a search for greater security within a cohort of like-minded parties and states. Stalin also feared American designs on East Asia and viewed an alliance with Beijing as a bulwark against such encroachment. Accordingly, the Sino-Soviet entente emerged out of geopolitical as well as ideological rationales.[51]

And each of those considerations precipitated the chain of events that led to the outbreak of the Korean War. It is now virtually impossible to discount the role that Moscow and Beijing played in the genesis of that conflict. Although its causes were clearly rooted in Korean soil, both the timing of the war and the course it took were largely driven by extraterritorial dynamics, at least one of which was American in origin.[52] Secretary of State Dean Acheson's "defensive perimeter" speech at the National Press Club made a deep impression on both Chinese and Soviet observers. At the time of its delivery, Mao was in Moscow for the Sino-Soviet treaty negotiations, whereupon Stalin had Foreign Minister Viacheslav Molotov read aloud passages from the address to his assembled guests. Evidently, Stalin sought to illustrate American treachery in fomenting trouble between the Chinese and the Soviets, intimating that the United States would seek to deny Taiwan to the Chinese Communists. Accordingly, Mao interpreted such talk as a provocation that needed to be addressed.[53] Over the next several months, the Soviets, the Chinese, and the North Koreans would outline a response. While the KPA's invasion of South Korea sprang from its own set of dynamics, it was clearly contingent on Kim's consultation with his more powerful comrades.[54]

Those discussions would continue after the attack had commenced, often in a rancorous way. Much of that divisiveness—or skittishness, to be more exact—stemmed from gross miscalculations over the projected Western response and the ultimate length of the war. Yet the indecision and improvisation that marked the Communist counterattack—realities that were not so plainly evident to Western eyes at the time—reveal the extent of Communist collaboration throughout the summer and fall of 1950. Such intimacy, which Westerners had earlier taken for granted, now appears to be a proven fact. While the accompanying disagreements and hesitations suggest that the Communist machine was not without friction, they nevertheless lend credence to allied suspicions of conspiratorial planning, both before and after June 25—which, in turn, points to the rough functional equivalent, if not the literal presence, of a monolithic front.[55]

To some extent, that perception was replicated in the East, for the Soviets, too, believed in the existence of something that might loosely be called a "capitalist monolith." Stalin had long feared encirclement by the West, an outlook that was attributable to ideology and practice, and likely to Stalin's own paranoia as well. Memories of Western intervention in the Russian Civil War persisted in the U.S.S.R. as Soviet officials recalled U.S. and associated efforts to strangle the Bolshevik experiment at birth. A sense that the Munich Pact of 1938 had allowed Hitler to turn his guns east further encouraged Soviet leaders along these lines. Nor did such thinking abate during the heyday of the World War II "Grand Alliance"; Stalin assumed that delays in opening the Second Front in Europe stemmed from the worst of Western intentions. That fear of encirclement carried over into the postwar era, with Moscow constantly wary of a bloc led by Great Britain and United States, ready to go on the offensive. Soviet perceptions of Western perfidy frequently took this form, suggesting that—at least in the short run—capitalist coordination, if not capitalist monolithicity, would mark the Kremlin's understanding of Western behavior. And just as Western statesmen tried to crack the Communist monolith, so, too, did Soviet officials seek to drive wedges between the capitalist powers; a belief that the "contradictions" inherent among capitalist states would render them liable to such a policy was very much a part of Stalin's thinking as the Cold War took shape. With ideology coming to dominate perceptions of international behavior, and with so much uncertainty swirling about the respective motives of East and West, each side ascribed to the other an increasing degree of coordinated action.[56]

Communist and Non-Communist "Complementarity"

That image of virtual uniformity was not the only one that Westerners held of communism and its practitioners. As other studies as well as this one have illustrated, American and British officials commented frequently on the presence of divisions in the Communist world. This finding comes as no surprise, inasmuch as several historians have already highlighted U.S. efforts to drive a "wedge" between the Soviets, the Chinese, and various other Communist states. They also divined fissures within the Communist bloc that policymakers might have exploited to widen breaches in the Soviet camp; those breaches, moreover, were thought to occur naturally, as part of the historical process of imperial decay.[57]

Yet nowhere did these statesmen posit the existence of an equally organic Communist movement divorced from the pull of Soviet Russia. Nor does the mere fact that policymakers were aware of tensions in the socialist camp point toward their liberation from the monolithic framework. Kennan, Bohlen, and their associates often described international communism as a Soviet-centric world, a view that was no less prevalent in government circles after the Tito split than before it took place. Even Charlton Ogburn and Ware Adams, the policymakers perhaps most interested in creating space for these developments, stopped short of identifying any current Communist regime as possessing such innate independence. In short, Kennan, as well as the vast majority of his colleagues in the State Department, believed that native Communists had to be weaned *away* from Moscow, extracted somehow from the Soviet grip. For those officials, the powers of attraction that lured Communists into the Soviet orbit were at least as elemental as the forces of repulsion that would presumably one day lead them out of it.

Given the assumption that the wedge strategy took as its goal the need to *reverse* the Soviet magnetic field, it is hard not to conclude that even the foremost proponents of the wedge strategy believed in the primacy, if not sustainability, of the monolithic force. Maintaining a belief in the ability, or at least desirability, of cracking the monolith was therefore in no way inconsistent with operating from a monolithic framework. Officials harboring these beliefs and objectives might best be described as embodying a "soft" monolithism distinct from the views of their more hard-line colleagues. Yet whether they embraced a "soft" or "hard" monolithism, British and American audiences were in many ways conditioned by their own pasts to see monolithic forces at work in the world. Considering the actions taken and statements uttered on behalf of international communism, the presumption of monolithic behavior on the part of that movement—even by the most sophisticated of diplomatic minds—appears to have been a rational, reasoned response to the events of the day.

As previously suggested, the U.S. and British officials were not necessarily wrong for embracing these precepts. Aside from the Tito split, the likelihood that additional schisms would take place within the Eastern Bloc was slim, as most policymakers realized. Even with talk about the shakiness of the Soviet empire and the prospect of further defections, officials continued to run up against a formidable obstacle: the nature of Titoism itself. For Titoism was a product of time and place, born of particular conditions. Local control of the army, state sovereignty over the security forces, and effective mastery of the intelligence network— the trappings of autonomous power that Kennan had touched on in June 1948—were absent among the European satellites.

Asian parties, however, did possess these capabilities and deployed them in bids for national independence and political power. Communist leaders in China, Indonesia, and Burma were all insulated from the levers of Soviet control, and Vietnamese Communist Ho Chi Minh seemed particularly well positioned to strike a Titoist pose. Ho had impeccable Communist credentials: he was a founding member of the French Communist Party, a member of the Comintern, and the driving force behind the Indochinese Communist Party. Yet he was equally committed to a program of independence for Vietnam.

The question of whether Ho's communism or nationalism held primacy bedeviled Western statesmen, who commented on the matter repeatedly during the early postwar years. British officials were generally more partial to the nationalist explanation, whereas American statesmen, particularly from 1949 onward, were increasingly drawn to darker appraisals. Perhaps neither appreciated the extent to which Ho's nationalism and communism could coexist and inform his actions. While the same could not be said of his colleagues atop the Vietminh hierarchy, Ho seemed comfortable, both politically and ideologically, espousing the centrality of both objectives, relying on Lenin's theory of "federations" to bridge the gap between the realization of national and international revolutions. Indeed, Ho personified the theory of Communist "complementarity" put forward by John Paton Davies. Not unlike the phenomenon whereby light assumed the properties of both particle and wave, Ho's behavior, more so even than Tito's, manifested both national and international qualities. The possibility that these impulses could live side-by-side within the same individual was hardly unique to Ho. As this study has tried to illustrate, several Western statesmen, even those most attuned to complexity and nuance in the Communist world, were themselves "complementarians," seeking to crack the monolith while remaining largely beholden to its precepts.[58]

Yet those nationally oriented Communists also seemed to be doing Moscow's bidding, as well as their own, in regions far afield from Soviet strength. Although individuals such as Ho Chi Minh sometimes acted contrary to the wishes of Soviet leaders, they nevertheless appeared to be furthering Soviet geostrategic objectives. Many had trained in the U.S.S.R., declared their ideological solidarity with Moscow, proclaimed their subservience to Stalin, and sided with Russia in its attacks on Tito. Still, the West had reason for hope: Chinese Communists, in particular, faced the daunting task of administering their newfound gains, a project that would compromise their ability to project Soviet power. Mao might also balk at furthering Soviet power—or at least in being a pawn of Soviet rule—thereby limiting Moscow's imperial reach. Yet each of these hypotheses seemed equally plausible, for not even the China specialists in the Foreign Office and the State Department were convinced that Mao would ultimately take an independent line. With so much uncertainty, and with Western statesmen interpreting the actions and rhetoric of Communist officials as one might decipher the textures of tea leaves, each new development appeared to foretell the shape of things to come.

By February 1951, senior officials in the State Department had concluded that "the encouragement of communist heresy in the satellites, as an intermediate stage between Kremlin domination and democratic freedom, had been proven to be an unrewarding and unrealistic policy." It was thus time to revisit NSC 58/2 and devise a new approach to the Soviet satellites in Eastern Europe.[59] Any such plan, however, would have to factor in American hostility toward the very notion of schismatic communism. As a recent departmental survey had noted, there was a widespread belief that "Communists in any country are under Russian control," including the 80 percent of the nation that held Moscow responsible for Beijing's intervention in Korea.[60] With Americans in no mood to consider the breakaway tendencies of Communist regimes, the wedge strategy remained an initiative with scant popular support. The phenomenon of McCarthyism ensured that it would remain so.

Policy for a Nonmonolithic World

But what difference would it have made if the public had conceived of communism in a nonmonolithic fashion? Did the absence of such a belief, or even a conversation about it, work to the detriment of U.S. or British foreign policy? Would such a dialogue have made it easier for policymakers to pursue a wedge strategy? Even if they could have pursued one, was it likely to have worked?

Broader interest in exploring tensions within international communism might not have yielded immediate benefits, but such a conversation might also have opened up diplomatic avenues closed off by the monolithic framework. From time to time, U.S. officials such as Kennan, Bohlen, Davies, Adams, and Ogburn did, in fact, call for a frank and sophisticated approach to public education for that very purpose. Rarely, however, did the State Department seek to engage Americans in a conversation about the monolithic and nonmonolithic aspects of international communism. As a result, a persistent and uncontested belief in a Communist monolith, solidified in no small measure by the vagaries of domestic politics, took root in the public culture, narrowing the creativity of U.S. policymakers and heightening the partisanship of American politics. Especially in light of the China recognition controversy, there is little doubt that such thinking constrained U.S. diplomacy during the Cold War.

British policymakers, who were less beholden to the whims of popular sentiment, had correspondingly little reason to stump for any such policy. The hawkish, anti-Communist cast of both the Russia Committee and the Information Research Department, moreover, militated against promotion of that position. To be fair, the temporal window for doing so was narrow; prior to June 1948, such talk would have fallen on deaf ears. Even after the Tito affair, a discussion of that sort would likely have been brief, given the subsequent hardening of the bloc. Stalin's purges in Eastern Europe, Mao's decision to "lean" toward the Kremlin in the Cold War, the signing of the Sino-Soviet treaty, the

North Korean invasion of South Korea, China's entrance into the Korean War—each seemed to be manifestations of a trajectory and a movement that would have inhibited efforts to portray communism as anything but monolithic. When Britain did embark on such a potentially bloc-busting policy, as with its recognition of the PRC, Beijing's rejection of that offer suggests that, at least for the scope of this study, both East and West were erecting roadblocks to a more sophisticated brand of diplomacy.

Vietnam, however, is one case in which a discussion of this sort might have mattered. Various observers, including scholars and government officials, have argued that the United States missed a golden opportunity to foster amicable relations with Ho. The purge of the "China Hands," moreover, members of the foreign service responsible for policy toward China up through its civil war, removed from circulation those statesmen most sensitive to particularity and difference in the Communist world. Consequently, the argument runs, when it came time to evaluate the Vietnamese Communists and their relationship to the PRC, the absence of such expertise led America further into the quagmire that became the Vietnam War. A corresponding and more general contention has been that the failure to detect splits between Moscow and Beijing prolonged the Cold War's bipolarity, thereby limiting the flexibility and effectiveness of U.S. policy.[61]

During the early postwar years, U.S. policymakers were, in fact, approaching Vietnam from a position that could have formed the basis for such a dialogue. Several officials with responsibility for the area recognized Ho's nationalist appeal and pro-American sentiments. The State Department, moreover, was loath to support French and British efforts to reinstall Paris as the colonial overlord of Indochina. Even the hardening of the Cold War in Europe and the declining fortunes of the Chinese Nationalists in Asia were not enough to tip the scales in favor of France. Only in 1949, after Paris had made its most fulsome pledge of independence for a united Vietnam, did the United States offer its rhetorical support for the French mission. Still, American largess did not materialize until both Mao and Stalin had recognized Ho's government in early 1950 and then, more dramatically, following the outbreak of the Korean War later that June. In that fluid situation, in which antipathy for the French project in Southeast Asia coexisted with competing visions of Ho and the Vietminh, a greater appreciation for regional and cultural particularity might have created political space at home for a more enlightened policy toward Vietnam.

It is not at all clear, however, whether such an approach would have been reciprocated by Hanoi. Ho was in several ways an outlier among the Vietminh leadership, with many of his comrades much more reticent than he about making common cause with the United States. Even were he to have won them over and forged a working relationship with Washington, his doctrinal affinity for Moscow and Beijing probably would have rendered exceedingly tenuous any such ties he was able to form. Moreover, key U.S. officials, such as Secretary of State Dean Acheson and Ambassador to France Jefferson Caffery, were highly dubious of Ho's Titoist potential and were unlikely to have shed those fears, especially given the emergence of a Communist China. Even those more sympathetic to Ho presumed that the political immaturity of DRV officials and citizens rendered both easy prey for the ideological and geopolitical ambitions of Moscow and/or Beijing.[62] Therefore, not only is it improbable that Ho would have steered his country toward the West and away from the Communist world, but hardly any U.S. official in a position of responsibility put much stock in that process in the first place. American policymakers were simply too cowed by the power of French communism during the period 1945 through 1947 and 1948 to have challenged Paris on its program of colonial reconquest, and then were too worried about the orientation of Vietnamese communism in subsequent years to have explored with any seriousness the possibility of adopting a pro-DRV stance.[63]

Broader knowledge of the Sino-Soviet split might well have led U.S. policymakers to rethink their assumptions about the Vietnamese insurgency, but there is also reason to doubt this claim. By the 1960s, the U.S. government was well aware of heightening tension within the Communist world and had considered many of the arguments the ousted China Hands would likely have made regarding the break-up of the socialist bloc.[64] Presidents John F. Kennedy and Lyndon B. Johnson were familiar with reports of division among the Vietnamese Communists, the parlous state of the South Vietnamese regime, the independent actions of Moscow, Beijing, and Hanoi, and the rifts developing among them. Furthermore, the purge that allegedly wiped out an entire class of Asian experts did not touch China specialist Everett S. Drumright or officials schooled in Japanese affairs, nor did it affect those who recognized these fissures, such as Alan Whiting, who rose to prominence within the department at a later date. Moreover, by the mid-1950s, the CIA had begun to furnish a steady stream of reports on intrabloc tension, going so far as to declare in 1960 that the break between Moscow and Beijing was irrevocable. Much of that information was reaching the State Department at the very moment the United States began to escalate its military commitment to Vietnam. The government, therefore, possessed a significant amount of competence on Asia and the Sino-Soviet split. Moreover, there is emerging evidence that the fractiousness of the socialist world was itself exacerbating the challenges in Southeast Asia. The Sino-Soviet split was thus hardly a boon for Western policymakers, for Soviet and Chinese Communists were offering greater amounts of support to Vietnam precisely because of the ideological competition they were waging.[65]

Although the monolithic framework might not have altered the actual practice of U.S. foreign policy, it seems to have had an impact on less overt aspects of American diplomacy. It might well have damaged the effectiveness of U.S. counterintelligence during the Cold War; it almost certainly hurt the morale of those conducting it. The CIA's top counterspy, James Jesus Angleton, never believed in the authenticity of the Sino-Soviet split, nor did he accept as fact either the Albanian-Soviet or Yugoslav-Soviet rifts. He would maintain those convictions even in the face of contradictory evidence provided by the agency itself. According to Donald Zagoria, a former CIA analyst of Soviet affairs, Angleton was one of a number of "true believers" who "needed to believe in the Communist monolith."[66]

The monolithic framework might have had its greatest impact, however, on domestic affairs. In an ironic twist, the willingness of the State Department to act on the assumptions of the wedge strategy during the mid-1940s backfired on the Truman administration, locking in the more rigidly monolithic mindset that arose later in the decade. The thought that the U.S. government could get along or at least do business with the Chinese Communists—a belief that was inherent in a host of initiatives, including Marshall's efforts to construct a power-sharing arrangement in 1946, administration reluctance in aiding Chiang, and official comment on the potential for a Soviet-CCP schism—emerged out of the notion that the United States could wean Mao and his ilk away from the Kremlin. It was the alleged fatuousness of that belief, as demonstrated by Mao's increasing affinity for Moscow, that the "primitives," to use Dean Acheson's phrase, used to discredit the very idea of a breakaway Communist movement.[67] While the image of a pliable Mao was both a politically acceptable and, it now appears, generally accurate representation of the CCP and its leanings in the immediate postwar period, it would morph into political dynamite by the end of the decade.

It would seem, therefore, that Truman's critics had turned the wedge strategy against the administration itself, hardening an already static view of communism and poisoning the domestic political climate. Of course, other dynamics made it equally difficult to pursue a wedge strategy: anti-New Deal Republicans had their own reasons for attacking Truman; the administration's inability to clarify its objectives hampered its flexibility; and the Chinese Communists themselves, we now know, were none too interested in American entreaties after 1946.[68] Yet, in retrospect, the demise of the wedge strategy seems at least partly attributable to its very implementation. Its inability to deliver China into American arms allowed the administration's critics to discredit its fundamental assumptions, leaving the wedge strategy and the ideas supporting it with little backing among the public at large.

Suffice it to say, the Communist monolith has had a curious existence. In the abstract, it connoted images of both stasis and change, possessing all the cohesiveness of an implacable, impervious foe as well as the immutable might of an insistent creeping force. More concretely, it alluded to the political realities of Eastern Europe, where Moscow had imposed its will and arrayed substantial power to maintain its hegemony. But it also referred to the actions of Soviet minions, be they loyal comrades aping Stalin's line behind the Iron Curtain or fifth column movements doing his bidding out beyond it. The image, therefore, held descriptive as well as predictive power, illuminating the present conditions of Communist states and forecasting the future behavior of Communist parties.

American and British statesmen, among others, found the Communist monolith a highly compelling concept during the early days of the Cold War. Their obeisance to a monolithic framework stemmed from dynamics that were deeply embedded as well as close to the surface of their respective political cultures. The publics they represented were similarly beholden to that interpretive lens. Although numerous observers in both countries would comment on fissures in the Communist world, practically all of them did so from a monolithic perspective, interpreting schismatic movements as a residual development rather than a primal condition of the Communist life cycle. Hardly anyone in a position of responsibility assumed that Communist parties were "born free" of the Soviet pull. Given the combination of a shared historical consciousness, the weight of contemporary evidence, the uncertainties of the age, and the politics that went along with them, it is hard to see how great numbers of those living at the time could have done otherwise.

Notes

Index

Notes

Abbreviations

AC	Advertising Council
AHR	*American Historical Review*
CAB	Records of the Cabinet Office
CAF	Country and Area Files
CCF	Congress for Cultural Freedom
CCP	Chinese Communist Party
CFM	Council of Foreign Ministers
CFR	Council on Foreign Relations
CFRP	Council on Foreign Relations Papers
CIA	Central Intelligence Agency
CIG	Central Intelligence Group
CM	Cabinet Minute
CP	Cabinet Paper
CPGB	Communist Party of Great Britain
CPUSA	Communist Party, USA
CWIHP	Cold War International History Project
DBPO	*Documents on British Policy Overseas*
DDRS	Declassified Documents Reference System
DRV	Democratic Republic of Vietnam
DSB	*Department of State Bulletin*
ECCI	Executive Committee of the Communist International
ERP	European Recovery Program
FO 371	Foreign Office, Political Departments
FO 800	Foreign Office, Private Office, Various Ministers' and Officials' Papers
FO 953	Foreign Office, Information Policy Department

FO 975	Foreign Office, Information Research Department, Information Reports
FO 1110	Foreign Office, Information Research Department, General Correspondence
FRUS	*Foreign Relations of the United States*
HSTL	Harry S. Truman Library and Museum
INR	Bureau of Intelligence and Research
IRD	Information Research Department
JCWS	*Journal of Cold War Studies*
JFKL	John F. Kennedy Library and Museum
JIC	Joint Intelligence Committee
KPA	Korean People's Army
LBJL	Lyndon B. Johnson Library and Museum
LM	Library Microfilm
NARA	National Archives and Records Administration, College Park
NIE	National Intelligence Estimate
NSC	National Security Council
NS&N	*New Statesman & Nation*
OASSPA	Office of the Assistant Secretary of State for Public Affairs
OCA	Office of Chinese Affairs
OIR	Office of Intelligence Research
OPA	Office of Public Affairs
OPOS	Office of Public Opinion Studies
ORE	Office of Research and Evaluation/Office of Reports and Estimates
OSS	Office of Strategic Services
PCF	Parti Communist Français
PCI	Partito Comunista Italiano
POF	President's Office Files
PPP: GWB	*Public Papers of the Presidents: George W. Bush, 2002*
PPP: HST	*Public Papers of the Presidents of the United States: The Papers of Harry S. Truman, 1945–1953*
PPPS	Papers of the Policy Planning Staff
PREM	Records of the Prime Minister's Office
PRO	Public Record Office
PSF	President's Secretary's Files
RC	Russia Committee
RG 59	General Records of the State Department
RG 263	Records of the Central Intelligence Agency
RPPS	Records of the Policy Planning Staff
SDPPSP	State Department Policy Planning Staff Papers
SF	Subject Files
SGMML	Seeley G. Mudd Manuscript Library, Princeton University
TNA	The National Archives, United Kingdom
YCP	Yugoslav Communist Party

Introduction

1. "Questions for Possible Study by S/P," 12 January 1950, NARA, RPPS 1947–1953, Box 44, Adams Chronological.
2. Melvyn P. Leffler, "The American Conception of National Security and the Beginnings of the Cold War, 1945–48," *American Historical Review* 89, no. 2 (April 1984): 348–381; John Lewis Gaddis, "The Insecurities of Victory: The United States and the Perception of the Soviet Threat after World War II," in *The Truman Presidency,* ed. Michael J. Lacey (New York, 1989), 236–239, 258–260, 263–268.
3. Scholarship on the power of symbols suggests that people interpret events not only according to their own psychological backgrounds but against larger cultural schemes. The meaning of an event, therefore, becomes refracted through various prisms on both the individual and societal level. See Marshall Sahlins, *Islands of History* (Chicago, 1985), 153.
4. Robert L. Ivie argues that metaphors, "as the source of arguments and first principles, provide the linguistic mechanism for grasping similarities among dissimilarities." Ivie, "Cold War Motives and Rhetorical Metaphor: A Framework of Criticism," in *Cold War Rhetoric: Strategy, Metaphor, and Ideology,* ed. Martin Medhurst et al. (East Lansing, Mich., 1997), 73. See also John Ziman, *Reliable Knowledge: An Exploration of the Grounds for Belief in Science* (New York, 1978), 24; Deborah Welch Larson, *Origins of Containment: A Psychological Explanation* (Princeton, N.J., 1985), 52–57.
5. See, for example, Howard Zinn, *Vietnam: The Logic of Withdrawal* (Boston, 1967), 83-84; Thomas G. Paterson et al., *American Foreign Policy: A History since 1900,* 2nd ed. (Lexington, Mass., 1983), 457, 463; Paterson, *Meeting the Communist Threat: Truman to Reagan* (New York, 1988), ix, 52, 128; Stephen M. Walt, *The Origins of Alliances* (Ithaca, N.Y., 1990), ix; Warren I. Cohen, *The Cambridge History of American Foreign Relations,* vol. 4, *America in the Age of Soviet Power, 1945–1991* (New York, 1993), 44; Gary A. Donaldson, *America at War since 1945: Politics and Diplomacy in Korea, Vietnam, and the Gulf War* (Westport, Conn., 1996), 12; Ngaire Woods, *Explaining International Relations since 1945* (New York, 1996), 183; James T. Miller, *On Our Own: Americans in the Sixties* (Lexington, Mass., 1996), 10; Michael H. Hunt, *Lyndon Johnson's War: America's Cold War Crusade in Vietnam, 1945–1968* (New York, 1997), 41; Fraser J. Harbutt, *The Cold War Era* (Malden, Mass., 2002), 68.
6. For some of the more noteworthy examples of each of these studies, see Larson, *Origins of Containment;* Richard M. Freeland, *The Truman Doctrine and the Origins of McCarthyism: Foreign Policy, Domestic Politics, and Internal Security, 1946–48* (New York, 1975); Thomas Paterson, *Meeting the Communist Threat: Truman to Reagan* (New York, 1988); Jack Snyder, *Myths of Empire: Domestic Politics and International Ambition* (Ithaca, N.Y., 1991), especially 255–304. While other volumes, such as John Lewis Gaddis's *The United States and the Origins of the Cold War* (New York,

1972) and Melvyn P. Leffler's *The Specter of Communism, 1917–1991* (New York, 1994), portray the emerging Cold War mind-set as a product of longer-term historical forces, neither does so against the backdrop of a more long-term, and more deeply ingrained, historical consciousness. Michael Hogan does indeed locate America's "national security discourse" in its "republican" identity, but he refrains from exploring that heritage in any fundamental way. Michael J. Hogan, *A Cross of Iron: Harry S. Truman and the Origins of the National Security State, 1945–1954* (New York, 1998), xi.

7. See Michael Donelan, *The Ideas of American Foreign Policy* (London, 1963); Michael H. Hunt, *Ideology and U.S. Foreign Policy* (New Haven, Conn., 1987); Anders Stephanson, *Manifest Destiny: American Expansion and the Empire of Right* (New York, 1995); Scott Lucas, *Freedom's War: The American Crusade against the Soviet Union* (New York, 1999). The most imaginative of this grouping is Frank Ninkovich's *Modernity and Power: A History of the Domino Theory in the Twentieth Century* (Chicago, 1994). Ninkovich offers a compelling account of how changing conceptions of time and space contributed to the crisis mentality of Cold War American statesmen.

8. Stephen J. Whitfield, *The Culture of the Cold War* (Baltimore, Md., 1991, 1996); Lary May, ed., *Recasting America: Culture and Politics in the Age of Cold War* (Chicago, 1989); Elaine Tyler May, *Homeward Bound: American Families in the Cold War Era* (New York, 1988).

9. John Lewis Gaddis, *The Long Peace: Inquiries into the History of the Cold War* (New York, 1987), 148; Gordon H. Chang, *Friends and Enemies: The United States, China, and the Soviet Union, 1948–1972* (Stanford, Calif., 1990), 3; see also David Allan Mayers, *Cracking the Monolith: U.S. Policy against the Sino-Soviet Alliance, 1949–1955* (Baton Rouge, La., 1986).

10. Andrew Ezergailis, "'Monolithic' vs. 'Crumbling' Communism," *Problems of Communism* 19, no. 1 (January/February 1970): 1; Ian H. Birchall, *Workers against the Monolith: The Communist Parties since 1943* (London, 1974); "What's Causing the Cracks in the Communist Monolith?" *U.S. News & World Report*, 1 November 1976, 66; Lyman H. Legters, "The Communist System: Monolithic or Diverse?" *Intellect* 104, no. 2375 (May/June 1976): 563; Evelyn Geller, *Communism: End of the Monolith?* (New York, 1978); Rhonda Smither Blunt, "The Mythical Monolith: American China Policy and the Sino-Soviet Split, 1945–1972" (Master's thesis, College of William and Mary, 1978); Malvin Magnus Helgesen, "The Origins of the Party-State Monolith in Soviet Russia: Relations between the Soviet and Party Committee in the Central Provinces, October 1917–March 1921" (Ph.D. dissertation, State University of New York at Stony Brook, 1980).

11. Mayers, *Cracking the Monolith*; Gaddis, *The Long Peace*, 147–194.

12. Chang, *Friends and Enemies*; Michael Scammel, *The Solzhenitsyn Files: Secret Soviet Documents Reveal One Man's Fight against the Monolith* (Chicago, 1995); Peter Stavrakis et al., eds., *Beyond the Monolith: The Emergence of Regionalism in Post-Soviet Russia* (Washington, D.C., 1997); Eugene B. Rumer, *The End of a Monolith: The Politics of Military Reform in*

the Soviet Armed Forces (Santa Monica, Calif., 1991); Boris Kagerlitsky, *The Disintegration of the Monolith* (New York, 1992).

13. "Cover Story: The TV Monolith—Slowest to Change," *Far Eastern Economic Review* 128, no. 20 (May 1985): 36; Hilton Kramer, Confronting the Monolith," in *Our Country, Our Culture: The Politics of Political Correctness,* ed. Edith Kurzweil and William Phillips (Boston, 1994); Charles Ramirez Berg, "Cracks in the 'Macho' Monolith: Machismo, Man, and Mexico in Recent Mexican Cinema," *New Orleans* Review 16, no. 1 (Spring 1989): 67; Allan White, "Dismantling the Monolith: A Retrospective View of the Papal Visit," *New Blackfriars* 64, no. 756 (June 1983): 252; Deroy Murdock, "Black America Must Shed Monolithic Thinking," *Human Events* 46, no. 15 (12 April 1985): 9; Goodwin H. Harding, "Monolithic Daddyism: An Autobiographical Account of Death," *Life-Threatening Behavior* 3, no. 2 (Summer 1973): 155.

14. John Fousek, *To Lead the Free World: American Nationalism and the Cultural Roots of the Cold War* (Chapel Hill, N.C., 2000), ix.

15. Philip D. Zelikow, "Terrorism and America's New War," retrieved 4 January 2007, *Miller Center Forum,* <http://millercenter.virginia.edu>; Walter LaFeber et al., "The Road to and from September 11th: A Roundtable," *Diplomatic History* 26, no. 4 (Fall 2002): 543–647; Mary L. Dudziak, *September 11 in History: A Watershed Moment?* (Durham, N.C., 2003); Joanne Meyerowitz, *History and September 11th* (Philadelphia, 2003); Melvyn P. Leffler, "9/11 and the Past and Future of American Foreign Policy," *International Affairs* 79 (2003): 1045–1063; John Lewis Gaddis, *Surprise, Security, and the American Experience* (Cambridge, Mass., 2004); Norman Podhoretz, "World War IV: How It Started, What It Means, and Why We Have to Win," *Commentary* (September 2004): 17–54; Peter Beinart, "A Fighting Faith," *The New Republic,* 13 December 2004, 17; James Mann, *Rise of the Vulcans: The History of Bush's War Cabinet* (New York, 2004), 313, 330.

16. "State of the Union Address," 29 January 2002, *Public Papers of the Presidents: George W. Bush, 2002* (hereafter *PPP: GWB*) (Washington, D.C., 2003), 131. According to Bush speechwriter David Frum, the phrase morphed from an "axis of hatred," comprising Iraq and Iran, to an "axis of evil" involving those two nations, and then to the final inclusion of North Korea as a member of the trio. Frum, *The Right Man: The Surprise Presidency of George W. Bush* (New York, 2003), 238. See also John R. Bolton, "Beyond the Axis of Evil: Additional Threats from Weapons of Mass Destruction," 6 May 2002, retrieved 18 December 2006, www.state.gov/t/us/rm/9962.htm; Paul Berman, *Terror and Liberalism* (New York, 2003).

17. *Survey by Newsweek and Princeton Survey Research Associates, January 31–February 1, 2002,* retrieved June 24, 2008, from the iPOLL Databank, The Roper Center for Public Opinion Research, University of Connecticut, <http://www.ropercenter.uconn.edu/ipoll.html>; *Survey by Cook Political Report and IPSOS-Reid, February 1–February 3, 2002,* ibid.; *Survey by Fox News and Opinion Dynamics, February 12–February 13, 2002,* ibid.; *Survey by Democracy Corps and Greenberg Quinlan Rosner Research, February*

26–March 3, 2002, ibid.; *Survey by Pew Research Center for the People & the Press, International Herald Tribune, and the Council on Foreign Relations and Princeton Survey Research Associates, April 3–April 8, 2002*, ibid. See also David W. Moore, " 'Axis of Evil' Countries Seen as America's Greatest Enemies," 23 February 2005, retrieved 24 June 2008 from the Gallup News Service, www.gallup.com; Lydia Saad, " 'Axis of Evil' Countries Dominate U.S. Perceptions of Greatest Enemy," 22 February 2007, ibid.

18. Thomas E. Ricks, *Fiasco: The American Military Adventure in Iraq* (New York, 2006), 308; Jeffrey Record, "Bounding the Global War on Terrorism," Strategic Studies Institute, Army War College, December 2003; Fareed Zakaria, "Mao & Stalin, Osama & Saddam," *Newsweek,* 18 September 2006, 39; Philip H. Gordon, *Winning the Right War: The Path to Security for America and the World* (New York, 2007), 22–29, 103.

19. "State of the Union Address," 28 January 2003, retrieved 24 June 2008, www.whitehouse.gov/news/releases/2003/01/20030128-19.html; "Address to the Nation Announcing Strikes against Al Qaida Training Camps and Taliban Military Installations in Afghanistan," 7 October 2001, *PPP: GWB,* 2001, vol. 2, 1201–1202. Bush softened this rhetoric in his "Remarks to the United Nations General Assembly," 10 November 2001, ibid., 1375–1379.

20. See Frank Ninkovich, *The Wilsonian Century: U.S. Foreign Policy since 1900* (Chicago, 1999), 8–11.

1. The Inheritance

1. Henry Luce, "The American Century," *Life,* 17 February 1941, 61–66. For a reappraisal of Luce's article, see the roundtable in *Diplomatic History* 23, no. 2 (Spring 1999), 157–370; Robert Herzstein, *Henry R. Luce: A Political Portrait of the Man Who Created the American Century* (New York, 1994), 176–185, 232.

2. The classic statement of the Whig perspective is found in Herbert Butterfield, *The Whig Interpretation of History* (London, 1951).

3. Jack P. Greene, *The Intellectual Construction of America: Exceptionalism and Identity from 1492 to 1800* (Chapel Hill, N.C., 1993); Sacvan Bercovitch, *The American Jeremiad* (Madison, Wis., 1978); Richard Hofstadter, *The Paranoid Style in American Politics* (New York, 1967, 1965); David Brion Davis, ed., *The Fear of Conspiracy: Images of Un-American Subversion from the Revolution to the Present* (Ithaca, N.Y., 1971); Richard O. Curry and Thomas M. Brown, eds., *Conspiracy: The Fear of Subversion in American History* (New York, 1972).

4. See Peter H. Buckingham, *America Sees Red: Anti-Communism in America, 1870s to 1980s* (Claremont, Calif., 1988), 11–19; M. J. Heale, *American Anticommunism: Combating the Enemy within, 1830–1970* (Baltimore, Md., 1990), 42–59; John Stevenson, *British Society 1914–45* (London, 1984), 55–57. Alan Dawley, *Changing the World: American Progressives in War and Revolution* (Princeton, N.J., 2003), 268–276, compares U.S. and British

responses to this challenge, as does Markku Ruotsila, *British and American Anticommunism before the Cold War* (London, 2001), 3–66.

5. See Helmut Gruber, *International Communism in the Era of Lenin: A Documentary History* (Ithaca, N.Y., 1967), 53–116; Franz Borkenau, *World Communism: A History of the Communist International* (Ann Arbor, Mich., 1962), 57–79.

6. Fraser Harbutt, *The Iron Curtain: Churchill, America, and the Origins of the Cold War* (New York, 1986), 25, 29. On Labour, see C. L. Mowat, *Britain between the Wars, 1918–40* (Chicago, 1955), 151–153.

7. Richard Gid Powers, *Not without Honor: The History of American Anticommunism* (New York, 1995), 20–21; William K. Klingaman, *1919: The Year Our World Began* (New York, 1987), 207–208, 331; N. Gordon Levin Jr., *Woodrow Wilson and World Politics: America's Response to War and Revolution* (New York, 1968), 189–197.

8. Theodore Draper, *The Roots of American Communism* (Chicago, 1985, 1957), 262–264. That declaration notwithstanding, American Communists saw themselves less as agents of a foreign power than as members of a single organization located in Moscow. For more on this period, see Harvey Klehr, John Earl Haynes, and Kyrill M. Anderson, eds., *The Soviet World of American Communism* (New Haven, Conn., 1998), 14–31; Borkenau, *World Communism*, 206–207; Helmut Gruber, *Soviet Russia Masters the Comintern: International Communism in the Era of Stalin's Ascendancy* (New York, 1974), 3–9; Kevin McDermott and Jeremy Agnew, *The Comintern: A History of International Communism from Lenin to Stalin* (New York, 1997), 1–40.

9. Powers, *Not without Honor*, 29–30, 64–65; Melvyn Leffler, *The Specter of Communism: The United States and the Origins of the Cold War, 1917–1953* (New York, 1994), 16; John Lewis Gaddis, *Russia, the Soviet Union, and the United States: An Interpretive History* (New York, 1990, 1978), 106–108; Buckingham, *America Sees Red*, 19–38; James Weinstein, *The Decline of Socialism in America, 1912–1925* (New Brunswick, N.J., 1984, 1967), 310–323.

10. Mowat, *Britain between the Wars*, 188–194; Curtis Keeble, *Britain and the Soviet Union, 1917–89* (New York, 1990), 95–108; F. S. Northedge and Audrey Wells, *Britain and Soviet Communism: The Impact of a Revolution* (London, 1982), 42–46; Andrew J. Williams, *Labour and Russia: The Attitude of the Labour Party to the U.S.S.R., 1924–1934* (Manchester, 1989), 17–45.

11. Gruber, *Soviet Russia Masters the Comintern*, 175–200; Kevin McDermott, "Bolshevisation 'from Above' or 'from Below'? The Comintern and European Communism in the 1920s," *Communism: National and* International, ed. Tauno Saarela and Kimmo Rentola (Helsinki, 1998), 105–118. Uninterested in granting true independence to Communist parties outside the U.S.S.R., the Kremlin was no more willing to tolerate such parochialism within the bounds of the Soviet Union itself. See Roman Smal-Stocki, "The Origins of National Communism," *Ukrainian Quarterly* 14, no. 4 (December 1958):

319; Mikhail Heller and Alexander Nekrich, *Utopia in Power: A History of the Soviet Union from 1917 to the Present* (New York, 1986), 151–157, 298–301.

12. Adam B. Ulam, *A History of Soviet Russia* (New York, 1976), 59–87; Martin Malia, *The Soviet Tragedy: A History of Socialism in Russia, 1917–1991* (New York, 1994), 250–252; McDermott and Agnew, *The Comintern*, 41–157; Walter A. Kemp, *Nationalism and Communism in Eastern Europe and the Soviet Union* (New York, 1999), 87–88.

13. Malia, *The Soviet Tragedy*, 167–171; Richard Pipes, *Russia under the Bolshevik Regime* (New York, 1995), 456.

14. Roy Medvedev, *Let History Judge: The Origins and Consequences of Stalinism* (New York, 1971), 387.

15. Nathan Leites, "Interaction: The Third International on Its Changes of Policy," in *Language of Politics: Studies in Quantitative Semantics*, ed. Harold Lasswell (New York, 1949), 333.

16. Kermit E. McKenzie, *Comintern and World Revolution, 1928–1943* (New York, 1964), 55.

17. Dmitri Volkogonov, *Stalin: Triumph and Tragedy* (New York, 1991), 218. Though "iron discipline" had been a central tenet of the early Bolshevik era, it was even more highly prized after Lenin, and embraced by dictators from Left to Right. Jane Degras, ed., *The Communist International, 1919–1943: Documents*, vol. 2 (New York, 1969), 106, 198, 464.

18. Leon Trotsky, *The Struggle against Fascism in Germany* (New York, 1971), 110; see also Fernando Claudin, *The Communist Movement: From Comintern to Cominform*, vol. 1 (New York, 1975), 120–121, and especially the chapter on "Monolithicity," 103–125.

19. Joseph Stalin, *Foundations of Leninism* (New York, 1932), 118.

20. Gene Dennis, "The Bolshevization of the Communist Party of the United States in the Struggle against the Imperialist War," *The Communist* 19, no. 5 (May 1940): 416; I would like to thank Steven Schwartz for this reference. See also Anton Antonov-Ovseyenko, *The Time of Stalin: Portrait of a Tyranny* (New York, 1980), 225.

21. Eugenio Reale, "The Founding of the Cominform," in *The Comintern: Historical Highlights, Essays, Recollections*, ed. Milorad M. Drachkovitch and Branko Lazitch (New York, 1966), 263; Irwin M. Wall, *French Communism in the Era of Stalin: The Quest for Unity and Integration, 1945–1962* (Westport, Conn., 1983), 5–6.

22. "Soviet Activity," *Times*, 13 February 1924, 14; "Soviet Purge of Trotskyists," *Times*, 27 August 1936, 11; "Yesterday's Heroes," *Times*, 14 June 1937, 15; "Where Stalin Is Master," *Times*, 12 December 1939, 7. See also "Moscow Leaders' Dissensions," *Times*, 12 May 1924, 8.

23. Louis Fischer, "The Passing of Trotsky," *Nation*, 21 December 1927, 703. Underscoring the term's flexibility, the journal would invoke it ten years later to describe the workings of the modern capitalist corporation. See "Map of Today," *Nation*, 10 July 1937, 32.

24. Herbert L. Matthews, "Rome Sees a Victory," *New York Times,* 14 August 1939, 1; see also Leon Trotsky, "Stalin in Retreat, Trotsky Declares," *New York Times,* 30 January 1937, 2; Anne O'Hare McCormick, "Seven Capitals in Search of a Policy," *New York Times,* 18 April 1937, 127; Henry B. Armstrong, "Demands of Monolithic States," *New York Times,* 26 June 1938, 84; Anne O'Hare McCormick, "Stunned Nations in the Nazi Shadow," *New York Times,* 109.

25. "New Diplomacy," *Washington Post,* 3 February 1944, 8; see also "The Nazis Move Left," *Washington Post,* 26 June 1939, 10; "Misunderstanding," *Washington Post,* 17 February 1944, 10.

26. On the language of communism and the importance of the monolithic idea, see Morten Thing, "The Signs of Communism—Signs of Ambiguity: Language and Communism," in *Communism: Nationalism and Internationalism,* ed. Saarela and Rentola, 246–247.

27. Martin H. Folly, *Churchill, Whitehall, and the Soviet Union, 1940–45* (New York, 2000), 16; Eduard Mark, "October or Thermidor? Interpretations of Stalinism and the Perception of Soviet Foreign Policy in the United States, 1927–1947," *American Historical Review* (hereafter *AHR*) 94 (October 1989): 938–941. See also Eduard Mark, "The Interpretation of Soviet Foreign Policy in the United States, 1928–1947" (Ph.D. diss., University of Connecticut, 1978), 51.

28. Folly, *Churchill, Whitehall, and the Soviet Union,* 54; Mark, "The Interpretation of Soviet Foreign Policy," 6, 55–57, 67; Henderson memorandum, 22 July 1939, *FRUS: The Soviet Union, 1933–39* (Washington, D.C., 1952), 773–775.

29. K. W. Watkins, *Britain Divided: The Effect of the Spanish Civil War on British Political Opinion* (New York, 1963), 84, 88–89; Noreen Branson and Margot Heinemann, *Britain in the 1930's* (New York, 1971), 255, 275–280, 308–322; P. M. H. Bell, *John Bull and the Bear: British Public Opinion, Foreign Policy and the Soviet Union, 1941–1945* (New York, 1990), 28–29; Winston Churchill, *Step by Step* (London, 1939), 37. Churchill refers specifically to a "Communist Spain spreading its snaky tentacles," but given his understanding of communism, the ultimate beneficiary of such a development would have likely been Moscow.

30. Bell, *John Bull,* 29; Mowat, *Britain between the Wars,* 579–581. For the impact of Spain on the Left, see *The God that Failed,* ed. Richard Crossman (New York, 1949).

31. For a description of cultural creation as a social process, see Clifford Geertz, *The Interpretation of Cultures: Selected Essays* (New York, 1973), 213–220; Michael Kammen, *Mystic Chords of Memory: The Transformation of Tradition in American Culture* (New York, 1991), 13; Robert Dallek, *Franklin D. Roosevelt and American Foreign Policy, 1932–1945* (New York, 1979), 136–137.

32. Kammen, *Mystic Chords,* 299–527; Alfred Kazin, *On Native Grounds: An Interpretation of Modern American Prose Literature* (New York, 1942),

502; Charles C. Alexander, *Here the Country Lies: Nationalism and the Arts in Twentieth-Century America* (Bloomington, Ind., 1980), 192–241.

33. Branson and Heinemann, *Britain in the 1930's,* 251–275; Mowat, *Britain between the Wars,* 480, 525–528.

34. Richard Pells, *Radical Visions and American Dreams: Culture and Social Thought in the Depression Years* (New York, 1973), 297–298; Branson and Heinemann, *Britain in the 1930's,* 278–280, 308–309.

35. Kazin, *On Native Grounds,* 504; see also Stephen Spender, *The God that Failed,* 231–272.

36. Malcolm Cowley, "The Puritan Legacy," *New Republic,* 26 August 1936, 80. See also Constance Rourke, "In Time of Hesitation," *Nation,* 18 February 1939, 206–207; Abbott Gleason, *Totalitarianism: The Inner History of the Cold War* (New York, 1995), 45–46; Pells, *Radical Visions,* 292–319; John P. Diggins, *The Rise and Fall of the American Left* (New York, 1992), 175–186; Benjamin L. Alpers, *Dictators, Democracy, and American Public Culture: Envisioning the Totalitarian Enemy, 1920s–1950s* (Chapel Hill, N.C., 2003), 144–146.

37. See Thomas R. Maddux, "Red Fascism, Brown Bolshevism: The American Image of Totalitarianism in the 1930s," *The Historian* 40 (November 1977), 97; Winston Churchill, "The Terrible Twins," *Collier's,* 30 September 1939, 22; Alan Bullock, *The Life and Times of Ernest Bevin,* vol. 1 (London, 1960), 527; see also Martin Kitchen, *British Policy towards the Soviet Union during the Second World War* (London, 1986), 20. In March 1940, the Labour Party would issue a public statement declaring that "Fascism and Bolshevism have identical political systems." See C. R. Attlee et al., "The Russian-Finnish War: A Statement of Facts," *Labour's Aims in War and Peace* (London, 1940), 74.

38. Maddux, "Red Fascism," 86–96; Gleason, *Totalitarianism,* 38–45; Alpers, *Dictators,* 129–156.

39. Gleason, *Totalitarianism,* 33, 38–45.

40. Pells, *Radical Visions,* 361; Kazin, *On Native Grounds,* 518.

41. For a brief historiography on "Red Fascism," see Thomas G. Paterson and Les K. Adler, "Red Fascism: The Merger of Nazi Germany and Soviet Russia in the American Image of Totalitarianism, 1930s–1950s," *AHR* 75, no. 4 (April 1970): 1046–1064, and letters in *AHR* volumes 75, no. 7 (December 1970): 2155–2164; 76, no. 2 (April 1971): 575–580; and 76, no. 3 (June 1971): 856–858. See also Daniel M. Smith, "Authoritarianism and American Policy Makers in Two World Wars," *Pacific Historical Review* 43, no. 3 (August 1974): 303–323; Maddux, "Red Fascism," 85–103.

42. F. H. Hinsley and C. A. G. Simkins, eds., *British Intelligence in the Second World War,* vol. 4 (London, 1990), 306; Klehr et al., *The Soviet World of American Communism,* 71–80; Guenter Lewy, *The Cause that Failed: Communism in American Political Life* (New York, 1990), 32.

43. Mark, "October or Thermidor?" 944; See also Thomas R. Maddux, *Years of Estrangement: American Relations with the Soviet Union, 1933–1941*

(Tallahassee, Fla., 1980), 102–106, 167; Kitchen, *British Policy towards the Soviet Union*, 16; Keeble, *Britain and the Soviet Union*, 159–160.

44. Victor Rothwell, *Britain and the Cold War, 1941–1947* (London, 1982), 84, 88–89, 98; Anthony Glees, *The Secrets of the Service: British Intelligence and Communist Subversion, 1939–1951* (London, 1987), 41–58; Lawrence Aronsen and Martin Kitchen, eds., *The Origins of the Cold War in Comparative Perspective: American, British, and Canadian Relations with the Soviet Union, 1941–48* (New York, 1988), 86–99; Folly, *Churchill, Whitehall, and the Soviet Union*, 6–7; for a later stage in the war, see Graham Ross, *The Foreign Office and the Kremlin: British Documents on Anglo-Soviet Relations, 1941–45* (New York, 1984), 147–155, 159–161; Mark, "October or Thermidor?" 946; Dennis J. Dunn, *Caught between Roosevelt and Stalin; America's Ambassadors to Moscow* (Lexington, Ky., 1998), 3–6.

45. John Lewis Gaddis, *The United States and the Origins of the Cold War, 1941–1947* (New York, 1972), 33, 47–49, 50; "Moscow Offensive," *Washington Post*, 24 May 1943, 10.

46. McDermott and Agnew, *The Comintern*, 204–211; Eduard Mark, "Revolution by Degrees: Stalin's National-Front Strategy for Europe, 1941–1947," *Cold War International History Project*, Working Paper no. 31 (Washington, D.C., February 2001), 18, 33–38; Alexander Dallin and F.I. Firsov, *Dimitrov and Stalin, 1934–1943: Letters from the Soviet Archives* (New Haven, Conn., 2000), 255.

47. "American Attitudes toward Russia: A Review, October 1943–October 1944," 1 December 1944, NARA, RG 59, OPOS, Special Reports on Public Attitudes toward Foreign Policy, Box 1; "Popular Opinion and Information about Russia," 22 February 1945, ibid.; see also Hadley Cantril and Mildred Strunk, *Public Opinion, 1935–1946* (Princeton, N.J., 1951), 962, 1169. For Britain, see Bell, *John Bull*, 7, 88–96.

48. "American Attitudes toward Russia," NARA, RG 59, OPOS, Box 1; see also Alpers, *Dictators*, 220–249.

49. "From Leninism to Stalinism," *Life*, 29 March 1943, 36 (see also Ralph Parker, "A Guy Named Joe," *Look*, 27 June 1944, 74); "Russia and European Federation," *New Republic*, 6 September 1943, 320; Joseph E. Davies, "The Soviets and the Post-War," *Life*, 29 March 1943, 49; "Hitler's Appeasement Offensive," *New Republic*, 15 February 1943, 200; see also Richard H. Pells, *The Liberal Mind in a Conservative Age: American Intellectuals in the 1940s and 1950s* (New York, 1985), 36–37; Gaddis, *Origins of the Cold War*, 38.

50. T. Michael Ruddy, *The Cautious Diplomat: Charles E. Bohlen and the Soviet Union, 1929–1969* (Kent, Ohio, 1986), 33; Gaddis, *Origins of the Cold War*, 51–52.

51. Along with the State Department's Division of European Affairs, Murphy had written a primer on Nazism during the war. See *National Socialism: Basic Principles, Their Application by the Nazi Party's Foreign Organization, and the Use of Germans Abroad for Nazi Aims* (Washington, D.C.,

1943). Murphy was special assistant to Director of European Affairs H. Freeman Matthews.

52. Raymond E. Murphy, "Possible Resurrection of Communist International, Resumption of Extreme Leftist Activities, Possible Effect on United States," 2 June 1945 (hereafter Murphy Report), *FRUS, The Conference of Berlin, 1945*: I (Washington, D.C., 1960), 269, 271–278.

53. Bell, *John Bull*, 96–100, 185; Aronsen and Kitchen, *The Origins of the Cold War*, 88–89; Rothwell, *Britain and the Cold War*, 104; Folly, *Churchill, Whitehall, and the Soviet Union*, 65–67; see also Hinsley and Simkins, *British Intelligence in the Second World War*, 285.

54. Rothwell, *Britain and the Cold War*, 92, 98.

55. Winston S. Churchill, *His Complete Speeches, 1897–1963*, ed. Robert Rhodes James, vol. 6 (New York, 1974), 6161.

56. For a treatment of such fears, see James Harris, "Encircled by Enemies: Stalin's Perceptions of the Capitalist World, 1918–1941," *Journal of Strategic Studies* 30, no. 3 (2007): 513–545.

57. William R. Caspary, "United States Public Opinion during the Onset of the Cold War," *Peace Research Society*, Papers 9, Cambridge Conference (1968), 26.

58. Ross, *The Foreign Office and the Kremlin*, 173–175; Folly, *Churchill, Whitehall, and the Soviet Union*, 61, 141, 147; Martin Kitchen argues that Soviet ideology "was totally discounted" in Foreign Office analyses of Moscow's likely postwar behavior. Kitchen, *British Policy towards the Soviet Union*, 27.

59. Lord Gladwyn, *The Memoirs of Lord Gladwyn* (London, 1972), 146.

60. John Lewis Gaddis, *The Long Peace: Inquiries into the History of the Cold War* (New York, 1987), 149–150; George F. Kennan, "Russia's International Position at the Close of the War with Germany," in Kennan, *Memoirs*, vol. 1 (Boston, 1967), 532–546, especially 536–537.

61. David Littlejohn, *The Patriotic Traitors: A History of Collaboration in German-Occupied Europe, 1940–1945* (London, 1972), 15; Peter Davies, *Dangerous Liaisons: Collaboration and World War II* (London, 2004), 6; Hans Fredrik Dahl, *Quisling: A Study in Treachery* (Cambridge, 1999), front matter.

62. Indeed, Kennan believed that Soviet control over international communism was as strong as ever. Gaddis, *Origins of the Cold War*, 296–298.

63. Gillian Peele, *Revival and Reaction: The Right in Contemporary America* (Oxford, 1984), 23; William L. O'Neill, *A Better World: The Great Schism: Stalinism and the American Intellectuals* (New York, 1982), 44–45; Alan M. Wald, *The New York Intellectuals: The Rise and Decline of the Anti-Stalinist Left from the 1930s to the 1980s* (Chapel Hill, N.C., 1987).

64. See Caffery to Byrnes, 29 May 1945, NARA, RG 59, Box 4071, Earl Browder, 1 January 1945—31 December 1949; Klehr et al., *The Soviet World of American Communism*, 91–106; Murphy Report, 268, 270–271, 277–278.

2. Appraising the Enigma

1. Paul Winterton, "The Aims of the U.S.S.R. in Europe," *International Affairs* 22, no. 1 (January 1946): 27.
2. "Bertrand Russell and the Problems of Peace," in *PicturePost, 1938–1950,* ed. Tom Hopkinson (London, 1984), 174.
3. "America and Russia," *Life,* 30 July 1945, 20.
4. "Statement on the Foreign Policy of the U.S.S.R.," 24 July 1945, SGMML, CFRP, vol. 17, Records of Groups–US-Soviet; "Digest of Sixth Meeting," 23 October 1945, ibid., vol. 16, Folder D.
5. John Lewis Gaddis, *Strategies of Containment: A Critical Appraisal of Postwar American National Security Policy during the Cold War,* rev. and exp. ed. (New York, 2005), 16–17; Alonzo L. Hamby, *Man of the People: A Life of Harry S. Truman* (New York, 1995), 314.
6. Ritchie Ovendale, *The English-Speaking Alliance: Britain, the United States, the Dominions and the Cold War, 1945–51* (London, 1985), 16–17; Victor Rothwell, *Britain and the Cold War, 1941–1947* (London, 1982), 226; Francis Beckett, *Clem Attlee* (London, 1997), 139; Kenneth Harris, *Attlee* (New York, 1982), 134–135, 292–296; Terry H. Anderson, *The United States, Great Britain, and the Cold War, 1944–1947* (Columbia, Mo., 1981), 84–86, 182; Alan Bullock, *Ernest Bevin: Foreign Secretary, 1945–1951* (New York, 1983), 25–30, 105–107.
7. "UNO: It May Work," *Time,* 11 February 1946, 24; Bullock, *Bevin,* 105–107, 193.
8. Brimelow Minute, 29 August 1945, *Documents on British Policy Overseas* (hereafter *DBPO*), ser. I, vol. 6, ed. M. E. Pelly et al. (London, 1991), 46.
9. "The Capabilities and Intentions of the Soviet Union as Affected by American Policy" (hereafter Bohlen-Robinson Report), in *Diplomatic History* 1, no. 4 (Fall 1977): 395, 391; Robert L. Messer, "Paths Not Taken: The United States Department of State and Alternatives to Containment, 1945–1946," *Diplomatic History* 1, no. 4 (Fall 1977): 297–319; T. Michael Ruddy, *The Cautious Diplomat: Charles E. Bohlen and the Soviet Union, 1929–1969* (Kent, Ohio, 1986), 57–60.
10. Mark A. Stoler, *Allies and Adversaries: The Joint Chiefs of Staff, the Grand Alliance, and U.S. Strategy in World War II* (Chapel Hill, N.C., 2000), 215–216, 245.
11. Forrestal to Lippmann, 7 January 1946, *The Forrestal Diaries,* ed. Walter Millis (New York, 1951), 128; see also John Lewis Gaddis, *The United States and the Origins of the Cold War, 1941–1947* (New York, 1972), 298–299.
12. Townsend Hoopes and Douglas Brinkley, *Driven Patriot: The Life and Times of James Forrestal* (New York, 1992), 266–269.
13. Forrestal to Luce, 6 January 1946, *Forrestal Diaries,* 128.
14. Edward Willett, "Dialectical Materialism and Russian Objectives," 14 January 1946, HSTL, PSF, SF, Foreign Affairs File (Russia-1), Russia, 1945–1948.
15. Hugh Thomas, *Armed Truce: The Beginnings of the Cold War, 1945–46*

(New York, 1987, 1986), 7–15; Gaddis, *Origins of the Cold War,* 299–301; Arnold A. Offner, *Another Such Victory: President Truman and the Cold War, 1945–1953* (Stanford, Calif., 2002), 128–129.

16. Kennan to Byrnes, 22 February 1946, *FRUS,* 1946, vol. 6 (Washington, D.C., 1969), 696–709; Wilson Miscamble, *George Kennan and the Making of American Foreign Policy, 1947–1950* (Princeton, N.J., 1992), 25–28; Gaddis, *Origins of the Cold War,* 302–304.

17. Kennan to Byrnes, 22 February 1946, *FRUS,* 1946, vol. 6, 703–704.

18. Gaddis, *Origins of the Cold War,* 303–304; Louis J. Halle, *The Cold War as History* (New York, 1967), 105; John Lewis Gaddis, *The Long Peace: Inquiries into the History of the Cold War* (New York, 1987), 39–40.

19. Gaddis, *Origins of the Cold War,* 304–306; see also Thomas, *Armed Truce,* 491–492; Melvyn P. Leffler, *A Preponderance of Power: National Security Policy in the Truman Administration* (Stanford, Calif., 1992), 107; Arthur H. Vandenberg, *The Private Papers of Senator Vandenberg* (Boston, 1952), 243–251.

20. Hadley Cantril and Mildred Strunk, *Public Opinion, 1935–1946* (Princeton, N.J., 1951), 963; George Gallup, *The Gallup Poll: Public Opinion, 1935–71,* vol. 1 (New York, 1972), 567.

21. For instance, the U.S. chargé in Belgrade, Harold Shantz, would describe the Yugoslav ideologue Moshe Pijade as the "Goebbels" of Tito's regime. Shantz to Byrnes, 12 August 1946, *FRUS,* 1946, vol. 6, 917; "The Barbarians Take Vienna," *Chicago Tribune,* 9 May 1946, 18.

22. Agnes Smedley, "We're Building a Fascist China," *Nation,* 31 August 1946, 236; Irving M. Engel, "Rankin and the Republicans," *Nation,* 26 October 1946, 465; I. F. Stone, "Swastika over the Senate," *Nation,* 9 February 1946, 158; Stanley Ross, "Peron: South American Hitler," *Nation,* 16 February 1946, 189; Manuel Sanchez Sarto, "Spain a Nazi Colony," *Nation,* 16 March 1946, 307. Although the *New Republic* found it acceptable to comment on the "Gestapo methods" of Western governments, both that journal and the *Nation* frowned on attempts to apply the analogy to the Soviet Union. M. J. Coldwell, "Gestapo Methods in Canada," *New Republic,* 13 May 1946, 691–692. Likewise, if the *New Republic* spoke of "satellites" at all, it was in relation to those of the former Axis powers. See "Clashes outside Paris," *New Republic,* 26 August 1946, 211.

23. Winston S. Churchill, "Alliance of English-Speaking Peoples," *Vital Speeches of the Day* 12, no. 11 (15 March 1946): 329–332; Fraser J. Harbutt, *The Iron Curtain: Churchill, America, and the Origins of the Cold War* (New York, 1986), 183–197; Gaddis, *Origins of the Cold War,* 306–309; Leffler, *A Preponderance of Power,* 107–110.

24. Churchill, "Alliance of English-Speaking Peoples," 329–332.

25. Harbutt, *The Iron Curtain,* 205; Lynn Boyd Hinds and Theodore Otto Windt Jr., *The Cold War as Rhetoric: The Beginnings, 1945–1950* (Westport, Conn., 1991), 108–113, 144; Rebecca Benson Pels, "The Coalescence of a Cold War Consensus: The Evolution of Fears Regarding the Soviet

Union as Expressed in Selected Popular Magazines, 1944–1947" (Master's thesis, University of Virginia, 1993), 106–108; John Fousek, *To Lead the Free World: American Nationalism and the Cultural Roots of the Cold War* (Chapel Hill, N.C., 2000), 107–111.

26. George Gallup, *The Gallup International Public Opinion Polls: Great Britain, 1937–1975* (New York, 1976), 128; Alan Foster, "The British Press and the Coming of the Cold War," in *Britain and the First Cold War,* ed. Anne Deighton (New York, 1990), 28–30; Raymond Smith, "A Climate of Opinion: British Officials and the Development of British Soviet Policy, 1945–1947," *International Affairs* (1988): 638–639.

27. Kenneth M. Jensen, ed., *Origins of the Cold War: The Novikov, Roberts, and Kennan "Long Telegrams" of 1946* (Washington, D.C., 1993), 54, 63; Sean Greenwood, "Frank Roberts and the 'Other' Long Telegram: The View from the British Embassy in Moscow, March 1946," *Journal of Contemporary History* 25 (1990): 110; Rothwell, *Britain and the Cold War,* 247–252.

28. Anne Deighton, *The Impossible Peace: Britain, the Division of Germany, and the Origins of the Cold War* (New York, 1990), 224; Rothwell, *Britain and the Cold War,* 251–252; Greenwood, "Frank Roberts," 113–120.

29. For background, see Ray Merrick, "The Russia Committee of the Foreign Office and the Cold War, 1946–47," *Journal of Contemporary History* 20 (1985): 453–468; John Zametica, "Three Letters to Bevin: Frank Roberts at the Moscow Embassy, 1945–46," in *British Officials and British Foreign Policy, 1945–50,* ed. John Zametica (New York, 1990), 81–87; Smith, "A Climate of Opinion," 631–647.

30. Warner Memorandum, "The Soviet Campaign against This Country and Our Response to It," 2 April 1946, *DBPO,* ser. 1, vol. 6, 345–352; Deighton, *The Impossible Peace,* 59; Robin Edmonds, *Setting the Mould: The United States and Britain, 1945–1950* (Oxford, 1986), 158.

31. "The Soviet Campaign against This Country," 350–351.

32. Anderson, *The United States, Great Britain, and the Cold War,* 84, 90–95; Andrew Defty, *Britain, America, and Anti-Communist Propaganda, 1945–1953: The Information Research Department* (New York, 2004), 30–37; Ovendale, *The English-Speaking Alliance,* 30–36.

33. Merrick, "The Russia Committee," 456; see also Minutes of RC Meeting, 18 June 1946, TNA/PRO/FO 371/56885, N183/5169/38; Orme Sargent, 13 May 1946, ibid., N6274/5169/G38.

34. "The Soviet Campaign against This Country," 345–352; Robertson Memo, undated, TNA/PRO/FO 371/56885, N8467/5169/G38; Mack to Bevin, rec. 14 January 1946, TNA/PRO/FO 371/56776, N573/137/38; British Embassy, Prague, Date Unknown, PRO/FO 371/56777, N11515/137/38.

35. Maurice Peterson, 22 July 1946, TNA/PRO/FO 371/56776, N9719/137/38; Roberts to Warner, 2 August 1946, ibid., N10671/137/38.

36. Minutes of RC Meeting, 7 November 1946, TNA/PRO/FO 371/56886, N14607/5169/G; Minutes of RC meeting, 28 November 1946, PRO/FO 371/56887, N15458/5169/G38.

37. Hankey to Cavendish-Bentinck, Date Unknown, TNA/PRO/FO 371/56835, N14143/605/38; Warner note on possible revival of the Comintern, Date Unknown, ibid.; J.I.C. (46)70(0), 23 September 1946, "The Spread of Communism and the Extent of Its Direction from Moscow," PRO/CAB 130/17.

38. Barnes to Byrnes, 27 February 1946, FRUS, 1946, vol. 6, 83; Schoenfeld to Byrnes, 6 June 1946, ibid., 303; Barnes to Byrnes, 5 November 1946, ibid., 167; Lane to Byrnes, 8 October 1946, ibid., 507; Keith to Byrnes, 25 November 1946, ibid., 522; Berry to Byrnes, 15 June 1946, ibid., 605; Steinhardt to Byrnes, 3 July 1946, ibid., 205; Smith to Byrnes, 31 May 1946, NARA, LM 177, Reel 1.

39. "Soviet Foreign Policy: A Summation," ca. March/April 1946, in Documentary History of the Truman Presidency, ed. Dennis Merrill (hereafter Documentary History), vol. 7 (Ann Arbor, Mich., 1996), 117–121; "Background of Soviet Foreign Policy," 14 March 1946, ibid., 98–101; ORE 1, "Soviet Foreign and Military Policy," 23 July 1946, Enclosure "A," NARA; see also ORE 1/1, "Revised Soviet Tactics in International Affairs," 6 January 1947, 4, NARA, which maintained the original argument.

40. See, for example, "Soviet Foreign Policy toward Western Europe," 21 March 1946, Merrill, Documentary History, 113.

41. Richard J. Aldrich, "Putting Culture into the Cold War: The Cultural Relations Department (CRD) and British Covert Information Warfare," Intelligence and International Security 18, no. 2 (June 2003): 112–119; Aldrich, The Hidden Hand: Britain, America, and Cold War Secret Intelligence (New York, 2001), 122–128; Joël Kotek, Students and the Cold War (New York, 1996), 62–106; JIC (46)I(0) Final (Revise), 1 March 1946, DBPO, ser. 1, vol. 6, 300; Defty, Britain, American, and Anti-Communist Propaganda, 49.

42. "American Relations with the Soviet Union (Clifford-Elsey Report)," in Merrill, Documentary History, 284–285; Clark M. Clifford, Counsel to the President: A Memoir (New York, 1991), 126. See also Leffler, Preponderance of Power, 131–138; Arthur Krock, Memoirs: Sixty Years on the Firing Line (New York, 1968), 474.

43. "Digest of Fight Meeting Meeting," 25 September 1945, SGMML, CFRP, vol. 16, Folder D; George Franklin Jr., "Report for the Study Group on United States Relations with the U.S.S.R.," 8 April 1946, ibid., vol. 17.

44. Tang Tsou, America's Failure in China, 1941–50 (Chicago, 1963), 181–183, 202–203, 208. John Carter Vincent, director of the Office of Far Eastern Affairs from 1945 to 1947, later remarked that he did not believe such an affinity existed until sometime during the Marshall mission in 1946. See ibid., 221–222.

45. United States Relations with China, with Special Reference to the Period 1944–1949 (Stanford, Calif., 1967), 92; Tsou, America's Failure in China, 200–201.

46. See "The China Crisis," New York Times, 1 November 1944, 22; "The Far Eastern Muddle," New Republic, 13 March 1944, 335. See also "Will China Win Her War?" New Republic, 13 November 1944, 616, and Richard Watts

Jr., "The Chinese Giant Stirs," *New Republic*, 28 May 1945, 735; "Our Choice in China," 10 September 1945, *New Republic*, 781; Tsou, *America's Failure in China*, 223–224.

47. Harrison Forman, *Report from Red China* (New York, 1945), 177; see also Tsou, *America's Failure in China*, 223–236.

48. Proposed Message to MacArthur, 28 February 1946, *FRUS*, 1946, vol. 8 (Washington, D.C., 1971), 645; Smith to Byrnes, 15 June 1946, NARA, RG 59, LM 177, Reel 1; ORE 1, "Soviet Foreign and Military Policy," 23 July 1946, in *Assessing the Soviet Threat: The Early Cold War Years*, ed. Woodrow J. Kuhns (Washington, D.C., 1997), 63; ORE 5/1, "The Situation in Korea," 3 January 1947, 2, 8–9, NARA; Gaddis, *Origins of the Cold War*, 318–323.

49. William J. Duiker, *Sacred War: Nationalism and Revolution in a Divided Vietnam* (New York, 1995), 44–56; William J. Duiker, *Ho Chi Minh* (New York, 2000), 349–350, 378.

50. Acheson to Reed, 9 October 1946, *FRUS*, 1946, vol. 8, 61; Acheson to Reed, 5 December 1946, ibid., 67.

51. Clayton to Reed, 9 September 1946, *FRUS*, vol. 8, 57; O'Sullivan to Byrnes, 1 November 1946, ibid., 62; Caffery to Byrnes, 29 November 1946, ibid., 63; O'Sullivan to Byrnes, 3 December 1946, ibid., 64.

52. Byrnes to Certain Missions Abroad, 17 December 1946, *FRUS*, vol. 8, 72; Marshall to Embassy in France, 3 February 1947, *FRUS*, 1947, vol. 7 (Washington, D.C., 1972), 68; William J. Duiker, *U.S. Containment Policy and the Conflict in Indochina* (Stanford, Calif., 1994), 39–46.

53. Mark Atwood Lawrence, "Transnational Coalition Building and the Making of the Cold War in Indochina, 1947–1949," *Diplomatic History* 26, no. 3 (Summer 2002): 459; Mark Atwood Lawrence, "Forging the Great Combination: Britain and the Indochina Problem, 1945–1950," in *The First Indochina War: Colonial Conflict and Cold War Crisis*, ed. Fredrik Logevall and Mark Atwood Lawrence (Cambridge, 2007), 108, 121; Nicholas Tarling, *Britain, Southeast Asia and the Onset of the Cold War, 1945–1950* (Cambridge, 1998), 153–156. For Ho's links with other CPs, see C. M. Anderson, 25 February 1946, TNA/PRO/FO 371/63549, F2829/2616/61.

54. Aron Shai, *Britain and China, 1941–47: Imperial Momentum* (London, 1984), 132; Christopher Thorne, *Allies of a Kind: The United States, Britain and the War against Japan, 1941–1945* (New York, 1978), 184, 320.

55. Bradley F. Smith, *The War's Long Shadow: The Second World War and Its Aftermath—China, Russia, Britain, America* (New York, 1986), 198.

56. Minutes of RC/1, 2 April 1946, TNA/PRO/FO 371/56885, N5169/-/G38; James Tuck-Hong Tang, *Britain's Encounter with Revolutionary China, 1949–54* (New York, 1992), 18; Thorne, *Allies of a Kind*, 441, 560–561. See also Brian Porter, *Britain and the Rise of Communist China: A Study of British Attitudes, 1945–1954* (New York, 1967), 5–6; Evan Luard, *Britain and China* (Baltimore, Md., 1962), 65–66.

57. "Chinese 'Communism' in Action," *Times*, 25 January 1945, 5; "Communism in China," *Times*, 17 January 1946, 5; "The Prospect in China," *New*

Statesman & Nation (hereafter *NS&N*), 7 July 1945, 4; Luard, *Britain and China*, 65–67.

58. Thorne, *Allies of a Kind*, 320, 560–561; Shai, *Britain and China*, 132; E. L. Woodward, *British Foreign Policy in the Second World War* (London, 1962), 528–530.

59. Minutes of RC Meeting, 7 May 1946, TNA/PRO/FO 371/56885, N6092 /5169G38; 31 December 1945, PRO/FO 371/54052, F6208.

60. Stevenson to Dening, 31 December 1946, TNA/PRO/FO 371/63282, F1169; Stevenson to Attlee, 23 November 1946, *DPBO*, ser. 1, vol. 8, 71. See also Dening to Bevin, 18 October 1946 and Kitson Minute, 30 July 1947, ibid., 59, 105–106.

61. J.I.C. (46)70(0), "The Spread of Communism and the Extent of Its Direction from Moscow."

62. "The Prospect in China," *NS&N*, 20 July 1946, 37.

63. Leffler, *Preponderance of Power*, 138–140; Gaddis, *Origins of the Cold War*, 338–341.

64. Trevor Burridge, *Clement Attlee: A Political Biography* (London, 1985), 228; Kenneth O. Morgan, *Labour in Power, 1945–1951* (New York, 1984), 63–64.

65. Harold B. Laski, "The Secret Battalion," *Plain Talk*, ed. Isaac Don Levine (New Rochelle, N.Y., 1976), 9–12; Philip Deery, "A Very Present Menace? Attlee, Communism, and the Cold War," *Australian Journal of Politics and History* 44, no. 1 (1998): 82; Robert Hewison, *In Anger: British Culture in the Cold War, 1945–60* (New York, 1981), 24; John Lewis, *The Left Book Club: An Historical Record* (London, 1970), 120–121.

66. Daniel L. Lykins, *From Total War to Total Diplomacy: The Advertising Council and the Construction of the Cold War Consensus* (Westport, Conn., 2003), 54–56; Les K. Adler, *The Red Image: American Attitudes toward Communism in the Cold War Era* (New York, 1991), 94–111.

67. Robert W. Merry, *Taking on the World: Joseph and Stewart Alsop: Guardians of the American Century* (New York, 1996), 158; Donald A. Ritchie, *Reporting from Washington: The History of the Washington Press Corps* (New York, 1995), 138–139.

68. Adler, *The Red Image*, 78.

69. See also Harbutt, *The Iron Curtain*, 156.

70. Foster, "The British Press and the Coming of the Cold War," 26. See also Foster, "The Beaverbrook Press, Eastern Europe, the Soviet Union, and the Coming of the Cold War," *Media, Culture & Society* 8, no. 1 (1986): 103–123.

71. Maurice Edelman, "Peace with Russia," *NS&N*, 6 July 1946, 4; "What Does Stalin Want?" *NS&N*, 16 February 1946, 113; "The Clash of Ideologies," *NS&N*, 23 March 1946, 203–204.

72. "Getting Tough with Russia," *Life*, 18 March 1946, 36.

73. Definition of a Liberal," *New Republic*, 27 January 1947, 6; see also Edward Montgomery, "United Nations: East and West," *New Republic*, 22 April 1946, 571. This impulse to dichotomize was hardly limited to those in the West, for it was part and parcel of Communist doctrine. Stalin had reasserted

that teaching in the course of his election speech; Tito had done much the same in August when he identified the world's only two competing fronts as the reactionary and the democratic. See CIG, Special Study, no. 3, 24 August 1946, "Current Soviet intentions," in Kuhns, *Assessing the Soviet Threat*, 77–80.

74. "The Clash of Ideologies," *NS&N*, 23 March 1946, 203–204; see also "Reorientations: The Munich Analogy," *NS&N*, 31 August 1946, 147–148.

75. Roberts to FO, 17 March 1946, in Jensen, *Origins of the Cold War*, 53–54, 57.

3. Supporting Free Peoples

1. "The History of Western Culture," *Life*, 3 March 1947, 69. Chambers, however, was not the author of the first article. See also Sam Tanenhaus, *Whittaker Chambers: A Biography* (New York: 1997), 194–199.

2. Walter Millis, ed., *The Forrestal Diaries* (New York, 1951), 251; Joseph M. Jones, *The Fifteen Weeks* (New York, 1955), 151.

3. See Walter Isaacson and Evan Thomas, *The Wise Men: Six Friends and the World They Made* (New York, 1986), 394–396; Arthur Vandenberg, *The Private Papers of Senator Vandenberg* (Westport, Conn., 1974, 1952), 340; Millis, *Forrestal Diaries*, 248–249; Alonzo L. Hamby, *Man of the People: A Life of Harry S. Truman* (New York, 1995), 389–392; Dean G. Acheson, *Present at the Creation: My Years in the State Department* (New York, 1969), 219; John Lewis Gaddis, *The United States and the Origins of the Cold War, 1941–1947* (New York, 1972), 349; Jones, *Fifteen Weeks*, 142.

4. Special Message to the Congress on Greece and Turkey: The Truman Doctrine, 12 March 1947, *Public Papers of the Presidents of the United States: Papers of Harry S. Truman, 1945–1953* (hereafter *PPP:HST*) (Washington, D.C., 1961–1966), 176–180.

5. Abbott Gleason, *Totalitarianism: The Inner History of the Cold War* (New York, 1995), 73–77.

6. President's Special Conference with the Association of Radio News Analysts, 13 May 1947, *PPP: HST*, 238. See also Margaret Truman, *Harry S. Truman* (New York, 1973), 343; Robin Edmonds, *Setting the Mould: The United States and Britain, 1945–1950* (Oxford, 1986), 157.

7. Gleason, *Totalitarianism*, 74–76; Michael Leigh, *Mobilizing Consent: Public Opinion and American Foreign Policy, 1937–1947* (Westport, Conn., 1976), 140–141.

8. "Red-Hunting," *Life*, 3 March 1947, 32; Winston Churchill, "If I Were an American," *Life*, 14 April 1947, 107; James Burnham, "Struggle for the World," *Life*, 31 March 1947, 59; "Struggle for the World," *Life*, 21 April 1947, 38.

9. Hubert Kay, "Comintern Agent," *Life*, 17 February 1947, 99, 108; "Red Hunt, 1947," *Collier's*, 18 January 1947, 78; Robert M. LaFollette Jr., "Turn the Light on Communism," *Collier's*, 8 February 1947, 22; Leo Cherne, "How to Spot a Communist," *Look*, 4 March 1947, 21; Richard M. Freeland, *The Truman Doctrine and the Origins of McCarthyism: Foreign*

Policy, Domestic Politics, and Internal Security, 1946–1948 (New York, 1975), 115–150.

10. George Gallup, *The Gallup Poll: Public Opinion, 1953–71* (New York, 1972), 593–594, 639; Truman Press Conference, 3 April 1947, *PPP: HST*, 191.

11. Thompson's comments in Balfour to Warner, 28 March 1947, TNA/PRO/ FO 371 N4045/49/38.

12. Bohlen to Carter, comments on War Department paper, "Communism in America," 29 May 1947, NARA, BP, Box 5, Memos 1947; "U.S. Relations with the Curtain States," 10 July 1947, ibid., Box 6, Bohlen Speeches.

13. "Weekly Summary Excerpt," 21 March 1947, in *Assessing the Soviet Threat: The Early Cold War Years,* ed. Woodrow J. Kuhns (Washington, D.C., 1997), 107; see also Hooker Memo, 12 May 1947, NARA, BP, Box 6, SF 1944–52, Communism.

14. Jones, *Fifteen Weeks,* 152; Reinhold Niebuhr, "Religion around the World," *Life,* 10 March 1947, 116; Tanenhaus, *Chambers,* 197–198; Arnold A. Offner, *Another Such Victory: President Truman and the Cold War, 1945–1953* (Stanford, Calif., 2002), 458, 461.

15. Acheson, *Present at the Creation,* 226–230; Charles E. Bohlen, *Witness to History, 1929–1969* (New York, 1973), 261; Leigh, *Mobilizing Consent,* 145; Jones, *Fifteen Weeks,* 194, 208, 237; Freeland, *The Truman Doctrine, 1946–48* (New York, 1975), 103–114; Melvyn P. Leffler, *A Preponderance of Power: National Security Policy in the Truman Administration* (Stanford, Calif., 1992), 147–164; Acheson to Marshall, 28 May 1947, *FRUS, 1947,* vol. 3 (Washington, D.C., 1972), 232–233.

16. Jones to Acheson, 20 May 1947, cited in Acheson to Marshall, *FRUS, 1947,* vol. 3, 233, fn. 5. The administration, however, was not unanimous on this issue. While Acheson and Kennan were trying to deflect attention from matters of ideology, other officials thought those debates should be front and center. For instance, the State Department's Robert Hooker, of the East European Division, lamented the absence of a comprehensive and systematic attempt by the government to educate the public about the nature and appeal of communism. See Hooker Memo, 12 May 1947, NARA, BP, Box 6, SF, 1944–1952, Communism.

17. Victor Rothwell, *Britain and the Cold War, 1941–1947* (London, 1982), 435–439; Terry H. Anderson, *The United States, Great Britain, and the Cold War, 1944–1947* (Columbia, Mo., 1981), 180–181; Lord Gladwyn (Gladwyn Jebb), *The Memoirs of Lord Gladwyn* (London, 1972), 199–203.

18. "Mr. Truman's Challenge," *Times,* 13 March 1947, 5; "The Changing World," *Manchester Guardian Weekly,* 20 March 1947, 2. Karen Potter argues that with the *Times* existing as a quasi-official mouthpiece, its generally favorable review suggests that the Truman Doctrine went over fairly well with British audiences. See Potter, "British McCarthyism," in *North American Spies: New Revisionist Essays,* ed. Rodri Jeffreys-Jones and Andrew Lownie (Lawrence, Kans., 1991), 150. Tony Shaw, "The British Popular Press and the Early Cold War," *History* 83, no. 269 (January 1998): 76–77;

"Political Sitzkrieg," *New Statesman & Nation* (hereafter *NS&N*), 26 April 1947, 287.

19. George Gallup, *The Gallup International Public Opinion Polls: Great Britain, 1937–1975* (New York, 1976), 159.

20. "Soviet Union Quarterly Report, Oct–Dec 1946," 22 February 1947, TNA/PRO/FO 371/66384, N2153/389/38, PRO. See also Anderson, *The United States, Great Britain, and the Cold War*, 180.

21. "Organisation of Communist Parties in Relation to Soviet Control," TNA/PRO/CAB 130/17; Roberts Letter, 3 February 1947, ibid.

22. Clarke to Warner, 27 March 1947, TNA/PRO/FO 371/66295, N3923/49/38; Inside note from Hogg, ibid.

23. Hope-Jones, FO Minute, 24 March 1947, TNA/PRO/FO 371/66294, N3581/49/38; Pink to Warner, 27 March 1947, ibid., N3917/49/38; Nichols to Warner, 14 April 1947, PRO/FO 371/66295, N4492/49/38; Brimelow Minute on "Organisation of Communist Parties Outside U.S.S.R.," 8 April 1947, PRO/FO 371/66295, N4045/49/38.

24. Peake to Warner, 15 April 1947, TNA/PRO/FO 371/66295, N5210/49/38; Bevin Circular, December 1949 (referencing Warner's letters of 26 February 1947 and 18 March 1947), PRO/FO 371/77594, N10752/10124/38G.

25. R. H. S. Crossman et al., *Keep Left* (London, 1947), 34–36; Denis Healey, "Cards on the Table," in *When Shrimps Learn to Whistle: Signposts for the Nineties* (London, 1990), 107.

26. Amy Knight, *How the Cold War Began: The Gouzenko Affair and the Hunt for Soviet Spies* (Toronto, 2005); Peter Hennessy, *The Secret State: Whitehall and the Cold War* (London, 2002), 20–21; Richard J. Aldrich, *The Hidden Hand: Britain, America, and Cold War Secret Intelligence* (London, 2001), 116–118.

27. Jones, *Fifteen Weeks*, 281–284.

28. Randall Woods and Howard Jones, *Dawning of the Cold War: The United States' Quest for Order* (Athens, Ga., 1991), 159–165; John Lewis Gaddis, *The Long Peace: Inquiries into the History of the Cold War* (New York, 1987), 154–158. For Kennan and the origins of the Policy Planning Staff, see Wilson D. Miscamble, *George F. Kennan and the Making of American Foreign Policy, 1947–1950* (Princeton, N.J., 1992), 6–11.

29. Rothwell, *Britain and the Cold War*, 283–284.

30. "Memorandum of conversation, London," 24 June 1947, *FRUS*, 1947, vol. 3, 268; Gaddis, *The Long Peace*, 156.

31. Caffery to Marshall, 1 July 1947, *FRUS*, 1947, vol. 3, 302–303; Edmonds, *Setting the Mould*, 168; Rothwell, *Britain and the Cold War*, 279–280.

32. Draft Minute by Warner to Sargent, 25 June 1947, TNA/PRO/FO 371/66370, N7458/271/38; Vladislav Zubok and Constantine Pleshakov, *Inside the Kremlin's Cold War: From Stalin to Khrushchev* (Cambridge, Mass., 1996), 104–108; Leffler, *Preponderance of Power*, 184–186; Scott Parrish and Mikhail M. Narinsky, "New Evidence on the Soviet Rejection of the Marshall Plan, 1947: Two Reports," *CWIHP*, Working Paper No. 9 (March 1994), 27.

33. "Summary of Soviet Tactics," 25 June 1947, TNA/PRO/FO 371/66295, N7365/49/38; Gaines to FO, 27 June 1947, PRO/FO 371/66202, N8714/574/55; Watson to FO, 29 July 1947, PRO/FO 371/66296, N8755/49/38; Peterson to FO, 20 June 1947, PRO/FO 371/66370, N7457/271/38; Hankey minute, 26 June 1947, ibid. In an updated version of his comments, Hankey omitted his previous reference to the Comintern; Warner and Sargent subsequently approved the edited marginal comments. For Warner's earlier comments on the Comintern, see Balfour to Warner, 28 March 1947, PRO/FO 371/66295, N4045/49/38.

34. See Jones, *Fifteen Weeks*, 195–197.

35. Kitson Minute, 27 July 1947, TNA/PRO/FO 371/63325, F90121; Sprouse Memorandum, 1 August 1947, *FRUS*, 1947, vol. 7 (Washington, D.C., 1972), 696; Lanxin Xiang, *Recasting the Imperial Far East: Britain and America in China, 1945–1950* (London, 1995), 109–110, 114. British public opinion also was critical of the American position on China, though it attacked U.S. policy from an opposite direction. In early July 1947, the *Times* rejected arguments that Moscow was aiding the Chinese Communists. See Xiang, *Recasting the Imperial Far East*, 126.

36. Vincent to Marshall, 20 June 1947, *FRUS*, 1947, vol. 7, 849; Vincent Memorandum, 27 June 1947, ibid., 854.

37. Xiang, *Recasting the Imperial Far East*, 113; JCS Memorandum, "Study of the Military Aspects of United States Policy toward China" (hereafter JCS Memorandum), 9 June 1947, *FRUS*, vol. 7, 839.

38. Marshall to Stuart, 26 June 1947, *FRUS*, 1947, vol. 7, 202–203; "Relationship between Chinese Communists and Soviet Communists," 31 July 1947, included in memo from William T. Turner, 4 August 1947, NARA, RG 263, MP, Box 24, Folder 38; "Overall Political Situation in China," 24 July 1947, ibid.

39. See, for instance, "Minutes of Meeting of the Secretaries of State, War, and Navy," 26 June 1947, *FRUS*, 1947, vol. 7, 851; JCS Memorandum, 9 June 1947, ibid., 840, 842, 845.

40. Nanking Embassy to Langdon, 8 August 1947, NARA, RG 263, MP, Box 24, Folder 38; Ludden to Wedemeyer, 23 July 1947, *FRUS*, 1947, vol. 7, 656–657.

41. Melby, "Sino-Soviet Relations," 31 July 1947, *FRUS*, 1947, vol. 7, 679. See also "Relationship between Chinese Communism and Soviet Communists"; "Overall Political Situation in China." Wedemeyer himself agreed that evidence of aid was immaterial to his evaluation of the CCP-Soviet relationship. Wedemeyer to Marshall, 8 August 1947, ibid., 713–714.

42. Wedemeyer to Truman, 19 September 1947, *United States Relations with China, with Special Reference to the Period 1944–49* (New York, 1968), 764–814, citing 766, 769, 777, 814. See also Leffler, *Preponderance of Power*, 246–247.

43. "Political Information: Dissidence in Chinese Communist Party—Differences of Opinion between Mao Tse Tung and Chang Wen-t'ien," 25 July 1947,

NARA, RG 263, MP, Box 24, Folder 3; ORE 45, "Implementation of Soviet Objectives in China," 15 September 1945, NARA. See also Enclosure B, "Evidence of Recent Soviet Aid to the Chinese Communists," ibid.

44. "The Strategic Importance of China Proper and Manchuria to the Security of the U.S.," Office of Intelligence Research Report no. 4517, 18 September 1947, *FRUS, 1947,* vol. 7, 287.

45. JCS Memorandum, 9 June 1947, *FRUS, 1947,* vol. 7, 838.

46. Caffery to Marshall, 3 March 1947, *FRUS, 1947,* vol. 6 (Washington, D.C., 1972), 76; Caffery to Marshall, 19 July 1947, ibid., 118–119; Caffery to Marshall, 31 July 1947, ibid., 127–128; Caffery to Marshall, 31 August 1947, ibid., 133–134; Mark Philip Bradley, *Imagining America and Vietnam: The Making of Postcolonial Vietnam, 1919–1950* (Chapel Hill, N.C., 2000), 166–169.

47. Reed to Marshall, 27 February 1947, *FRUS, 1947,* vol. 6, 76; Reed to Marshall, 14 June 1947, ibid., 105; Reed to Marshall, 24 June 1947, ibid., 107; Reed to Marshall, 11 July 1947, ibid., 114–115; Reed to Marshall, 24 July 1947, ibid., 124–125.

48. O'Sullivan to Marshall, 3 July 1947, *FRUS, 1947,* vol. 6, 108; O'Sullivan to Marshall, 19 July 1947, ibid., 120; O'Sullivan to Marshall, 21 July 1947, 121–123; O'Sullivan to Marshall, 15 September 1947, ibid., 136. See also William J. Duiker, *U.S. Containment Policy and the Conflict in Indochina* (Stanford, Calif., 1994), 58–59.

49. Mark Atwood Lawrence, "Forging the Great Combination: Britain and the Indochina Problem, 1945–1950," in *The First Indochina War: Colonial Conflict and Cold War Crisis,* ed. Fredrik Logevall and Mark Atwood Lawrence (Cambridge, Mass., 2007), 121; Nicholas Tarling, *Britain, Southeast Asia, and the Onset of the Cold War, 1945–1950* (Cambridge, 1998), 153–156, 241.

50. Rothwell, *Britain and the Cold War,* 275–276.

51. Joint Intelligence Sub-Committee, "Soviet Interests, Intentions and Capabilities," J.I.C.(47) 7/1, August 1947, 1, located in NARA, RG 59, LM 1, Reel 177.

52. Shaw, "The British Popular Press," 73; Crossman, *Keep Left,* 33.

53. Durbrow to Marshall, 10 June 1947, *FRUS, 1947,* vol. 4, 567–569.

54. Peterson to FO, 20 June 1947, TNA/PRO/FO 371/66370, N7458/271/38; Durbrow to Marshall, 10 June 1947, *FRUS, 1947,* vol. 4, 569.

55. X [George Kennan], "The Sources of Soviet Conduct," *Foreign Affairs* 25 (July 1947): 575. For the genesis of the "X Article," see Kennan, *Memoirs,* vol. 1 (Boston, 1967), 354–367. For excerpts, see *Life,* 28 July 1947, 53.

56. Walter Lippmann, *The Cold War: A Study in U.S. Foreign Policy* (New York, 1947), 40. Emphasis in the original.

57. See, for example, Ernest K. Lindley, "Significance: The Gravest Crisis since the War," *Newsweek,* 10 March 1947, 24; Joseph B. Phillips, "The Truman Move through Russian Eyes," *Newsweek,* 24 March 1947, 46; "Reds: Not Bombs but a Fifth Column," *Newsweek,* 7 April 1947, 21; "Stalin's Future Empire," *Newsweek,* 22 September 1947, cover and 38.

58. Harold J. Laski, "Why Does Russia Act That Way?" *Nation*, 1 March 1947, 240.

59. Jock Balfour, for instance, in March 1947, remarked on a conversation with the State Department's Llewellyn Thompson, in which Thompson claimed that China "was probably the one country in which the leaders of the local Communists could not be regarded as mere instruments of Kremlin policy." Balfour to Warner, 28 March 1947, TNA/PRO/FO/371 66295, N4045/49/38; Brimelow Minute, 8 April 1947, ibid.

60. The Central Intelligence Group, for example, had detected a split within the Czech Communist Party, but failed to identify it as being between nationalists and internationalists. "Weekly Summary Excerpt," 7 March 1947, in Kuhns, *Assessing the Soviet Threat*, 103–104.

4. The Cominform

1. Richard M. Fried, *The Russians Are Coming, the Russians Are Coming: Pageantry and Patriotism in Cold-War America* (New York, 1998), 33–34, 43; Daniel L. Lykins, *From Total War to Total Diplomacy: The Advertising Council and the Construction of the Cold War Consensus* (Westport, Conn., 2003), 70–77; "Don't Miss the Freedom Train," *Collier's*, 18 October 1947, 118. On the emergence of a public-private network, see Scott Lucas, *Freedom's War: The American Crusade against the Soviet Union* (New York, 1999).

2. Andrei Zhdanov, "The Two-Camp Policy," in *From Stalinism to Pluralism: A Documentary History of Eastern Europe since 1945,* ed. Gale Stokes (New York, 1991, 1996), 38–42.

3. See Smith to Marshall, 3 October 1947, *FRUS*, 1947, vol. 4 (Washington, D.C., 1972), 594, fn. 1; Griffis to Marshall, no. 1618, 6 October 1947, NARA, RG 263, MP, Box 149, Folder 420; see also "Summary of Telegrams" for 6, 8, 9, 13, October, and 19 December 1947, HSTL, PSF, Box 206.

4. CIA 2, "Review of the World Situation as It Relates to the Security of the United States," 14 November 1947, 1, HSTL, PSF, Intelligence Files; NSC Special Evaluation #21, "Implications of the New Communist Information Bureau," 13 October 1947, in *Assessing the Soviet Threat: The Early Cold War Years,* ed. Woodrow J. Kuhns (Washington, D.C., 1997), 141–144; "Summary of Telegrams," 10 November 1947, HSTL, PSF, Box 206; see also "Summary of Telegrams," 8 October 1947, and 5 November 1947, ibid.

5. "Monthly Survey of American Opinion on International Affairs," October 1947, NARA, RG 59, OPOS, 1943–1975, Monthly Surveys of Public Opinion on International Affairs 1944–1948, Box 11, Fortnightly Survey, March–December 1947.

6. "Daily Summary of Opinion Developments," 6 October 1947, NARA, RG 59, OPOS, OPA, DPS, Box 3; Press Release, No. 809, 8 October 1947, RG 59, RPPS 1947–1953, SF, Box 8, Communism, 1947–1951. See also Proposed Lovett Statement, 8 October 1947, RG 59, BP, Box 5, Memos, 1947.

7. "Daily Summary of Opinion Developments," 7 October 1947, NARA, RG 59, OPA, DPS, OPOS, Box 3.

8. Ibid., 8 October 1947; see also "Initial Reaction to Formation of a New Nine-Nation Communist Organization," 13 October 1947, NARA, RG 59, OPOS, Public Opinion on Foreign Countries and Regions, Box 45, Russia, November 1943–October 1947.

9. George Gallup, *The Gallup Poll: Public Opinion, 1935–1971* (New York, 1972), 682–683, 690, 721, 736, 743.

10. Roberts to FO, 6 October 1947, TNA/PRO/FO 371/66475, N11554 /11494/38 and Hankey Minute, ibid.; see also N11723/11494/38 and N12187/11494/38 in ibid.; Victor Rothwell, *Britain and the Cold War, 1941–1947* (London, 1982), 104–105.

11. Rothwell, *Britain and the Cold War,* 287; Victor Rothwell, "Robin Hankey," in *British Officials and British Foreign Policy, 1945–1950,* ed. John Zametica (New York, 1990), 169; Ray Merrick, "The Russia Committee of the Foreign Office and the Cold War, 1946–1947," *Journal of Contemporary History* 20 (1985): 464; see also Cooper to FO, 10 October 1947, TNA/PRO/FO 371/67682, Z8930/58/17; Cooper to FO, 6 November 1947, ibid., Z9772/58/17; Gallman to Marshall, no. 5440, 9 October 1947, and no. 5431, 9 October 1947, NARA, RG 59, Box 4071, 800.00b, Communist International, 1 January 1945–21 October 1947.

12. Rothwell, *Britain and the Cold War,* 373–374; Sargent Minute, 29 October 1947, TNA/PRO/FO 371/66476, N12356/11494/38.

13. Roberts to Bevin, 7 October 1947, TNA/PRO/FO 371/66475, N11723/ 11494/38. See also Hankey Minute, 15 October 1947, N12187/11494/38 in ibid.; Hankey Minute, 7 October 1947, ibid., N11554/11494/38.

14. "Two Worlds," *Times,* 7 October 1947, 5; "Two Camps," *Manchester Guardian Weekly,* 9 October 1947, 2; "The Cold War," *Manchester Guardian Weekly,* 18 December 1947, 3; "Another Great Illusion," *New Statesman & Nation* (hereafter *NS&N*), 6 December 1947, 443; see also "The Cominform," *NS&N,* 11 October 1947, 283.

15. Roberts to FO, 6 October 1947, PRO/FO 371/66475, N11554/11494/38; Hankey Minute, 7 October 1947, ibid.; Rothwell, *Britain and the Cold War,* 286–287.

16. Rothwell, "Robin Hankey," 169; Merrick, "The Russia Committee," 463–464.

17. Lambert Minute, 7 November 1947, TNA/PRO/FO 371/66373, N12755/ 271/G38.

18. Clutton to FO, December 1947, TNA/PRO/FO 371/66297, N14886/49/ 38G.

19. Hankey to Clutton, 24 December 1947, ibid. In a November paper on Communist policy, the FO concluded that Yugoslavia "is already largely a 'monolithic' totalitarian state," responsive to the will of Moscow and the Cominform. "Paper on Communist Policy," November 1947, ibid., N13619/49/G38. The following month, it declared Yugoslavia to be "the

most 'monolithic' state among the satellites." See "Monthly Review of Soviet Tactics," 9 December 1947, ibid., N14048/49/38.

20. "Monthly Review of Soviet Tactics," 9 December 1947, ibid., N14048/49/38; see also Rothwell, *Britain and the Cold War,* 452.

21. See, for instance, Minutes of RC Meeting, 4 June 1946, TNA/PRO/FO 371/56885, N7517/5169/G38; "Policy in Eastern Europe," 5 February 1947, TNA/PRO/FO 953/4E, P198/198/950. See also W. Scott Lucas and C.J. Morris, "A Very British Crusade: The IRD and the Beginning of the Cold War," in *British Intelligence, Strategy and the Cold War, 1945–51,* ed. Richard J. Aldrich (New York, 1992), 94–95.

22. "Future Foreign Publicity Policy," 8 January 1948, TNA/PRO/CAB 129/23, CP(48)8; see also "The First Aim of British Foreign Policy," 4 January 1948, PRO/CAB 129/23, CP(48)6; Lucas and Morris, "A Very British Crusade," 98.

23. Minutes of a Meeting, 29 November 1947, TNA/PRO/FO 371/66297, N14645/49/G38; Minutes of RC Meeting, 15 January 1948, PRO/FO 371/71687, N765/765/G38.

24. "Future Foreign Publicity Policy"; "The First Aim of British Foreign Policy"; Lucas and Morris, "A Very British Crusade," 93–95.

25. Bevin Memorandum, "Review of Soviet Policy" (date unknown, but most likely between 4 and 8 January 1948), PRO/CAB 129/23, CP(48)7; see also Minutes of a Meeting, 29 November 1947, TNA/PRO/FO 371/66297, N14645/49/G38; "Communism—New Publicity Policy," 12 February 1948, PRO/FO 1110/24, PR41/41/G.

26. "Summary of Telegrams," 17 November 1947, HSTL, PSF, Box 206. William Stone, the head of the U.S. Overseas Information Committee, told his British colleagues that the State Department had drawn up a policy similar to Britain's "almost a year ago" but that Marshall "had decided against its adoption at that time." Francis Stevens had spoken with British officials and relayed the information that the State Department had reached similar conclusions toward the end of November. FO Minute, March 1948, TNA/PRO/FO 1110/24, PR41/41 G. See also Walter L. Hixson, *Parting the Curtain: Propaganda, Culture, and the Cold War, 1945–1961* (New York, 1997), 5–13.

27. Gallup, *The Gallup Poll,* 683.

28. McDermott to Marshall, 6 November 1947, NARA, RG 59, BP, Box 6, Information Policy; see also "Substance of Recent and Current Criticisms of the Department's Information Policies," 6 November 1947, ibid.; "Monthly Survey of American Opinion on International Affairs," October 1947, RG 59, OPOS, 1943–1975, Monthly Surveys of Public Opinion on International Affairs, 1944–1948, Box 11, Fortnightly Survey, March–December 1947.

29. Rusk Memorandum, 24 October 1947, "Request of National Conference of Editorial Writers for Background Information," NARA, RG 59, BP, Box 6, Information Policy; see also James Reston, "Inadequate Public Relations Hamper State Department," *New York Times,* 28 October 1947, 13.

30. Hickerson to McDermott and Russell, 30 October 1947, NARA, RG 59, BP, Box 6, Information Policy; Bohlen to McDermott and Russell, 3 November 1947, ibid.

31. Lykins, *From Total War to Total Diplomacy*, 82, 87–88.

32. Michael Wala, "Selling the Marshall Plan at Home: The Committee for the Marshall Plan to Aid European Recovery," *Diplomatic History* 10, no. 3 (Summer 1986): 250; see also Lucas, *Freedom's War*, 39–40.

33. *Public Papers of the Presidents of the United States: Harry S. Truman, 1945–1953* (hereafter *PPP: HST*) (Washington, D.C., 1961–1966), 516; Forrest C. Pogue, *George C. Marshall: Statesman, 1945–1959* (New York, 1987), 240, 247; Bohlen Speech, 3 January 1948 (delivered on 5 January 1948), NARA, RG 59, BP, Box 6, Bohlen Speeches. See also Richard M. Freeland, *The Truman Doctrine and the Origins of McCarthyism: Foreign Policy, Domestic Politics, and Internal Security, 1946–48* (New York, 1975), 252–264.

34. Smith to Marshall, 15 November 1947, *FRUS*, 1947, vol. 4, 619–622. Lovett's comments are in footnote 7 on 622. For documents on the Nazi-Soviet discussions and pact, see *FRUS*, 1947, vol. 3 (Washington, D.C., 1972), 640–653.

35. Freeland, *The Truman Doctrine*, 255–256; "U.S. Decides to Print Record to Counter Russian Attacks," *New York Times*, 22 January 1948, 1; "U.S. Publishes Documents on Nazi-Red Pact," *Washington Post*, 22 January 1948, 1.

36. Wala, "Selling the Marshall Plan at Home," 262. See also Committee on Un-American Activities, U.S. House of Representatives, "100 Things You Should Know about Communism in the U.S.A" (Washington, D.C.), NARA, RG 59, BP, SF, 1944–1952, Box 6, Communism.

37. "U.S. Public Comment on Nazi-Soviet Documents," 9 February 1948, NARA, RG 59, OPOS, 1943–1975, Public Opinion on Foreign Countries and Regimes, Soviet Union and Eastern Europe, 1943–1965, Box 45, Russian Reports, Miscellaneous 1948. See also "Initial U.S. Press and Radio Reaction to Russian Statement of February 9 on Nazi-Soviet Documents," ibid.

38. Notes of Meeting, "Security Measures Taken or to Be Taken in Europe by the Five," 7 July 1948, NARA, RG 59, RPPS, CAF, Box 27, Europe, 1947–1948; see also Stevens to Savage, 3 June 1948, ibid., Box 23.

39. PPS/20, "Effect upon the United States If the European Recovery Plan Is Not Adopted," Statement, 22 January 1948, in *The State Department Policy Planning Staff Papers* (hereafter *SDPPSP*) ed. Anna K. Nelson (New York, 1983), vol. 2, 77; "The Political Strategic Background of U.S. Aid Programs," February 1948, NARA, RG 59, BP, Box 6, Information Papers.

40. Gallup, *The Gallup Poll*, 683, 708–709; see also Freeland, *The Truman Doctrine*, 261–264; Thomas C. Christensen, *Useful Adversaries: Grand Strategy, Domestic Mobilization, and Sino-American Conflict, 1947–1958* (Princeton, N.J., 1996), 54–58.

41. Christensen, *Useful Adversaries*, 62–75.

42. *United States Relations with China with Special Reference to the Period 1944–1949* (hereafter *The China White Paper*) (New York, 1968), 371–387;

Alfred Kohlberg, "Issues in China," *New York Times*, 2 November 1947, sec. E, 8; "New Peril Seen in China," *New York Times*, 16 November 1947, 45; Harold B. Hinton, "China Issue Worry to Administration" *New York Times*, 23 December 1947, 5.

43. ORE 45, "Implementation of Soviet Objectives in China," 15 September 1947, NARA, RG 263, Office of Research and Estimates, Box 1.

44. *Life* also publicized the article in several eastern newspapers. Office of Public Affairs, "Daily Summary of Opinion Developments," 10 October 1947, NARA, RG 59, OPA, OPOS, DPS, Box 3.

45. See Marshall to Stuart, 26 June 1947, *FRUS*, 1947, vol. 7 (Washington, D.C., 1972), 202–203, fn. 79.

46. Stuart to Marshall, 29 October 1947, *FRUS*, 1947, vol. 7, 344; Durbrow to Marshall, 9 December 1947, *FRUS*, ibid., 396–397; Ward to Marshall, 11 December 1947, ibid., 401–402; Rice to Butterworth, 18 December 1947, ibid., 405. Cabot to Butterworth, 6 February 1948, *FRUS*, 1948, vol. 8 (Washington, D.C., 1973), 467–471.

47. Clubb to Stuart, 25 October 1947, *FRUS*, 1947, vol. 7, 336–341; ORE 45, "Implementation of Soviet Objectives in China," 2.

48. "The Political Strategic Background of U.S. Aid Programs," February 1948, NARA, RG 59, BP, Box 6, Information Papers; Davies to Kennan, 15 December 1947, RG 59, RPPS, 1947–1953, SF, Box 8, Communism, 1947–1951.

49. Christensen, *Useful Adversaries*, 62–75; Nancy Bernkopf Tucker, *Patterns in the Dust: Chinese-American Relations and the Recognition Controversy, 1949–1950* (New York, 1983), 162–163.

50. FO to Nanking, no. 903, 25 November 1947, TNA/PRO/FO 1110/33, PR1137/71/913.

51. Minutes of RC Meeting, 19 February 1948, TNA/PRO/FO 371/71687, N8166/765/G38; Evan Luard, *Britain and China* (Baltimore, Md., 1962), 65–66.

52. Stevenson to Bevin, 2 February 1948, *Documents on British Policy Overseas* (hereafter *DBPO*), ser. I, vol. 8, ed. S. R. Ashton et al. (London, 2002), 124.

53. See FO Minutes, March 1948, TNA/PRO/FO1110/33; "The Facts of Soviet Expansionism," PRO/FO 975, Document 8, 1948 (exact date unknown); 1 June 1948, PRO/FO 1110/33, PR421/71/913G.

54. "Memorandum by China Department on Chinese Communists," April 1, 1948, *DBPO*, 133–136; Dening to Stevenson, 8 April 1948, *DBPO*, 137–140.

55. Lovett to Moscow, 18 November 1947, NARA, RG 59, Box 4071, Folder 800.00b, Communist International, 22 October 1947–31 December 1947; Durbrow to Marshall, 21 November 1947, ibid.; Pilcher (Shanghai) to Marshall, 24 November 1947, ibid.; Siebens (Changchun) to Marshall, 28 November 1947, ibid.; see also U.S. Consul-General, Shanghai, "Far Eastern Cominform," 29 December 1947, ibid.

56. Hillenkoetter to Truman, 31 March 1948, *Declassified Documents Reference System* (hereafter *DDRS*), Fiche 267C, Document 49. See also Siebens to Marshall, no. 2, 8 January 1948, NARA, RG 59, Box 4072, 800.00b, Communist International, Decimal File, 1945–1949, 14 January 1948–10 May 1948; Smith to Marshall, 23 January 1948, ibid. But see also Marshall to Saigon, 5 February 1948, ibid.; Sebald to Marshall, "Far Eastern Cominform," 14 May 1948, NARA, ibid.

57. CIA, 4–48, "Review of the World Situation," 8 April 1948, *DDRS,* Fiche 179C, 7; NSC, Special Evaluation #29, "Possible Communist Tactics in the Far East," 31 March 1948, HSTL; NSC 6, "Draft Report of the National Security Council on the Position of the United States Regarding Short-Term Assistance to China," 24 March 1948, *FRUS,* 1948, vol. 8, 46.

58. For studies that generally reject the official British and America line, see Philip Deery, "Malaya 1948: Britain's 'Asian Cold War'?" *The Cold War as Global Conflict,* Working Paper no. 3, International Center for Advanced Studies, New York University (April 2002), 7–9; Tanigawa Yoshihiko, "The Cominform and Southeast Asia," in *The Origins of the Cold War in Asia,* ed. Yonosuke Nagai and Akira Iriye (New York, 1977), 352–377; see also John Cady Oral History, 35, 37–39, HSTL, www.trumanlibrary.org/oralhist/cadyjf.htm, accessed 19 December 2007.

59. Stephenson to Bevin, 2 February 1948, *DBPO,* ser. I, vol. 8, 123.

60. See John Lewis Gaddis, *The Long Peace: Inquiries into the History of the Cold War* (New York, 1987), 157; "Monthly Survey of American Opinion on International Affairs," October 1947, NARA, RG 59, OPOS, 1943–1975, Monthly Surveys of Public Opinion on International Affairs, 1944–1948, Box 11, Fortnightly Survey, March–December 1947.

61. Walter Isaacson and Evan Thomas, *The Wise Men: Six Friends and the World They Made* (New York, 1986), 439; Millis, *Forrestal Diaries,* 395; Pogue, *Marshall,* 249.

62. Arthur H. Vandenberg Jr., ed., *The Private Papers of Senator Vandenberg* (Boston, 1952), 389–391.

63. Christensen, *Useful Adversaries,* 54–75; Gallup, *The Gallup Poll,* 721.

64. *The China White Paper,* 387–390.

65. Bevin Memorandum, "The Threat to Western Civilisation," 3 March 1948, TNA/PRO/CP(48)72.

66. Lucas and Morris, "A Very British Crusade," 94–100. For more on the early IRD, see Hugh Wilford, *The CIA, the British Left and the Cold War: Calling the Tune?* (London, 2003), 48–81; Richard J. Aldrich, *The Hidden Hand: Britain, America and Cold War Secret Intelligence* (New York, 2001), 131–134; Andrew J. Defty, *Britain, American, and Anti-Communist Propaganda, 1945–1953: The Information Research Department* (New York, 2004), 74–94.

67. "The Practice of Stalinism," 24 March 1948, TNA/PRO/FO 975, Document 21.

68. Peterson to Bevin, 24 March 1948, included in Smith to Marshall, 5 April

1948, NARA, RG 59, Box 4072, Decimal File, 1945–1949, 800.00b, Communist International, 14 January 1948–10 May 1948.

69. Defty, *Anti-Communist* Propaganda, 70, 102–108.

70. "Points of Resemblence [*sic*] between Fascism and Communism," April 1948, TNA/PRO/FO 1110/40, PR140; see also "The Real Condition in Soviet Russia," 11 March 1948, PRO/FO 1110/29, PR57/57/913.

71. Noel Annan, *Our Age: The Generation that Made Postwar Britain* (London, 1995, 1990), 256; British Embassy, Washington, Aide-Memoire, 11 March 1948, NARA, RG 59, RPPS, 1947–1953, CAF, Box 27, Europe, 1947–1948.

72. "The Foundations of Stalinism," 1948, TNA/PRO/FO 975, Document 22.

73. FO Minute, 21 June 1948, TNA/PRO/FO 1110/74, PR494/494/913.

74. Alonzo L. Hamby, *Man of the People: A Life of Harry S. Truman* (New York, 1995), 418–438.

75. Allen Yarnell, *Democrats and Progressives: The 1948 Presidential Election as a Test of Postwar Liberalism* (Berkeley, Calif., 1974), 32–33; Adler, *The Red Image,* 374–410; Robert Griffith, *The Politics of Fear: Joseph R. McCarthy and the Senate* (New York, 1978, 1970), 46; Athan Theoharis, "The Rhetoric of Politics: Foreign Policy, Internal Security, and Domestic Politics in the Truman Era, 1945–1950," in *Politics and Policies in the Truman Administration,* ed. Barton Bernstein (Chicago, 1970), 221.

76. See Freeland, *The Truman Doctrine,* 307–318.

77. "United States Foreign Policy," 28 April 1948, NARA, RG 59, BP, Box 6, Bohlen Speeches; see also Gaddis, *The Long Peace,* 150; John E. Moser, *Twisting the Lion's Tail: Anglophobia in the United States, 1921–1948* (London, 1999), 176; Caroline Antsey, "Foreign Office Publicity, American Aid, and European Unity: Mobilising Public Opinion, 1947–1949," in *Power in Europe: Great Britain, France, Italy, and Germany in a Postwar World, 1945–1950,* ed. Josef Becker and Franz Knipping (New York, 1986), 373–394.

78. "United States Foreign Policy," 28 April 1948, NARA, RG 59, BP, Box 6, Bohlen Speeches.

79. Fried, *The Russians Are Coming!,* 52–54; Gallup, *The Gallup Poll,* 736.

80. David Caute, *The Great Fear: The Anti-Communist Purge under Truman and Eisenhower* (New York, 1978), 20–21, 85–86.

81. For studies of American moralism and exceptionalism, see Ernest Lee Tuveson, *Redeemer Nation: The Idea of America's Millennial Role* (Chicago, 1968); Seymour Martin Lipset, *American Exceptionalism: A Double-Edged Sword* (New York, 1995). For a brief comparison of postwar British and American anticommunism, see Reg Whitaker, "Fighting the Cold War on the Home Front: America, Britain, Australia, and Canada," in *The Socialist Register 1984: The Uses of Anti-Communism,* ed. Ralph Miliband et al. (London, 1984), 23–67.

82. Peter Hennessy, *The Secret State: Whitehall and the Cold War* (London, 2002), 83–89; Robert Hewison, *In Anger: British Culture in the Cold War, 1945–60* (New York, 1981), 25.

83. Philip Deery, " 'A Very Present Menace'? Attlee, Communism and the Cold War," *Australian Journal of Politics and History* 44, no. 1 (1998): 85–86; Francis Beckett, *The Enemy Within: The Rise and Fall of the British Communist Party* (London, 1995), 119.

84. Kenneth O. Morgan, *Labour in Power, 1945–1951* (London, 1984), 64–68.

85. See, for example, Text of Roberts Speech, 2 April 1948, TNA/PRO/FO 1110/41, PR151/142/913.

86. Minutes of Russia Committee Meeting, 10 June 1948, TNA/PRO/FO 371/71687, N7350/765/G38; "Basic Directive on Combating Communist Propaganda in Germany," 1 June 1948, PRO/FO 1110/9, PR379G.

87. Randall Woods and Howard Jones, *Dawning of the Cold War: The United States' Quest for Order* (Chicago, 1994, 1991), 207.

88. Karen Potter, "British McCarthyism," in *North American Spies: New Revisionist Essays,* ed. Rodri Jeffreys-Jones and Andrew Lownie (Lawrence, Kans., 1991), 143–157.

89. For the argument that both the U.S. and British press rejected the idea that the Cominform was a revival of the Comintern, see Roberts, TNA/PRO/FO 371/66476, N12302/11494/38; for evidence that Moscow itself sought to portray the Cominform as different from the Comintern, see *Pravda* editorial cited in *FRUS,* 1947, vol. 4, 595, footnote 2. See also Durbrow to Marshall, 10 October 1947, NARA, RG 59, LM 176, Reel 2.

90. Edwards to Warner, March 1948, TNA/PRO/FO 1110/24, PR41/41 G; Memorandum of Conversation, 9 February 1948, NARA, Confidential U.S. State Department Central Files: Great Britain, Foreign Affairs, 1945–1949, LM 166, Reel 5, frames 0357-0362; Defty, *Anti-Communist Propaganda,* chs. 2–3.

91. Warner Note, 19 March 1948, TNA/PRO/FO 1110/24, PR41/41 G; see also Edwards to Warner, March 1948, ibid.

92. "100 Things You Should Know about Communism in the U.S.A.: The First of a Series on the Communist Conspiracy and Its Influence in This Country as a Whole on Religion, on Education, on Labor and on Our Government" (Washington, D.C., 1948), Albert and Shirley Small Special Collections Library, University of Virginia.

93. Fried, *The Russians Are Coming!* 19–22; Adler, *The Red Image,* 103–105; Michael Barson and Steven Heller, *Red Scared: The Commie Menace in Propaganda and Popular Culture* (San Francisco, 2001), 145.

94. CIA, 6–48, "Review of the World Situation," 17 June 1948, *DDRS,* Fiche 179D.

95. "Paper on Communist Policy," November 1947, TNA/PRO/FO 371/66297, N13619/49/G38; CIA 6–48, "Review of the World Situation," 17 June 1948, *DDRS,* Fiche 179D.

5. A Break in the Bloc

1. NSC 17, "The Internal Security of the United States," 28 June 1948, HSTL, 6, 20.

2. See, for instance, Cannon to Marshall, 9 June 1948, NARA, RG 59, Box 4072, 800.00B, Decimal File, 1945–1949, 11 May 1948–15 July 1948; Steinhardt to Marshall, nos. 1000 and 1010, 23 June 1948, ibid.

3. Minute of Meeting of NSC, 6th Meeting, 2 February 1948, *Declassified Documents Reference Series* (hereafter *DDRS*), Reel 1, frame 35.

4. Beatrice Heuser, *Western "Containment" Policies in the Cold War: The Yugoslav Case, 1948–53* (New York, 1989), 36; Lorraine M. Lees, *Keeping Tito Afloat: The United States, Yugoslavia, and the Cold War* (University Park, Penn., 1997), 47–48. For the argument that U.S. representatives were caught off guard, see Robert Blum, "Surprised by Tito: The Anatomy of an Intelligence Failure," *Diplomatic History* 12 (Winter 1988): 39–57.

5. Cannon to Marshall, 9 June 1948; Cochran to Marshall, 25 June 1948, ibid.; see also Reams to Marshall, 18 June 1948, *FRUS*, 1948, vol. 4 (Washington, D.C., 1974), 1073.

6. Peake to FO, 17 June 1948, TNA/PRO/FO 371/70229, W3817/676/803. See also Bennett Note, 26 January 1948, PRO/FO 371/74183, R1558/5/67; Bateman Minute, 6 February 1948, ibid., R1875/5/67; Watson, Wallinger, and Hankey Minutes, 4, 5, and 9 February 1948, PRO/FO 371/72162, R1984/5/67.

7. "Clues to a Communist Split: Text of Cominform's Attack on the Tito Regime," *U.S. News & World Report*, 9 July 1948, 59–61. For a brief record of the correspondence between Moscow and Belgrade leading up to the rift, see Gail Stokes, *From Stalinism to Pluralism: A Documentary History of Eastern Europe since 1945* (New York, 1996, 1991), 58–65.

8. Wisner to Harriman, 22 July 1948, *FRUS*, vol. 4, 1096; see also Reams to Marshall, 30 June 1948, ibid., 1078.

9. PPS 35, "The Attitude of This Government toward Events in Yugoslavia," 30 June 1948, *FRUS*, 1948, vol. 4, 1079–1081; Policy Planning Staff, 219th Meeting, 30 June 1948, NARA, RG 59, RPPS, Minutes of Meetings, Box 32, Minutes, 1947–1948. See also Lorraine M. Lees, "The American Decision to Assist Tito, 1948–1949," *Diplomatic History* 2 (Fall 1978): 410; Wilson D. Miscamble, *George F. Kennan and the Making of American Foreign Policy, 1947–1950* (Princeton, N.J., 1992), 189–192.

10. Marshall, outgoing telegram, 30 June 1948, NARA, RG 59, RPPS, Box 24, Yugoslavia.

11. See Bruins to Marshall, no. 1041, 30 June 1948, NARA, RG 59, Box 4072, 800.00B, Decimal File, 1945–1949, 11 May 1948–15 July 1948; Caffery to Marshall, no. 3485, 1 July 1948, ibid.; Crocker to Marshall, no. 955, 3 July 1948, ibid.; Reams to Marshall, 7 July 1948, *FRUS*, 1948, vol. 4, 623.

12. Smith to Marshall, 1 July 1948, *FRUS*, 1948, vol. 4, 1082; Hillenkoetter memorandum, 29 June 1948, *DDRS*, fiche 285B, doc. 141; see also Hillenkoetter memorandum, 30 June 1948, ibid., fiche 285C, doc. 142.

13. Reams to Marshall, 31 August 1948, *FRUS*, 1948, vol. 4, 1102–1103; Reams to Marshall, 15 September 1948, ibid., 1109.

14. King to FO, 30 June 1948, TNA/PRO/FO 371/72579, R7751/407/92; see also King to FO, 29 June 1948, ibid., R7655/407/92.

15. 1 July 1948, TNA/PRO CM 46 (48) 3; Alan Bullock, *Ernest Bevin: Foreign Secretary, 1945–1951* (New York, 1983), 599. Elisabeth Barker argues that the Foreign Office shared Bevin's doubts about the break, though she admits that individual diplomats held "differing views." Barker, *The British between the Superpowers, 1945–50* (Toronto, 1983), 111.

16. See Victor Rothwell, "Robin Hankey," in *British Officials and British Foreign Policy, 1945–1950*, ed. John Zametica (New York, 1990), 174; Heuser, *Western Containment Policies*, 58. See also Minutes of RC Meeting, 8 July 1948, TNA/PRO/FO 371/71687, N8172/765/G38.

17. Jebb to Hayter, 5 August 1948, TNA/PRO/FO 1110/92, PR603/603/913.

18. CIA 8–48, "Review of the World Situation," 19 August 1948, HSTL, PSF, Intelligence Files; ORE 20–48, "Soviet and Satellite Grain," 2 August 1948, www.foia.cia.gov, accessed 22 June 2008.

19. Bastion Paper, 25 August 1948, TNA/PRO/FO 371/72196, R10197/8476/67/G.

20. Smith to Marshall, 1 July 1948, *FRUS, 1948*, vol. 7 (Washington, D.C., 1973), 333; Stuart to Marshall, 27 July 1948, ibid., 377–378. See also Stuart to Marshall, 15 July 1948, ibid., 360–361; Marshall to Stuart, 21 July 1948, ibid., 374.

21. PPS/38, "United States Objectives with Respect to Russia," 18 August 1948, in *The State Department Policy Planning Staff Papers*, vol. 2, ed. Anna K. Nelson (New York, 1983), 391; Davies to Marshall, 11 August 1948, draft report from 252nd Meeting, NARA, RG 59, RPPS, Minutes of Meetings, Box 32, Minutes, 1947–1948.

22. Stuart to Marshall, 17 July 1948, *FRUS, 1948*, vol. 7, 366; Smith to Marshall, 30 June 1948, *FRUS, 1948*, vol. 1, pt. 2 (Washington, D.C., 1976), 584.

23. ORE 45–48, "The Current Situation in China," 22 July 1948, *DDRS*, document number CK3100529808, accessed 22 June 2008. Its remarks on the subject, published after the Tito split became public, were based on reporting completed prior to emergence of the rift itself.

24. "The Break-Up of the Colonial Empires and Its Implications for US Security," ORE 25–48, 3 September 1948, in *Estimative Products on Vietnam, 1948–1975*, ed. David F. Gordon (Washington, D.C., 2005), 1–16; see also Robert J. Hanyok, "Ho Chi Minh: Stooge for Moscow or Nationalist? A Perspective from U.S. State Department Intelligence, 1945–1947," paper presented at annual conference of the Society for Historians of American Foreign Relations, 5–7 June 2003, George Washington University, Washington, D.C., 12.

25. Marshall to Embassy in China, 2 July 1948, *FRUS, 1948*, vol. 6 (Washington, D.C., 1974), 28; Marshall to Embassy in France, 3 July 1948, ibid., 30; "Department of State Policy Statement on Indochina," 27 September 1948, ibid., 45, 48; Abbott to Marshall, 5 November 1948, ibid., 54. See also William J. Duiker, *Sacred War: Nationalism and Revolution in a Divided Vietnam* (New York, 1995), 69; Duiker, *U.S. Containment Policy and the Conflict in Indochina* (Stanford, Calif., 1994), 65–68; Marilyn Young, *The Vietnam Wars, 1945–1990* (New York, 1991), 23.

26. "Daily Summary of Opinion Developments," 29 June, 1 and 2 July 1948, NARA, RG 59, OPA, OPOS, DPS, Box 3; "Monthly Survey of American Opinion on International Affairs," July 1948, RG 59, OPOS, 1943–1975, Monthly Survey of Public Opinion Studies on International Affairs, 1944–1948, Box 11, Fortnightly Survey 1948.

27. Raymond Daniell, "Communism, Held in the West; Strikes in the East," *New York Times,* 26 December 1948, 3; see also C. L. Sulzberger, "Heresy— The Great Bogy of the Kremlin," *New York Times Magazine,* 10 October 1948, 7; Sulzberger, "Kremlin Acts to Halt Spread of Tito Heresy," *New York Times,* 12 September 1948, sec. E, 3; Sulzberger, "Cominform Orders Red Party Purges," *New York Times,* 19 December 1948, 21.

28. M. S. Handler, "Other Satellites Snap at Yugoslavia's Heels," *New York Times,* 3 October 1948, sec. E, 4; see also Sulzberger, "Heresy," 70; M. S. Handler, "Yugoslavs Back Soviet," *New York Times,* 8 November 1948, 4; "Russia Twice Condemned," *New York Times,* 29 November 1948, 22.

29. "The Periscope," *Newsweek,* 4 October 1948, 13; "Longer the Shadows of Danger," *Newsweek,* 32; *Newsweek,* 9 August 1948, 32; "The Secret Plans for the Satellites," *Newsweek,* 11 October 1948, 43; *Newsweek,* 18 October 1948, 26; "The Periscope," *Newsweek,* 25 October 1948, 21. See also "Portents in Stalin-Tito Feud," *U.S. News & World Report,* 9 July 1948, 14; "People of the Week," *U.S. News & World Report,* 39; "Key to Soviet Ruler's Control," *U.S. News & World Report,* 23 July 1948, 26; "Newsgram," *U.S. News & World Report,* 30 July 1948, 7; "Signs of Trouble in Russian Bloc," *U.S. News & World Report,* 6 August 1948, 24; *U.S. News & World Report,* "Worldgram," 20 August 1948, 29.

30. "Soviet's 30-Year Rise to Empire: Grabbing a Fifth of the Earth," *U.S. News & World Report,* 17 December 1948, 12; "Rising Resistance to Moscow," *U.S. News & World Report,* 17 September 1948, 24.

31. "Tito and the Kremlin," *Nation,* 10 July 1948, 33; Del Vayo, "Family Fight," *Nation,* 47. See also "The Shape of Things," *Nation,* 17 July 1948, 58–59; Alexander Werth, "Yugoslavia: Test of Nerves," *Nation,* 4 September 1948, 253.

32. "The Soviet Sphere Quakes," *New Republic,* 12 July 1948, 5; Alexander Kendrick, "Marx Overlooked This," *New Republic,* 12 July 1948, 8; "Outside America," *New Republic,* 20 December 1948. See also Alexander Kendrick, "The Tito Generation," *New Republic,* 9 August 1948, 6; Kendrick, "The Red Danube," *New Republic,* 23 August 1948, 6; Alexander Werth, "Tito, the Unrepentant," *Nation,* 7 August 1948, 147–149; Werth, "Yugoslavia: Neither East Nor West," *Nation,* 27 November 1948, 600–601.

33. William O. Douglas, "The Way to Win without War," *Reader's Digest,* July 1948, 87.

34. "Good News from Europe," *Life,* 12 July 1948, 32; "Three Weeks in Tito's Yugoslavia," *Life,* 25. Its September 13 issue, which featured a picture of Tito on its cover, included a statement from theologian Reinhold Niebuhr

alleging that Russian power was "not so monolithic as is generally assumed." Niebuhr, "For Peace, We Must Risk War," *Life,* 20 September 1948, 38. See also "A Visit to Tito," *Life,* 13 September 1948.

35. Walter L. Briggs, "Is China Different?," *New Republic,* 28 June 1948, 15. Henry A. Wallace, the *New Republic*'s star contributing editor, did paint the Chinese Communists as essentially agrarian reformers in a 5 July article, but he never addressed the question that Briggs raised the previous week. Wallace, "American Fiasco in China," *New Republic,* 5 July 1948, 11.

36. Henry R. Lieberman, "China's Reds Back Attack upon Tito," *New York Times,* 12 July 1948, 10.

37. "'Cold War' Has Two Fronts," *New York Times,* 10 October 1948, 8. See also Henry R. Lieberman, "China Communist Gains Have Big Implications," *New York Times,* 7 November 1948, sec. E, 9; Lieberman, "The Man Who Would Be China's Lenin," *New York Times Magazine,* 19 December 1948, 11.

38. Henry R. Lieberman, "Goal of China Communists Is Same as Russia's," *New York Times,* 21 November 1948, sec. E, 3.

39. "Moscow's Orders," *Times,* 1 July 1948, 5.

40. "Tito's Defiance," *Economist,* 7 August 1948, 213; see also *Economist,* 17 July 1948, 98; "The Trials of Tito," *Economist,* 20 November 1948, 822–823; "The Tactics of Peace," *New Statesman & Nation* (hereafter *NS&N*), 2 October 1948, 273; "The French Strikes," *NS&N,* 16 October 1948, 317; "Mr. Churchill's Defeatism," *NS&N,* 16 October 1948, 319; "Mr. Horner's Dilemma," *NS&N,* 23 October 1948, 337; "Trade Union Problems," *NS&N,* 27 November 1948, 455.

41. "Communism in Europe," *Times,* 1 July 1948, 5; "Belgrade and Moscow," *Times,* 5 August 1948, 5; "Titoism," *Times,* 31 December 1948, 5.

42. "Chip off the Eastern Bloc," *Economist,* 3 July 1948, 2–3; "No Peace—No War," *Economist,* 25 September 1948, 481.

43. "Communist Victory in China," *NS&N,* 6 November 1948, 387. See also "China Outlook," *Economist,* 13 November 1948, 415–416; "A Question of Color," *Economist,* 11 December 1948, 515.

44. "Communism in the Far East," *NS&N,* 7 August 1948, 106. See also "Defence of Malaya," *Times,* 5 August 1948, 5; "Terrorists in Malaya," *Times,* 27 August 1948, 5. Pieces by Kingsley Martin would occasionally cast doubt on the alignment of various Communist parties, but most articles reflected the belief that Moscow was calling the shots. See Martin, "U Tin Tut," *NS&N,* 25 September 1948, 253. "Divided Korea," *NS&N,* 25 September 1948, 250; "Communism in Indonesia," *NS&N,* 30 October 1948, 367.

45. "China in the Balance," *Times,* 20 November 1948, 5; "The China Communists," *Times,* 4 December 1948, 5; see also "Crossroads in China," *Times,* 8 November 1948, 5; "Nature of Chinese Communism," *Times,* 17 December 1948, 4; "Chinese Struggle for Power," *Times,* 31 December 1948, 5.

46. "Crisis in China," *Economist,* 13 November 1948, 779. "Rally in China," *Economist,* 11 September 1948, 405.

47. Minutes of RC Meeting, 14 October 1948, TNA/PRO/FO 371/71687,

N11144/765/G38; Philip Deery, "Malaya, 1948: Britain's 'Asian Cold War'?" *JCWS*, vol. 9, no. 1 (Winter 2007): 33–35.

48. Watson Cover Note, 25 August 1948, TNA/PRO/FO 371/72588, R9853/407/92; Minutes of RC(16)48, 25 November 1948, PRO/FO 371/71687, N13016/765/G38; Minutes of RC Meeting, 30 September 1948, PRO/FO 371/71687, N10730/765/G38.

49. Bevin Memorandum, 13 December 1948, TNA/PRO/CAB 128/13, CAB 80(48)3, CM 48.

50. Bevin Memorandum, "Recent Developments in the Civil War in China," 9 December 1948, TNA/PRO/CAB 129/31, CP(48)299.

51. Bevin Memorandum, 13 December 1948; see also Minutes RC(24)48, 10 December 1948, TNA/PRO/FO 371/71687, N13469/765/G38.

52. Minutes of RC(16)48, 25 November 1948, TNA/PRO/FO 371/71687, N13016/765/G38.

53. Bevin Memorandum, 9 December 1948, CP(48)299, CAB 129/31; Mark Atwood Lawrence, "Transnational Coalition Building and the Making of the Cold War in Indochina, 1947–1949," *Diplomatic History* 26, no. 3 (Summer 2002): 470–471; Karl Hack, *Defence and Decolonisation in Southeast Asia: Britain, Malaya, and Singapore, 1941–1968* (Richmond, Va., 2001), 63–64; Nicholas Tarling, *Britain, Southeast Asia, and the Onset of the Cold War, 1945–1950* (Cambridge, 1998), 243–244, 302–305.

54. Heuser, *Western Containment Policies*, 56.

55. Bevin to Marshall, 22 December 1948, TNA/PRO/FO 371/74183, AN308/1053/45G.

56. John Paton Davies Jr., *Foreign and Other Affairs* (New York, 1966, 1964), 142. As Davies noted, "It was not generally seen as revelatory of nationalism alive within the monolith." Ibid.

57. "Daily Summary of Opinion Developments," 13 July 1948, NARA, RG 59, OPA, OPOS, DPS, Box 3.

58. Reams to Marshall, 15 September 1948, *FRUS*, 1948, vol. 4, 1109; FO Minute, 30 August 1948, TNA/PRO/FO 371/72588, R10071/407/92.

59. See John Lewis Gaddis, *The Long Peace: Inquiries into the History of the Cold War* (New York, 1987), 161–164; CIA, 11–48, "Review of the World Situation," 17 November 1948, HSTL.

60. Robert L. Beisner, *Dean Acheson: A Life in the Cold War* (New York, 2006), 181.

61. Gaddis, *The Long Peace*, 153–155.

62. Smith to Marshall, 10 May 1948, NARA, RG 59, RPPS, 1947–1953, CAF, Box 27, Europe, 1947–1948; see also press release, no. 361, 11 May 1948, ibid., Box 23.

63. Stuart to Marshall, 26 October 1948, *FRUS*, 1948, vol. 7, 519; Cabot to Butterworth 30 December 1948, *FRUS*, 1948, vol. 7, 714. Cabot argued that "such a course of action, of course, depends for success on pressing Communist exigencies, the inherent nature of things here in China, and above all on the theory that the Chinese Communists are not a monolithic bloc in their

subservience to Moscow. I grant you I'm not over-sanguine of success. But what are the alternatives?" Ibid.

64. Cabot to Butterworth, 30 December 1948, *FRUS, 1948*, vol. 7, 718. John Gaddis notes that the demands of the moment "helps to account for the less-than arduous efforts" of policymakers "to explain the 'wedge' strategy in public, or to try to build a domestic base of support for improving relations with communist states not under Moscow's control." Gaddis, *The Long Peace*, 194.

65. Joseph and Stewart Alsop, "The Tito Trouble—III," *Washington Post*, 5 July 1948, 5; Harold E. Stassen, "Make Tito 'Earn' Our Help, Stassen Urges," *Washington Post*, 11 July 1948, 2B. Constantin Fotitch, "Behind the Soviet Tito Split," *Washington Post*, 7 July 1948, 10.

66. Gaddis, *The Long Peace*, 194.

67. Thomas C. Christensen, *Useful Adversaries: Grand Strategy, Domestic Mobilization, and Sino-American Conflict, 1947–1958* (Princeton, N.J., 1996), 54–75.

68. Robert Hooker, October 1948, NARA OASSPA, OPA, SF, 1945–1952, Box 2, Communism, 1946–1951.

69. "Observations on the Policy that the USA Should Follow in View of the Break between Stalin and Tito," 16 November 1948, NARA, RG 59, Miscellaneous Lot Files Relating to Yugoslav Affairs, 1948–1953, 59 D 383, Box 35, Yugoslavia, 1948–1949; PPS 35, 30 June 1948, codified as NSC 18, 2 September 1948, *FRUS, 1948*, vol. 4, 1079, fn 1.

6. The Wedge Strategy

1. J. S. Steele, 1 June 1946, FO 371/56885, N8467/5169/G38, PRO. According to Maurice Peterson, Britain's ambassador in Moscow, the distinction between communism and the Soviet Union "will not of course be possible invariably to maintain and this need not worry us." Smith had made these comments to Maurice Peterson, Britain's ambassador to Russia. Peterson to FO, 20 June 1947, TNA/PRO/FO 371/66370, N7457/271/38.

2. Douglas to Marshall, 24 July 1947, *FRUS, 1947*, vol. 4 (Washington, D.C., 1972), 348–349.

3. The Central Intelligence Group, for example, had detected a split within the Czech Communist Party but failed to identify it as being between nationalists and internationalists. "Weekly Summary Excerpt," 7 March 1947, in *Assessing the Soviet Threat: The Early Cold War Years*, ed. Woodrow J. Kuhns (Washington, D.C., 1997), 103–104.

4. Brimelow Note, 1 September 1947, TNA/PRO/FO 371/66296, N9445/49/G38; Hankey to Warner, 6 September 1947, ibid.

5. Watson to FO, 29 July 1947, TNA/PRO/FO 371/66296, N8755/49/38; Brimelow Note, 1 September 1947, ibid., N9445/49/G38; Brimelow Note, 1 September 1947, ibid., N9942/49/G38; Rumbold to Warner, 22 August 1947, ibid., N9941/49/G; Mack to FO, 20 August 1947, ibid.,

N9942/49/G38; Clarke to FO, 23 September 1947, ibid., N11201/49/G38; Victor Rothwell, *Britain and the Cold War, 1941–1947* (London, 1982), 276.

6. For background on U.S. and British reaction to the split, see Robert M. Blum, "Surprised by Tito: Anatomy of an Intelligence Failure," *Diplomatic History* 12, no. 1 (Winter 1988): 39–57; Beatrice Heuser, *Western "Containment" Policies in the Cold War: The Yugoslav Case, 1948–53* (New York, 1989); Lorraine Lees, *Keeping Tito Afloat: The United States, Yugoslavia, and the Cold War* (University Park, Penn., 1997).

7. "Daily Summary of Opinion Developments," 6 July 1948, NARA, RG 59, OPA, OPOS, DPS, Box 3; see also "Portents in Stalin-Tito Feud," *U.S. News & World Report,* 9 July 1948, 14.

8. Partridge and Sweetser to Marshall, 29 June 1948, *FRUS,* 1948, vol. 4, 1077; Draper to Royall, 6 July 1948, ibid., 1085–1087; Reams to Marshall, 31 August 1948, ibid., 1104–1105.

9. PPS/35, "The Attitude of this Government toward Events in Yugoslavia," 30 June 1948, *FRUS,* 1948, vol. 4, 1079–1081; Marshall to Royall, 7 July 1948, *FRUS,* 1948, vol. 4, 1087.

10. Editorial Note, *FRUS,* 1948, vol. 4, 1093; Wisner to Harriman, 22 July 1948, *FRUS,* 1948, vol. 4, 1095–1096.

11. PPS/38, "United States Objectives with Respect to Russia," 18 August 1948, in *The State Department Policy Planning Staff Papers,* vol. 2 (hereafter *SDPPSP*), ed. Anna K. Nelson (New York, 1983), 386.

12. NSC 20/1, "U.S. Objectives with Respect to Russia," 18 August 1948, *FRUS,* 1948, vol. 1 (Washington, D.C., 1975), 609–611; NSC 20/4, "Report by the National Security Council on U.S. Objectives with Respect to the USSR to Counter Soviet Threats to U.S. Security," 23 November 1948, ibid., 667–669.

13. King to FO, 29 June 1948, TNA/PRO/FO 371/72579, R7655/407/92; King to FO, 30 June 1948, ibid., R7751/407/92.

14. Minutes of RC(16)48, 25 November 1948, TNA/PRO/FO 371/71687, N13016/765/G38; Heuser, *Western Containment Policies,* 77.

15. Minutes of RC Meeting, 21 November 1948, TNA/PRO/FO 371/56886, N15456/5169/938. For a subsequent exchange between Warner and Ronald, see Minutes of RC meeting, 28 November 1946, PRO/FO 371/56887, N15458/5169/G38.

16. Annex A, Russia Committee Terms of Reference, 24 November 1948, TNA/PRO/FO 371/71687, N13016/765/G38.

17. Hickerson to Lovett, "Supplement to Instructions to Field Setting Forth 'U.S. Attitude toward Events in Yugoslavia' Embodied in S/P's Paper of June 30, 1948," 2 December 1948, NARA, RG 59, RPPS, Box 24, Yugoslavia; M. S. Handler, "U.S. Help at Once Held Vital to Tito," *New York Times,* 29 December 1948, 10; Hickerson to Kennan, 26 November 1948, *FRUS,* 1948, vol. 4, 1117–1118; see also ibid., fn. 4, 1118.

18. NSC 18/2, "National Security Council Progress Report by the Secretary of State on the Implementation of Economic Relations between the United States and Yugoslavia," 11 April 1949, in *U.S. Diplomatic Records on Relations*

with Yugoslavia during the Early Cold War, 1948–1957, ed. Nick Ceh (New York, 2002), 73–74.

19. Wisner to Harriman, 22 July 1948, *FRUS, 1948,* vol. 4, 1095; Heuser, *Western Containment Policies,* 81–86.

20. Bevin Memorandum, "Communism in Countries outside the Soviet Orbit," 24 March 1949, TNA/PRO/CAB 129/34, CP(49)72; Minutes of RC/78/49, 24 May 1949, PRO/FO 371/77623, N4901/1052/38G; Bevin Memorandum, 23 August 1949, PRO/CAB 129/36, CP(49)180.

21. RC/15/49, "The Progress of Consolidation of the Soviet Orbit in Europe in 1948," TNA/PRO/FO 371/77566, N1225/1016/38; Minutes of RC/11/49, 21 January 1949, PRO/FO 371/77623, N847/1052/38G; see also RC/6/49, "Progress of Consolidation of Soviet Orbit in Europe in 1948," cited in ibid.; see also Wallinger Minute, 15 February 1949, PRO/FO 371/78716, R2168/1051/92G.

22. Cabot to Butterworth, 30 December 1948, *FRUS, 1948,* vol. 7 (Washington, D.C., 1973), 711–714; Stuart to Marshall, 4 August 1948, *FRUS, 1948,* vol. 7, 399; see also Stuart to Marshall, 10 July 1948, ibid., 346–347; Lovett to Stuart, 16 November 1948, ibid., 574; PPS 39/2, "United States Policy toward China," 25 February 1949, in Nelson, *SDPPSP,* vol. 3, 28.

23. Minutes of RC(16)48, 25 November 1948; Bevin Memorandum, 13 December 1948, PRO/CAB 128/13, CAB 80(48)3, CM48; see also Minutes of RC/11/49, 21 January 1949, PRO/FO 371/77623, N847/1052/38G.

24. Bevin Memorandum, "The Situation in China," 4 March 1949, TNA/PRO/CAB 129/32, CP(49)39; Bevin Memorandum, 8 March 1949, PRO/CAB 128/15, CM18(49)2.

25. NSC 34/2, "U.S. Policy toward China," 28 February 1949, *FRUS, 1949,* vol. 9 (Washington, D.C., 1974), 494.

26. Minutes, Policy Planning Staff, 32nd Meeting, 23 February 1949, NARA, RG 59, PPPS, 1947–1953, Minutes 1949, Box 32; Minutes, Policy Planning Staff, 36th Meeting, 1 March 1949, ibid.

27. Davies to Kennan, 25 January 1949, NARA, RG 59, RPPS, 1947–1953, Box 45, Davies, 1947–1949; see also Nancy Bernkopf Tucker, *Patterns in the Dust: Chinese-American Relations and the Recognition Controversy, 1949–1950* (New York, 1983), 29.

28. Adams to Kennan, 8 March 1949, NARA, RG 59, RPPS, 1947–1953, SF, Box 8, Communism 1947–51. The primary author of the paper is unclear. A subsequent memo found in Adams's files, which contains similar arguments, suggests that Adams was the original author. Nevertheless, records of the Policy Planning Staff note that John Davies submitted a draft paper on the subject of international communism at virtually the same moment. Minutes, Policy Planning Staff, 42nd Meeting Wednesday, 11 March 1949, RG 59, PPPS, 1947–1953, Minutes 1949, Box 32. See also Minutes of 46th meeting, ibid. For additional evidence that points to Adams as the author, see "Questions for Possible Study by S/P," 12 January 1950, RG 59, RPPS, 1947–1953, Box 44, Adams Chronological, NARA.

29. All of the following quotes are from "United States Policy toward Communism," Draft Working Paper, 8 March 1949, NARA, RG 59, RPPS, 1947–1953, SF, Box 8, Communism, 1947–1951.
30. Nevertheless, Adams thought such a practice might also have helped stiffen resistance to Communist encroachment.
31. I have uncovered no further references to it in the PPS or State Department files.
32. Memorandum, Joyce to Savage, 1 April 1949, *FRUS*, 1949, vol. 5 (Washington, D.C., 1976), 10–13.
33. Minutes of RC/11/49, 21 January 1949, TNA/PRO/FO 371/77623, N847/1052/38G; see also Minute RC/29/49, 1 March 1949, ibid., N2190/1052/38G.
34. "Memorandum on the Use of Words in Publicity about Communism," March/April 1949, TNA/PRO/FO 1110/191, PR704/14/G; Attlee memo March/April 1949, ibid.
35. "Memorandum on the Use of Words in Publicity about Communism," March/April 1949; Murray to Warner, 5 August 1949, TNA/PRO/FO 1110/191, PR704/14/G; Warner note, 7 August 1949, ibid.
36. Bevin Memorandum, "Peace Offensive: Tactical Deviation, or Change of Long-Term Policy?" 13 May 1949, TNA/PRO/FO 800/503; Minutes of RC/56/49, 12 April 1949, PRO/FO 371/77623, N3583/1052/38G.
37. Minutes of RC/78/49, 24 May 1949, TNA/PRO/FO 371/77623, N4901/1052/38G.
38. For background on these developments, see Carolyn Eisenberg, *Drawing the Line: The American Decision to Divide Germany* (New York, 1996); R. W. Smyser, *From Yalta to Berlin: The Cold War Struggle over Germany* (New York, 1999); Thomas Parrish, *Berlin in the Balance, 1945–1949: The Blockade, the Airlift, the First Major Battle of the Cold War* (Reading, Mass., 1998); Lawrence S. Kaplan, *The United States and NATO: The Formative Years* (Lexington, Ky., 1984); Joseph Smith, ed., *The Origins of NATO* (Exeter, 1990).
39. See John Earl Haynes and Harvey Klehr, *Early Cold War Spies: The Espionage Trials That Shaped American Politics* (New York, 2006), chs. 4, 6. Allen Weinstein, *Perjury: The Hiss-Chambers Case* (New York, 1997); Michal R. Belknap, *Cold War Political Justice: The Smith Act, the Communist Party, and American Civil Liberties* (Westport, Conn., 1977); David Caute, *The Great Fear: The Anti-Communist Purge under Truman and Eisenhower* (New York, 1978).
40. Richard M. Fried, *Nightmare in Red: The McCarthy Era in Perspective* (New York, 1990), 87–113. In 1949, loyalty oaths were prescribed for Oklahoma University, the University of California, and Texas higher education; the University of Washington fired three professors for suspected Communist activities. Ibid., 101–02, 105–06, 108–09. HUAC also scoured bibliographies from scores of universities, looking for Communist propaganda. Ibid., 100.

41. U.S. Department of State, Bulletin (hereafter *DSB*), 6 February 1949 (Washington, D.C., 1949), 174; Richard M. Fried, *The Russians Are Coming! The Russians Are Coming! Pageantry and Patriotism in Cold-War America* (New York, 1998), 56–57.

42. Donald S. Crosby, S.J., "The Politics of Religion: American Catholics and the Anticommunist Impulse," in *The Specter: Original Essays on the Cold War and the Origins of McCarthyism*, ed. Robert Griffith (New York, 1974), 18–38; Patrick McNamara, *A Catholic Cold War: Edmund A. Walsh, S.J. and the Politics of American Catholic Anticommunism* (New York, 2005), 137, 141, 148; Allen Yarnell, *Democrats and Progressives: The 1948 Presidential Election as a Test of Postwar Liberalism* (Berkeley, Calif., 1974), 36–37, 57–60.

43. Diane Kirby, "Divinely Sanctioned: The Anglo-American Cold War Alliance and the Defence of Western Civilization and Christianity, 1945–48," *Journal of Contemporary History* 35, no. 3 (2000): 389, 392; Kirby, "Ecclesiastical McCarthyism: Cold War Repression in the Church of England," *Contemporary British History* 19, no. 2 (June 2005): 187–203. See also Caroline Antsey, "The Projection of British Socialism: Foreign Office Publicity and American Opinion, 1945–50," *Journal of Contemporary History* 19 (July 1984): 417–451.

44. Fried, *The Russians Are Coming!* 87–88; 101; *Public Papers of the Presidents: Harry S. Truman, 1945–1953* (hereafter *PPP: HST*) (Washington, D.C., 1961–1966), 294.

45. "Tito's National Communism," *New York Times,* 3 January 1949, 22; "Monthly Survey of American Opinion on International Affairs," no. 94, February 1949, NARA, RG 59, OPA, DPS, Monthly Survey. See also "Popular Attitudes toward Greater Trade with Yugoslavia," 18 February 1949, RG 59, OPOS, 1943–1975, Public Opinion on Foreign Countries and Regions: Soviet Union and Eastern Europe, 1943–1965, Box 45, Yugoslavia; "Economic Support by this Government for Marshal Tito" (date unknown, probably early 1949), RG 59, Miscellaneous Lot Files Relating to Yugoslav Affairs, Box 35, NSC 18 Series.

46. See, for instance, several articles in *New Statesman & Nation,* including "The Dictatorship of the Proletariat," 24 September 1949, 317; Alexander Werth, "Back to Belgrade," *NS&N,* 8 October 1949, 376–377; Kingsley Martin, "Communist Trials," *NS&N,* 15 October 1949, 416–417. See also "Nationalism and Communism," *Times,* 31 May 1949, 5.

47. Kenneth O. Morgan, *Labour in Power, 1945–1951* (Oxford, 1984), 68; Philip Deery, " 'A Very Present Menace'? Attlee, Communism and the Cold War," *Australian Journal of Politics and History* 44, no. 1 (1998): 73.

48. Andrew Defty, *Britain, America, and Anti-Communist Propaganda, 1945–53: The Information Research Department* (New York, 2004), 118–119.

49. "Text of Bevin's Speech on the Atlantic Pact," *New York Times,* 2 April 1949, 4; E. L. Woodward, "The Heritage of Western Civilization," *International*

Affairs 25, no. 2 (April 1949): 137–148; Woodward, "1939 and 1949—Two Momentous Years," *New York Times Magazine*, 16 January 1949, 11.

50. Defty, *Britain, America, and Anti-Communist Propaganda*, 118–119, 138.

51. Andrew J. Rotter, *The Path to Vietnam: Origins of the American Commitment to Southeast Asia* (Ithaca, N.Y., 1987), 60–63; Mark Atwood Lawrence, "Transnational Coalition Building and the Making of the Cold War in Indochina, 1947–1949," *Diplomatic History* 26, no. 3 (Summer 2002): 470–471, 475; Kathryn C. Statler, *Replacing France: The Origins of American Intervention in Vietnam* (Lexington, Ky., 2007), 17.

52. Warner to Strang, 13 January 1949, *DBPO*, ser. I, vol. 8, ed. S. R. Ashton et al. (London, 2002), 195–196, 199; Scarlett Minute, 15 February 1949, ibid., 203; Bevin Memorandum, 4 March 1949, ibid., 213; JIC(49)48, ibid., 369, 377; Karl Hack, *Defence and Decolonisation in Southeast Asia: Britain, Malaya, and Singapore, 1941–1968* (Richmond, Va., 2001), 67–68; Nicholas Tarling, *Britain, Southeast Asia, and the Onset of the Cold War, 1945–1950* (Cambridge, 1998), 375–376, 378–379; Rotter, *The Path to Vietnam*, 158.

53. William J. Duiker, *Sacred War: Nationalism and Revolution in a Divided Vietnam* (New York, 1995), 69–70; Duiker, *U.S. Containment Policy and the Conflict in Indochina* (Stanford, Calif., 1994), 69–71.

54. Caffery to Acheson, 16 March 1949, *FRUS*, 1949, vol. 7, pt. I (Washington, D.C., 1975), 13–14; Acheson to Saigon, 10 May 1949, ibid., 24; Stanton to Acheson, 14 June 1949, ibid., 50–53.

55. Robert M. Blum, *Drawing the Line: The Origin of the American Containment Policy in East Asia* (New York, 1982), 120; Marilyn Young, *The Vietnam Wars* (New York, 1991), 23–24; Acheson to Hanoi, 20 May 1949, *FRUS*, 1949, vol. 7, pt. I, 29.

56. "Economic Support by this Government for Marshal Tito;" "Monthly Survey of American Opinion on International Affairs," no. 94, February 1949; no. 98, June 1949, RG 59, OPA, DPS, Box 12, Monthly Survey.

57. Ross Koen, *The China Lobby in American Politics* (New York, 1974); "Mao's Reply: 'I Am No Tito,'" *China Monthly* 10, no. 7 (July 1949): 140–141; see also "Those 'Agrarian Reformers,'" *China Monthly* 10, no. 3 (March 1949): 58.

58. Walter Sullivan, "Mao Expects No Help from West; Hails Soviet as China's True Ally," *New York Times*, 1 July 1949, 1; "Mao Settles the Dust," *Time*, 11 July 1949, 22.

59. Blum, *Drawing the Line*, 76–79; Thomas C. Christensen, *Useful Adversaries: Grand Strategy, Domestic Mobilization, and Sino-American Conflict, 1947–1958* (Princeton, N.J., 1996), 88–89; Tucker, *Patterns in the Dust*, 47, 149–150; Warren I. Cohen, *America's Response to China: A History of Sino-American Relations* (New York, 1990), 164–165.

60. "The China White Paper," *China Monthly* 10, no. 8 (August 1949): 160–161; Blum, *Drawing the Line*, 94–95. By September 1949, both the contents and even the very existence of the "China White Paper" were still a

mystery to a solid majority of the American population. See Tucker, *Patterns in the Dust,* 156.

61. U.S. Department of State, *U.S. Relations with China,* xvi. In an interesting twist on the use of Red Fascist rhetoric, the CCP regarded U.S. efforts to drive a wedge between Soviet and Chinese Communists as amounting to the construction of a "fifth column" in China itself. Steven M. Goldstein, "Chinese Communist Policy toward the United States: Opportunities and Constraints, 1944–1950," in *Uncertain Years: Chinese-American Relations, 1947–1950,* ed. Dorothy Borg and Waldo Heinrichs (New York, 1980), 265.

62. Gordon H. Chang, *Friends and Enemies: The United States, China, and the Soviet Union, 1948–1972* (Stanford, Calif., 1990), 50–59. Everett Case, president of Colgate University, was also a departmental consultant in the exercise.

63. Bevin Memorandum, "China," 23 August 1949, TNA/PRO/CAB 129/36, CP(49)180.

64. Lees, *Keeping Tito Afloat,* 66–79; Heuser, *Western Containment Policies,* 81–124; "Public Comment on Yugoslavia," 31 August 1949, NARA, RG 59, OPOS, Public Opinion on Foreign Countries and Regions: Soviet Union and Eastern Europe, 1943–1965, Box 45, Yugoslavia, 1945–1952.

65. See Lees, *Keeping Tito Afloat,* 66–79; Heuser, *Western Containment Policies,* 81–124.

66. "Public Opinion on Yugoslavia," 29 September 1949, NARA, RG 59, OPOS, 1943–1975, Public Opinion and Foreign Countries and Regions: Soviet Union and Eastern Europe, 1943–1965, Box 45, Yugoslavia, 1945–1952; "Monthly Surveys of Public Opinion," no. 100, August 1949, RG 59, OPA, DPS, Box 12, Monthly Surveys; "Monthly Surveys of Public Opinion," no. 101, September 1949, ibid.

67. "Public Comment on Yugoslavia," 31 August 1949; Minutes RC/84/49, 8 June 1949, TNA/PRO/FO 371/77623, N5326/1052/38G.

68. Minutes of RC/90/49, 21 June 1949, PRO/FO 371/77624, N5675/1052/38G; Mackenzie Minute, 10 June 1949, PRO/FO 371/77566, N5134/1016/38; see also "British Policy towards Soviet Communism," 28 July 1949, TNA/PRO/FO 371/77622, N1107/1051/38G, PUSC/31.

69. "British Policy towards Soviet Communism," 28 July 1949.

70. NSC 58/2, "United States Policy toward the Soviet Satellite States in Eastern Europe," 8 December 1949, *FRUS,* 1949, vol. 5, 54; NSC 58, "United States Policy toward the Soviet Satellite States in Eastern Europe," 14 September 1949, in *Containment: Documents on American Policy and Strategy, 1945–1950,* ed. Thomas H. Etzold and John Lewis Gaddis (New York, 1978), 223.

71. Jürg Martin Gabriel, *The American Conception of Neutrality after 1941* (New York, 1988); David P. Kilroy, "The Legacy of Neutrality: U.S.-Irish Relations in World War II and the Early Cold War," paper presented at a meeting of the Society for Historians of American Foreign Relations, College Park, MD, 25 June 2005.

72. NSC 28/1, "The Position of the United States with Respect to Scandinavia," 3 September 1948, *FRUS,* 1948, vol. 3 (Washington, D.C., 1974), 233; T. Michael Ruddy, "Complementary Interests: U.S. Policy Toward Finland in the Early Cold War," paper presented at a meeting of the Society for Historians of American Foreign Relations, College Park, MD, 25 June 2005; Jussi M. Hanhimaki, *Scandinavia and the United States: An Insecure Friendship* (New York, 1997); Hanhimaki, *Containing Coexistence; American, Russia, and the "Finnish Solution," 1945–1956* (Kent, Ohio, 1997); Ruddy, "Neutralism," *Encyclopedia of American Foreign Policy,* 2nd ed., vol. 2, ed. Alexander De Conde, et al. (New York, 2002), 542–552.

73. James Reston, "U.S. Asserts Soviet Forces Formation of Atlantic Group," *New York Times,* 15 January 1949, 1; "Invitation to Scandinavia," *New York Times,* 2 February 1949, 26; "The Fallacy of Neutrality," 30 May 1950, 5; but also see "American Policy," *Times,* 10 February 1950, 7. At the time, Soviet officials actually condemned neutralism as an "imperialist plot." See Robert J. McMahon, *Cold War on the Periphery: The United States, India, and Pakistan* (New York, 1994), 46.

74. Chester J. Pach, *Arming the Free World: Origins of the U.S. Military Assistance Program* (Chapel Hill, N.C., 1991), 210; SANACC 360/14, "Appraisal of U.S. National Interests in South Asia," 19 April 1949, *FRUS,* 1949, vol. 6 (Washington, D.C., 1977), 12–13.

75. Juhana Aunesluoma, *Britain, Sweden, and the Cold War, 1945–54* (Basingstoke, 2003), xiv–xix, 24–104, 154–161; Harto Hakovirta, *East-West Conflict and European Neutrality* (Oxford, 1988), 113–118.

76. "Teacher 'Neutrality'" on U.S. Ideals Barred," *New York Times,* 28 March 1949, 15; "Jansen Stresses Democracy Study," *New York Times,* 1 February 1949, 8; Lawrence E. Davies, "Union Heads Score Formula in Hawaii," *New York Times,* 30 June 1949, 5.

77. McMahon, *Cold War on the Periphery,* 15–16, 40–52; Anita Inder Singh, *The Limits of British Influence: South Asia and the Anglo-American Relationship, 1947–1956* (New York, 1993), 46–71.

78. See, for example, Grady to Marshall, 20 March 1948, *FRUS,* 1948, vol. 5, pt. 1 (Washington, D.C., 1975), 498; Memorandum of a Conversation, 2 April 1948, ibid., 502–503; Satterthwaite to the Acting Secretary of State, 6 June 1949, *FRUS,* 1949, vol. 7, pt. 2, 1146.

79. "Communism in Western Europe," No. 5, July–September 1949, TNA/PRO/FO 371/77569, N10939/G.

80. Wallinger to Rumbold, 22 June 1949, TNA/PRO/FO 371/78521, R6319/10110/21; C.R.A. Rae, 11 February 1949, PRO/FO 371/77566, N1025/1016/38.

81. "Memorandum on the Use of Words in Publicity about Communism," March/April 1949.

82. Murray to Warner, 5 August 1949, TNA/PRO/FO 1110/191, PR704/14/G.

83. Schwartz to Smith ("G," UN), 21 September 1949, NARA, RG 59, RPPS, Box 33, Chronological 1949.

84. Memorandum of a Conversation, 19 February 1949, *FRUS,* 1949, vol. 5, 872. The meeting involved Secretary of State Dean Acheson, ECA administrator Paul Hoffman, and Economic Affairs official Willard Thorp.

85. Russell, "The Function of Public-Opinion Analysis in the Formulation of Foreign Policy," *DSB,* 6 March 1949, no. 505, 277.

7. Anti-Stalinist Communism

1. Chester J. Pach Jr., *Arming the Free World: The Origins of the United States Military Assistance Program* (Chapel Hill, N.C., 1991), 221–325; Robert L. Beisner, *Dean Acheson: A Life in the Cold War* (New York, 2006), 159; Paul Boyer, *By the Bomb's Early Light: American Thought and Culture at the Dawn of the Atomic Age* (Chapel Hill, N.C., 1994, 1985), 336–337.

2. Arthur Schlesinger Jr., *The Age of Jackson* (New York, 1945), ix; Schlesinger, *The Vital Center: The Politics of Freedom* (Boston, 1949).

3. *Arthur Koestler, The God that Failed,* ed. R.H.S. Crossman (New York: 1949), 25–82; George Orwell, *Nineteen Eighty-Four: A Novel* (New York, 1949). Richard H. Pells cites Schlesinger's *The Vital Center* as the key political treatise of the age. Pells, *The Liberal Mind in a Conservative Age: American Intellectuals in the 1940s and 1950s* (New York, 1985), 131.

4. Schlesinger, *The Vital Center,* 2, 8, 59–60. Schlesinger even represents the forces on the left in terms of a binary relationship. Liberals were "forced to choose between the New Dealer and the Doughface," between the legacy of Jackson and that of the utopians. Ibid., 160.

5. Ibid., 98, 100–101.

6. The *New Leader* was one such publication trumpeting these themes that appealed to intellectuals in both nations. Featuring writers such as Irving Kristol, Melvin Lasky, and Daniel Bell, the journal repeatedly identified communism as an aggressive, monolithic movement, using several strands of Red Fascist imagery to that end. See Hugh Wilford, *The CIA, the British Left, and the Cold War: Calling the Tune?* (London, 2003), 123–147.

7. Richard Pells notes that Schlesinger was one of a number of intellectuals and writers who contributed to a "celebration of America." Pells, *The Liberal Mind,* 130.

8. "Weekly Summary of Comment on China," 25–31 August 1949, NARA, RG 59, OPOS, Public Opinion on Foreign Countries and Regions, Box 26, China; "Monthly Survey of Public Opinion," no. 105, January 1950, RG 59, OPA, DPS, Box 12, Monthly Surveys, 1950.

9. "Mao in Moscow," *Washington Post,* 20 December 1949, 14; "Mao Makes His Pilgrimage," *New York Times,* 18 December 1949, sec. E, 8; "Monthly Surveys of Public Opinion," no. 102 (October 1949), no. 103 (November 1949), no. 104 (December 1949), NARA, RG 59, OPA, DPS, Box 12, Monthly Surveys. The quote is from survey no. 103; comments from the *New York Herald Tribune* appear in survey no. 104.

10. Leonard A. Kusnitz, *Public Opinion and Foreign Policy: America's China*

Policy, 1949–1979 (Westport, Conn., 1984), 25; Russell to Sargeant, "Policy Information Paper on China," 4 January 1950, NARA, RG 59, OASSPA, SF, 1945–1952, Box 2, China, 1949–1951.

11. Acheson, "Basic Principles of U.S. Policy toward the Far East," U.S. State Department, *Bulletin* (hereafter *DSB*), 15 August 1949, 236; Smith, "Europe as a Bulwark of Peace," ibid., 20 June 1949, 872; Peurifoy, "The Department of State: A Reflection of U.S. Leadership," ibid., 31 October 1949, 673.

12. See, for example, U.S. Senate, Committee on Foreign Relations, *Reviews of the World Situation*, Historical Series, 1949–1950 (Washington, D.C., 1974), 97.

13. Acheson, "United States Policy Toward Asia," *DSB*, 27 March 1950, 468; Dulles, "New Aspects of American Foreign Policy," ibid., 8 May 1950, 720.

14. See also George McGhee, *DSB*, 28 November 1949, 825; Kennan, "Is War with Russia Inevitable?" *Reader's Digest*, March 1950, reprinted in *DSB*, 20 February 1950. The *Digest's* sponsorship of this argument is significant, given the journal's doctrinaire appraisals of communism and Communist states. See Joanne P. Sharp, *Condensing the Cold War: "Reader's Digest" and American Identity* (Minneapolis, 2000), 83–106.

15. Hamilton Fish Armstrong, "Tito and Stalin," *Atlantic* 184, no. 4 (October 1949): 35–36.

16. "Conclusions and Recommendations of the London Conference of October 24–26 of United States Chiefs of Mission to the Satellite States" (hereafter "London Conference"), undated, *FRUS*, 1949, vol. 5 (Washington, D.C., 1976), 30–31; NSC 58/2, "United States Policy toward the Soviet Satellite States in Eastern Europe," 8 December 1949, ibid., 43–44.

17. Swihart to Schwinn, 11 October 1949, NARA, RG 59, OASSPA, OPA, SF, Box 9, Russia, 1947–1951.

18. NSC 58/2, "United States Policy toward the Soviet Satellite States in Eastern Europe," *FRUS*, 1949, vol. 5, 51–53; U.S. Senate, *Reviews of the World Situation*, 87, 97.

19. See Gordon H. Chang, *Friends and Enemies: The United States, China, and the Soviet Union, 1948–1972* (Stanford, Calif., 1990), 58, fn. 39, 309–310.

20. Evan Thomas, *The Very Best Men: Four Who Dared. The Early Years of the CIA* (New York, 1995), 38–39; Richard J. Aldrich, *The Hidden Hand: Britain, America, and Cold War Secret Intelligence* (London, 2001), 152–154, 160–162; Scott Lucas, *Freedom's War: The American Crusade against the Soviet Union* (New York, 1999), 66–67.

21. Nevertheless, various sources including the Hearst press continued to voice reservations over such a policy. See "Monthly Surveys of Public Opinion," no. 102 (October 1949), no. 103 (November 1949), no. 104 (December 1949), NARA, RG 59, OPA, DPS, Box 12, Monthly Surveys; "London Conference," 28–31. See also Perkins to Acheson, 7 November 1949, ibid., 36–38.

22. NSC 58/2, *FRUS*, 1949, vol. 5, 54; Samuel L. Sharp, "Tito Now a Delicate Problem for Us," *Washington Post*, 25 September 1949, B2; Thomas C. Christensen, *Useful Adversaries: Grand Strategy, Domestic Mobilization, and Sino-American Conflict, 1947–1958* (Princeton, N.J., 1996), 89–95;

Nancy Bernkopf Tucker, *Patterns in the Dust: Chinese-American Relations and the Recognition Controversy* (New York, 1983), 163–165.

23. NSC 58/2, *FRUS, 1949*, vol. 5, 47.

24. Davies lecture to the National War College, 16 December 1949, NARA, RG 59, Box 45, Davies, 1945–1949.

25. "Britain and China," *Times,* 7 January 1950, 7; Michael Lindsay, "Chinese Communists, IV—The Pro-Russian Alignment," *New Statesman & Nation* (hereafter *NS&N*), 24 December 1949, 751; "The Lessons of 1949," *NS&N*, 31 December 1949, 769; "China," *Manchester Guardian Weekly,* 20 October 1949, 8–9; Robert Guillan, "China under the Red Flag," *NS&N*, 29 December 1949, 5.

26. Minutes of RC/159/49, 6 December 1949, TNA/PRO/FO 371/77624, N10521/1052/38G. At the same time, however, he also thought that the younger generation of Chinese Communists tended "to look mainly towards Russia." See also Harrison to Nicholls, 15 December 1949, ibid.

27. RC/4/50, "Draft Summary of Indications Regarding Soviet Foreign Policy, no. 46," 5 January 1950, TNA/PRO/FO 371/86750, NS1052/3/G. The final draft of the document, completed on 9 January 1950, appears as RC/7/50, ibid.; RC/17/50, "Summary of Indications Regarding Soviet Foreign Policy, no. 48," 4 February 1950, ibid., NS1052/10G. See also Minutes of RC Meeting, RC/2/50, 5 January 1950, ibid., NS1052/1/G.

28. Kelly to FO, 12 December 1949, TNA/PRO/FO 371/86750, NS1052/1/G; see also RC/13/50, "Trends of Communist Propaganda, 17 December 1949–24 January 1950," 31 January 1950, ibid., NS1052/7/G; RC/25/50, "Summary of Indications regarding Soviet Foreign Policy, no. 49," 18 February 1950, PRO/FO 371/86751, NS1052/18G.

29. Kennan to Acheson, 17 February 1950, *FRUS, 1950*, vol. 1 (Washington, D.C., 1977), 160–161; Minutes of Policy Planning Staff, 3rd Meeting, 11 January 1950, NARA, RG 59, PPPS, Box 32, Minutes, 1950.

30. NSC 48/2, "The Position of the United States with Respect to Asia," 30 December 1949, *FRUS, 1949*, vol. 7, pt. 2 (Washington, D.C., 1977), 1219; Beisner, *Acheson,* 199, 200, 275; Walter Lippmann, "After Containment, What?" *Washington Post,* 12 January 1950, 13; Lippmann, "The Dust Has Settled," *Washington Post,* 16 January 1950, 7.

31. For the origin of this paper, see Minutes of RC/153/49, 22 November 1949, TNA/PRO/FO 371/77624, N10086/1052/38G. For iterations of this document, see RC/5/50, 6 January 1950, FO 371/86750, NS1052/4/G; RC/15/50, 2 February 1950, ibid., NS1052/9/G; RC/22/50, 11 February 1950, ibid., NS1052/13.

32. RC/27/50, "Anti-Stalinist Communism," 21 February 1950, TNA/PRO/FO 371/86751, NS1052/19/G; NSC 58/2, *FRUS, 1949.* vol. 5, 42–54; see footnote 1 for versions of the document.

33. P.M.(50)12, Bevin to Attlee, 18 March 1950, TNA/PRO/FO 371/86751, NS1052/19/G; "Copy of Minute by the Prime Minister," 23 March 1950, ibid.; Bevin circular no. 027, "Anti-Stalinist Communism," 27 March 1950, PRO/FO 371/86899, NS2191/34G, PRO.

34. RC/24/50, 14 February 1950, TNA/PRO/FO 371/86761, NS1053/6G; British Embassy, Washington, to FO, 10 January 1950, 2191/1/50, PRO/FO 371/86898, NS2191/6G. On 20 December 1949, the State Department delivered a top-secret aide-mémoire summing up the conclusions of NSC 18/4, which outlined U.S. policy on the Soviet-Yugoslav dispute, to the British Embassy in Washington. See *FRUS*, 1950, vol. 4 (Washington, D.C., 1975), 1341, fn. 1.

35. RC/24/50, 14 February 1950, TNA/PRO/FO 371/86761, NS1053/6G; see also FO to Washington, 17 January 1950, NS1053/2/G; Minutes of RC/19/50, 7 February 1950, ibid., NS1053/5/G. For British empiricism and pragmatism, see Joseph Frankel, *British Foreign Policy, 1945–1973* (London, 1975), 112–115.

36. Minutes of Policy Planning Staff, 4th Meeting, 13 January 1950, NARA, RG 59, PPPS, Box 32, Minutes, 1950.

37. Joyce, "The Attitude of the United States towards Titoism and 'National Communism,' " 24 January 1950, NARA, RG 59, Miscellaneous Lot Files Relating to Yugoslav Affairs, 1948–1956, Box 35, Tito Ideological.

38. "Cohesiveness in the World Communist Movement: A Preliminary Estimate," 31 January 1950, NARA, RG 59, Miscellaneous Lot Files, Yugoslav Affairs, 1948–1956, Box 35, Tito Ideological; "Present Capabilities of the World Communist Movement outside the Soviet Union," RG 59, Records of Intelligence Bureau, Office of the Director, 1949–1959, Box 4, EG/UM (Communism). A note atop the first page suggests that the paper was originally prepared in May, but that "this revision, though completed just prior to June 25, seems sound enough to justify its being polished and published as an EG estimate." The date atop the first page is 20 October 1950.

39. "Cohesiveness in the World Communist Movement: A Preliminary Estimate"; Marc Trachtenberg, "A Wasting Asset: American Strategy and the Shifting Nuclear Balance, 1949–1954," in *History and Strategy* (Princeton, N.J., 1991), 100–152.

40. Richard M. Fried, *Nightmare in Red: The McCarthy Era in Perspective* (New York, 1990), 123–127; Robert P. Newman, *Owen Lattimore and the "Loss" of China* (Berkeley, Calif., 1992), 217.

41. Editorial, "McCarthy and the Past," *Life*, 10 April 1950, 32; Editorial, "The Conservative Revival," *Life*, 15 May 1950, 38. For British reactions to McCarthy, see John Brown, "The Causes and Effects of McCarthyism," *Political Quarterly* 26, no. 2 (April–June 1955): 178–185; John P. Rossi, "The British Reaction to McCarthyism, 1950–1954," *Mid-America* 70, no. 1 (1988): 5–18; Jussi M. Hanhimaki, " 'The Number One Reason': McCarthy, Eisenhower and the Decline of American Prestige in Britain," in *Twentieth-Century Anglo-American Relations*, ed. Jonathan Hollowell (Basingstoke, 2001), 104–123.

42. Lisle Abbott Rose, *The Cold War Comes to Main Street: America in 1950* (Lawrence, Kans., 1998), 145–165.

43. The World Congress for the Partisans of Peace was founded in April 1949 and met in Stockholm from March 15 to 19, 1950. Maclaren Minute, 18

August 1950, TNA/PRO/FO 1110/296, PR 22/29/G; "A Soviet 'Peace' Maneuver," *New York Times*, 23 June 1950, 24; see also Philip Deery, "The Dove Flies East: Whitehall, Warsaw and the 1950 World Peace Congress," *Australian Journal of Politics and History* 48, no 4 (2002): 449–468; Lucas, *Freedom's War*, 97; Richard H. Pells, *Not Like Us: How Europeans Have Loved, Hated, and Transformed American Culture since World War II* (New York, 1997), 65–76.

44. Truman, "Going Forward with a Campaign of Truth," *DSB*, 1 May 1950, 669–672. In March, Senator William Benton, the former assistant secretary of state for public affairs, had called for a similar program, which he labeled a "Marshall plan in the field of ideas." Editorial Note, *FRUS*, 1950, vol. 4, 315. For the text of the resolution and Acheson's commentary on it before the Senate Foreign Relations Committee, see *DSB*, 17 July 1950, 100–102.

45. Andrew Defty, *Britain, America, and Anti-Communist Propaganda, 1945–1953: The Information Research Department* (New York, 2004), 139. See also James Reston, "Acheson Acts to Increase Foreign Policy Information," *New York Times*, 3 November 1949, 1.

46. Lewis Wood, "Truman Proclaims World-Wide Fight to Crush Red Lies," *New York Times*," 21 April 1950, 1.

47. See also Anders Stephanson, "Liberty or Death: The Cold War as U.S. Ideology," in *Reviewing the Cold War: Approaches, Interpretations, Theory*, ed. Odd Arne Westad (London, 2001, 2000), 81–100.

48. See "U.S. Views on Capturing Initiative in Psychological Field" (undated, but circulated within State Department on 14 April 1950 as FM D-H-1), *FRUS*, 1950, vol. 4, 296–302.

49. Editorial Note, *FRUS*, 1950, vol. 4, 306–307. Full documentation of the meetings is in *FRUS*, 1950, vol. 3 (Washington, D.C., 1977), 828ff.; Acheson to Certain Diplomatic and Consular Offices, 15 July 1950, *FRUS*, 1950, vol. 4, 318–319; Defty, *Anti-Communist Propaganda*, 106, 143–147.

50. Rose, *The Cold War Comes to Main Street*, 162–163; Richard M. Fried, *The Russians Are Coming! The Russians Are Coming! Pageantry and Patriotism in Cold-War America* (New York, 1998), 67–86.

51. NSC 68, "United States Objectives and Programs for National Security," 14 April 1950, *FRUS*, 1950, vol. I, 247, 260, 285, 289.

52. RC/35/50, "Sovietisation and 'Purges' in Eastern Europe," 2 March 1950, TNA/PRO/FO 371/86752, NS1052/24G. For the centrality of this theme in British reporting, see, for instance, "Communism in Latin America," RC/28/50, 20 February 1950, PRO/FO 371/86751, NS1052/16G; "Strengthening of Soviet Political Control in Eastern Europe," RC/43/50, 16 March 1950, PRO/FO 371/86752, NS1052/29G; "Consolidation of Communism in Eastern Europe 1948–50," 16 June 1950, PRO/FO 371/86146, N10112/1, MIS/19/50.

53. "Note by the Executive Secretary to the National Security Council on United States Policy toward the Soviet Satellite States in Eastern Europe, Reference: NSC 20/4," 14 September 1949, HSTL, PSF, Box 201. I would like to thank

Robert Beisner for this reference. See also Beisner, *Acheson*, 303, for a postadministration mention.

54. NSC 68, *FRUS*, 1950, vol. 1, 247.

55. U.S. Senate, *Reviews of the World Situation*, 109.

56. "Report on 'Soviet Intentions' Prepared by the Joint Intelligence Committee, American Embassy, U.S.S.R" (hereafter "Soviet Intentions"), 25 April 1950, *FRUS*, 1950, vol. 4, 1168–1169. See also accompanying memo from Ambassador Alan G. Kirk, ibid., 1164–1168; "U.S. Views on Capturing Initiative in Psychological Field," *FRUS*, 1950, vol. 4, 296–297.

57. Rusk to Nitze, 23 February 1950, *FRUS*, 1950, vol. 1, 168. Kennan to Acheson, 17 February 1950, ibid., 162; Rose, *The Cold War Comes to Main Street*, 138; see also John C. McCloy, "The German Problem and Its Solution," *DSB*, 10 April 1950, 587; Acheson, "Peace through Strength: A Foreign Policy Objective," ibid., 13 June 1950, 1038.

58. RC/72/50, 9 May 1950, TNA/PRO/FO 371/86761, NS1053/17G.

59. Acheson, " 'Total Diplomacy' to Strengthen U.S. Leadership for Human Freedom," *DSB*, 20 March 1950, 427–430.

60. "Soviet Intentions," 25 April 1950, *FRUS*, 1950, vol. 4, 1168–1169, and Kirk Memo, ibid., 1164–1168.

61. NSC 68, *FRUS*, 1950, vol. 1, 235–292, but especially 237–244. See also comments by Emily Rosenberg and Zara Steiner in *American Cold War Strategy: Interpreting NSC 68*, ed. Ernest R. May (New York, 1993), 160–164, 181.

62. Michael J. Hogan, *A Cross of Iron: Harry S. Truman and the Origins of the National Security State, 1945–1950* (Cambridge, 1998), 14, 465. Acheson, "Threats to Democracy and Its Way of Life," *DSB*, 1 May 1950, 674–677. Frank Ninkovich makes this argument central to his understanding of the "domino theory" and its hold on U.S. presidents during the modern era. Ninkovich, *Modernity and Power: A History of the Domino Theory in the Twentieth Century* (Chicago, 1994).

63. "Publicizing Foreign Policy," *New York Times*, 4 November 1949, 26; Richard H. Parke, "Baruch Sponsors Total-Peace Drive," *New York Times*, 1 April 1950, 1; Truman, "Going Forward," 670.

64. Marshall to the Embassy in India, 22 January 1947, *FRUS*, 1947, vol. 3 (Washington, D.C., 1972), 139; Grady to Marshall, 20 March 1948, *FRUS*, 1948, vol. 5, pt. 1 (Washington, D.C., 1975), 498; Memorandum of Conversation, 10 May 1948, ibid., 509; Walter H. Waggoner, "Nehru Bars Neutrality in Injustice; Talk Suggests India as Conciliator," *New York Times*, 14 October 1949, 1; Robert J. McMahon, *The Cold War on the Periphery: The United States, India, and Pakistan* (New York: 1994), 40–59; H. W. Brands, *The Specter of Neutralism: The United States and the Third World, 1947–1960* (New York, 1989), 32–33; Jacqueline Dix, "The United States and India: The Challenge of Neutralism to Bipolarity," in *Deconstructing and Reconstructing the Cold War*, ed. Alan Dobson (Brookfield, Vt., 1999), 152–177.

65. Douglas to Acheson, 15 June 1949, *FRUS*, 1949, vol. 7, pt. 1 (Washington,

D.C., 1975), 56; Webb to Embassy in India, 18 June 1949, ibid., 60; Acheson to Embassy in India, 20 June 1949, ibid., 67; Butterworth Memorandum, 9 September 1949, ibid., 77; O'Sullivan Memorandum, 28 September 1949, ibid., 84–85. At the same time, Nehru was unwilling to believe that Ho's communism made him a tool of Moscow. See Butterworth to Acheson, 20 October 1949, ibid., 92–93. That position put the Indian leader at odds with Sir Girja Shankar Bajpai, secretary general of India's Department of External Affairs; see Henderson to Acheson, 12 April 1950, *FRUS*, 1950, vol. 6 (Washington, D.C., 1976), 779.

66. Brands, *Specter*, 39.
67. Barrett, "The American People's Part in U.S. Foreign Policy," *DSB*, 24 April 1950, 646; "Finis to Neutrality," *New York Times*, 25 June 1950, 128; see also C.P. Trussell, "Day of Neutrality Declared at End," *New York Times*, 23 June 1950, 10; "Mr. Hoover and the U.N.," *New York Times*, 29 April 1950, 8.
68. Walter Lippmann, "Breakup of the Two-Power World," *Atlantic Monthly* 185, no. 4 (April 1950): 25–30. See also British Embassy to Northern Department, 5 April 1950, TNA/PRO/FO 371/81632.
69. See, for instance, Russell to Barrett, 6 March 1950, *FRUS*, 1950, vol. 1, 186.
70. Acheson, "Crisis in Asia: An Examination of U.S. Policy," *DSB*, 23 January 1950, 114; Acheson, "United States Policy toward Asia," *DSB*, 27 March 1950, 472.
71. See, for instance, Truman, "Making Democracy Work and Defending It from Its Enemies," *DSB*, 6 March 1950, 347–350; Webb, "Streamlining the Department of State," *DSB*, 13 February 1950, 237.
72. Acheson to Consulate, 20 May 1949, *FRUS*, 1949, vol. 7, pt. 1, 29; Butterworth to Acheson, 20 October 1949, ibid., 93; Acheson to the Embassy in Yugoslavia, 7 February 1950, *FRUS*, 1950, vol. 4, 1365; see also Beisner, *Acheson*, 71, 169, 249, 268–272; Mark Atwood Lawrence, *Europe and the American Commitment to War in Vietnam* (Berkeley, Calif., 2005), 172–173.
73. See, for example, Abbott to Acheson, 31 January 1950, *FRUS*, 1950, vol. 6, 707; "Military Aid for Indochina," 1 February 1950, ibid., 713; Folsom to Lacy, 9 March 1950, ibid., 758; Henderson to Acheson, 12 April 1950, ibid., 779.
74. Lacy to Peak, 4 April 1950, in reference to OIR Report no. 5181.4, "The Status of Organized Labor in Southeast Asia: Indochina," NARA, RG 59, Bureau of Intelligence Research, INR, 1945–60, Lot 58 D 776, Box 6, Forms to Comment On; Acheson, "Kremlin Recognizes Communist Movement in Indonesia," *DSB*, 13 February 1950, 244; Jessup, "Report to the American People on the Far East," *DSB*, 24 April 1950, 627. See also See Truman, "Going Forward," 669; Acheson, "'Total Diplomacy,'" 428; Acheson, "United States Policy toward Asia," *DSB*, 27 March 1950, 469–472.
75. William J. Duiker, *U.S. Containment Policy and the Conflict in Indochina* (Stanford, Calif., 1994), 83; Bruce to Acheson, 11 December 1949, *FRUS*, 1949, vol. 7, pt. 1, 106.

76. William J. Duiker, *Ho Chi Minh* (New York, 2002), 425; Duiker, *U.S. Containment Policy*, 93–94.

77. Andrew J. Rotter, *The Path toward Vietnam: Origins of the American Commitment to Southeast Asia* (Ithaca, N.Y., 1987), 60–63, 142, 146, 149, 153, 158; William J. Duiker, *Sacred War: Nationalism and Revolution in a Divided Vietnam* (New York, 1995), 71–72; Duiker, *U.S. Containment Policy*, 92; Karl Hack, *Defense and Decolonisation in Southeast Asia: Britain, Malaya, and Singapore, 1941–1968* (Richmond, Va., 2001), 68.

78. In that regard, Britain sought to maintain a dual policy of accommodating Chinese communism while resisting it in Southeast Asia, with Bevin maintaining that there was "no inconsistency in a policy which recognized Beijing while intensifying resistance to Indochinese communism. Bevin Memorandum, CP(49)244[CAB 129/37], 26 November 1949, *DBPO*, ser. I, vol. 8, 411–412; Nicholas Tarling, *Britain, Southeast Asia, and the Onset of the Cold War, 1945–1950* (Cambridge, 1998), 389–391.

79. Mark Atwood Lawrence, "Transnational Coalition Building and the Making of the Cold War in Indochina, 1947–1949," *Diplomatic History* 26, no. 3 (Summer 2002): 453–480; Lawrence, "Forging the 'Great Combination': Britain and the Indochina Problem, 1945–1950," in *The First Vietnam War: Colonial Conflict and Cold War Crisis*, ed. Fredrik Logevall and Mark Atwood Lawrence (Cambridge, Mass., 2007), 105–129.

80. Philip Deery, "The Terminology of Terrorism: Malaya, 1948–52," *Journal of Southeast Asian Studies* 34, no. 2 (June 2003): 5–8. See also Hack, *Defence and Decolonisation*, 67–68; Tarling, *Britain*, 386, 391; Susan L. Carruthers, *Winning Hearts and Minds: British Governments, the Media and Colonial Counter-insurgency, 1944–1960* (New York, 1995), 72–127.

81. Peter Hennessy, *The Secret State: Whitehall and the Cold War* (London, 2002), 90–96; Peter Hennessy and Gail Brownfeld, "Britain's Cold War Security Purge: The Origins of Positive Vetting," *Historical Journal* 25, no. 4 (1982): 969.

82. "Principles Governing U.S. Relationships with the 'Free World' and the 'Soviet World,'" 13 February 1950, NARA, RG 59, RPPS 1947–53, Box 44, Adams Chronological.

83. "Monthly Survey of Public Opinion," no. 107, March 1950, NARA, RG 59, OPA, DPS, Box 12, Monthly Surveys 1950.

84. U.S. Senate, *Reviews of the World Situation*, 108–110. To solidify Tito's position, the State Department secured a $20 million Export-Import loan for Yugoslavia on 1 March 1950. See Acheson to Embassy in France, 22 February 1950, *FRUS*, 1950, vol. 4, 1373.

85. "Second Bipartite Ministerial Meeting," 9 May 1950, TNA/PRO/PREM 8/1204; "Western Measures to Counter Soviet Expansion and Indications of Their Effect," RC/78/50, 20 May 1950, revised on 3 June and 21 June, PRO/FO 371/86755, N1052/50G.

86. See "Present Capabilities of the World Communist Movement outside the Soviet Union." See also *FRUS*, 1950, vol. 4, 318, fn. 5.

87. NSC 68, *FRUS*, 1950, vol. 1, 260; Davies Memorandum, 2 February 1950,

FRUS, 1950, vol. 6, 305–306. At the same time, Davies thought the wedge strategy called for a more belligerent tone on the part U.S. officials. As he argued in May 1950, "it would seem incumbent on the P area (Public Affairs) to sound a little more of the Old Testament note rather than the Sermon on the Mount in its proselytization of the new heathen in China." Davies to Nitze, 25 May 1950, NARA, RG 59, Box 45, Davies, 1950–1951.

88. "The London Conference, May 1950, Annex: South East Asia," May 1950, TNA/PRO/PREM 8/1202.

89. Barrett, "Forging a Free World with a Truth Campaign," *DSB*, 17 July 1950, 104; Russell, "Where We Stand Today," *DSB*, 112; Acheson to Johnson, 28 April 1950, *FRUS*, 1950, vol. 6, 632. See also Acheson to Sawyer, 8 June 1950, ibid., 638.

90. Rusk to Acheson, 30 May 1950, *FRUS*, 1950, vol. 6, 349; Ogburn Memo, 2 June 1950, ibid., 353–356.

91. Britain and the United States displayed subtle differences in their appraisal of the Chinese situation. Whereas U.S. officials thought that Titoism still overshadowed the establishment of the PRC, British officials seemed to take the opposite view. See Acheson to Certain Diplomatic Offices, 26 April 1950, *FRUS*, 1950, vol. 4, 1184. This is somewhat difficult to pin down precisely due to the ambiguous wording of Acheson's telegram. His exact words are as follows: America's position was that "while Kremlin now dominates many more people and much larger area than it did at end of war, development of Titoism and its ramifications probably largely offset for present Communist victory in China in Kremlin's evaluation of its power position." He then stated that "Brit consider Communist successes in China more than offset Tito disaffection." Acheson's comments seem to be a paraphrase of a similar passage in NSC 68. See *FRUS*, 1950, vol. 1, 260. Americans stationed at the embassy in Moscow, however, agreed with British officials and placed greater weight on developments in China than on Titoism. Kirk to Acheson, 28 April 1950, *FRUS*, 1950, vol. 4, 1186.

92. RC/9/50, "Draft Summary of Indications Regarding Soviet Foreign Policy No. 47," 21 January 1950, TNA/PRO/FO 371/86750, NS1052/6/G; RC /49/50, "Summary of Indications Regarding Soviet Foreign Policy no. 51," 23 March 1950, PRO/FO 371/86752, NS1052/33G.

8. Korea

1. "Manifesto of Congress for Cultural Freedom," in Peter Coleman, *The Liberal Conspiracy: The Congress for Cultural Freedom and the Struggle for the Mind of Postwar Europe* (New York: 1989), 251; Sidney Hook, "The Berlin Congress for Cultural Freedom," in *A Partisan Century: Political Writings from Partisan Review*, ed. Edith Kurzweil (New York, 1996), 108–115.

2. Truman Statement, 27 June 1950, U.S. Department of State, *Bulletin* (hereafter *DSB*), 3 July 1950, 5; Acheson, "Act of Aggression in Korea," in *DSB*, 10 July 1950, 46; Dulles, "A Militaristic Experiment," ibid., 49.

3. "Roundtable: The Korean War: A Fifty-Year Perspective," annual convention of the American Historical Association, Chicago, 9 January 2000.

4. Truman, "Justice Based on Human Rights: A Threat to Tyranny," *DSB*, 24 July 1950, 123; Dulles, "U.S. Military Action in Korea," ibid., 88; see also Acheson, "Charging South Korea as Aggressor Reminiscent of Nazi Tactics," ibid., 17 July 1950, 87.

5. Ernest K. Lindley, "Korea: Austria of the Next War?" *Newsweek*, 3 July 1950, 16; "U.S. Throws Forces into Korean War," *Newsweek*, 11; *Time*, 3 July 1950, 15; *Time*, 10 July 1950, 14; "Weekly Summary of Comment on Far East," 22–28 June 1950, NARA, RG 59, OPOS, Public Opinion on Foreign Countries and Regions, Box 26, 1950.

6. "War in Korea," *Times*, 26 June 1950, 5; "Hotting the Cold War," *New Statesman and Nation* (hereafter *NS&N*), 1 July 1950, 3–4; "How to Limit the War," *NS&N*, 8 July 1950, 31–32.

7. See Cabinet minutes, 27 June 1950, TNA/PRO/CAB 128/17 39 (50) 4, CM 39(50)27; FO to Washington, 27 June 1950, PRO/FO 371/84057 FK 1015/50; Tony Shaw, "The Information Research Department of the British Foreign Office and the Korean War, 1950–53," *Journal of Contemporary History* 34, no. 2 (1999): 266; Alan Bullock, *Ernest Bevin: Foreign Secretary, 1945–1951* (New York, 1983), 791; Michael F. Hopkins, "The Price of Cold War Partnership: Sir Oliver Franks and the British Military Commitment in the Korean War," *Cold War History* 1, no. 2 (January 2001): 35; Leon D. Epstein, *Britain—Uneasy Ally* (Chicago, 1954), 213.

8. Bullock, *Bevin*, 791; RC/102/50, "The Soviet Union and Korea," 1 July 1950, TNA/PRO/FO 371/86756, NS1052/68G; FO Note, 1 August 1950, PRO/FO 371/86757, NS1052/79G; Callum MacDonald, "The Diplomacy of Restraint: The Attlee Government and the Korean War," in *Contemporary British History, 1931–1961: Politics and the Limits of Policy*, ed. Anthony Gorst et al. (New York, 1991), 219–220; Hopkins, "The Price of Cold War Partnership," 34, 39–41, 43–44.

9. Shaw, "The IRD and the Korean War," 267–268; Brian Porter, *Britain and the Rise of Communist China: A Study of British Attitudes, 1945–1954* (New York, 1967), 95–96, and Appendix 3, Sections D1 and D2, 167.

10. RC/109/50, "Western Measures to Counter Soviet Expansion," 14 July 1950, PRO/FO 371/86757, NS1052/72G; RC/118/50, "Summary of Indications Regarding Soviet Foreign Policy, no. 60," 10 August 1950, ibid., NS1052/78G; "Soviet Aggressive Policy," PRO/FO 371/86760, NS1052/102; see especially speech of 22 August 1950. For further comment on the IRD's role in disseminating these arguments during the Korean War, see Shaw, "The IRD and the Korean War," 263–281.

11. Acheson to Embassy in the United Kingdom, 28 July 1950, *FRUS*, 1950, vol. 6 (Washington, D.C., 1976), 396; Acheson to Embassy in the United Kingdom, 13 August 1950, ibid., 433; Kennan Memorandum to Acheson, 8 August 1950, *FRUS*, 1950, vol. 4 (Washington, D.C., 1981), 1227; Robert L. Beisner, *Dean Acheson: A Life in the Cold War* (New York, 2006), 268–270;

Heath to Acheson, 15 October 1950, *FRUS, 1950*, vol. 6 (Washington, D.C., 1976), 896; Lacy Memorandum, 30 October 1950, *FRUS, 1950*, vol. 6, 911.

12. William J. Duiker, *U.S. Containment Policy and the Conflict in Indochina* (Stanford, Calif., 1994), 98–99; Kathryn C. Statler, *Replacing France: The Origins of American Intervention in Vietnam* (Lexington, Ky., 2007), 26.

13. William J. Duiker, *Sacred War: Nationalism and Revolution in a Divided Vietnam* (New York, 1995), 72–73; NIE-5, "Indochina: Current Situation and Probable Developments," 29 December 1950, *FRUS, 1950*, vol. 6, 960, 963; Duiker, *U.S. Containment Policy*, 99.

14. See Gordon H. Chang, *Friends and Enemies: The United States, China, and the Soviet Union, 1948–1972* (Stanford, Calif., 1990), 50–77, for a discussion of how the "hard" policy that Charles Yost recommended won out over the "benign" policies of Everett Case and Raymond Fosdick. The phrase "watchful waiting" is Fosdick's and is cited in ibid., 55.

15. Minutes of a Meeting by Representative of France, the United Kingdom and the United States in Paris, 4 August 1950, *FRUS, 1950*, vol. 6, 421.

16. Truman, "Preserving Our Basic Liberties and Protecting the Internal Security of the United States," *DSB*, 21 August 1950, 295; Truman, "Aims and Objectives in Resisting Aggression in Korea," *DSB*, 11 September 1950, 407; Austin, "President Malik's Continued Obstruction Tactics in the Security Council," *DSB*, 28 August 1950, 326; Austin, "Exposing Soviet Propaganda Tactics," *DSB*, 4 September 1950, 371; Ross, "The Threat of Communist Imperialism," *DSB*, 380–381; see also Dulles, "U.S. Military Action in Korea," *DSB*, 17 July, 89.

17. These papers were produced by the department's Public Affairs Policy Advisory Staff. See "Information Policy Guidance Paper," Special Guidance no. 50, 27 July 1950, *FRUS, 1950*, vol. 4, 320, fn. 1.

18. See editorial note, *FRUS, 1950*, vol. 4, 315; see also Senate Resolution 243, *DSB*, 17 July 1950, 102; Russell, "Where We Stand Today," *DSB*, 17 July 1950, 115.

19. For text of the PSB announcement, see *DSB*, 28 August 1950, 335; "Letter from Senatorial Group to the President," 18 August 1950, *DSB*, 11 September 1950, 424; Sara L. Sale, *The Shaping of Containment: Harry S. Truman, the National Security Council, and the Cold War* (St. James, N.Y., 1998), 186–187; see also Scott Lucas, *Freedom's War: The American Crusade against the Soviet Union* (New York, 1999), 83–106, 128–162; Andrew Defty, *Britain, America, and Anti-Communist Propaganda, 1945–1953: The Information Research Department* (New York, 2004), 139–143; Gregory Mitrovich, *Undermining the Kremlin: America's Strategy to Subvert the Soviet Bloc, 1947–1956* (Ithaca, N.Y., 2000), 59–61; Sargeant to Webb, 12 October 1949, NARA, OASSPA, OPA, SF, Box 9, Russia, 1947–1951; Walter L. Hixson, *Parting the Curtain: Propaganda, Culture, and the Cold War, 1945–1961* (New York, 1997), 11–13, 32–36.

20. David L. Larson, *United States Foreign Policy toward Yugoslavia, 1943–1963* (Washington, D.C., 1979), 216; Lorraine M. Lees, *Keeping Tito*

Afloat: The United States, Yugoslavia, and the Cold War (University Park, Penn., 1997), 88; Melbourne to Yost, Reinhardt, 26 July 1950, NARA, RG 59, Records Relating to State Department Participation in NSC, 1935–1962, 61 D167, Box 46, Yugoslavia NSC 18 Series.

21. Ogburn, "Recapturing Propaganda Initiative from Soviets—Part II," 15 September 1950, NARA, RG 59, PPS, 1947–1953, Lot 64D563, SF, Box 11A, Political and Psychological Warfare, 1947–1950.

22. Truman, "Aims and Objectives in Resisting Aggression in Korea," *DSB,* 11 September 1950, 407–409; Kirk to Acheson, no. 649, 8 September 1950, *FRUS,* 1950, vol. 4, 1242–1243. See Ogburn, "Recapturing Propaganda Initiative from Soviets—Part II."

23. Chancery, British Embassy, Moscow, 21 July 1950, TNA/PRO/FO 953/1005, PG13834/2. Bevin, for his part, had wavered on whether British propaganda should attack communism or Soviet imperialism. For Bevin's statements, see "Publicity Policy in the Far East," Circular no. 0116, 31 July 1948, PRO/FO 1110/12, PR554/G. The Russia Committee believed that attacks on communism itself might be counterproductive, especially in Asia and the Middle East. See minutes of Russia Committee Meeting, 10 June 1948, PRO/FO 371/71687, N7350/765/G38. As noted in Chapter 6, the Russia Committee, by the spring of 1949, was recommending that ministers avoid using the word "Communist" in their attacks on Soviet policy "because of its vague attraction for many waverers." See "Memorandum on the Use of Words in Publicity about Communism," March/April 1949, PRO/FO 1110/191, PR704/14/G.

24. Chancery, British Embassy, Moscow, 21 July 1950, TNA/PRO/FO 953/1005, PG13834/2; Warner marginal comments on letter from Murray, 7 August 1950, PRO/FO 1110/191, PR704/14/G.

25. William Stueck, *The Korean War: An International History* (Princeton, N.J., 1995), 85–126.

26. CIA, "Current Reassessment of the Tito-Soviet Break," Intelligence Memorandum no. 325, 13 September 1950, NARA, RG 59, Records of the Policy Planning Staff relating to State Participation in NSC, 1935–1962, 61 D 167, Box 46, Yugoslavia NSC 18 Series; Lees, *Keeping Tito Afloat,* 81–101; Beatrice Heuser, *Western "Containment" Policies in the Cold War: The Yugoslav Case, 1948–53* (New York, 1989), 149–154, 184–192.

27. See Editorial Note, *FRUS,* 1950, vol. 4, 1438–1439.

28. Lees, *Keeping Tito Afloat,* 92–93; "Public Comment on U.S. Policy toward Yugoslavia," 31 October 1950, NARA, RG 59, OPOS, 1943–1975, Public Opinion on Foreign Countries and Regions, Soviet Union and Eastern Europe, 1943–1965, Box 45, Yugoslavia 1945–62; see also a similar report on 10 November 1950, ibid.

29. Acheson, "Foreign Policies toward Asia," *DSB,* 18 September 1950, 464. See also Acheson, "Plowing a Straight Furrow," *DSB,* 27 November 1950, 851.

30. Davies Paper on Political Warfare, 27 October 1950, Section III E, Annex 8, NARA, RG 59, Box 45, Davies, 1947–1949; Davies to Rusk and Clubb, 30

October 1950, ibid. As part of that communiqué, Davies had taken umbrage with a 26 October memo from O. Edmund Clubb in which the Asian specialist lumped together the aims of Communists throughout the world. In response, Davies had also sought to differentiate Stalin from Hitler, describing the Soviet leader as a "supreme opportunist and realist." Adding a rhetorical twist to the depiction of "national Communism," Davies thought U.S. officials might seek to promote the term *exceptionalism* rather than *Titoism*, given the indigenous factors involved and the outcome they would generate.

31. Stueck, *The Korean War*, 111–119; Melvyn P. Leffler, *A Preponderance of Power: National Security Policy in the Truman Administration* (Stanford, Calif., 1992), 376–380, 398–399.

32. Leffler, *Preponderance of Power*, 376; NIE-3, "Soviet Intentions and Capabilities," 15 November 1950, NARA, RG 59, USSR, 1946–1950, Box 23; "Weekly Summary of Comment on Far East," 8 November 1950, RG 59, OPOS, 1943–1965, Public Opinion on Foreign Countries and Regions, China and Far East, 1949–1950, Box 26, China Telegrams, July–December 1950.

33. Truman, "Chinese Communist Attack on Korea Demands Strengthening of Free World's Defenses," *DSB*, 11 December 1950, 925–926; Beisner, *Acheson*, 411–412; Rusk, "Security Problems in Far East Areas," *DSB*, 4 December 1950, 889–891; Kathryn Weathersby, "The Soviet Role in the Korean War: The State of Historical Knowledge," in *The Korean War in World History*, ed. William Stueck (Lexington, Ky., 2004), 61–92.

34. "China and Korea," *Times*, 10 November 1950, 7.

35. RC/147/50, "Summary of Indications Regarding Soviet Foreign Policy (with an Annex Regarding Chinese Policy in the Far East), no. 67," 7 November 1950, TNA/PRO/FO 371/86759, NS1052/95/G; RC/152/50, "Soviet World-Wide Policy and Intentions," no. 68, 21 November 1950, PRO/FO 371/86760, NS1052/96/G; Bevin Memorandum, 10 November 1950, PRO/CAB 129/43, CP(50)267.

36. Porter, *Britain and the Rise of Communist China*, 104–106; Stueck, *The Korean War*, 131.

37. Minutes of Meeting, 4 December 1950, TNA/PRO/PREM 8, 1200; Minutes of Meeting, 5 December 1950, ibid.; Beisner, *Acheson*, 414–419; Stueck, *The Korean War*, 131–132.

38. See Acheson to Certain Diplomatic and Consular Office, 8 December 1950, *FRUS*, 1950, vol. 6, 676; Acheson to All Diplomatic Offices, 16 December 1950, ibid., 682–683.

39. Truman, "Chinese Communist Attack on Korea Demands Strengthening of Free World's Defenses," *DSB*, 11 December 1950, 925–926; see also Truman, message to Congress, 1 December 1950, *DSB*, 926–927; Barrett, "Need for Public Assistance in the Campaign of Truth," *DSB*, 18 December 1950, 968–969.

40. "Public Comment on U.S. Policy toward Yugoslavia," 7 December 1950, NARA, RG 59, OPOS, 1943–1975, Public Opinion on Foreign Countries

and Regions: Soviet Union and Eastern Europe, 1943–1965, Box 45, Yugo-slavia, 1945–1952.

41. OIR, "Strength and Weaknesses of the World Communist Movement outside the Soviet Union," 7 November 1950, 4, NARA, RG 59, Intelligence Bureau, Office of the Director, 1950–1959, Miscellaneous Lot Files, 1944–1959, Box 64. The OIR report was the final version of the May 1950 report; NIE-3, "Soviet Intentions and Capabilities."

42. Heuser, Western "Containment" Policies, 184–186; Lees, Keeping Tito Afloat, 94–97; U.S. Diplomatic Records on Relations with Yugoslavia during the Early Cold War, 1948–1957, ed. Nick Ceh (New York, 2002), 214–240.

43. George W. Perkins testimony before House Committee on Foreign Affairs, 29 November 1950, DSB, 11 December 1950, 938; U.S. Congressional Record, 81st Congress, 2d Session, vol. 96, pt. 12 (27 November 1950 to 2 January 1951), 16337, 16342.

44. Congressional Record, 16478–16480, 16347–16348, 16354; Larson, United States Foreign Policy toward Yugoslavia, 234.

45. Truman, "The National Emergency," DSB, 25 December 1950, 999; Truman, "Crisis in World Affairs, a Challenge to the Youth of Today," ibid., 1009–1010.

46. Truman, "Partnership of World Peace," DSB, 30 October 1950, 685; Truman, "The Liberty Bell-Symbol of Freedom," DSB, 20 November 1950, 802; Truman, "Preserving Our Basic Liberties and Protecting the Internal Se-curity of the United States," DSB, 21 August 1950, 294; Truman, "Making Democracy Work and Defending it from Its Enemies," DSB, 6 March 1950, 347–350; Acheson, "Fulfillment of Responsibility in a World in Peril," DSB, 16 October 1950, 614.

47. See Jessup, "Let Freedom Ring," DSB, 9 October 1950, 583–585; Truman, "Aims and Objectives in Resisting Aggression in Korea," DSB, 11 September 1950, 407.

48. 30 November 1950, Journal of the Parliaments of the Commonwealth 31, no. 4 December 1950, 670; 28 March 1950, ibid., no. 2, June 1950, 167.

49. "Soviet Aggressive Policy," Notes for Speech by the Secretary of State for Commonwealth Relations at Brierly Hill on 17 December, TNA/PRO/FO 371/86760, NS1052/102.

50. Truman, "The National Emergency," DSB, 25 December 1950, 1000; Sanders, "Peaceful Coexistence—Fact and Fiction," DSB, 11 December 1950, 921, 923.

51. Memorandum of a Conversation, 6 April 1950, FRUS, 1950, vol. 4, 293.

52. "The Position of the Department of State with Respect to the Internal Secu-rity Act of 1950," 22 November 1950, FRUS, 1950, vol. 1 (Washington, D.C., 1977), 901.

53. OIR, "Strength and Weaknesses of the World Communist Movement outside the Soviet Union."

54. Truman, "The Liberty Bell-Symbol of Freedom," DSB, 20 November 1950, 802; Connally, "Reviewing American Foreign Policy since 1945," DSB, 9

October 1950, 563; Barrett, "Need for Public Assistance in the Campaign of Truth," *DSB*, 18 December 1950, 968; Acheson, "The Peace the World Wants," *DSB*, 2 October 1950, 524; "The Strategy of Freedom," *DSB*, 18 December 1950, 964; for Rusk, see "Fundamentals of Far Eastern Foreign Policy," *DSB*, 18 September 1950, 466.

55. Susan L. Carruthers, "A Red under Every Bed? Anti-Communist Propaganda and Britain's Response to Colonial Insurgency," *Contemporary Record* 9, no. 2 (Autumn 1995): 303.

56. Warner marginal comments on letter from B. Ratheven-Murray, 7 August 1950, TNA/PRO/FO 1110/191, PR704/14/G.

57. Russell, "Toward a Stronger World Organization," *DSB*, 7 August 1950, 222; Barrett, "Expanding Techniques for a Truth Strategy," *DSB*, 11 December 1950, 945–946; Barrett, "Truth Campaign Needs Support of Private and government Groups," *DSB*, 6 November 1950, 736. For additional references to Soviet "blunders," see Barrett, "USIE Capitalizes on Soviet Propaganda Blunders," *DSB*, 11 September 1950, 414.

58. Stephenson Note, 28 July 1950, TNA/PRO/FO 371/88260, RY1072/11.

59. Coleman, *The Liberal Conspiracy*, 251.

60. "Public Attitudes on Dealing with the Soviet Union's Role in Communist Aggression," 29 September 1950, NARA, RG 59, OPOS, Public Opinion on Foreign Countries and Regions, Soviet Union and Eastern Europe, 1943–1965, Box 45, Russia: March–December 1950.

61. Ogburn, "Recapturing Propaganda Initiative from Soviet—Party II." Among those receiving the memo were Dean Rusk in the Bureau of Far Eastern Affairs, George McGhee in Near Eastern Affairs, George Perkins in European Affairs, Edward Barrett in Public Affairs, and John Hickerson in UN Affairs. Watts to Rusk et al., 10 October 1950, NARA, RG 59, PPS, Lot 64D563, SF, Box 11A, Political and Psychological Warfare, 1947–1950.

62. For the Russia Committee judgment on Sino-Soviet coordination, see RC/155/50, "Soviet World-Wide Policy and Intentions," 8 December 1950, TNA/PRO/FO 371/86760, NS1052/99G; for the IRD, see Shaw, "The IRD and the Korean War," 270.

63. Kelly to Rumbold, 21 July 1950, TNA/PRO/FO 371/88260, RY1072/11.

64. IRD to Moscow Chancery, 23 August 1950, TNA/PRO/FO 953/1005, PG13834/2.

Conclusion

1. George F. Kennan, "Totalitarianism in the Modern World," in *Totalitarianism: Proceedings of a Conference Held at the American Academy of Arts and Sciences*, ed. Carl J. Friedrich (New York, 1954), 19–20; Karl W. Deutsch, "Cracks in the Monolith: Possibilities and Patterns of Disintegration in Totalitarian Systems," in ibid., 308–333.

2. See, for example, Arthur F. Wright, "The Chinese Monolith, Past and Present," *Problems of Communism* 4, no. 4 (July/August 1955): 1; "The

Chinese Monolith: Past and Present," *Far Eastern Economic Review* 19, no. 10 (8 September 1955): 289; John Davy, "Monolith in the Melting Pot," *Twentieth Century* (January/June 1957): 215.

3. Michael Terpack, "The Monolithic Myth of the USSR: The Nationalities Problem," *Vital Speeches of the Day* 26, no. 10 (1 March 1960): 313; Walter Laqueur, "The End of the Monolith: World Communism in 1962," *Foreign Affairs* 40, no. 3 (April 1962): 360–373; Marshall D. Shulman, "Is the Monolith Cracking?" *Institute on United States Foreign Policy,* University of Wisconsin, Milwaukee, recording (Westinghouse Broadcasting Company, 1963); Robert V. Daniels, "How Monolithic Was the Monolith?" *Problems of Communism* 13, no. 2 (March/April 1964): 40; Franklin W. Houn, "The Communist Monolith versus the Chinese Tradition," *Orbis* 8, no. 4 (Winter 1965): 894; J.D.B. Miller, ed., *The Disintegrating Monolith* (Canberra, 1965); Thomas A. Bailey, "The Mythmakers of American History," *Journal of American History* 55, no. 1 (1968): 5–21.

4. Arthur Schlesinger Jr., "The Varieties of Communist Experience," in *The Politics of Hope* (Boston, 1963), 265, 283, 290; Schlesinger, *The Vital Center: The Politics of Freedom* (Boston, 1949), 120.

5. Schlesinger, *Vital Center,* 3; "Principles Governing U.S. Relationships with the 'Free World' and the 'Soviet World,' " 13 February 1950, NARA, RG 59, RPPS, 1947–1953, Box 44, Adams Chronological.

6. Walter A. McDougall, *Promised Land, Crusader State: The American Encounter with the World since 1776* (Boston, 1997), 11; Anders Stephanson, *Manifest Destiny: American Expansionism and the Empire of Right* (New York, 1995), 61–67.

7. David Brion Davis, *The Fear of Conspiracy: Images of Un-American Subversion from the Revolution to the Present* (Ithaca, N.Y., 1971), xv; Michael J. Hogan, *A Cross of Iron: Harry S. Truman and the Origins of the National Security State, 1945–1950* (Cambridge, 1998), 17–18, 468.

8. Richard Hofstadter, *The American Political Tradition and the Men Who Made It* (New York, 1948), xxiii–xxiv; Schlesinger, *Vital Center,* 1, 52. See also Robert Hewison, *In Anger: British Culture in the Cold War, 1945–60* (New York, 1981), 4–12.

9. Eric Goldman, *The Crucial Decade, 1945–1955* (New York, 1956), 14. For more on these themes, see Robert Booth Fowler, *Believing Skeptics: American Political Intellectuals, 1945–1964* (Westport, Conn., 1978).

10. Louis J. Halle, *The Cold War as History* (New York, 1967), 102–103.

11. See Deborah Welch Larson, *Origins of Containment: A Psychological Explanation* (Princeton, N.J., 1985), 53–54. For more on the Munich analogy, see Yuen Foong Khong, *Analogies at War: Korea, Munich, Dien Bien Phu, and the Vietnam Decisions of 1965* (Princeton, N.J., 1995), 184–187; Joseph M. Siracusa, "The Munich Analogy," in *Encyclopedia of American Foreign Policy,* 2nd ed., vol. 2, ed. Alexander DeConde et al. (New York, 2002), 443–454.

12. David Littlejohn, *The Patriotic Traitors: A History of Collaboration in German-Occupied Europe, 1940–1945* (London, 1972), 15; Peter Davies,

Dangerous Liaisons: Collaboration and World War II (London, 2004), 6; Hans Fredrik Dahl, *Quisling: A Study in Treachery* (Cambridge, 1999), front matter.

13. Thomas E. Cronin and Michael A. Genovese, *The Paradoxes of the American Presidency* (New York, 1998), 75–76; Brigitte Lebens Nacos, *The Press, Presidents, and Crises* (New York, 1990), 4; Leonard A. Kusnitz, *Public Opinion and Foreign Policy: America's China Policy, 1949–1979* (Westport, Conn., 1984), 3–7; Ralph D. Levering, *The Public and American Foreign Policy, 1917–1978* (New York, 1978), 93–106; J. Michael Sproule, *Propaganda and Democracy: The American Experience of Media and Mass Persuasion* (New York, 1997), 213–217.

14. Placards depicting bolshevism as a knife-wielding skeleton, as well as posters calling on Germans to guard against Russian bolshevism, were regular features of the public dialogue. Rudi Feld, "Die Gefahr des Bolshevism" ("The danger of Bolshevism") and "Deutsche! Schuetzt die Grenzen Eures Vaterlandes gegen russiche Bolschwisten!" ("Germans! Protect the borders of your Fatherland against the Russian Bolsheviks!"), Freikorps Plakat, 1919, in *Politische Plakate der Weimar Republik, 1918–1933*, Ausstellung vom 18. September 1980 bis 23. November 1980 (Darmstadt, 1980), 10, 27.

15. In 1930, SPD leader Kurt Schumacher described the KPD as the "Oststehenden Heere der sowjetrussiche Aussenpolitik" (standing east armies of Soviet Russia's foreign policy). Dieter Dowe, hg., *Kurt Schumacher and der "Neubau" der Deutsche Sozialdemokratie nach 1945* (Bonn, 1996), 137.

16. Examples of this genre include "Von Hitler zu Pieck" (From Hitler to Pieck), "von der NS Frauenschaft zum kommunistischen DFD" (From the National Socialist Women's League to the Communist Democratic Women's Federation of Germany), and the label "Kreml-Kreaturen" (Kremlin Creatures). The first two examples were poster-size materials, and the third can be found in the SPD political pamphlet, "12 Fragen and das Politbüro der SED," located in Friedrich Ebert Stiftung, Bonn. Perhaps the most famous example of Germans invoking monolithic themes came from Konrad Adenauer and his Christian Democratic Party (CDU). Maintaining its hostility toward Left-leaning political solutions, the CDU declared that "Alle Wege des Marxismus führen nach Moskau!" (All Marxist roads lead to Moscow!) during the 1953 general election. *Erlebnis Geschichte: Das Buch zur Austellung: Haus der Geschichte der Bundesrepublik Deutschland* (Gustav Luebbe Verlag), 94. I would like to thank Jeff Verhey for providing access to SPD archives and archivists.

17. To cite just one other example, Nehru—a figure not disposed to carrying America's water—declared in 1948 that "Indian voters repudiated Communists because they served Moscow, not India." Marshall to Lovett, 16 October 1948, *FRUS*, 1948, vol. 5, 517.

18. For British usage, see Royal Institute of International Affairs, "The Tito-Stalin Correspondence," *The World Today* (December 1948): 531. For more on "pendulum swings," see Geir Lundestad, *The American "Empire" and*

Other Studies of U.S. Foreign Policy in a Comparative Perspective (New York, 1990), especially 117–141.

19. "United States Policy toward Communism," Draft Working Paper, 8 March 1949, NARA, RG 59, RPPS, 1947–1953, SF, Box 8, Communism, 1947–1951. Emphasis in original.

20. Seymour Martin Lipset, *American Exceptionalism: A Double-Edged Sword* (New York, 1996), 289. For explorations of the "exceptionalism," see Daniel T. Rodgers, "Exceptionalism," in *Imagined Histories: American Historians Interpret the Past,* ed. Anthony Molho and Gordon S. Wood (Princeton, N.J., 1998), 21–40; Michael Kammen, "The Problem of American Exceptionalism," *American Quarterly* 45, no. 1 (March 1993): 1–43. One member of Parliament, Sir Waldron Smithers, did seek to create such a committee on un-British activities. For background, see Peter Hennessy and Gail Brownfield, "Britain's Cold War Security Purge: The Origins of Positive Vetting," *Historical Journal* 25, no. 4 (1982): 965–973.

21. Nevertheless, Bevin believed there to be "a great opportunity for well-directed propaganda and the right treatment of the Chinese to contribute towards keeping China form lining up permanently with Soviet Russia." See "Debate in House of Commons," 14 December 1950, *Journal of the Parliaments of the Commonwealth* 31, no. 4 (December 1950): 686.

22. "Outline of Communist Strategy in South-East Asia," 15 August 1950, TNA/PRO/FO1110/189, PR2887/11/913.

23. See Eduard Mark, "Revolution by Degrees: Stalin's National-Front Strategy for Europe, 1941–1947," *CWIHP* Working Paper No. 31 (February 2001), 18.

24. Irwin M. Wall, *French Communism in the Era of Stalin: The Quest for Unity and Integration, 1945–1962* (Westport, Conn., 1983), 38–40, 46–47. For a vigorous discussion of the PCF and Vietnam, see the H-Diplo thread of November and December 2000, "Ho Chi Minh and National Communism," at www.h-net.org/~diplo/, accessed 31 December 2007.

25. Elena Aga-Rossi and Victor Zaslavsky, "The Soviet Union and the Italian Communist Party, 1944–8," in *The Soviet Union and Europe in the Cold War,* ed. Francesca Gori and Silvio Pons (New York, 1996), 165–170; Galina Murashko and Albina F. Noskova, "Stalin and the National-Territorial Controversies in Eastern Europe, 1945–47 (pts. 1 & 2)," *Cold War History* 1, no. 3 (April 2001): 161–172, and vol. 2, no. 1 (October 2001): 145–157; Walter A. Kemp, *Nationalism and Communism in Eastern Europe and the Soviet Union: A Basic Contradiction?* (New York: 1999), 101; Sheldon Anderson, *A Cold War in the Soviet Bloc: Polish-East German Relations, 1945–1962* (Boulder, Colo., 2001), 10–95.

26. Aldo Agosti, "Recasting Democracy? Communist Parties Facing Change and Reconstruction in Postwar Europe," in *Transnational Moments of Change: Europe 1945, 1968, 1989,* ed. Gerd-Rainer Horn and Padraic Kenney (New York, 2004), 11.

27. Peter Grieder, *The East German Leadership, 1946–73: Conflict and Crisis* (Manchester, 1999), 8–52.

28. Aga-Rossi and Zaslavsky, "The Soviet Union and the Italian Communist Party," 166–170.

29. Vojtech Mastny, *The Cold War and Soviet Insecurity: The Stalin Years* (New York, 1996), 18; Alexander Dallin and F.I. Firsov, *Dimitrov and Stalin, 1934–1943: Letters from the Soviet Archives* (New Haven, Conn., 2000), 254–262.

30. Donald L.M. Blackmer and Annie Kriegel, *The International Role of the Communist Parties of Italy and France* (Cambridge, Mass., 1975); Marc Lazar, "The Cold War Culture of the French and Italian Communist Parties," *Intelligence and National Security* 18, no. 2 (June 2003): 213–224; Wall, *French Communism in the Era of Stalin*, 53–109; Lazar, "The French Communist Party between Nation and Internationalism," in *Communism: National and International*, ed. Tauno Saarela and Kimmo Rentola (Helsinki, 1998), 41–59.

31. Aga-Rossi and Zaslavsky, "The Soviet Union and the Italian Communist Party," 165–170; see also Aldo Agosti, "Palmiro Togliatti, the Italian Communist Party and International Communism," in *Communism*, ed. Saarela and Rentola, 141–158.

32. Kevin Morgan, "Harry Pollitt, the British Communist Party, and International Communism," in *Communism*, ed. Saarela and Rentola, 183–206.

33. Mastny, *The Cold War*, 26, 19, 21; Csaba Békés, "Soviet Plans to Establish the COMINFORM in Early 1946: New Evidence from the Hungarian Archives," *CWIHP Bulletin* 10 (March 1998): 135–136; Melvyn P. Leffler, "The Cold War: What Do 'We Now Know'?" *American Historical Review* 104, no. 2 (April 1999): 501–524; see also Norman Naimark, *The Russians in Germany: A History of the Soviet Zone of Occupation, 1945–1949* (Cambridge, Mass., 1995).

34. See Norman Naimark and Leonid Gibianskii, *The Establishment of Communist Regimes in Eastern Europe, 1944–1949* (Boulder, Colo., 1997), for a country-by-country account of Communist ascendancy in the region.

35. See Wilfried Loth, "Stalin's Plans for Post-War Germany," in *The Soviet Union and Europe in the Cold War*, ed. Gori and Pons, 26; Vladimir O. Pechatnov, " 'The Allies Are Pressing on You to Break Your Will . . . ,' " Foreign Policy Correspondence between Stalin and Molotov and Other Politburo Members, September 1945–December 1946, *CWIHP*, Working Paper No. 26 (September 1999), 11; Mark, "Revolution by Degrees," 13–14.

36. Vladimir O. Pechatnov, "The Big Three after World War II: New Documents on Soviet Thinking about Post War Relations with the United States and Great Britain," *CWIHP*, Working Paper No. 13 (July 1995), 4–5, 13; see also Mark, "Revolution by Degrees"; Vladislav M. Zubok, *A Failed Empire: The Soviet Union from Stalin to Gorbachev* (New York, 2007), 17–18, 20, 48.

37. See Scott D. Parrish and Mikhail M. Narinsky, "New Evidence on the Soviet Rejection of the Marshall Plan, 1947: Two Reports," *CWIHP*, Working Paper no. 9 (Washington, D.C., March 1994); Mastny, *The Cold War*, 28–29; Parrish, "The Marshall Plan and the Division of Europe," in *The Establishment*

of Communist Regimes, ed. Naimark and Gibianskii, 284–286; Melvyn P. Leffler, *For the Soul of Mankind: The United States, the Soviet Union, and the Cold War* (New York, 2007), 65–66.

38. Mastny, *The Cold War,* 26, 31; Csaba Békés, "Soviet Plans to Establish the COMINFORM," 135–136.

39. Mastny, *The Cold War,* 30. Moscow's delay in creating the Cominform also apparently stemmed from its desire to promote the interests of comrades in France, Czechoslovakia, and Romania. With elections upcoming in each of those nations, Stalin did not want to provide the non-Communist parties with a ready-made campaign issue prior to the vote. Thus, while it appears that Stalin had long been interested in reviving the Comintern, as Raymond Murphy had argued in June 1945, Stalin's own thoughts on the matter might not have jelled until after the war had ended.

40. Mastny, *The Cold War,* 31–34; Parrish, "The Turn toward Confrontation," 32, 39.

41. Odd Arne Westad, *Brothers in Arms: The Rise and Fall of the Sino-Soviet Alliance, 1945–1963* (Washington, D.C., 1998), 5–7.

42. Michael M. Sheng, "The Triumph of Internationalism: CCP-Moscow Relations before 1949," *Diplomatic History* 21, no. 1 (Winter 1997): 98.

43. Westad, *Brothers in Arms,* 6–7; Michael M. Sheng, *Battling Western Imperialism: Mao, Stalin, and the United States* (Princeton, N.J., 1997), 5–7.

44. Westad, *Brothers in Arms,* 8; Westad, *Decisive Encounters: The Chinese Civil War, 1946–1950* (Stanford, Calif., 2003), 52, 119–120, 165–167; Hua-yu Li, *Mao and the Economic Stalinization of China, 1948–1953* (New York, 2006), 3–7, 187–189.

45. Westad, *Decisive Encounters,* 119, 232, 236, 269; Niu Jun, "The Origins of the Sino-Soviet Alliance," in *Brothers in Arms,* 63, 70; Sheng, "The Triumph of Internationalism," 98; Sheng, *Battling Western Imperialism,* 7; Mercy A. Kuo, *Contending with Contradictions: China's Policy toward Soviet Eastern Europe and the Origins of the Sino-Soviet Split, 1953–1960* (New York, 2001), 12–13, 20.

46. Niu, "The Origins of the Sino-Soviet Alliance," 72; Westad, *Decisive Encounters,* 120, 165–167, 232; Chen Jian, *Mao's China and the Cold War* (Chapel Hill, N.C., 2000), 52–53.

47. Sheng, "The Triumph of Internationalism," 95; Chen, *Mao's China,* 44–48; Westad, *Decisive Encounters,* 236; Sheng, *Battling Western Imperialism,* 7. Chen Jian, "The Myth of America's 'Lost Chance' in China: A Chinese Perspective in Light of New Evidence," *Diplomatic History* 21, no. 1 (Winter 1997): 80–81.

48. Chen, "The Myth of America's 'Lost Chance' in China," 85; Chen, *Mao's China,* 38–48; Sheng, *Battling Western Imperialism,* 191; Westad, "The Sino-Soviet Alliance and the United States," in Westad, *Brothers in Arms,* 168.

49. See Westad, *Brothers in Arms,* 10; Westad, *Decisive Encounters,* 267–269. The emphasis is Stalin's.

50. Niu, "Origins of the Sino-Soviet Alliance," 73.

51. Though anti-imperialism had long been a trait of Leninist thought, Mao's hostility to Western dominance seems to have sprung from cultural realities as much as from material or ideological reasoning. See Westad, "The Sino-Soviet Alliance and the United States," 165, 167; Sheng, *Battling Western Imperialism*, 5–7; Chen, *Mao's China*, 50.

52. John Lewis Gaddis, *We Now Know: Rethinking Cold War History* (New York, 1997), 70–75; for the most comprehensive analysis of the war as a Korean-centered conflict, see Bruce Cumings, *The Origins of the Korean War*, 2 vols. (Princeton, N.J., 1981–1990).

53. Westad, "The Sino-Soviet Alliance and the United States," 171.

54. For material on the nature and extent of those discussions, see Kathryn Weathersby, "Korea 1949–50: To Attack or Not to Attack? Stalin, Kim Il-sung and the Prelude to War," *CWIHP Bulletin* 5 (Spring 1995): 1, 2–9; Weathersby, "New Findings on the Korean War," *CWIHP Bulletin*, no. 3 (Fall 1993): 1, 14–18; Weathersby, "New Russian Documents on the Korean War," *CWIHP Bulletin*, nos. 6 and 7 (Winter 1995/1996): 30–35; Stueck, *The Korean War: An International History* (Princeton, N.J., 1995), 10–46; Chen Jian, *China's Road to the Korean War: The Making of the Sino-American Confrontation* (New York, 1994); Weathersby, "The Soviet Role in the Korean War," in *The Korean War in World History,* ed. Stueck (Lexington, Ky., 2004), 61–92; Shen Zhuihua, "Sino-Soviet Relations and the Origins of the Korean War: Stalin's Strategic Goals in the Far East," *JCWS* 2, no. 2 (2000): 44–68.

55. Indeed, Mao's support for other Communist movements, such the Vietminh's effort to evict the French from Indochina, evoke those images of coordinated, conspiratorial behavior. Apparently, Mao was even more interested in assisting Indochina than in liberating Taiwan. See Westad, "The Sino-Soviet Alliance and the United States," 169; see also Douglas J. Macdonald, "Communist Bloc Expansion in the Early Cold War: Challenging Realism, Refuting Revisionism," *International Security* 20, no. 3 (Winter 1995–1996): 152–188; on the virtues of speaking of a Communist "order," see Robert Service, *Comrades! A History of World Communism* (Cambridge, Mass., 2007), 8–9.

56. Arthur Schlesinger Jr., "Some Lessons from the Cold War," in *The End of the Cold War: Its Meaning and Implications,* ed. Michael J. Hogan (New York, 1992), 55; James Harris, "Encircled by Enemies: Stalin's Perceptions of the Capitalist World, 1918–1941," *Journal of Strategic Studies* 30, no. 3 (June 2007): 513–545; Zubok, *A Failed Empire,* 6, 17–18, 26, 33, 48, 60; Gaddis, *We Now Know;* 195–196; Leffler, *For the Soul of Mankind,* 15, 27, 65–67, 79–83; Robert Jervis, *Perception and Misperception in International Politics* (Princeton, N.J., 1976), especially 321–342.

57. See Gordon H. Chang, *Friends and Enemies: The United States, China, and the Soviet Union, 1948–1972* (Stanford, Calif., 1990), especially 5–115; John Lewis Gaddis, *The Long Peace: Inquiries into the History of the Cold War* (New York, 1987), 147–194; David Allan Mayers, *Cracking the Monolith: U.S. Policy against the Sino-Soviet Alliance, 1949–1955* (Baton Rouge, La., 1986).

58. Marilyn Young, *The Vietnam Wars, 1945–1950* (New York, 1991), 22–24; Kathryn Statler, *Replacing France: The Origins of American Intervention in Vietnam* (Lexington, Ky., 2007), 17–26; Mark Atwood Lawrence, "Forging the Great Combination: Britain and the Indochina Problem, 1945–1950," in *The First Indochina War: Colonial Conflict and Cold War Crisis,* ed. Fredrik Logevall and Mark Atwood Lawrence (Cambridge, Mass., 2007), 121; William J. Duiker, *Ho Chi Minh* (New York, 2000), 122–124.

59. Bohlen to Barbour, 15 May 1952, NARA, RG 59, RPPS, 1947–1953, Lot 64 D 563, CAF, Box 29, East Europe, 1949–1953.

60. "Memorandum on American Attitudes toward Russian Government and Russian People," 5 March 1951, NARA, RG 59, OPOS, Public Opinion on Foreign Countries and Regions, 1943–1965, Box 45, Russia, 1950.

61. See Archimedes Patti, *Why Vietnam? Prelude to America's Albatross* (Berkeley, Calif., 1980); William J. Duiker, *U.S. Containment Policy and the Conflict in Indochina* (Stanford, Calif., 1994), 48–49; Duiker, *Ho Chi Minh,* 573; E. J. Kahn, *The China Hands: America's Foreign Service Officers and What Befell Them* (New York, 1975), 8, 224, and Ernest May's appraisal of Kahn's argument in "The China Hands in Perspective: Ethics, Diplomacy, and Statecraft," in *The China Hands' Legacy: Ethics and Diplomacy,* ed. Paul Gordon Lauren (Boulder, Colo., 1987), 97–99, 107–117; Bernard S. Morris, *Communism, Revolution, and American Policy* (New York, 1966, rev. 1987), 133–137

62. Mark Philip Bradley, *Imagining Vietnam: The Making of Postcolonial Vietnam, 1919–1950* (Chapel Hill, N.C., 2000).

63. Duiker, *U.S. Containment Policy,* 48–50; Duiker, *Ho Chi Minh,* 573–574.

64. See, for example, the secret recordings of Presidents Kennedy and Johnson, including Tape 25, JFKL, POF, Presidential Recordings Collection; Tape 60, ibid.; Tape 102.2, ibid.; WH6506.08, #8206, LBJL, Recordings of Telephone Conversations—White House Series, Recordings and Transcripts of Conversations and Meetings; WH6405.10, #3521, ibid.

65. May, "The China Hands in Perspective," 107–117; Harold P. Ford, "Calling the Sino-Soviet Split," *Studies in Intelligence* (Winter 1998–1999): 61, 65–67; Noam Kochavi, *A Conflict Perpetuated: China Policy during the Kennedy Years* (Westport, Conn., 2002); Thomas J. Christensen, "Worse than a Monolith: Disorganization and Rivalry within Asian Communist Alliances and U.S. Containment Challenges, 1949–1969," *Asian Security* 1, no. 1 (2005), 80–127.

66. Tom Mangold, *Cold Warrior: James Jesus Angleton: The CIA's Master Spy Hunter* (New York, 1991), 112–113, 321–322; Ford, "Calling the Sino-Soviet Split," 64–65; Ray S. Cline, *Secrets, Spies, and Scholars: Blueprint of the Essential CIA* (Washington, D.C., 1976), 151.

67. Dean G. Acheson, *Present at the Creation: My Years in the State Department* (New York, 1969), 354.

68. Goldman, *The Crucial Decade,* 55–57, 115; Gaddis, *The Long Peace,* 194; Gaddis, *We Now Know,* 62–63.

Index